VEGETABLES

The Ultimate Cookbook

This book may be ordered by mail from the publisher. Please include $5.99 for
postage and handling. Please support your local bookseller first!
Books published by Cider Mill Press Book Publishers are available at special
discounts for bulk purchases in the United States by corporations, institutions,
and other organizations. For more information, please contact the publisher.

Cider Mill Press Book Publishers
"Where good books are ready for press"
PO Box 454
12 Spring Street
Kennebunkport, Maine 04046
Visit us online!
cidermillpress.com

Typography: Adobe Garamond, Brandon Grotesque, Lastra, Sackers English Script
Front Endpaper Image: Cold Zucchini Soup, see page 387
Back Endpaper Image: Basic Red Cabbage Slaw, see page 481

Printed in China
2 3 4 5 6 7 8 9 0

VEGETABLES

The Ulitmate Cookbook

LAURA SORKIN

CIDER MILL PRESS

BOOK PUBLISHERS
KENNEBUNKPORT, MAINE

THIS BOOK IS FOR HENRY,
THE MOST FEARLESS COOK I KNOW.

CONTENTS

INTRODUCTION

The course of my life was steered by a tomato. Not just any tomato: a summer-ripe, lusciously flavorful tomato doused with vinaigrette and flecked with torn basil. My parents were avid gardeners who cultivated a small garden behind our house in Connecticut. They were very content to spend hours tending and weeding the patches of beans and carrots. My sister, brother, and I, not so much. Whenever the small harvest would land on our plates, my mother would always make a point to mention that they were "our beans" or "our lettuces." Big deal, I thought, it was still a green vegetable that was taking up space on the plate where I would have preferred rice, pasta or, truthfully, chocolate.

At some point around age 10 or 11, my palate matured, and I specifically remember picking one of our garden tomatoes and preparing it very simply: sliced, with a little bit of salt, oil, and balsamic and a few of "our basil leaves." It was a revelation—the absolute best thing I had ever put in my mouth. How had I not noticed before? Other things from our garden began to have more appeal, too. The lettuces were more tender than the ones from the store or even, gak, school. The carrots had more snap and the herbs more zing. And, truly, few things were sweeter than standing on bare soil, eating raw peas from a just-picked pod.

Cooking became an obsession from my teen years on. My post-college career veered and swayed, as it does in your 20s, but I always returned to food. After a brief stint at a magazine, I went to the French Culinary Institute (now called the International Culinary Center) in New York City. But after putting in some time as a garde manger in some of New York's better restaurants, I felt I ought to have a more

reliable career and went to graduate school to study environmental management. I tried to focus on saving the world one habitat at a time, but I still found that all of my energies were focused on what I could make for dinner. A new passion was also emerging: How to get back to that original, incredible tomato?

It was the late '90s, and although Alice Waters was heralding the superiority of fresh, seasonal produce in California, the farm-to-table movement was still only found in pockets elsewhere. I started to become obsessed with growing fruits and vegetables. Just a little bit of research unearthed myriad varieties of produce that sounded so much better than what you found at the supermarket. I wanted to try them all. My husband, Eric, and I had always discussed having a farm in our retirement years, but the yearning to grow things on a large scale became overwhelming. We left our jobs in the environmental nonprofit world and jumped into the adventure of our lives with strong bodies, optimism, and, most agreed, complete naivete.

In 1999, we moved to Vermont and started looking for land. I interned at an organic farm in central Vermont for one summer, and then we found our property. It had not been farmed since the 1940s and even then, it was used as pasture for sheep, not cultivated for crops. I soon discovered why. Most of the fields had returned to forest and the only bit of open land was what surrounded the circa-1860s farm-house, but even that had been overgrown by a thicket of blackberry brambles and weeds, locally known as "puckerbrush." Our first investment was a high-powered mower that could cut through 2-inch saplings. Starting just outside the house, one of us would steer the mower into the puckerbrush, which was head-high on a tall man, until we bumped into something. That was how we found the beauti-ful stone walls that ran throughout the property.

The house and backyard were manageable messes, but the real challenge was converting the fields. First, we had to remove the trees and roots that had grown back in the old sheep pastures. Then came a crash course in dirt. Eric took care of all of the infrastructure and mechanics of the farm while I was the grower. All of my experience in gardens and on farms had been with good soil; I had never started with virgin land. Our newly acquired soil was rocky and very acidic, with hardly any organic matter. I spent the next 10 years in, on, and covered by that dirt, coaxing it into better con-dition. This is a cookbook focused on vegetable preparation, not botany, but it needs to be said that there is no more important factor in the taste of food than healthy agricultural land. Weather and pests can also play a part, but the mantra I came up with over the years to explain any sort of success or disaster fit into the acronym ISS: It's the soil, stupid.

Once my soil-improvement plans were underway and a few greenhouses had been put up, I set out to grow everything that one can grow in northern New England and a few things that experts said I couldn't. I had a 2-acre perennial field with berries, asparagus, fruit

trees, and flowers; a 6-acre field that held all of the annual crops; and greenhouses devoted to nursery crops and tomatoes. When choosing varieties, I ignored any advisory regarding how well or large they grew; my only criteria was how they purportedly tasted. That the butternut squash grew under drought conditions or resisted disease meant very little to me. If the seed company did not exalt the taste in the catalog description, I skipped to the next.

I learned a lot of hard lessons those first few seasons, and after many years I'm still getting schooled by the bugs, fungi, beasts, and weather. I trialed hundreds of different varieties of vegetables and discovered what grew well in my soils (tomatoes, blueberries, eggplant), and what would have to be dropped from the roster (celery, pumpkins, broccoli). I learned how foolish it is to ignore the disease resistance or general heartiness of a variety because you can't taste it if you have no crop to start with. I dropped my bias against hybrids when I found those that combined excellent flavor with high yields. And, like every other farmer, I swelled with pride when I managed to grow a cauliflower bigger than your head or a softball-sized onion. The flavor of the produce remained paramount, however, and if it wasn't the best damned squash, tomato, bean, or blueberry I'd ever tried, then it was out.

We started our Community Supported Agriculture the second year on the farm with about 30 members from our small town. Since I was growing unusual vegetables like kohlrabi, I began writing a newsletter to go in the weekly basket that would include news from the farm and a recipe on how to cook the oddballs. No matter how busy I was, I really enjoyed sitting for an hour and writing about the week's harvest. This was the start of my food writing career. I later picked up a column in the *Burlington Free Press* and freelanced for *Edible Green Mountains*, *Modern Farmer*, *Better Homes & Gardens*, and *Local Banquet*. I wrote about what was coming out of the ground that week, the challenges of growing it this season, and great ways to prepare it. Sometimes the writing

forced me to experiment with a vegetable that I had never cooked or to expand my own repertoire beyond the same old, same old. I still enjoy learning about vegetables and sharing what I've learned, and this book has allowed me to play with several I previously had little exposure to, such as taro.

In 2009, my husband started a maple operation on our property, and he shifted his focus to full-time production of maple syrup. We had two young children, and I was ready to stop running myself into the ground balancing farming and motherhood. So over the next several years, I reduced the number of crops I produced until the only thing left to tend was blueberry bushes. I grew my last commercial crop of about a quarter-acre of garlic in 2016 and presently have shifted to an ever-expanding kitchen garden that I fuss over with my son, who has inherited my passion for growing. I don't miss the heat or black flies, but I do miss the thrill of spying a row of seedlings pop up from the earth or the satisfaction of seeing my stand chockablock with fresh veggies at the farmers market. And our maple operation, Runamok Maple, has taken off to the extent that it is more than full-time year-round.

This book is meant to share what I have learned about vegetables, both from a farmer's and a cook's perspective. I have tried to include tips on cooking with them so as to bring out their best flavor and really celebrate their character. I have drawn on my own experience in cooking both professionally and at home, but I've also included recipes from other cooks. With a global economy allowing for imports of not only vegetables but tastes and trends from all over the world, I wanted as many different perspectives as possible. I still consider the summer-ripe tomato one of the best things on the planet, but there is so much more at the vegetable stand that could potentially ignite the passion of a lifelong vegetable lover. I hope this book will be helpful both for those who already enjoy veggies and those who are looking to learn more.

Laura Sorkin

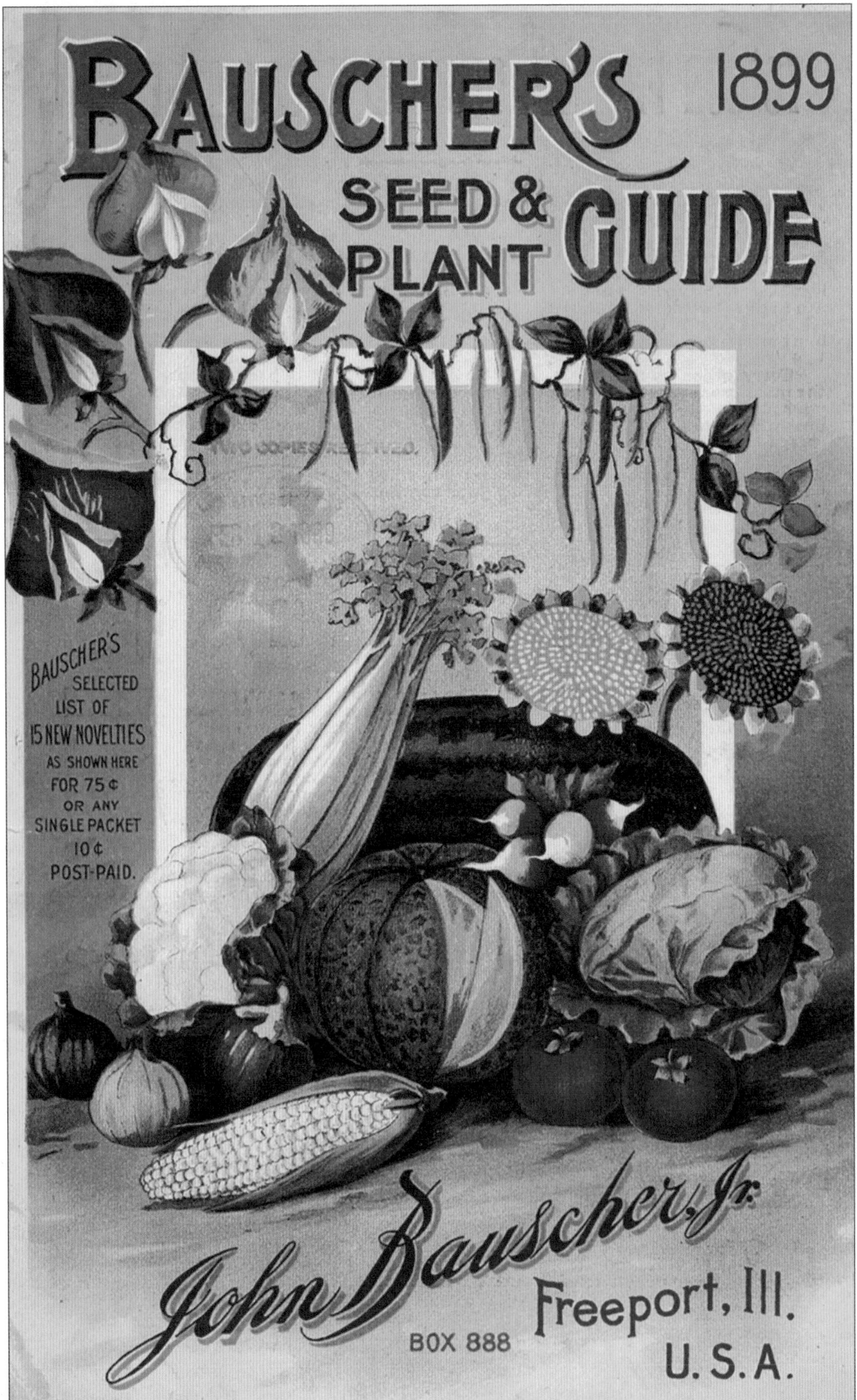
BAUSCHER'S 1899
SEED & PLANT GUIDE
BAUSCHER'S SELECTED LIST OF 15 NEW NOVELTIES AS SHOWN HERE FOR 75¢ OR ANY SINGLE PACKET 10¢ POST-PAID.
John Bauscher, Jr.
BOX 888
Freeport, Ill.
U.S.A.
COPYRIGHTED JOHN BAUSCHER, JR. 1899.

LET'S TALK ABOUT VEGETABLES

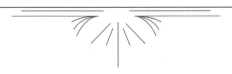

OMNIVORE VS. VEGETARIAN

The debate over which diet is superior—omnivore, vegetarian, or vegan—is endless. Thanks to the internet, if you have a strong opinion about the matter, you can find multiple studies to reassure yourself, and anyone else across the table from you, that your diet choice is the best. "Meat is bad for you, inhumane, and bad for the planet." "Vegetarians do not get a complete diet, and grazing is important for a balanced ecosystem." "Vegans are a nightmare as Thanksgiving guests." Diet choices are highly personal, but here are some definitions and points to consider.

An omnivore is the easiest to define. They eat everything: meat, fish, dairy, and vegetables. Personally, I am an omnivore, but I admire those who choose to be vegetarian. There is no doubt that industrial livestock farms are damaging the environment. Runoff from animal waste is detrimental to waterways, and methane from cows is contributing to climate change. There is also the issue of how animals raised for meat are treated, which is an ongoing problem that should continue to be addressed. And the American diet is far too dependent upon meat. A USDA report showed the American consumption of meat to be at an all-time high

in 2018, with the average citizen eating 222.2 pounds of beef and poultry that year. With diabetes and obesity at staggering levels, is it any coincidence that the acronym for our eating habits is SAD (Standard American Diet)?

Eating more vegetables is the obvious answer, but vegetarians do not get to claim faultless environmental stewardship, either. Growing vegetables also creates runoff that can pollute waterways, and many crops are water hogs. The drought in California brought to light water data that we probably otherwise would not have learned about. Vegetarians are quick to point out that it takes about 1,700 gallons of water to produce a pound of beef but less vocal about how it takes roughly 1,900 gallons of water to grow a pound of almonds. There are plenty of crops that have much lower water needs, such as chickpeas (501 gallons/lb.) and sweet potatoes (46 gallons/lb.), but all crops will have some sort of impact on the land they are growing on.

Vegans do not eat anything derived from animals, including milk, eggs, and honey. Their diet is very admirable but challenging to execute. Though many restaurants are introducing vegan options, and all-vegan restaurants are becoming easier to find in cities and university towns, vegan options for eating out can be limited. Traveling abroad and finding all-vegan meals can also be difficult. And animal products can figure into things that may be a necessity; consider that many medicines are administered in capsules that contain animal-derived gelatin. In other words, omitting all things that come from animals and living in the industrial world takes some work.

I like Michael Pollan's approach to diet, described in his book *In Defense of Food: An Eater's Manifesto*: "Eat food. Not too much. Mostly plants." This is a wonderfully concise way of saying: stay away from processed foods, reduce our notoriously huge portions, and cut back on all that meat. He makes arguments both for and against eating meat, but he recommends, if you choose to eat meat, enjoying it only occasionally. I love this approach, as I would miss the flavor of meat, but I don't need a 32 oz. porterhouse to feel satisfied. There are many cuisines that use meat as a flavoring agent rather than the central component, such as Chinese dishes. The recipe for Dry-Fried Beans (see page 614) incorporates ground pork for texture and flavor, but the savory green beans are the star. In other Chinese recipes, dried shrimp are a common ingredient that impart a briny, umami flavor to otherwise vegetable-based dishes.

This book is not strictly vegetarian. Instead, it is meant to celebrate vegetables and how they are prepared around the world. Some of the dishes contain small amounts of meat—like the recipe mentioned in the above paragraph—or include a meat broth, but it is really about vegetables in all of their sumptuous glory. For too long, vegetables have been perceived as just a side, and that makes us consider them incidental or, worse, obligatory. Yet I can't stop thinking of the time my husband and I ordered Fried Brussels Sprouts with Maple-Cider Glaze (see page 474) at our favorite BBQ joint and I regretted having ordered the pulled pork as well since the Brussels were so intoxicatingly good. I can think of many meals where my order was decided by potato gratin being included "on the side." And though I love roast turkey, for me Thanksgiving is all about the myriad vegetable dishes that accompany it.

The recipes in this book are, simply, really good food; how you decide to serve them is up to you. I can make a meal out of a plate of summer tomatoes and fresh mozzarella with vinaigrette. But if you have hearty eaters, consider putting some Chili-Dusted Cauliflower & Chickpea Salad (see page 420) on the plate, too. For my fellow omnivores, the dishes in this book are intended to make it easier to attain Pollan's goal. Put some effort into the vegetable part of the meal. Make it such a showstopper that it gets the pole position on the plate, relegating the meat portion to an also-ran. Or lose the meat altogether.

And, for a recommendation that applies to *all* diets, let's make an effort to reduce food waste. Recent studies show that a quarter of all food produced gets wasted. As a farmer, I get particularly riled up over this because I know exactly how much work went into growing it. According to a study by the Meridian Institute, the amount of greenhouse gases generated worldwide by producing food that never gets eaten is third in line behind the greenhouse gases created by the two worst offenders: China and the United States. We can reduce waste by being a little more open to fruit and vegetables that appear damaged. In most cases, you can cut the unwanted part off and the rest is fine. And just because a carrot looks gnarled doesn't mean it isn't perfectly good to eat.

Also, remember the adage that your eyes are often bigger than your stomach. Don't load up your plate only to scrape half of it into the garbage when you realize you are full. This is especially true for children, so help them learn to choose reasonable portions. By cutting back on food waste, we reduce the amount of resources needed to grow it, the money it costs to buy it, and the landfill to deal with the aftermath. And compost if you are able. Since Pollan already coined the perfect phrase for healthy eating, this is my addendum for the planet:

Only take what you are going to eat. Imperfect doesn't mean inedible. Leftovers rock.

This is a diet mantra we can all get on board with. And to help make sure you don't toss that last half of a zucchini, I have included a few recipes that help use up the bits and pieces in the vegetable bin.

THE SALAD REVOLUTION

The ever-blossoming cultural diversity of the United States has rescued us from dreary, dead veggies. Sure, crisp and crunchy fresh summer salads have been around for a while, but so too have boiled veggies denigrated to flavorless mush. Indian Americans brought spices and hot peppers, and Chinese arrivals introduced the concept of quick searing in a hot pan to caramelize. The cuisines of Mediterranean Spain, Greece, and Italy incorporated the garlic, citrus, and olive oil that bring so many dishes to life. Mexican cuisine continues to be a dominant influence in American cooking with its use of cilantro, beans, peppers, and salsas. (Does any family not have a taco night?)

These ingredients had the happy circumstance of being spread throughout a country with considerable potential for growing excellent produce. The farming regions of California and Florida alone ensure that fresh vegetables are available year-round. The combination of a diverse population and prolific farms has vastly improved vegetable preparation in the U.S., and

there is no longer any reason to boil your vegetables into submission.

Unless you had a garden in your backyard, a fresh green salad was not a big component of the American diet until refrigeration became common in the 1930s. A Batavian type of lettuce, which is like a typical red- or green-leaf head, was the most commonly grown lettuce in the country at that time, but it didn't travel well. Around the 1940s, growers developed a variety of crisphead lettuce called Iceberg, which could withstand the journey from the fields of California to the East Coast without wilting. Iceberg lettuce is indeed crisp but tastes mostly of its main component—water—and is substantially less nutritious than most other salad greens. Nevertheless, for home cooks in the middle of the 20th century, "green salad" in America meant Iceberg lettuce, and enthusiasm for it was as tepid as its taste.

In the 1970s, farm stands in California started offering a mix of baby greens consisting of peppery arugula, sweet Bibb lettuce, fiery mustards, and hearty kale. Mesclun had been a fixture in France for some time, but the green blends were new to American palates. Once people tried them, the concept took off.

Americans were particularly enamored with the convenience of a prewashed, pre-cut mix that could go from bag to plate in a matter of seconds. They also had so much flavor that the green salad made a roaring comeback on menus and in households. Not only are mesclun greens the base for limitless toppings, they have also become a complementary companion to many dishes. For example, it would now be unthinkable to serve a slice of quiche without a piquant mesclun salad alongside to balance the rich egg and cheese.

The salad has now become acceptable as a meal unto itself. Start with a really good mix of greens and then add some crunch (nuts, seeds, croutons), protein (chicken, tofu, steak, beans), maybe some fat (cheese, avocado), and a fabulous dressing. There is no limit to creativity considering the possible combinations of a salad. My only recommendation is that you balance sweet, salty, herbaceous, and sour when considering your components. And of course, the freshest produce will result in the liveliest salad, so take advantage of farmers markets during your region's growing season for best results.

THE DRY-HEAT REVOLUTION

Another recent change in our perception of how delicious vegetables can be is the "discovery" of the roasted vegetable. For too long, many an American vegetable was subjected to the long boil for its preparation. The result: generations of children (and adults) pushing bland and mushy peas and carrots around their plates or just foregoing vegetables all together. Around the dawn of the new millennium, there was a noticeable shift away from the pot of water to the oven. Certainly, potatoes had been roasted in American kitchens, but home cooks and chefs discovered that all sorts of other vegetables, from cauliflower to turnips, needed only a little oil and some dry heat to bring out their best attributes.

When I was a kid, my mother cooked Brussels sprouts and cauliflower according to the style of the time—by boiling them—and I absolutely detested the smell, texture, and taste. I'm not sure exactly when the roasting revolution began, but I can trace my own uprising to the early 2000s, when my husband, of all people, introduced me to roasted Brussels sprouts. By my mid-30s, I had embraced most vegetables, but the memory of metallic-tasting boiled Brussels sprouts preserved a strict prohibition against them in my kitchen. Eric is a devoted carnivore, so I was shocked when he swooned over one of the few vegetables I hated. I owe him big. The roasted Brussels sprout was a revelation; sweet and nutty with a hint of cabbage-tinged tanginess. The outside leaves became slightly crispy while the interior remained tender. They were scrumptious with just a sprinkling of salt but also took on other flavors well, such as Parmesan cheese, bacon, or a tart balsamic glaze. It turned out that those roasted Brussels sprouts were a gateway for many other vegetables that I had not fully embraced, particularly in the brassica family. Roasted broccoli is wonderful, especially when the little florets become a touch crispy. Roasting turnips tames their aggressive sourness to a mellow tang, and roasted cauliflower has become nothing less than a national sensation, showing up on menus everywhere.

Grilling and sautéing also produce a nice sear on veggies. Eggplant and zucchini are especially good candidates for the grill. A quick spritz of some oil and seasoning keep them moist and flavorful without getting too greasy. You can grill nearly any vegetable, including romaine lettuce. Just keep in mind that the denser veggies, such as carrots and potatoes, should be steamed or parboiled first to make sure their interiors get cooked through.

I am partial to sautéing because it gives me maximum control. The rule is to keep everything in one layer so each piece gets a good sear. Vegetables have considerable amounts of water in them, so if you pile them up in the pan, they will steam, not brown. This is especially true for mushrooms and onions, where you are really looking for that nice caramelizing effect to obtain maximum flavor. On the other hand, if your pan is too big and there are just a few items in it, you will have empty hot spots that will result in burned oil. It is worthwhile to invest in a variety of pan sizes so they are always the right proportion for the meal you are cooking.

In spite of the dry-heat revolution, not all veggies should be banned from the pot. Green

beans and asparagus, for example, are excellent after a quick parboil in salty water, though some veggies are best with a long simmer, such as collards. A steamed artichoke served with mayonnaise or melted butter is among the best appetizers I can think of. The trick is to not overcook them, as they will lose their texture and flavor. Steaming is also recommended when you want to retain crunch and nutrients in foods like broccoli and carrots. And then there is edamame, or edible soybeans. You will find no recipes for edamame in this book because one cannot improve on the simple procedure of boiling them in their pods in salty water for 3 minutes and then serving them up with another sprinkle of salt. They are perfection in their simplest form.

In a few instances, it turns out no cooking is required at all. Corn, for example, has been overlooked as a raw vegetable. Yes, it is wonderful boiled and buttered, but the next time you have access to just-picked corn, try husking it and eating it raw off the cob. I was not aware how great raw corn was until I started growing sweet corn on my farm. One of my experienced employees grabbed an ear off the stalk, shucked it right there in the field, and began munching away. I was a little appalled, but after I gave it a try there was no going back. After introducing my children to raw corn, they were so enamored they went evangelical about it, taking all their friends out to the field when they would visit to insist they try this new, magical food. As long as the corn is very fresh, there is no need to cook it, and incorporating the kernels in salads adds a sweet, crisp element. I feel the same way about shell peas, but those are a little trickier. There are few things finer than standing in the garden eating fresh peas out of the shell. But the sugars in peas turn to starch very quickly, so if you are going to use them raw, they should be picked the same day.

THE FARM STAND

Another factor in how our vegetable world is broadening is the proliferation of farmers markets. In the U.S., their number has grown from under 2,000 in 1994 to over 8,600 registered with the USDA as of 2019. They have introduced a world of new varieties and types of vegetables to the public—and, in the process, opened the eyes of consumers as to how good vegetables can be. Supermarkets are restricted to vegetables that ship well and have a decent shelf life; flavor is a factor, but the first two criteria get priority. Farmers who sell their crops at local markets can grow anything that does well in their climate, opening the door to heirloom or more fragile varieties that may lack in durability but have excellent flavor.

The best example of this dichotomy is the Sungold tomato. The Sungold is an orange-colored cherry tomato that is sublime—intense sugars with just the right balance of acid and rich tomato taste. Most people who try them say they taste like candy. Sungolds are prolific and grow without much trouble, but they are highly prone to cracking. Before harvest, while still on the vine, and after harvest just hanging out in the pint, some will just spontaneously split open. Customers who are familiar with Sungolds accept this about them because they are so damned good, but there is no way a produce manager in a supermarket would put them out on the floor, because they look like damaged goods. Most of my customers were aware of the Sungold's tendency to crack, but didn't care because they were the best-tasting tomato they had ever tried, and they were always the most popular item at the stand. Someday, breeders may develop a new hybrid with Sungold flavor that doesn't split. Until then, the best-tasting tomato on the planet is only available at a farmers market.

So many of the other varieties that one can find at a farmers market are not at a supermarket because they are too perishable, odd, or new. Larger farms that grow on contract for supermarkets are less likely to take a chance on a variety of eggplant that has a shape the American public is not accustomed to or a shell bean that has unusual markings. A small-market farmer can plant a short row of that strange eggplant to try it for herself and see if there is any market for it among chefs or her customers. Or perhaps a crop was requested by a chef who asked for something like salsify (a largely forgotten root vegetable once common in European cooking) and a portion of the crop is made available on the stand. You never know what is going to be available at your local farmers market, and the anticipation of making a discovery is half the fun. If the market is truly local, you can bet that the produce will be fresh and the flavor, not endurance, will be paramount.

Not everyone has access to a farmers market, though, and I am not as much of a market snob as I may sound. The produce aisles of your average supermarket have vastly improved over the last few decades. Demand for greater diversity and better quality has resulted in gourmet markets like Whole Foods and Fresh Market where the vegetable section is a sea of gorgeous, perfect produce, much of it sourced locally. But even the midrange markets have upped their veggie game, offering things like escarole or cassava because consumers learn of new ingredients on TV, the web, or a local restaurant and want to try them at home. For many regions in the U.S., we are living at a time of abundance and choice for which we should be grateful.

For regions that lack availability of fresh produce, also known as food deserts, there is a lot of work to be done. There is no excuse in a country as wealthy as ours for people not to have access to good, quality food. I am not oblivious to the fact that some do not have the money to afford fresh produce or the time or knowledge to prepare it. There are heroes out there who see the connection between a healthy diet and the overall health of a community and who are trying to address the issue of food deserts and nutrient-poor diets. It is my aim to support those heroes in putting out as many delicious recipes of all kinds of vegetables— fresh, frozen, canned, or dried—to increase our collective knowledge of good veg prep and healthy diets for all. As a country, we can do better.

Die-hards will tell you that fresh produce requires only minimal preparation, and I would agree with them wholeheartedly. A tomato from the garden only needs a light sprinkle of salt to bring out the depth of its character and can be a divine experience. But we don't always have garden-fresh tomatoes available, plus, winter happens. If I had to choose between a supermarket tomato in January or a canned one, there is no question I would start looking for my can opener. There is also the fact that nearly any vegetable tastes great with a quick turn in the skillet in a little olive oil, finished with some fresh garlic or perhaps a squeeze of lemon. But no one buys a cookbook for 300 recipes of veggies sautéed in garlic. This book is meant to celebrate the diversity of flavors vegetables have to offer and to show off some of the very best ways of preparing them from around the world.

VEGETABLES A TO Z

*T*he following section profiles over 50 different vegetables. There are many more delicious types of plants that are grown and processed for consumption all over the world, but the following pages cover the produce that can reliably be found in a U.S. market, along with a few vegetables that are becoming more prevalent. Each entry includes a little background—where the veggie originated, who grows the bulk of it, and how it is celebrated—along with some points of historical interest. If it is something I've grown, I toss in some stories of my own experiences.

A word for those hung up on semantics: I know that many of the vegetables in this book are technically fruits (something that emanates from a flower). But many of those fruits, like avocados, eggplants, tomatoes, and squash, are most commonly used for savory dishes and considered vegetables. Plus, other non-vegetables, like mushrooms and seitan, are a regular part of vegetable fare, so we'll keep it simple and call them all vegetables.

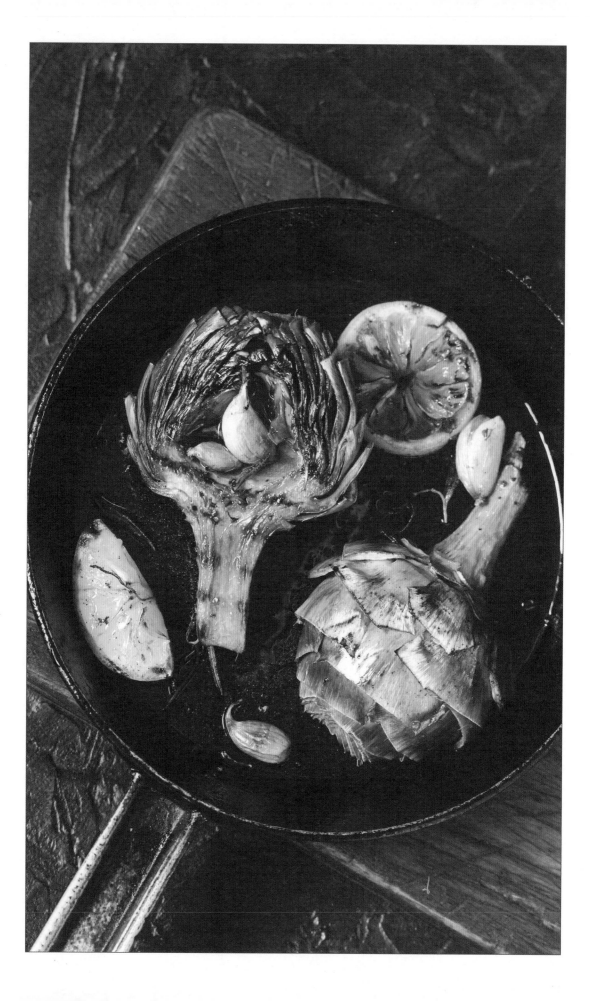

ARTICHOKES

Every spring, my family and I look forward to steamed fresh artichokes. I put out a small bowl of mayonnaise and we dip the leaves in, scraping the tender "meat" off with our teeth. When we have worked through all of the thick leaves, we pull off the remainder of the inner folds and scrape out the choke, leaving the heart, which is cut into pieces and dunked in the remaining mayo. For those of you who enjoy lobster, this is akin to starting with the tantalizing little tidbits from the knuckles and then saving the great hunk of meat from the tail for last. It's some work getting to the good stuff, but it is worth it.

Artichokes are the flower of a type of thistle plant. They are indigenous to the Mediterranean region and especially revered in Italy. In fact, Italy is the largest producer of them worldwide, followed by Egypt and Spain. Italian markets are always stocked with fresh artichokes, ranging from large and green to small and purple. Given that they are technically thistles, you have to be careful with the thorny tips, but under the layers of leaves and fibrous "choke" is a delicious core called the heart, which some describe as manna from heaven.

The majority of the artichokes produced in the U.S. are grown in California (some say 100 percent, but I know a few Eastern farmers who would contest that). In fact, in 2013 it was named California's official state vegetable by popular vote, which says a lot given the staggering variety of vegetables grown in the state. Most of the crop is grown in Castroville, which has the perfect climate for it: cool with just enough rain. Castroville has long celebrated its primary industry by having an Artichoke Festival each May where you can visit the world's largest artichoke sculpture, 20 feet tall and 12 feet across, and check in to see who is crowned the Artichoke Queen. The first one was named in 1947, a Miss Norma Jeane Mortenson, who later moved to Hollywood and changed her name to Marilyn Monroe.

Americans enjoy artichokes but mostly cook with some packaged variety. Doing a quick web search on artichoke recipes, I found that nine out of ten home cooks use canned or frozen artichokes instead of fresh. I understand how a cumbersome thistle bud can be intimidating, but the fresh versions are worth the effort to prepare. The easiest way is to boil the artichokes in water spiked with a little lemon juice for about 20 minutes or until the core is tender. Once cooked, you can remove the leaves and chokes to get at the hearts, which you can add to pasta, grilled cheese, lasagna, or simply fry in some olive oil and a pinch of salt.

I have grown artichokes on my farm, but the process is tricky. It is a perennial, so botanically

Artichoke.
The Blackwell delin. sculp. et Pinx.   Cinara.

it wants to produce a flower after being in the ground for at least a year. That is not going to work for a tender plant in an area that sees -25°F in January, so you have to trick the artichoke into thinking it has gone through a whole growing season in its first year by varying the temperature around it. This is done by taking the potted seedling out of a warm greenhouse into 40°F weather for a time. It's a funny thing to mess with the psyche of a plant, but most years I was successful, and to see a genuine artichoke growing in a Vermont field felt triumphant.

If you don't harvest the artichoke when the leaves are still tight—technically the bud phase—it produces a gorgeous flower in lilac purple. My friend Dave, a fellow farmer, always left his artichokes to flower, which drove me crazy. It took such effort to grow a real artichoke in Vermont, I would always give him a hard time for not harvesting it to eat. Upon seeing those huge, fluorescent flowers in early fall, however, it was hard not to argue that they make a spectacular ornamental.

Artichokes are at their peak in the U.S. in midspring. Look for ones that are green all around, without any brown spots. If you don't

have access to fresh artichokes, I prefer the frozen ones to the canned variety, but either one should be rinsed well before using.

Tab.33.

Eruca, latifolia, alba, sativa Dioscoridis. C.B.Pin.93. J.R.H.227
Ital.Ruchetta di Orto. __ Gall.Roquette

ARUGULA

Thank goodness for arugula—the peppery green that adds zip to any dish, hot or cold. Bland pasta or tepid salad? Add some arugula. Have a rich cut of meat that needs balance? Top it off with arugula. Even pizza or a boring sandwich can be improved with arugula.

Native to the Mediterranean area, arugula dates back so many centuries that there are even references to it in the Old Testament (II Kings 4:39). It has always been popular in Europe, where it is called *rucola* in Italy, *roquette* in France, and *rocket* in England. Americans didn't really discover its merits until it started showing up as a component in mesclun mixes in the 1970s. I would argue that it was arugula and its leafy mustard cousins that revitalized the American appetite for salad in general. But arugula's popularity really took off in the 1990s, when cooks learned that apart from mesclun, the green was a great way to punch up the flavor of any dish. Now it has broken out of the salad category and is used as an herb or a general flavor booster.

In the summer months, arugula is grown in many areas of the U.S., but in particular in northern California, where it stays cooler. November through March, 90 percent of the arugula and the other greens enjoyed in the U.S. come from Yuma, Arizona. Given our national appetite for salad, one might ask how it is that such a large amount of water-hungry crops are grown in the desert. Salad greens require sun, moderate warmth, and irrigation. Yuma holds the Guinness World Record for the sunniest place on earth, so check off the first box. It also has perfect salad-growing temperatures in winter and very fertile soils. What sets Yuma apart from much of the rest of the southwest is its access to the Colorado River, not to mention a large population of skilled workers who cross the border from Mexico daily to work in the fields. All of these conditions result in nine salad processing plants that produce up to 2 million pounds of bagged lettuce and salad mixes each and every day during the height of the winter season.

This massive production keeps us in leafy greens year-round, which is a good thing, considering how many ways you can use arugula. It shines best when contrasted with something mild or sweet. It will pep up eggs nicely, so I've tossed it in an omelet with creamy ricotta, salty olives, and sun-dried tomatoes (see page 591). It also goes well with fruit, as seen in the Arugula, Nectarine, Farro & Goat Cheese Salad with White Balsamic Vinaigrette (see page 403). Arugula pesto has many uses besides pasta; you can swirl it in bean soup or top a sandwich with it. Dressing pizza with arugula is a trend that I hope is here to stay, since it cuts through rich cheese well. And lastly, its peppery taste is the perfect foil for rich, fatty meats such as flank steak or pork belly.

The intensity of arugula increases as it gets more mature, so if you are looking for less peppery greens, pick the very young, tender bunches. The older greens pack a punch, which is great for pesto or cooking but can be a bit much for eating raw. Always keep arugula cold, preferably in a reusable plastic bin to help retain moisture.

ASPARAGUS

Spring at our house means the sap will be running, the mud will be deep, and asparagus will be on the dinner table at every opportunity. I love asparagus but am very picky about the quality and will only buy it in season. Though it is now available year-round from sources across the globe, it is at its best when harvested as close to home as possible between the months of March and June (in northern regions). When it is finally available locally, I celebrate its return by steaming, roasting, and grilling it to the point where the family need not ask what's for dinner; the answer is _____ and asparagus.

Asparagus is a perennial, which means it is a plant that stays in the ground and regrows every year. When the weather warms in spring, the crown (root) sends up green shoots that have tender, sweet stalks and tight buds at their tips. These are handpicked at ground level. The plant will continue to send up new shoots, the number and size of which depend on the age of the plant. Eventually, the stalks become very slender, the buds open, and the farmer will let them continue to their full growth as a shrub with beautiful, feathery, fern-like tops that can reach 6 feet in height. It is this part of the plant that absorbs energy from the sun and feeds the crown for next year's shoots. I once saw a garden that used asparagus as a decorative hedge and thought how clever this person was for planting a garden that offered edibles in the spring and privacy in summer.

Asparagus is thought to be indigenous to Europe, and references to it have been found in ancient Greek, Roman, and Egyptian texts. It is enjoyed all over the world and has been incorporated into local fare such as asparagus curry in India and asparagus stir-fry in China. But it is the Europeans who truly adore this sprout and celebrate the harvest annually. Germans are mad for white asparagus, and farmers bank dirt around the stalk to prevent the development of chlorophyll. They claim this is the sweetest, most tender of the species and even have a special name for the season: *Spargelzeit*. In the French region of Alsace, the Brotherhood of Asparagus of Village-Neuf has long declared that local soils make their crop of white asparagus the very best and have ceremonies and celebrations to prove it. The British also adore it, claiming English asparagus to be the very finest. The British Asparagus Growers Association has a very extensive website with a countdown page until harvest begins. In short, Europeans are devoted to the spear and it's likely that their frequency of cooking it during the season rivals mine.

Asparagus is a cousin of the onion, though the two have little in common in terms of taste. Growing asparagus can be a measure of maturity in that you get your reward up front but then have to take care of the plant for the rest of the season to reap anything the following year.

Given my love for it and the fact that it thrives in my climate, there was no question I was going to grow it on my farm. I planted a 100-foot row of crowns my first year and diligently took care of the small growth, resisting the urge to harvest anything until it was stronger. The following years were good harvests, but, like in any area of open soil, weeds moved in and had to be managed. When tomatoes needed harvesting and the third round of carrots needed weeding, it was hard to give my limited time to a crop that had already given me the goods in June. In the end, I had too many other things going on and replaced the asparagus with lower-maintenance blueberries.

Look for asparagus in markets starting in March. You will find them in both thick and thin spears, and which is better is a matter of taste. I find the thicker ones more tender and better for blanching or boiling, and those of medium thickness to be best for grilling. The thin ones are very elegant to steam and use in a crudités platter. White asparagus are less common in the States, but I have started to see them popping up in U.S. markets more often. You can use them in all the same recipes as green asparagus, but peeling the skin before cooking is recommended.

AVOCADOS

Avocados have had a meteoric rise in the past decade, one that is rivaled only by cauliflower and kale. Once considered an expensive oddity, consumption of the avocado in the United States increased 300 percent from 2010 to 2015. It is now estimated that Americans consume about 7 pounds per person, per year. Though some of their popularity comes from an uptick in plant-based diets and the now-ubiquitous availability of delicious and authentic Mexican food nationwide, most point to a singular dish that is practically the symbol of millennial hipsterdom: the avocado toast. If you are among the three people on the planet who have not seen this dish on a menu recently, it is simply mashed avocado on bread with a topper such as egg or tomato. There are more elaborate renditions with everything from smoked salmon to

blueberries, and if you search for #avocadotoast on Instagram, the volume of internet space taken up with this simple dish is staggering. That could be because it is really good.

Avocados, of course, are excellent in many dishes other than avocado toast. They add welcome fat to salads and a creamy element to sandwiches. A perfect green slice in sushi enhances the flavor of fish or vegetables, and avocados are integral to Mexican cuisine, often served alongside grilled steak or chicken as well as on tacos and nachos. Guacamole is so popular that it is estimated 200 million avocados are consumed during the Super Bowl, an event that could be renamed Wings and Guacamole Day. I've always considered avocados to have a similar effect to butter; you can't necessarily define the taste, but it makes everything around it taste better.

The rise in avocado popularity has a darker side, though. Demand for the fruit was so high that large areas of Mexican forests were cleared to plant more avocado trees, destroying habitat, depleting local water supplies, and adding to the pesticide and fertilizer load in local waterways. Drug cartels also noticed the thriving industry and moved into towns with large orchards, extorting money from the farmers. Some towns in the Michoacán region, the largest avocado-growing area, fought back and formed their own militias to defend against the cartels. Avocado growers in California have their own problems dealing with 'cado rustlers who steal the high-cash crop right off of the trees. The California Avocado Commission now

devotes considerable energy to helping growers deter theft. For a creamy, delicious fruit, it has caused considerable strife.

Their popularity is not likely to wane anytime soon, though, because avocados are extraordinarily delicious. I prefer the taste of Hass avocados, which have a black, bumpy peel. The other variety you are likely to see is the Florida avocado, which is larger and has a smooth, green peel. The taste of the Florida variety is not as pronounced, but they can still produce excellent guacamole.

Picking a ripe avocado is tricky, and even experienced buyers end up with fruit that looks good on the outside but is rotten on the inside. If you are buying the Hass variety, look for avocados that are still hard but are just turning from dark green to black. I find taking home an unripe fruit and letting it ripen on the counter yields better results than subjecting a soft one

to the jostling of the shopping bag. If you need it that day and must find a ripe fruit, look for ones that are all black and have just a little give when squeezed.

Once you open an avocado, you must find a way to keep it from turning brown. You can either sprinkle some lemon juice on it or, if you are using it in a salad, put a little bit of the dressing on it. Lastly, I saw more injuries in a commercial kitchen due to removing avocado pits than any other calamities, including burns. The best way I have found is to slice open the fruit and hold the side with the pit in one hand. Take a knife in the other hand and tap the middle of the blade into the pit with as little force as needed to embed the knife edge, so if you miss the pit you do not hit your hand. Wiggle the pit until it comes loose and pull it out. If you question your coordination, use a spoon and dig out the pit.

BEETS

Beets are one of those love-em or hate-em foods. When I was very little, my mother convinced me to eat them by telling me they made my blood red. I didn't like them, but I was concerned about what color my blood might turn otherwise, so I dutifully ate them. Many people who don't enjoy beets find their earthiness overpowers all other flavors. ("They taste like dirt," says my husband.) For the rest of us, they are a sweet addition to salads, soups, and roasts, with a nice balance of mineral and vegetal.

There is really no other vegetable like them. Their sugar content is so high that the cultivar known as sugar beets (20 percent sugar) is grown strictly for processing and is responsible for one third of the world's sugar supply. Russia is the highest producer of sugar beets, with France, the U.S., and Germany following.

Table beets have 6 percent sugar content, and yet no one moons over their sweet flavor the way we do corn or winter squash. This may be because the majority of beets grown in this country are sent for processing to be canned or frozen. Only a small percentage is used for fresh market. If your only experience with beets is the rubbery cubes poured from a can into a salad bar, you should try them fresh from the farmers market. Their succulent sweetness is the perfect foil for a chalky chèvre, which is why beet and goat cheese salad is on repeat on so many menus. It just works. Their texture is also perfect after boiling or steaming; tender but with enough resistance to make the meal feel substantial. Eastern Europeans consume a lot of beets, and they are not afraid to toss them in any kind of soup or salad, even if they turn everything red or Valentine's Day pink. My go-to recipe for the famous Ukrainian soup borscht (see page 286) includes red cabbage as well as beets, just in case your bowl was not red enough.

There are two types of fresh beets that you will find at the market. The first type is almost always available, and those are storage beets. They are generally large and without their tops, but, like carrots, they store very well for months so they should taste fresh and have good texture. The other type is bunched beets, which are often smaller and with their greens still attached. They are also fresh-tasting and have the added bonus of the tops, which you can use as you would kale or chard. Both types come in a range of colors; garnet, gold, white, and striped. You can use the colors interchangeably but if you find a variety called Chioggia, be sure to use them raw in a dish where you can show off their internal stripes, which resemble a bull's-eye.

Though my mother was only interested in getting me to eat my vegetables, it turns out that her fib wasn't too far from the truth. Beets are high in nitrates, which your body turns into nitric oxide, a chemical important for maintaining healthy blood flow and blood pressure. They are also a very good source of folate and manganese. When it came time to get my own kids to eat them, I didn't expound on biochemistry, though. I looked them in the eye and told them with a serious face that eating beets kept their blood red. They didn't fall for it. I blame the internet.

JUST ARRIVED
Alfred Wright's
PERFUMERY
" Mary Stuart "
AND
" Wild Olive."
45 Cts. Per Bottle.

FOR SALE BY
SHARPLESS & SONS,
PHILADELPHIA.

Bok choy, aka pak choi, is a type of cabbage originally from south China. It is mild and sweet, consisting of a crunchy stalk and a leafy top. It is most often used in a stir-fry and takes very well to almost any sauce as well as simple seasonings. In markets, you will find a large bok choy with dark green leaves and a smaller version with lighter-colored leaves and stalks. The larger bok choy is considered the true bok choy and the smaller is often referred to as Shanghai or "baby" bok choy. When a recipe calls for bok choy, you can use either.

The cultivation of bok choy in China dates back as far as 5 CE. It is very popular throughout Asia and is widely grown in Japan, Malaysia, the Philippines, and Indonesia. It was brought to Europe in the mid-18th century and is also now commonly found in Europe and U.S. markets. European chefs often pair it with fish since its delicate taste does not overwhelm.

Napa cabbage is thought to be the natural cross of a turnip and bok choy and has been cultivated in China since the 15th century. Like bok choy, it is popular throughout all of Asia and has become a market staple from Korea to Singapore. I had always assumed the name meant it was grown in Napa, California, but in fact it comes from the Japanese word *nappa,* which refers to the leaves of any vegetable. Though this cabbage has a tighter head than bok choy, the flavor and uses are similar, as it has a mild cabbage flavor with lots of crunch. They are similar enough that in Chinese, Napa cabbage is called *da bai cai,* which means "big white vegetable," and bok choy is simply *bai cai* or "white vegetable."

Napa cabbage is especially important in Korean cuisine as the main ingredient in kimchi, the fermented vegetable pickle that is widely considered the national dish of both North and South Korea. There are many variations on kimchi, but one of the most common renditions contains Napa cabbage, daikon radish, chilies, scallion, ginger, and garlic. Koreans consider Napa cabbage such an important crop that extensive research has gone into plant breeding, and in the 21st century 880 varieties of it were registered by the Korea Seed and Variety Service. Kimchi, like fermented foods in general, has gained popularity in the States as well, and plenty of chefs have capitalized on its ability to put some kick into sandwiches, soups, and just about anything else it is added to.

Napa cabbage and bok choy are typical of other cabbage types in their growth habit; they prefer cool weather with plenty of water, but not too wet and not too cold. In the U.S., they are a feast for many types of pests, especially flea beetles, which don't kill the plant but put unsightly little pinholes in the leaves. These pests are managed in organic farming by putting hoops along the row and then a fabric cover over the hoops that lets in light and water but not pesky bugs. Since I am a huge fan of bok choy, I included it as part of the crop list my first year of farming. I thought I would attempt the season without the row cover but discovered I had a thriving population of flea beetles that were very appreciative of the food I provided them. Henceforth, the beetles were cut off from their favorite meal by the row covers, and I had very nice, whole heads of choy. If you see pristine-looking organic bok choy in the market, know that that it is some very pampered cabbage.

BROCCOLI

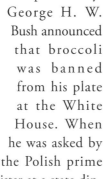

During the early years of his presidency, George H. W. Bush announced that broccoli was banned from his plate at the White House. When he was asked by the Polish prime minister at a state dinner to explain his boycott, Bush replied, "Just as Poland had a rebellion against totalitarianism, I am rebelling against broccoli and I refuse to give ground. I do not like broccoli, and I haven't liked it since I was a little kid and my mother made me eat it. And I'm president of the United States and I'm not going to eat any more broccoli." I actually have quite a few things in common with President Bush. We both come from the same part of Connecticut and went to the same high school (though decades apart, thank you very much). And though we did not share many opinions on politics, I agree with him 100 percent about broccoli. To put it in less presidential terms, blech.

But most Americans love broccoli, even children. Statistics from 2017 show that each person in the U.S. consumed about 7 pounds of broccoli per person in that year. Everyone I know likes broccoli, and I must confess it has a diverse repertoire. You can stir-fry it, blanch it, or steam it to make the most of its nutritional value. Or you can slather it in cheese sauce or feature it in a rich casserole, as it marries well with its surroundings. Like other brassicas, cooks have discovered that it is excellent roasted, especially when the little florets become crispy and almost blackened.

The majority of broccoli grown in the U.S. comes out of California, but it is grown commercially in most states and is even exported to Canada and, to a lesser extent, Japan. China and India are the world's largest producers, with the U.S. a distant third. If I'm tempted to grumble about the lack of nutritious eating in America, I certainly can't be discouraged by the popularity of broccoli. It is packed with vitamins, not the least of which are mega amounts of vitamins C, K, A, and folate. It is also thought to have many cancer-fighting compounds.

Broccoli is thought to originate in the eastern Mediterranean region and has been cultivated in Italy since Roman times. What you are eating is an immature flower head. If it is left unharvested, the tiny buds bloom into small yellow flowers. Italians have long prized its flavor. Though there are records of Thomas Jefferson experimenting with it in his garden, it

didn't become popular in the States until a large contingent of Italians arrived in the 1920s.

Not being a huge fan, I never put a lot of effort into growing broccoli on my farm. It is a demanding vegetable, requiring a great deal of space and fertilizer for a single head. It prefers cool weather but could theoretically be grown all summer long in Vermont if you made sure it had enough water. My lack of enthusiasm for it showed in the quality of the heads I grew. I remember one customer asking if I was intentionally growing mini broccoli (that's not a thing). After a few years I gave up on it, deciding my indifference to the vegetable showed in the final product.

Bush never did weaken the broccoli blockade. After his remarks to the Polish prime minister were made public, California's broccoli growers sent the White House 10 tons of broccoli. The president was steadfast, saying, "Barbara loves broccoli. She's tried to make me eat it. She eats it all the time herself. So she can go out and meet the caravan." I have relaxed my broccoli ban a tad and now accept that roasted broccoli is okay. The little florets get nice and crispy and the stems a little caramelized. Still, at a certain point in your life, I think it is all right to accept your dislikes as just a part of who you are. So for once, regarding this vegetable, I'm with George.

BRUSSELS SPROUTS

When I was a kid, the quickest way to ruin my day was to tell me we were having Brussels sprouts for dinner. I loathed them and knew that in keeping with our dinner rules I was going to have to finish every last smelly bite on my plate. As was the trend in the '70s, my mother boiled the sprouts, and the sulfuric cloud they produced wafted throughout the house, portending a long stint at the table until I could muster the courage to put sprout to fork and fork to mouth.

As I grew older, other vegetables that were on the Ick List gradually became more appealing and, one by one, I developed a love for nearly all of them. But not Brussels sprouts. Apparently, I'm not alone in that. A survey done by the Heinz company in 2008 showed Brussels sprouts to be the most hated vegetable in the U.S.

Of all people, it was my husband, a devoted carnivore, who turned me around on the sprouts. I was dutifully growing them for our CSA one September when Eric suggested making them for dinner. "No way," I responded, shivering a little at the thought. "They are really incredible roasted," he claimed. It was a rare occurrence for Eric to request vegetables in general, so I thought I would indulge him, assuming he just forgot how awful they were.

The roasted Brussels sprouts were a revelation. The crispy exterior was nutty and crunchy while the interior was tender and sweet. Just a little bit of salt was all you needed on a perfectly browned sprout, and you had a great counterpoint to roast pork or grilled chicken. That first tray I made disappeared quickly. For every subsequent batch I've made, I'll prepare extra, knowing I will snack on half of them before they even make it to the table. Once you've tried roasted Brussels sprouts in their pure form, add some bacon ends or perhaps a maple-balsamic glaze. Heaven.

Brussels sprouts are a cool-weather crop and are mostly grown in California, though you can find them locally in most places in the U.S. in the fall. They are not technically "sprouts" but are, in fact, little cabbages that grow along a thick stalk. Without leaves, a Brussels-sprout stalk looks a bit like a medieval club. The freshest way to buy them is to get the whole stalk and pick them off just before cooking. A good frost intensifies their sugars and makes them very sweet, so October and November are ideal times to buy them. They are very popular in Belgium, which is probably where their common name derived from.

I still believe their highest calling is to be roasted, but I've seen raw, shaved Brussels sprouts showing up on menus at trendier spots. This makes sense, since in their sliced, raw form, they are very much like coleslaw. Theoretically, one can steam or boil them, but I'm afraid I still haven't taken a shine to either method. If you are an unconditional fan of Brussels sprouts, have at it.

These little green guys are now on the trendy-vegetable list. Whereas they used to make a once-a-year appearance at Thanksgiving, today you find them on pizza, in grain bowls, and even at national chains such as Panera Bread. Statistics show that sales of Brussels sprouts were up 13 percent in 2018. It seems others have made the same discovery that I have: a roasted Brussels sprout is divine. I've become a roasted Brussels sprouts evangelist, spreading the word to all my fellow sprout-haters that not only are they not the bottom of the vegetable taste meter, they are very close to the top.

CABBAGES

Cabbage has found its way into kitchens across the globe, with each culture putting their own imprint on this adaptable vegetable. The cultivation of cabbage dates back to 4000 BCE in China and over 3,000 years ago in Europe. As explorers moved about, they brought it with them since it stores well, is very nutritious, and provides essential vitamin C to prevent scurvy. Once brought to a new region, it was incorporated into local cuisines. When considering which country has the best cabbage recipes, I'm at a loss. Eastern Europe loves a good braised cabbage. Koreans turn it into kimchi. Indians incorporate it into curries, and the Chinese use it in stir-fry. Americans are crazy for coleslaw and Germans are famous for sauerkraut. This incomplete list of the various uses of cabbage shows just how versatile it is.

It grows best in cool weather and fertile soil. China produces the most by volume, but Russia wins the prize of consuming the most per capita. Worldwide production in 2014 was 71.8 million tons. Red and green heads taste largely the same; choose one based on the color you would like. Because the color is so vibrant, I almost always

Brassica capitata alba, et viridis.
Ital. Cauolo. Bolognese. Gall. Chou

use red. Savoy cabbage has a similar taste, but the wrinkled leaves are slightly softer. Napa cabbage is somewhat different and is covered in the section on bok choy (see pages 46–47).

Iceberg lettuce used to be the standard topper for tacos and other dishes that needed a bit of fresh crunch, but red cabbage slaw has now replaced it. Cabbage offers more complexity of flavor, and if it is given a little time to soften with lime juice and salt, it has the perfect texture. Check out page 481 for a basic slaw recipe that can be used on top of tacos and nachos.

Sautéing cabbage is a quick and easy way to caramelize it, giving it the same treatment that chefs are applying to cauliflower and Brussels sprouts. I created a nice autumn dish with apples and fennel seed on page 482 that would be excellent alongside pork or cheesy rice. And if you are looking for ideas for cabbage in the summer, you could either grill it, like on page 478, or turn it into a tangy salad with tahini dressing. Finally, if you are thick in the middle of winter and looking for something hearty, there's Egg Noodles with Browned Onions & Cabbage (see page 633), a perfect dish for big appetites.

CARROTS

The carrot is the easiest vegetable to love. Crunchy, sweet, nutritious, and versatile, it is a staple in most kitchens. If kept cool and moist, it travels well in lunchboxes and goes with almost any dip. It is part of the flavor-building trio called a mirepoix that European cooks frequently employ in stocks, soups, and sauces. And it plays nice with nearly all other vegetables in salads, stir-fries, and curries, making it the second most popular vegetable in the world.

Though orange carrots are currently the norm and purple carrots are considered exotic, it used to be the other way around. In Europe and Asia Minor, where carrots are thought to have originated, most were purple or white and it wasn't until the 17th century that the orange carrot was developed, after which it became the dominant cultivar.

Multicolored carrots have made a comeback, and I highly recommend the purple ones for both cooked and raw preparations. They have excellent crunchy texture and an intense carrot flavor that is not too sweet. Plus, they are gorgeous on the plate. The white, red, and yellow varieties are milder in flavor and are best cooked. Use them in a dish where a robust sauce can boost them up a bit because the added color they provide is a boon to any table.

China produces the largest amount of carrots in tons per year, but California's Grimmway Farms and Bolthouse Farms are the largest individual producers of carrots in the world. They also dominate the market of the precut "baby carrots" that have taken over the fresh carrot market. Though I recommend full-size carrots for cooking at home, it is worth digressing into the baby carrot industry because, at the moment, they *are* the carrot market.

Baby carrots are, in fact, full-grown carrots that have been cut and peeled to be identical in size and shape. When the convenient little veggies were introduced in the 1990s, they immediately upended the carrot industry as a whole. Some fun facts from the Carrot Museum in the United Kingdom:

- In the U.S. over 172 million tons of carrots are processed into baby carrots each year.

- Sales of baby carrots exceed $400 million per annum.

- Overall carrot consumption in the U.S. has increased by 33 percent through the introduction of baby carrots.

- Baby carrots now account for over 70 percent of all retail carrot sales.

Baby carrots have been a hit with consumers from the start, but there have also been controversies. An approved chlorine solution is used to wash carrots in both the organic and nonorganic brands. There has been concern about

this added chemical, but without it, the public would be at risk of E. coli exposure. There has also been grumbling about food waste from all the peeling it takes to get that uniform shape, but the excised parts are used for either juicing or animal feed, not wasted. In fact, the baby carrot was first developed by farmer Mike Yurosek of Newhall, California, who was tired of tossing the odd-shaped carrots that didn't meet industry standards.

While I appreciate the public's environmental audit of this market disruptor, the statistic I focus on is the 33-percent increase in the overall consumption of carrots. We are eating more carrots, and that is a good thing.

Roasted carrots are among my favorite preparations. You can find a recipe on page 532 in which they are accompanied by parsnips, a honey glaze, and a North African spice blend called ras el hanout. Carrots are regulars in all kinds of salad, so I included one I make often in summer that includes jicama and a zesty ginger dressing (see page 431). One of my favorite carrot preparations comes from India, where grated carrots are braised in milk, sugar, and cardamom for a dessert called Halwa. I've made a savory version that is still plenty sweet, and is excellent alongside spicy lamb, on page 484.

CAULIFLOWER

Cauliflower has undergone nothing short of a renaissance. Once the ignored component on the crudités platter, one now finds it as the featured ingredient on menus, from roasted cauliflower steaks to cauliflower rice and tabbouleh. Like its cousins in the brassica family, cooks have discovered that roasting or browning cauliflower in a pan transforms the florets into nutty, sweet nuggets. But it does well as a puree as well, especially when combined with cream and turned into a soup or sauce.

Like cabbage, cauliflower is popular worldwide. China is the largest producer, growing 10.6 million tons in 2016. India grows quite a bit too, and the U.S. is a distant third. It is not the easiest vegetable to grow. It needs cool but not cold temperatures and very fertile soil. If conditions are not perfect, the heads can become stalky or small. I can only remember a few years when I could take pride in my big, beautiful cauliflower heads, and that was only after giving them prime spots in the field. Now when I see big heads in the market, I look on with admiration and more than a little envy.

There are color options besides white that can be fun. The orange variety, called Cheddar, was developed from a mutant found in a Canadian field in 1970. This type has a higher level of beta carotene, which is a bonus to an already nutritious vegetable. The purple types contain higher levels of anthocyanins, the same compounds that make blueberries and red wine so good for you. There are two types of green cauliflower: regular curd and Romanesco. The Romanesco types have the intricacy of coral, and mathematicians have celebrated their distinct fractal dimensions. I'm not exactly sure what that means, but suffice to say they look wicked cool. These different varieties of cauliflower all taste very similar, so I would choose one based on which would make the largest impact. Unlike other purple vegetables, the purple cauliflower will retain its color when cooked, though it might be muted. I would avoid using them for purees, as the color could turn to a dull gray.

CELERIAC

Celeriac gets its own section because it is very different from celery in almost every way. The taste is similar, but its texture, preparation, and end use are not. For starters, celery is the stalk of the plant, whereas celeriac is the root (and is sometimes referred to as celery root). But they are not the same plant, having gone in different breeding directions. Where celery is crisp and refreshing, celeriac is dense and creamy. Celery is best when it capitalizes on its crunchy, salty attributes in a salad or as the base for a soup. Celeriac is almost always cooked to tenderize its texture and draw out its sweet notes.

Celeriac is more commonly used in Europe, where it appears in creamy soup, in stews, and alongside roasts. The French really know how to bring out the best in it, turning it into a puree and using it as a side or a sauce under meats. It can also be combined with potatoes, either in a mash or as another component in a gratin. One of my favorite dishes is a remoulade in which grated celeriac is combined with tangy mayonnaise and served as a salad (see page 423).

In its harvested form, celeriac is not going to win any beauty contests. It can best be described as gnarly, and it looks like something that Bilbo just brought back to the Shire. To get to the good stuff you have to peel off the skin and all of the crannies where dirt can hide. Peeling away all of the unwanted parts can reduce it in size quite a bit, so be prepared to have considerably less than what you started with. Once peeled, the white interior can oxidize and turn brown. Keep it in a bowl of water with a bit of lemon juice in it in order to maintain its creamy color.

Celeriac is harvested in the fall and stores relatively well, so the best time to purchase it is September to March. Look for medium-sized bulbs, since the small ones will be too small once you are done peeling and the large ones may have something called "hollow heart," which is a result of overly dry growing conditions.

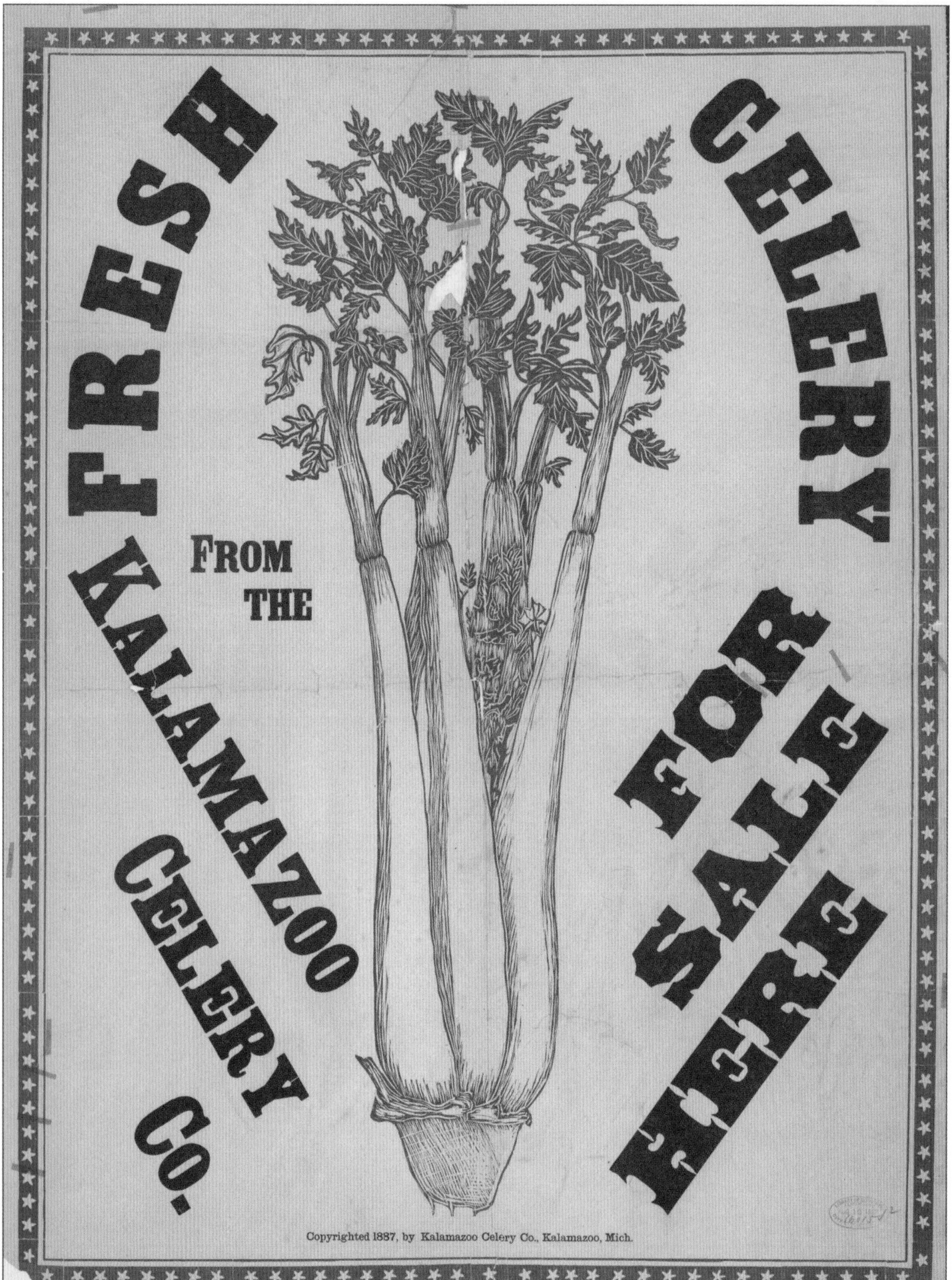

FRESH CELERY
FROM THE
KALAMAZOO CELERY CO.
FOR SALE HERE
Copyrighted 1887, by Kalamazoo Celery Co., Kalamazoo, Mich.

CELERY

People don't go gaga over celery. No one has ever said, "Darling, you have to try the celery, it's divine." The taste is somewhat salty and a little metallic. It is the cliché diet food that is rumored to require more calories to chew than it contains and, now that cauliflower is ascendant, it is always the last vegetable left on the crudités platter. A writer for the NPR food blog *The Salt* once wrote that, in her opinion, celery has "about as much flavor as a desk lamp." It is in many popular dishes but never cited for its contribution. Poor celery; always in the chorus and never given an aria.

But I will sing its praises. It is critical to a satisfying tuna salad and is de rigueur in chicken soup or a Bloody Mary. More importantly, it is one of the components that make up mirepoix along with onions and carrots. A mirepoix is the foundation of stocks and soups in French cooking and could be considered the place where flavor begins; the Italians call the trio *battuto* and also use it as a base for rich, complex sauces. In Louisiana's Creole and Cajun cuisines, many dishes are started with the Holy Trinity of celery, onions, and green peppers. One may not appreciate celery on its own, but some of the world's finest cooking wouldn't be as good without it.

Thought to be from the Mediterranean region, celery was first used as a food in Italy in the 1600s. Brought to the States in the 1800s, it was cultivated in the Midwest, where it became a very important crop for some towns. Celeryville, Ohio, for example, was so named for the dominant crop grown by Dutch settlers. The soils there are known to be so fertile that growers can produce twice as many crops as other regions, and yet they chose to not only grow the plebian celery but to name their town after it. There is also Portage, Michigan, where the Celery Flats Interpretive Center calls attention to the crop's importance in Kalamazoo County. Call me an agro-geek, but I would very much like to visit the working farm at the museum to unlock the secrets of a good-quality head of celery.

It is not an easy vegetable to grow. Unless it gets exactly what it wants, the stalks will end up bitter and stringy. What it wants is not too much heat, very rich soil, and lots and lots of water, which is why today the majority is grown in California and, to a lesser extent, Michigan. I tried growing it on my farm and barely managed a meager crop. After a great deal of effort, the stalks were skinny and tough, and the taste actually made my husband wince. The experience left me with much respect for celery farmers who do it well.

Celery might not inspire sonnets, but it adds an element to a dish that you would miss if it wasn't there. The salty flavor adds complexity, and there is even something about that metallic tang that adds an important note to the dish. And sometimes it can take center stage, such as in the salad on page 417. In addition, a celery soup can be a lovely first course when you've planned something heavy for the main course. The entire plant is edible, so use the leaves as well as the stalks.

COLLARDS

Collards are another member of the brassica family that can bring some backbone to any meal. Popular in Africa, South America, southern Europe, India, and southern parts of the United States, they are most commonly used as a side dish or in soup. In Portugal, the vegetable is an integral part of Caldo Verde (see page 313), a soup consisting of sausage, potatoes, and collards that is a strong candidate for the national dish. Indians in the Kashmiri region stew collards in spices for a dish called *haak*. In Brazil, they are sautéed with garlic and olive oil for a dish called *couve a mineira*. And in the southeastern U.S., they are slow cooked, often with pork and vinegar, for a side dish that is served alongside fried chicken, ribs, or pulled pork. You may notice a theme with all of the dishes above: collards can stand up to bold flavors and long cooking times. A delicate green they are not, but sometimes that is exactly what is called for.

Collards are easy to grow and dense with nutrients. They can withstand very cold temperatures, which makes them a good winter vegetable in the southern U.S. In fact, in 2011, collard greens were designated as the state vegetable of South Carolina, nominated by Mary Grace Wingard, a third-grader from Lexington. I'm very impressed with Ms. Wingard's good taste, and I can attest that South Carolina collards are excellent. My family has visited Hilton Head Island, South Carolina, for many years, and one of the things I look forward to most are the collard greens at A Lowcountry Backyard Restaurant. They are tangy, with a rich, salty broth that feeds both body and soul.

Collards are sacred in the American southeast and slowly gaining more attention elsewhere. All one has to do is mention that their high nutrient content qualifies them as a "superfood," and you've got the Californians on board. As a great-tasting green with some oomph, collards should continue to expand into more and more kitchens across the country.

CORN

When I was a kid, I used to visit my grandparents in Ohio. They had a beautiful house situated on the Maumee River near acres of cornfields that went right up to their suburban neighborhood. One time I was there in late August, when the corn was high, and asked my grandmother if we could go pick some for dinner. "Oh, we can't eat that corn," she said. Her local grocery store didn't have any local produce either. I looked around at the acres of crops that went for miles in every direction and thought, "What?"

Sweet corn is delicious and nutritious, but there is considerable confusion surrounding it. In 2018, farmers in the U.S. planted 88 million acres of corn. Though it is usually the largest-yield crop we grow (sometimes soybeans exceed it), nearly all of it is dent corn. If you break down the uses for the entire crop, 40 percent is converted to ethanol, 36 percent is used for animal feed, and almost all of the rest is exported. Within this massive agricultural system, only 1 percent of the corn grown in the U.S. is meant for direct human consumption. This subset of the market is known as sweet corn. The crop of dent corn is often caught up in politics such as subsidies and tariffs that have nothing to do with growing sweet corn as a fresh vegetable. To distinguish itself from its commodity relative, sweet corn is badly in need of a divorce.

Not that it has suffered in popularity. Come midsummer the whole country starts salivating over the prospect of luscious corn on the cob, bathed in butter with a sprinkle of salt. Simple boiling or steaming results in corn nirvana, but that doesn't stop us from switching it up with herb butters or trendy seasonings. When eating off the cob becomes old hat, we cut off the kernels and use them to make salads, salsas, corn-

bread, and fritters. And, as I have pointed out, if it is truly fresh, there is nothing better than to eat it raw as soon as you get your hands on it.

Corn is a type of grass. It is thought to have been first cultivated in Central America roughly 10,000 years ago from a species called teosinte. Over thousands of years, humans have developed corn, selecting for favorable traits and planting only the best seeds to the point that there is no resemblance to its original ancestor. The upshot of this ancient genetic project is that corn as we know it cannot exist in the wild and needs humanity to keep it going. With 88 million acres planted in this country alone, it's hard to see that dependence as any reason to be worried about it.

The sugars in sweet corn convert to starch very quickly, so it is best to buy it within a day or two of when you are going to eat it and keep it chilled in the fridge. It goes without saying that you are going to find the best corn from a local farmer. When looking for good ears, you don't have to pull the husk down to check if it is ripe. What farmers do is to gently pinch the top of the ear to see if the kernels at the tip are developed. If they are nice and plump, the ear is fully ripe.

In winter, frozen corn kernels are quite good, especially in soup or in corn bread. Producers are well aware they have a short window with it, so it is frozen soon after harvest. If you find yourself with extra ears in the summer, you can cut the kernels off and freeze them yourself. Just pop them in a freezer bag and label it with the date. And same goes for the cobs. They can be "milked" for their sweet liquid or used to make a subtly sweet corn stock.

I don't see the politics surrounding corn going away anytime soon. So keep in mind that sweet corn has nothing to do with corn syrup, ethanol, subsidies, animal feed, or exports. It is just a really good vegetable.

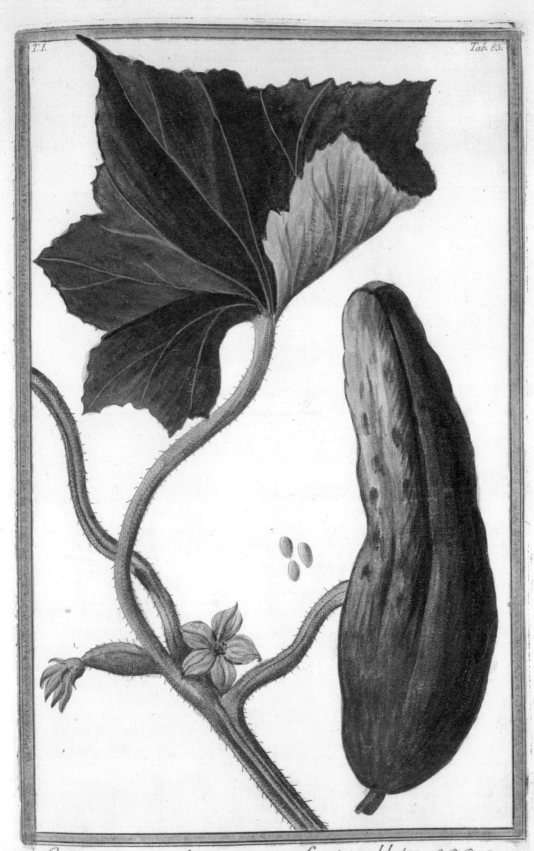

Cucumis satīus, vulgaris, maturo fructu subluteo. C.B.Pin.310.
Ital. Cetriuolo. — *Gall.* Cocombre ordinaire

CUCUMBERS

Cool as a cucumber. Since global temperatures are rising, let us take a moment to celebrate the vegetable that has always been associated with being cold. The cucumber owes its ability to acquire and hold a chill to its 95-percent water content. It is a mildly astringent and refreshing vegetable, just the thing for a crisp salad on a sweltering summer day. It is also high in the anti-inflammatory agent caffeic acid, which is why you see ladies at the spa with slices on their eyes. I encourage eating them over wearing them, especially when they have been pickled to perfection or fanned out on a plate alongside summer tomatoes.

Cucumbers are indigenous to South Asia but are now grown worldwide. Though the most common cucumbers in the U.S. are the green slicing and pickling varieties, many more fantastical shapes and colors are popular around the world. If you have a nearby farmers market with adventurous growers, you may get to sample some of these varieties, such as the Dragon's Egg or the Crystal Apple, both with round, white, sweet fruit. The Hmong Red and the Poona Kheera are good in a Thai salad. Many market farmers like to grow the Lemon variety (round, yellow, and a little fuzzy), which is sweet and doesn't contain any of the chemical that can make cucumbers bitter and hard to digest. But there is nothing wrong with Marketmore, the classic garden variety, to contribute a refreshing crunch to a summer salad.

China produces the majority of cukes for the global market, but most countries grow them since they are considered a staple. If the plants are healthy, they are prolific producers, sending up lateral vines, each with many flowers. I grew them on our farm and found that they did best in my greenhouse, especially if I provided a trellis for them to climb. Just a short row of plants would form a thick wall of foliage with the fruits hidden inside. When it comes to speedy growth, they rival zucchini in going from reasonable to outrageous in a short period of time, so we picked them daily to keep up. I still grow them for our family in order to make pickles, and every year I reduce the number of plants by one, thinking that will result in a reasonable amount. We are down to three plants and still end up giving away bushels in August.

Whichever varietal you choose to grow or purchase, pick cucumbers that are medium to small. The larger ones will be bitter and have a large cavity of hard seeds. Be aware that supermarkets wax or wrap them in plastic because they lose moisture quickly. To remove the wax, rinse the cucumbers under cool water and then soak them in a solution that is equal parts water and vinegar for 1 to 2 minutes. If you do get unwaxed ones at the farmers market or out of your garden, keep them in a plastic bag in the fridge or eat them within a few days.

When I add cucumbers to a salad, I generally remove the seeds, even if they are small, because they can make a dish very watery. Simply slice the cuke in half and scoop them out with a spoon, then slice the rest as you please. Their firm texture is also good for "zoodles," so if you have a spiralizer, you can have some fun making curly salads. The refreshing nature of cucumbers matches well with equally lively herbs like parsley, mint, and especially dill. The mint in the Thai Beef & Cucumber Salad (see page 427) will bring the cukes to life and the dill in the Quick Pickles (see page 193). . .well, there are few better combos than dill and cucumber.

DRY BEANS

Dry beans are a treasure. They are tasty, economical, ubiquitous, easy to prepare, and full of vitamins, protein, and fiber. Every culture around the world includes beans, also known as legumes, in their diet in some form: falafel in the Middle East, tofu in Asia, dal in India, rice and beans in South America, and baked beans in North America, just to scratch the surface. Beans are also critical for meeting global nutritional needs in that they provide an important source of protein in cultures that cannot afford, or choose not to, eat meat.

When I refer to "dry beans," I mean the kind that you find in bags or in the bulk food aisle, as well as the fully cooked canned beans. This includes lentils, chickpeas, split peas, soybeans, fava beans, and the rainbow of other dried beans from red kidneys to black turtle. There are over 40,000 types of beans in the world's seed banks, though only a small percentage are regularly cultivated. In 2005, over 25 million hectares of dry beans were planted worldwide, generating an estimated $11 billion.

The history and importance of beans in the world's diet is immense. They all belong to the *Fabaceae* family but evolved into different species on the evolutionary tree in different areas of the world. The typical dry bean found in baked beans (*Phaseolus vulgaris*) is from the New World. Favas (*Vicia faba*) and chickpeas (*Cicer arietinum*) have long been popular staples in the Mediterranean region, while soybeans (*Glycine max*) and adzuki (*Vigna angularis*) have thrived in Asia for at least 2,000 years.

Growing dry beans is a hoot. To start, there are so many more types of beans available to grow than one finds in the average supermarket. Though there is nothing wrong with a standard white cannellini bean, one can grow beans that are blue, pink, striped, speckled, and all of the above, all at once. Groups such as Seed Savers Exchange and the company Rancho Gordo have been reintroducing old varieties, and the color and diversity now available is dazzling.

When I first thought to plant dry beans on my farm, my husband noted that since they are among the cheapest items per pound that one can buy, it would be hard to make any profit selling them. But once I had a seed catalog in hand, it was too late, agronomics be damned. I was seduced by the fabulous colors and whimsical names. Perigion, an heirloom from Oregon, was a favorite that produced beans that were marbled in tan and navy. The most remarkable was Yin Yang: black and white in a near perfect facsimile of the yin-and-yang symbol, complete with the dots of opposing color. At the market, my customers were smitten with the diversity of the beans I had harvested, and they usually sold very well.

There have been countless cookbooks written about beans and the myriad ways they can be prepared. Every cook should have a recipe for a bean burger, and the one on page 585 is excellent. The same is true for a great hummus recipe like the one on page 198, a go-to rice and beans preparation, and a hearty pea soup. I've also included a few recipes with lentils since they take less time to cook than other legumes and make for fast, healthy meals.

I prefer working with dried beans that I soak and then cook myself because I like to have control over the texture, but canned beans are very convenient and, in many cases, just as good. Be sure to first drain canned beans in a colander and rinse them well under cold water before using, or they may end up tasting like the can they arrived in. If you are going to reconstitute the beans yourself, changing the soaking water a few times before cooking helps with reducing their gas-inducing nature. Also, do not cook the dried beans with any salt, baking soda (unless you are cooking chickpeas for hummus), or acid (such as tomatoes) because liquid will have a more difficult time penetrating the skins. Just simmer them in plain water and add your flavorings once they are fully tender.

EGGPLANT

Eggplant is a member of the *Solanaceae* family and is therefore a cousin to potatoes, tomatoes, and peppers. First cultivated in India and China, the bulbous fruit got its name from the fact that early cultivars were small and white and resembled eggs hanging about the garden. When Arabs brought eggplant to Europe and Africa at the start of the 15th century via trade routes, it was met with skepticism, rumored to be poisonous (as was the tomato) and cause insanity. Traders must have been aware of the old adage that "sex sells" because they soon created a reputation for the fruit of being an aphrodisiac. The rumor persists to this day, and the veg has been popular ever since. African and South American cultures were more welcoming to the eggplant. Thomas Jefferson introduced eggplant to America; it is likely that the white and purple varieties he lists in an 1812 journal entry were grown from seeds collected by Jefferson in France or brought from Africa by the slaves who were responsible for Monticello's abundant gardens. Today, there are now numerous cultivars of every shape and color available in temperate and tropical regions.

Cooking with eggplant can be a challenge because of its spongy texture. When cooking it in a pan, it seems like it can absorb an unlimited amount of oil and still be in danger of burning. For this reason, when sautéing, I try to keep the flame medium-low and stir often. Another option for Italian varieties is to brush with oil and then grill or bake. You can still achieve some nice browning without ending up with an oil-saturated mess. Of course, the beloved Eggplant Parmesan (a version of which appears on page 604) is traditionally made with slices that are breaded and deep-fried, then slathered with marinara and topped with melted mozzarella cheese. If you are looking for a meatless meal that will be fully embraced by carnivores, this is a go-to.

Asian types, also known as Japanese or Chinese eggplant, have a sweeter, less fibrous flesh. Though they take well to stir-frying, they are lovely steamed and doused with a tangy sauce. The texture becomes melt-in-your-mouth tender, and their mild flavor is a good platform for bold Asian sauces such as ginger, fermented black bean, and soy. Even when I switched from commercial farming to a small kitchen garden, I always made space for Asian eggplants because they are not always available in local markets and I had to ensure I had access to some.

China is by far the largest producer of eggplant, growing almost 60 percent of the world's supply. It is such a popular ingredient there that a traditional adage states that a woman must have 12 eggplant recipes if she is to be eligible for marriage. I probably have 12 different ways to prepare eggplant, though I've long suspected Eric married me because of my Blue Cheese Gratin (see page 540).

Eggplant is available year-round but will be at its freshest in late summer. The two most popular types that can be found in American markets are Italian and Asian. Look for fruits that are firm with no dents. Among the Italian varieties, you will find black, white, striped, and green types, all of which have a similar flavor and texture. Asian varieties tend to be long and slender and usually come in purple, but there are also white and green ones. You may be able to find the small, round Thai varieties that are commonly used in stir-fries and can be green, orange, and purple. Thai eggplants have more seeds than other types and are best cooked over high heat in a frying pan or simmered for a long time in a soup.

FENNEL

Fennel deserves more attention. It is terrific as both a main or supporting player in recipes, adding a subtle anise flavor when raw and sweetness when cooked. You can roast it alongside chicken or pork, and it caramelizes beautifully. Included in soups and stews, it adds depth of flavor.

Native to the Mediterranean region, fennel is most widely used in Italy. India has also taken to it and produces more than half of the world's crop, though a portion of it goes for fennel seed. The entire plant is edible, including the pollen from its flowers, but generally it is just the bulb and seeds that are eaten. The stalks are too tough to chew, but they are an excellent addition to stock, especially fish stock.

Fennel is not the most agreeable plant to grow. You may or may not have heard of companion planting, in which you situate certain crops near others because they create a mutually favorable habitat. A commonly known pairing is to plant marigolds next to tomatoes because marigold roots repel nematodes. Fennel is a companion to none and actively tries to kill its neighbors. The seeds emit a chemical called fenchone that inhibits root growth of nearby plants, a trait known as being allelopathic. I only witnessed its vegicidal nature once, because I usually planted fennel in one of the greenhouses and never saw any ill effects on its neighbors. But in the greenhouse there was ample space between rows. One year, I planted fennel in my kitchen garden, where space is limited. In midsummer, I seeded turnips next to the fennel in anticipation of the fall roasting season. The turnips, usually an easy crop, had

very poor germination and only produced two sad plants that struggled to gain size. Was it the heat? Old seed? Or was it the turf boss in the adjacent row? Dead turnips tell no tales.

In spite of its aggressive nature in the ground, it pairs beautifully with other vegetables on the plate. If you are roasting pork or chicken and have placed some carrots and potatoes alongside, add a sliced fennel bulb. It cooks at approximately the same rate, so it is a perfect addition to the usual roasting suspects. In soups, anywhere you would use celery, fennel makes an excellent alternative; you can either use it in place of celery or in addition to it. The taste is somewhat sweeter, with a hint of licorice, can often be found used in fish soup—most notably in Bouillabaisse (see page 328), France's famous saffron-laced seafood stew.

You may notice in the recipes in this book that citrus is a constant companion to fennel. There is something about the acidity in lemons, grapefruit, and oranges that brings out the best in it. The Browned Fennel with Orange Glaze (see page 512) is a good example of this.

When using fennel raw, it is best to slice it very thin since it can be somewhat fibrous. Invest in an inexpensive mandoline (the Japanese ones are excellent and often very reasonably priced) and slicing will become the quickest task at hand. When used raw it definitely asserts itself, so it is often paired with an equally strong counterpart, like grapefruit. I've included a fennel and grapefruit salad in this book (see page 432), which only needs the simplest of dressings and a sprinkling of pistachios.

Whether raw or cooked, you should always remove the triangular core, since it is too tough to eat. Simply cut the fennel in half and you will see the core just above the root. Make a triangular cut with a sharp knife to remove it and confidently use the rest.

Ferula faemina Plinii. C. B. Pu. 148. J. R. H. 321.
Ital. Finocchione Salvatico. Gall. La Ferule.

GARLIC

Where and when to cook with garlic is like asking where and when one should use butter: anytime, anywhere. Nearly any dish, save for the most delicate, includes a clove or two of garlic to give it backbone. Whether in a marinade or tossed straight into the pan, garlic imparts a sweet, rich, umami flavor and aroma that draws people into a kitchen. Americans didn't always embrace this allium and it wasn't in common use in home kitchens until the 1940s (save for the Italians, Chinese, and other communities whose cuisines knew better). We now consume about 260,000 tons (about 2 pounds per person) annually, and it is impossible to imagine modern American cuisine without it.

Garlic is thought to come from central Asia, and its use in both food and medicine dates back several thousand years. It was found in King Tutankhamun's tomb and was a well-known part of the diet of Greek and Roman soldiers. Explorers spread it worldwide, and now it is an integral part of cuisines from Brazil to Vietnam.

Today, garlic is an important commodity but is also at the center of some strife for farmers. The majority of the world's garlic is grown in China. The Chinese not only use it prolifically in cooking but also believe in its medicinal qualities. In the past several decades, China has been part of a trade war over garlic with the U.S. and the European Union. Several countries accused China of dumping huge quantities of cheap garlic on their markets, making it difficult for local growers to compete. In 1994, the U.S. enacted a whopping 377 percent tariff on Chinese garlic to protect U.S. production, most of which is grown in California, Oregon, and Nevada.

Along with politics, a fungal disease called white rot is a serious problem that is popping up in garlic-growing regions. It is a nasty pathogen that can remain in the soil for up to 40 years, even without a garlic or onion host to keep it alive. If a farmer's field is infected, they would have to stop growing garlic or onions all together.

I used to grow up to 600 pounds of 14 different varieties of garlic every year. There are German, Chinese, Russian, Spanish, and American-developed varieties of many different sizes, colors, and degrees of pungency. Customers were always surprised to see that there was more than the plain white variety they found in the supermarket. It is a crop well-suited to Vermont and is fairly easy to grow and market. Like potatoes, garlic is grown from garlic; you split the heads into individual cloves and plant the best of them to keep the quality high. I planted in late September through October because garlic likes to settle in for the winter and wake up in its own bed come spring. There have been many winters when I feared there was little

possibility that the crop survived the extreme cold, but every spring it popped up at the same time as the daffodils and heralded the start of the farming season.

There are a few things to remember about cooking with garlic. Keep in mind that it has a high oil content and burns easily. Burnt garlic can make a dish taste bitter, so keep an eye on it and turn down the heat or add the rest of your ingredients when you notice it starting to brown. It may be counterintuitive, but gar-lic is at its mildest when it is freshly harvested. The longer it has cured, the more intense the flavor. In uncooked sauces and dips, such as hummus, dressing, or pesto, I prefer to use one clove because it can overpower the other flavors. Garlic should be a team player and, when used raw, more than one makes it a prima donna. For dishes where it is cooked, such as in soups or stir-fry—don't hold back. Cooking mellows its zing but adds a sweet, robust flavor to any savory dish.

Green beans are the Steady Eddie of the vegetable world; people don't make a big fuss over them, but almost everyone likes them. I think they deserve more than just a polite nod of acknowledgment. Green beans are very versatile and can work well in a variety of dishes, from Indian curry to a cold French salad. They are also the star of one of my all-time favorite meals: Dry-Fried Beans (see page 614). This is a dish made with charred green beans that are tossed with ground pork, soy sauce, and garlic. Dry-fried beans is among my top-five favorite vegetable dishes, along with 20 others.

Green beans are of the species *Phaseolus vulgaris*, which includes the same plant that produces what we know as dry beans. The green bean is simply an immature version that one eats with the pod still on, just like snap peas are the edible, podded relative of shell peas. Breeders several centuries ago took the bean plant and selectively bred ones that had a tender, sweet pod and small interior beans. For a time, it was necessary to pull off a "string" at the seam of the pod because it was rather tough, but around the turn of the 19th century the string was successfully bred out. These days, all supermarket varieties are easy to prepare, though for some, the name "string beans" has stuck.

Along with green beans you can also find similar vegetables such as yard-long beans (*Vigna unguiculata*) and hyacinth beans (*Lablab purpureus*), which are also immature, podded beans, the yard-long being from Asia and the hyacinth hailing from Africa. The yard-long, or asparagus, bean needs long periods of hot weather and so is primarily grown in tropical climates and occasionally in the southern U.S. If you do run across yard-longs in your local market, prepare them the same way you would green beans, though I recommend cutting them down to a manageable size. Hyacinth beans need to be prepared in a very specific way or they can be poisonous. As a result, they are mainly used as an ornamental vine in the States.

China is by far the largest producer of green beans worldwide, growing over 16 million tons in 2012. The top producers in the States are Wisconsin, Florida, and New York. The common bush variety also comes in yellow and purple, though the purple color turns green when cooked. Breeders have also created types that are meant to be harvested very young, when they are slim and delicate. These are referred to as haricot verts, which in French means "green beans" but in America it implies the smaller type. They are delicious steamed with nothing more than a little butter. I used to grow haricot verts to sell at the farmers market. Given how thin they are, it would take hours to harvest an acceptable amount, but gourmet shoppers always snapped them up.

Green beans can be parboiled, steamed, stir-fried, deep-fried, baked, and even grilled. They are available year-round from all the usual export countries, but nothing beats a crisp bean that didn't travel far. They are available locally starting in midsummer, going through until first frost. Look for light green pods with no brown spots that snap when you bend them.

JICAMA

Jicama is a crunchy, sweet tuber that is excellent in cold salads and stir-fries. Native to Mexico and Central America, it is often eaten with chili powder and lime juice as a snack. Spaniards brought jicama to Asia, where it is also popular in Indonesia, the Philippines, Malaysia, and Singapore. Given its similarity to water chestnuts it is a natural for stir-fries and curries.

Jicama is in the legume family and produces long vines with bean-type pods. It requires at least nine months of hot weather to grow, making it only suitable for cultivation in the tropics. While the tuber is completely benign, the top portion of the plant is poisonous. The seeds contain the compound rotenone, which is used to kill fish and insects. I've always pondered how a culture determined that a particular food was edible when half of it was highly toxic, but jicama has been consumed in Mexico since the days of the Aztec empire. It is harvested in the fall and is ready in time to be used in important Mexican holidays such as the Day of the Dead and Christmas.

Include jicama in salads anywhere a carrot would be appropriate. It is also a great choice for a crudités platter since, unlike other white fruits and vegetables, jicama will not oxidize and turn brown. You must always peel the tubers, not only because the skin is tough but also because they are often treated with wax to keep in moisture. I've found a knife more effective than a peeler for this job.

KALE

I have a theory about the phenomenon I call Kale Mania. Kale had long been considered hippie food, something to be consumed atop virtuous whole grains while discussing Marx. If you weren't preparing for the revolution, you might see it as a curly little garnish perking up the meat counter, but few considered eating it. In the first decade of the new millennium, kale was, all of a sudden, everywhere. There was kale pesto, kale chips, kale Caesar salad, kale lasagna, even a BKT (bacon, kale, and tomato). And in 2016, McDonald's introduced the Kale Breakfast Bowl, finalizing the leafy green's acceptance into the American diet. It tastes good and is very versatile, but that has always been the case. So why the sudden frenzy?

My theory is that CSA farmers are at the root of the phenomenon because the plant is so productive. It is one of the first plants available for harvest in the spring and one of the last going in the fall. If you subscribe to a CSA, you likely have kale in your basket weekly. What to do with this hardy green that won't quit? It turns out, a lot.

Like others in the brassica family, kale is originally from the eastern Mediterranean area and Asia Minor, where it has been a food crop since at least 2000 BCE. It is very popular in Germany and other northern European countries, with the exception of France. In 2013, the *New York Times* published an article about a young American who was trying to encourage the French to embrace kale; the French response was largely, *Pourquoi?*

Because of its versatility, kale can be substituted for collards and cabbage in many dishes. The flavor is hearty but not so earthy that it tastes obligatory. If you are kale-wary, I recommend starting with kale chips. They are crispy and salty, something like a virtuous potato chip. Kale makes for a good addition in any multiplayer dish like curry or stir-fry. The leaves are excellent in soup, where they soften but remain robust, unlike spinach, which reduces substantially in size. If you want to have it in a salad, I recommend the small, younger greens, which are more tender. In fact, some cooks even suggest you massage the leaves to soften them up, but I find if they are young enough, that is not necessary.

Kale was a regular crop on my farm and one of the few things that grew successfully every year no matter how I treated it, which brings me back to my CSA theory. In my first few years of offering a CSA, I only had one suggestion for my members as to how to cook it: sautéed with garlic, olive oil, and lemon. This is a delicious preparation, but there is only so much one can eat of it, and, like Tribbles on the *Enterprise*, more kale just kept coming. In the early 2000s, CSAs were taking off. Given that it is a farmer favorite, I can only imagine this was a pattern being repeated across the country.

Around that same time, I noticed a T-shirt showing up all over Vermont that read: "Eat More Kale." It turned out to be the design of a man named Bo Muller-Moore, who printed T-shirts out of his garage in Montpelier and gave them to his friends at High-Ledge Farm, which had a huge crop that year. The T-shirts became all the rage in the locavore movement. Then Chick-fil-A, a southern-based fast food chain, claimed it looked too much like their "Eat mor chikin" logo and sued for trademark infringement. Muller-Moore won the lawsuit, and after media outlets like CNN and *The Economist* covered the story, Eat More Kale shirts took off nationally. Kale had arrived.

I'm not saying a T-shirt or my little state is responsible for putting kale in every vegetable bin and on every menu in the country. I think it was the combination of an increase of CSAs across the country, a movement for healthier food, and a desperate need to find ways to use a prolific green. Furthermore, I have no evidence whatsoever to back my theory other than a pair of eyes and an overabundance of kale. But the Eat More Kale shirts certainly brought attention to the vegetable and turned the garnish into a conversation piece.

Meanwhile, in 2016 Chick-fil-A put a kale salad on their menu—with a maple vinaigrette, no less.

KOHLRABI

Kohlrabi is among the most underappreciated vegetables out there. Literally translated from German as "cabbage turnip," it has a flavor similar to broccoli stems, only sweeter and juicier. When grated, it makes for a delicious slaw; when diced and sauteed, it is akin to water chestnuts. I cannot account for why kohlrabi has not caught on in the States other than that, since it looks like a tiny UFO landed in the garden, people just don't know what to make of it. To familiarize yourself with kohlrabi, I first recommend peeling it and cutting off a slice to try raw. Not bad, right?

Kohlrabi originated in northern Europe and is derived from the wild cabbage. It is commonly used in Germany and other parts of Europe, where it is roasted, stuffed, braised, or served raw. The most common preparation in German cuisine is to give it a quick boil and then cover it with a white sauce dotted with nutmeg. Kohlrabi is also popular in the Kashmir region of India as well as northern Vietnam. In these warmer climates, it is used in stir-fries, curries, and cold salads.

Before becoming a farmer, I had never seen it in a supermarket and only discovered it when paging through a seed catalog when I was looking for what may grow in Vermont. It is a gardener's delight in that it is fast-growing and only takes about 40 days from seed to harvest. It is also very practical, as not only are the bulbs edible but the huge leaves are also very good, nearly identical in flavor to collards. As kohlrabi is now showing up in large supermarkets more often, there is no excuse for America to not fall for its charms.

Kohlrabi comes in green and purple varietals, but the skin must be peeled, so it will always be pale green on the plate. The plants grow all summer long, so source them locally as soon as the weather warms up. Look for small-sized ones, 2 to 3 inches in diameter, as those will be the most tender. There are some breeds that reach gargantuan size—the Guinness World Record is 96 lbs. and 12 oz. While the big ones are fun to toss around and marvel at, there is a good chance they are very woody inside, so stick to the little ones for dinner. And if you find them in the produce section of a large chain supermarket, be sure to thank the produce manager for taking a chance on them. Then buy some and tell all of your friends to do the same so the shelves remain stocked with this most excellent vegetable.

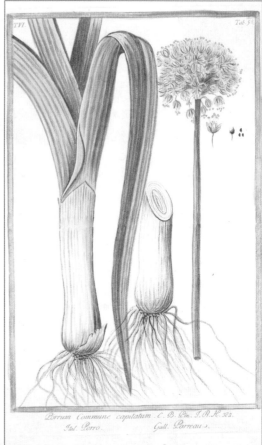

LEEKS

When September comes around, I always notice a malaise about the end of summer. While I will miss the open windows and sigh deeply when I have to return the ice scraper to the car, I'm also excited by what I feel is the best time of year for fresh vegetables. Summer vegetables are still thriving and fall crops are just beginning to appear. One of my favorite ingredients to welcome back into the kitchen is the leek. Leeks, to me, mean hot soup, thick stews, and luscious gratins. They offer an oniony flavor that is more refined than an onion and sturdier than a scallion. They are always cooked, since heat softens their texture and releases their flavor into the surrounding soup or sauce. They are also quite nutritious, being high in vitamins B, K, A, and C as well as iron.

Leeks fall into two categories: summer leeks and winter leeks. Summer leeks are usually ready by August and are more tender and delicate. Because they have thinner layers, they are good candidates for grilling. One can generally only find summer leeks at farmers markets since they don't keep as long as winter leeks. Make an effort to look for them so you can make the traditional Catalan dish of Charred Summer Leeks with Romesco Sauce (see page 520). Winter leeks are hardier and can withstand very cold weather. The leeks you find at the supermarket are most likely to be of the winter variety.

All leeks require excellent soil, regular inputs of fertilizer, and a weed-free existence. Ignoring these rules will result in pencil-sized stems, a fate I have seen many people consigned to, myself among them. I once grew a crop that was so small, my mother mistook them for scallions and chopped them for our salad. I can attest that they are pretty tough raw. They are also hilled as they grow, which means the farmer piles dirt along the shaft to create as much of the tender, white section as possible. Because of repeated hilling, there is often quite a bit of dirt in between the layers, so it is imperative that you slice the leeks lengthwise and rinse them well before using.

Although Americans are warming up to leeks, they are much more commonly used in Europe. The French love them and use them in everything from sauces to soups, like the classic Vichyssoise. Grilled and braised leeks often show up in Spanish tapas and, as mentioned, in Catalonia the leek variety known as *calçots* are charred over an open fire and dipped in romesco sauce. In Wales, however, they go one step further in their reverence: they wear them. Legend has it that in 633 CE, St. David distinguished his soldiers from the Saxons in the battle of Heathfield by having them wear a leek on their helmet, and so from the 16th century on, the leek has been the emblem of Wales. To this day the leek is worn on St. David's Day (March 1st), the Welsh national holiday. The Welsh also nominated the leek to represent them on the back of the 1985 British one-pound coin. I wonder what product of the vegetable world we would choose to represent the United States? (Would it be a cheap shot to say corn syrup?)

Leeks keep very well in the fridge for 4 to 6 weeks, provided they are good and cold with just a little humidity. One of the simplest ways to use them is in a creamy sauce over pasta, like in the preparation on pages 682–83. Frizzled Leeks (see page 522) are among my favorite toppings for a steak or piece of roasted tofu. They are like delicate, gourmet onion rings that melt in your mouth.

MUSHROOMS

When we first started our farm, my husband and I reclaimed an old sheep field that had returned to forest. The trees that had grown up were mostly birch, poplar, and ironwood, which we sold for timber or kept for our wood stove and mulch needs. When we were nearly done with the project, we had enough firewood for the year and a chip pile that was over my head, so I considered what we might do with the remaining wood. After some research, I learned that I had ideal sizes and species for log-grown shiitake and oyster mushrooms. Thus began a 20-year love affair with growing edible mushrooms.

I was new to organic farming, so mushrooms seemed no more or less intimidating than any of the other crops I was trying on my own for the first time. In rural Vermont, in a pre-YouTube era, I went old school and bought a book called *Growing Shiitake Mushrooms in a Continental Climate* by Joe Krawczyk and Mary Ellen Kozak. None of it made any sense. It is a well-written book, but the process of preparing shiitake logs feels awkward for someone accustomed to dirt and seeds. Every step of the way, I questioned how the method could possibly work. I followed it to the letter, however, and the mysterious ways of fungi took their course in spite of my doubts. A year later I was bringing up to 15 pounds of gorgeous shiitakes to market every week.

The topic of edible mushrooms is vast. The majority of mushrooms consumed in the U.S. are white or button mushrooms (*Agaricus bisporus*). These were originally discovered in the 1920s, a mutant of the common brown mushroom that we know as the portobello or cremini. The white ones had a "cleaner" look to

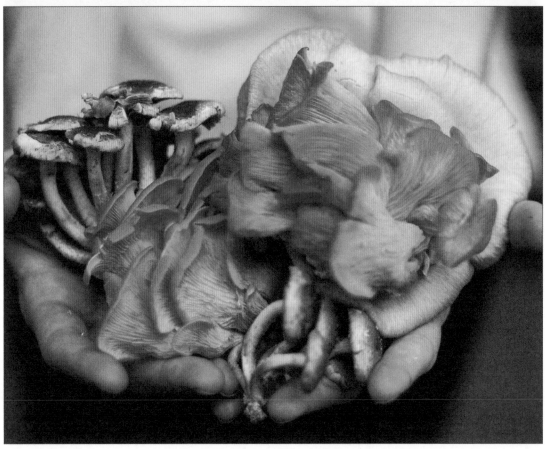

them and they have dominated the market ever since. Brown portobellos made a comeback in the 1980s, in part because they grow large caps that are excellent for grilling. *Agaricus* types are grown in soil, usually composted manure, in large grow houses under controlled conditions.

Many of what we call "wild" mushrooms are grown on wood, either whole logs or sawdust blocks. Among these are oysters, shiitakes, maitake, and lion's mane, all of which can be grown by farmers, using some type of wood as a substrate, with a good degree of success. Then there are the truly wild ones that have thus far eluded cultivation: morels, chanterelles, black trumpets, porcini, the ethereal truffles, and so many more. Many have tried to domesticate these, and some have claimed success; it is possible to purchase a grow kit for porcini (*Boletus edulis*), and some entrepreneurs are "planting" spores in orchards in anticipation of commercial-sized crops. But generally, one must go to the woods at the right time of year, under the right conditions, with a reliable field guide, to get the real thing.

China produces the largest portion of mushrooms worldwide, followed by Italy, the U.S., and the Netherlands. Poland is the fifth-largest producer, but they rank first in passion for them; their mushroom industry is growing larger every year. Mushroom hunting, for Poles, is a national pastime, enjoyed as a family outing, much like apple picking is for Americans. If you have considered looking for wild mushrooms yourself, I implore you to be extra careful, as there are fatalities from poisonous mushrooms every year. Varieties such as *Amanita bisporigera*, aka, the Destroying Angel, which causes liver and kidney failure, are as much a part of the landscape as choice edibles. Personally, I have always had a macabre fascination with poisonous mushrooms, but if I ever gave someone so much as mild indigestion from a mushroom I picked I would never forgive myself. So I stick to store-bought or the ones I have grown.

Fresh mushrooms are available year-round and, if you are lucky, your local market may carry oysters and shiitake. The white button mushroom gets a bad rap for being dull, but it can be plenty tasty if it is cooked properly. Portobellos are similar in flavor to the white mushroom but get more attention for their large size. I personally don't care for raw mushrooms of any kind, but that is a matter of taste, as some enjoy them on salads.

Dried mushrooms are excellent flavor boosters. One of the secrets of a really rich mushroom soup is to add dried porcini along with fresh mushrooms. Just make sure the dried ones are well chopped (once reconstituted), as the texture can be tough. Chinese cuisines use dried, pickled, and canned mushrooms in their soups and stir-fries, and you can discover many different types of mushrooms in Asian markets.

When cleaning them, it is heresy among mushroom lovers to even speak of rinsing them under water, and the general advice is to brush off any dirt with a towel. In my experience I have found that if the mushroom is really dirty, it is better to rinse them with water just before cooking than suffer grit in your dish. Any water that was absorbed by the mushroom will be cooked off if you immediately put it in a hot pan, but definitely do not soak them or wash them well in advance.

SHIITAKE HOW-TO

The Japanese have cultivated shiitake mushrooms on hardwood logs for centuries. The method begins with drilling holes in a 6-inch diameter log and then filling the holes with sawdust that has been inoculated with mycelium. The log is then left in a shady spot outside for a year. The mycelium will gradually inoculate the log, spreading throughout the sapwood.

When I took on the shiitake project, I had never done it myself or taken a class anywhere. The whole process felt odd, and during the week it took to do 200 logs, I kept thinking, "This couldn't possibly amount to more than a pile of hole-filled firewood." The fact that a seed planted will grow and create food or flower is miraculous enough, but most of us are at least familiar with the process. *Fungi* are in an entirely different kingdom from *Plantae* and, unlike planting a seed that you can see and hold in your hand, shiitakes grow from microscopic spores that present themselves as a colony of spongy, white fuzz. Instead of comforting and familiar soil, you "plant" into wood, a substrate that seems as likely as a rock to grow anything edible. And then, to ultimately test your trust and patience, you have to wait a year to see if you did it correctly. There is no fertilizer to apply, no weeding necessary, nothing you can actively do (other than keep them moist) but hope that under the bark the fungi are doing what you set them there to do.

After a year, when the weather has warmed, you take the log and soak it in cold, clean water overnight, then take it out and stand it up. In about 5 days, little pins will appear, and within another day or two they will grow into mushrooms. One 40-inch log can produce up to a pound of some of the best-tasting shiitakes you have ever tried. Once I got the hang of growing them, I started bringing a fully fruited log covered in mushrooms to the market with me so the customers could pick their shiitakes right off the log. But eventually I had to stop. People were so intrigued with the process that I spent all of my time describing how shiitakes are grown when I had baskets of other produce to sell.

Even after scaling down our farm, I still inoculate about 20 logs every other year. Once inoculated, those logs will fruit for about five years if you let them rest for a few months between soaking, so there are shiitakes growing near my house throughout the summer. If I ever decide to go back to school, I would study mycology since I find the ways of fungi fascinating. Because I am still just an amateur mushroom lover/grower, I choose to believe that the process is magic.

OKRA

Okra is an edible seed pod that is best fried or stewed. Though its origins are contested, many think it came from Ethiopia and records show it was cultivated in Egypt and other regions along the Mediterranean as early as the 12th century BCE.

A member of the mallow family, okra is unlike any other vegetable, literally. It is related to cotton, hibiscus, and hollyhock, but its particular parentage is unknown, as there are no similar plants like it growing in the wild. In my mind, this adds to its allure—that millennia ago, a strange cross or genetic mutation brought forth this beautiful and edible plant, its originators then disappearing like a pair of wizards in a pink cloud.

It grows best in tropical climates and is most commonly used there, particularly in Africa, Southeast Asia, the Caribbean, and the American South. Okra came to the States via the slave trade and has remained an important ingredient in Creole cooking. In America, the most well-known dish containing okra is gumbo, which may have derived its name from the Bantu word *(ki)ngumbo*. It is also used in other Creole dishes and frequently appears in the cuisine of the southeast.

While okra is treasured down South, it has yet to catch on with Yankees.

When cut, it releases a mucilaginous liquid, and some complain it is too slimy. While it is not a good candidate for use raw in a salad, the sticky liquid is actually a part of okra's usefulness because it is excellent in thickening stews like gumbo. I've also found that the sticky nature is helpful at catching and holding spices, salt, and breading, making frying up a well-seasoned nugget easy. And when you fry okra, there isn't any sliminess. Because it is unlike any other vegetable, it can be difficult to describe the taste, but I find okra has the flavor of eggplant with hints of green pepper. It can stand up to acids such as tomatoes and lemons and also handles spices like chili powder and cumin well.

You can buy okra fresh or frozen. When selecting it fresh, choose pods that are bright green with no black spots, which are a sign of age. They should snap when you bend them and appear dry. On that note, do not wash them until you are ready to use them, as they will become slimy. Lastly, don't bring up the slimy nature to an okra fan, because they are not having it. I came across one food blogger who wrote: "Remember, okra is slimy and sticky—it is supposed to be that way. If you object to this quality, don't eat okra. You can't get rid of this quality by soaking or overcooking. Accept it and like it. Or not." You've been warned.

Every good recipe starts with reaching for an onion. They are the start of a fresh salsa, a supporting player in any stir-fry or curry, and a member of the carrot-celery-onion triad that is the basis for many dishes in European cuisine. Simply put, we cannot make anything that really tastes good without them. Nevertheless, they are taken for granted, like a good foundation that is completely ignored once the house is built.

The United States grows a lot of onions. In fact, we are the third-highest producer in the world behind China and India. Onions are also the third most consumed vegetable (after tomatoes and potatoes), but one would probably not presume their prevalence because they are so overlooked.

Onions may be the proletariat of the kitchen, but they can be real divas in the field. For one, you can't just grow any type of onion anywhere you like. Some are referred to as "long-day" varieties and will only create bulbs in the north, where midsummer sees longer periods of sunshine. Others, often the sweeter ones, are short-day types that only grow in the south. In some cases, it is not just latitude that allows the growth of a certain variety, but trademarks. Walla Walla, Washington, and Vidalia, Georgia, have exclusive rights to the names of their onions. Georgia was the first state to realize that the soil and climate of certain counties, particularly Vidalia, grew exceptional sweet onions (the variety is actually the Yellow Granex) and in the early part of the 20th century, the reputation of the Vidalia onion spread. In 1989, the state passed the Vidalia Onion Act, trademarking the name. Farmers from outside the region were prohibited from calling their onions Vidalias even if they were of the same variety. The Vidalia Onion Committee even started a festival, created their own mascot

(Yumion), and successfully rallied to make it the official state vegetable. Their branding effort has paid off: the Vidalia is now a household name, prized for its sweet, complex flavor. In 2017, Georgia growers harvested 230 million pounds of them, which carried a value of more than $150 million. Walla Walla, Washington, growers have also trademarked their name and have their own festival, website, and T-shirt.

In the kitchen, onions are essential, but it is important to pay attention to detail with their preparation. Among storage-type, non-trademarked onions, I have found that red and yellow are interchangeable and you should select one more for color than for taste. White varieties tend to be sweeter and milder but do not store as long. For any onion, if using them raw, such as in a salad, it helps to soak the slices in cold water for 10 minutes to remove some of their bite. When using them as a compo-

nent in a soup, sauce, or stir-fry, they should always be sautéed on their own for a few minutes, as opposed to just being tossed in with all the other ingredients. And be sure to give the onions plenty of room in the pan so they brown and don't steam. This will add more flavor to the dish.

Lastly, when instructions call for caramelizing, put on your favorite music and grab a stool, because proper caramelizing takes time. The onions should be put in a pan on medium-low heat with oil and left to brown, stirred only occasionally to prevent burning. They are not finished until they are entirely brown and limp. If you've done it right, the result is a sweet tangle of ribbons that will bring complex flavor to any dish.

PARSLEY

Parsley is the unsung hero of the kitchen. Tasted on its own, it has a generic "herbal" flavor, but I have never been in a commercial kitchen that didn't use it liberally in everything from stock to salads because of its magical ability to make anything it touches taste better. There are a few dishes that feature parsley as the core element, such as tabbouleh, and many variations of parsley-based sauces. Brazil, Argentina, France, Italy, and Afghanistan all have their own versions of a parsley sauce that can turn a simple steak or pastry into a regional specialty. So it's about time this hero got some praise.

Parsley is thought to come from the Mediterranean region and has figured in the area's history in both sinister and uplifting ways. The botanical name *Petroselinum* comes from the Greek word for stone, informed by the fact that the plant grows well in rocky areas. The Greeks made wreaths for graves with it and considered it a symbol of death. The Romans didn't cook with it either but used it for covering up putrid smells and bad breath. Between the two cultures, it had some unpleasant associations. Jewish communities took a more favorable view of parsley, seeing it as a symbol of spring and using it in Passover celebrations. And both Charlemagne and Catherine de Medici were champions of it, giving the herb a rebirth of respectability.

Americans know parsley mostly as a garnish, but in Middle Eastern food it is given more prominence. The traditional Lebanese dish of tabbouleh is often seen in the States as a bulgur wheat salad with some parsley and mint tossed in, but the traditional preparation leans heavily on the parsley with the bulgur as backup. The result is an herbaceous, emerald-green salad that is a perfect accompaniment to hummus, grilled veggies, or labneh cheese.

Perhaps the most underutilized purpose for parsley is as a sauce. Basil pesto has hoarded all of the attention for herb-based sauces for a few decades, but I think it is time to show off parsley's attributes as an all-purpose condiment. Chimichurri (see page 805), the Argentinian sauce of parsley, vinegar, garlic, oregano, and red pepper, is among the most well-known. The French make a similar sauce, called persillade, with parsley and garlic, and the Italians have salsa verde, which is parsley, capers, anchovies, and garlic. The Italians also make gremolata (see page 327), parsley, garlic, and lemon, to go over traditional osso buco. In Afghanistan, they make a parsley-centric sauce to go with savory pastries called bolani (see page 209).

The parsley sauce I make is a variation of all of these, depending on what other herbs are looking good at the time and what I'm planning on making for dinner. I started making chimichurri years ago to go with grilled steak but found it was even better on sautéed potatoes. Since then, the chimichurri has morphed into a malleable sauce that goes with anything. If I'm serving chicken, I might add lemon and rosemary. If the entrée is grilled pork, I may steer toward cilantro and extra garlic. The additions vary, but every batch of chimichurri starts with a base of at least 1 full cup of large-leaf parsley, and there is never any left over because we slather it over everything. I have also found that while a basil pesto can go wrong in 10 different ways, the parsley sauce always tastes good, no matter what I put in it.

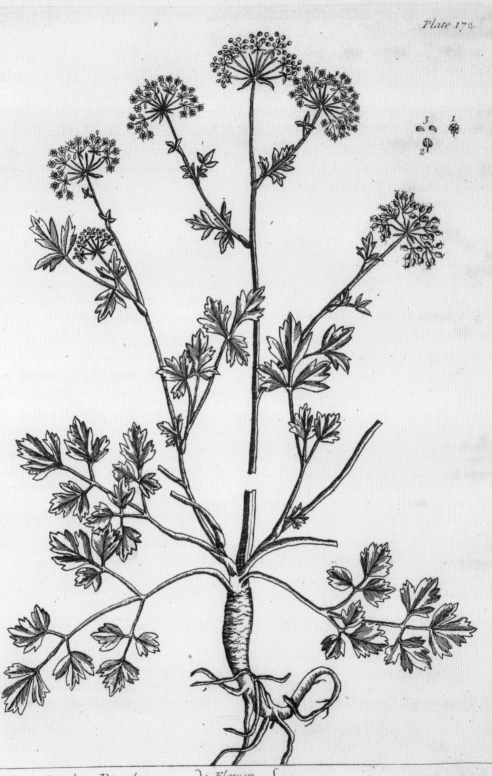

Plate 172.

Garden Parsley

}1. Flower.
{2. Seed Vessel. { *Apium hortense or Petroselinum.*

Eliz. Blackwell delin. sculp. et Pinx. }3. Seed.

PARSNIPS

Parsnips might best be referred to as the candy of the vegetable world. Never mind sweet corn or sweet potatoes, parsnips out-sugar both of those poseurs, especially when roasted. They have the reputation as a fall vegetable; indeed, they are fully grown by mid fall but those in the know (farmers) know that the best parsnips are those that are overwintered in the ground and harvested first thing in the spring. Just like with Brussels sprouts, cold temperatures allow the plant to develop its sugars. The result is a very sweet root that heralds the start of the thaw.

An irregular shape and a sometimes-woody core can make cooking with parsnips tricky. The parsnip has been largely ignored by breeders for some time, so there have been very few new varieties introduced that tackle these problems. Burpee's seed catalog, for example, features 18 different types of carrot and only one parsnip. Carrots have been bred to offer some uniformity, but parsnips are often very skinny on the bottom half, so when you peel them, there is little "meat" left. Also, the woody cores that are tough to eat aren't usually discovered until the parsnips are cooked; sometimes they are tender enough and sometimes not. Having once served roasted parsnips at a dinner party that had the texture of newly cut branches, I learned my lesson, and now I always cut out the core.

Given all of the issues with parsnips, one might ask, why bother? The answer is that they are exquisite. Their sweetness brings balance to any soup, roast, or salad. To deal with the core, I first peel them top to bottom and cut off the tapered part. The core in that slender section is usually fine, and I'll just chop it up or use it whole. For the upper part, once you slice off the very top you can see the core and cut around it. There is plenty of vegetable left to work with, and you can save the cores (and peels and other trimmings, for that matter) to make ice cream (see page 728).

In the U.S., Michigan, New York, and Oregon are the largest growing regions, likely because they get cold enough to produce a really sweet root. Parsnips are still most popular in Europe, where they originated. The roots, once more popular than potatoes or carrots were commonly consumed during the time of Lent when meat was forbidden. Given our global market, parsnips have been embraced by the rest of the world. You can find them in Indian curries and Chinese stir-fries among other international cuisines.

Though they are available year-round, parsnips will be fresh and firm starting in fall. But if you buy from a local farmer, ask if they overwinter any of them to get the sweetest harvest of the year in spring.

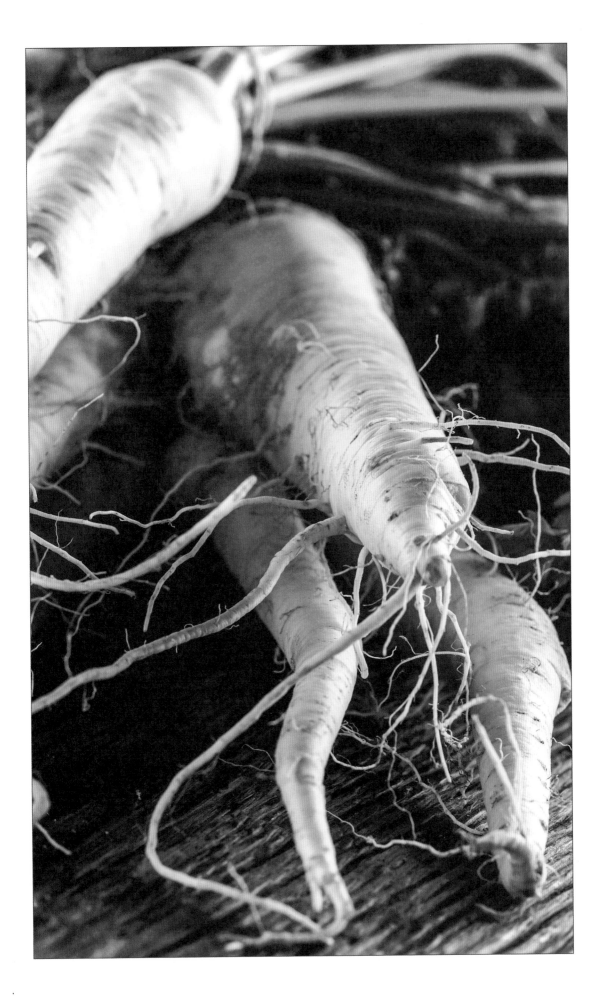

Tab. 66.

Capsicum fructu subrotundo, ventricoso dulci in summitate tetragono.
Ital. Peperoni di Spagna grandi, e dolci. — Gall. Poivre d'Inde ou de Guinée

PEPPERS

Both bell peppers and chili peppers are of the species *Capsicum annum*. The only difference is that chili peppers contain capsaicin, a compound that sets your tongue on fire. They are also one of the few vegetables that is commonly used as a spice. All peppers start green and then can eventually turn red, yellow, orange, purple, brown, and white. Members of the nightshade family, they are related to tomatoes, potatoes, and eggplant and are native to Mexico, Central America, and South America. Cuisines across the planet have embraced peppers, particularly in areas where spice is prized, like India and Southeast Asia.

China is the world's largest grower by volume, but the U.S. imports most of its peppers from Mexico. Within the States, the majority of peppers are grown in California because they need a long period of warmth to reach maturity. In 2017, the U.S. grew approximately 1.6 million pounds of bell peppers, with the crop valued at $642 million. Total chili pepper production in 2017 was 4.7 million pounds, valued at $143 million.

Fresh peppers are moderate contributors to the American diet. On average we consume 11.4 pounds of sweet peppers and 7.7 pounds of chili peppers per person, per year. They are excellent in salads, contributing not only sweetness and crunch but a nice array of colors as well. They are also part of the Cajun Holy Trinity, which consists of onion, celery, and bell peppers; crawfish etouffee, gumbo, and jambalaya all start with this trio. I love peppers of all kinds, but especially ones that have been roasted with their skins removed. They have a tangy sweetness and depth of flavor that is beautiful in any dish, hot or cold.

Peppers figure more prominently in other countries' cuisines as a spice, like in Mexico, Hungary, and Turkey. The chili powder that one finds in the store, more often than not, is a blend of ground chilies and other spices such as cumin. Chipotles are dried and smoked jalapeño peppers that either come powdered, in whole form, or canned in adobo sauce. I highly recommend the canned version because both the pepper and the sauce are useful in recipes. Ancho chilies are dried poblanos that are used for similar purposes as a seasoning. All of these types are described as "mild heat," but spice is a very subjective thing, so I recommend a small taste of any chili before adding it. There are hundreds of other varieties of chilies from Mexico, many of which can be found in powdered form.

Less familiar to Americans are types of paprika from Hungary. While Americans think of paprika as a spice that goes on deviled eggs and some potato recipes, in Hungary it is integral to many regional dishes, the most famous of which is goulash. Paprika is so important in Hungary that there are at least seven different grades to choose from, such as "delicate," "exquisite delicate," and "pungent exquisite delicate." Smoked paprika (also found in Spain and known as pimenton) is also a terrific seasoning that adds a rich, smoky flavor to dishes

but not a lot of heat, allowing you to taste the herbal notes of the pepper.

Another pepper seasoning that is just starting to make waves in the U.S. is Urfa biber, commonly called the Black Urfa pepper. Grown in the Urfa region of Turkey, it looks like a big, red poblano. After harvest, the peppers are laid in the sun and then put under plastic or tarps at night to preserve some of the oils and moisture. The result is a semi-dry flake that is quasi-cured and has incredible, rich flavor reminiscent of tobacco. It goes on anything from grilled meat to roasted vegetables. It was introduced to our household last year, and now my husband puts it on everything.

Fresh peppers are available year-round but will be the best locally at the end of the summer. Look for firm ones with thick walls. Don't wash them until you are ready to use them and keep them cool in the fridge until then. The seeds of sweet bell peppers are always removed before using; just cut the pepper in half and pull out the seed ball out with your fingers. Hot chilies are served with or without seeds, but it is a myth that this is where all of the heat comes from. In fact, it is the ribs, or white pith, that contains the most capsaicin, with some also in the walls of the peppers. The seeds pick up heat from their proximity to the ribs but are not inherently hot. If you want to reduce the heat of a chili pepper, cut out the white pith, but be aware there is still some in the walls.

POTATOES

The most consumed vegetable in the U.S. is the potato. On average, we gobble 50 pounds of spuds per person, per year, mostly in the guise of French fries. In fact, twice as many potatoes are consumed as the next most popular vegetable, tomatoes, and they are the fourth-largest food crop worldwide. This may give agita to dieticians and add extra inches to waistlines, but it is only because they are infinitely versatile and so darned good.

Potatoes come from South America and are part of the nightshade family, along with tomatoes, peppers, and eggplants. The Incas were known to cultivate potatoes as early as 8000 BCE. Modern-day Peruvians, Bolivians, and Ecuadorians still grow over 4,000 varieties. The Spanish brought potatoes back to Europe from their South American explorations in the 1500s, and Europeans adopted them as one of their staple crops, finding them both nutritious and delicious. Their reliance became a detriment in the 1800s, however, when a disease spread through the potato crop, causing widespread famine in Ireland. Over 1 million people died as a result of food shortages, and another million emigrated to escape the devastation. Hard lessons were learned about relying on one variety of one crop, but the popularity of the potato has endured, and it remains a staple worldwide.

Potatoes are grown from potatoes, not seed. I had always assumed this was common knowledge, but after an unscientific survey of three non-agrarian friends, I have found it is not. To grow a potato plant, one takes a regular potato that hasn't been treated with chemicals and puts it in the ground. You know those little buds that sometimes form if you leave a potato too long in the pantry? Those will send out roots below and foliage above, and eventually more potatoes (or tubers) will grow from the original one. Digging for potatoes on a small scale is like hunting for treasure, as you dig around with your shovel and come up with a pile of spuds. If your soil is good, you can get between 5 and 8 pounds of potatoes for every 1 pound you plant—not a bad return on investment.

As noted, there are thousands of varieties of potatoes that are still grown in South America, but in the States, we stick to less than 10. This is a shame, since the variety of shapes, flavors, and colors available is impressive. Luckily, Americans are now more accustomed to seeing blue and purple potatoes and have also embraced the sweet fingerling types. Farmers markets are a good source of more unusual varieties. I always planted as many different kinds as I had space for in my field because they made such a great display at market and because they are one of my favorite vegetables. Along with well-known favorites such as yellow Yukon Golds, there are types that are red both inside and out, like Adirondacks, and marbled-skinned kinds like Purple Vikings.

When considering what type to buy, choose based on what you plan on doing with them. Low-starch potatoes, or "new potatoes," are best for boiling or steaming because they are less likely to fall apart in water. High-starch, such as Idahos or Russets, are great for baking and frying because they are drier and the starch results in a crispy spud. Fingerling potatoes are considerably sweeter than regular varieties, so you should take that into account if you are adding a sweet sauce to your dish. For hundreds of other potato recipes out there like gratins, you really can't go wrong with any type of potato. The only rule I would suggest following is to not use blue potatoes for mashed potatoes, as they will turn an unappetizing gray.

The most common question I received at the farmers market was, "Is it sweet?" This would be asked of carrots, peas, cucumbers, and even onions, along with nearly every other offering under my tent. Customers would swoon over the Sungold tomatoes I grew, offering high praise by saying, "They taste like candy." Americans love their sugar, and it is an important part of the flavor profile of many foods. But bitterness can be just as exciting to the taste buds, especially when contrasted with so many sweet components. And yet the heroes of bitter, like radicchio, endive, and escarole, don't get much play in the States.

Radicchio in particular is a favorite of mine. Though it looks like a peculiar cabbage, it is a member of the chicory family. The flavor is unapologetically bitter, mellowed only by roasting or cooking. You can find it in high-quality mixes of mesclun because it balances the sweet bibb lettuce, earthy kale, and peppery arugula. In Italy, it is incorporated into risotto and pasta—an addition that will wake up the palate in extra-creamy dishes. Chefs have discovered its potential as an ingredient on the grill or in the oven. It is excellent when roasted and paired with fruit—the sweet and the bitter making for the perfect bite. You can serve it as a hot side to sausages and other rich, fatty meats or let it cool to room temperature and use it in a salad.

Most radicchio comes from northern Italy, where the climate is perfect for its growth. The region of Veneto boasts at least three varieties that have become world standards, named after the towns where they were developed: Chioggia, Traviso, and Castelfranco. The most common found in U.S. markets are the round heads of Chioggia. Growing radicchio is most peculiar, and one wonders how the method first evolved. There are some varieties that are grown in the field and harvested like any other type of head lettuce or cabbage. Others are harvested and brought into a large grow house where the roots are put in 60°F water and the entire plant is covered with a tarp. The water stimulates growth in the center while the lack of light halts photosynthesis, resulting in the intense white and red color. This latter type, Tardivo, is especially prized for its flavor but it is rarely seen Stateside.

Radicchio is at its best in fall and winter. Look for firm heads with bright red coloring. It is more expensive than many other greens, but given its bitterness, a little goes a long way.

RADISHES

Early spring is a bonanza for greens, but it doesn't produce too many vegetable superstars, with the notable exception of asparagus. If you approach a farm stand, there may be one pop of color in all that green: radishes. They are commonly found in salads or relegated to a supportive role, whether as a garnish or in spring rolls or sushi. Often, it is just a decoration. A little investigation into the life and times of the radish, however, reveals that it can do wondrous things. It can provide important vitamins, improve soil, produce vital oils, and even inspire an entire festival. The radish, as it turns out, has some gravitas.

Radishes were domesticated in Europe in pre-Roman times and today are consumed worldwide. In Europe and the Americas, we grow the common short-season radish, which comes in shades of red, purple, black, and white. They are a cinch to grow, taking only 25 days from seed to harvest. The only restriction in their production is that they become intensely bitter in the heat, making them spring- and fall-only crops.

In Asia, the longer-season daikon radish can be used raw, cooked, or pickled. We can also thank China for the watermelon radish, which has a plain white exterior that belies a stunning center of bright pink. Its Chinese name is *xin li mei*, which translates to "in one's heart beautiful," but I propose it be renamed "root that launched a million Instagram posts." A crosswise slice of watermelon radish is so visually arresting, it will elevate almost any dish just with its color.

All types of radishes are good sources of vitamin C, folic acid, and potassium. In addition, they are fat-free and provide a long list of micronutrients such as magnesium and copper. As well as being food for humans, it turns out that the radish is a good producer of oil and a remarkable soil improver. The oilseed radish, as its name would suggest, was developed for oil production. The seeds contain nearly 48 percent oil by weight, which is inedible to humans but may be a potential source of biofuel. More recently, the oilseed radish was discovered to be a good cover crop. A cover crop is meant to improve the soil by suppressing weeds, increasing biomatter or nutrients, or breaking up compacted soil. Farmers will seed overworked crop land with radishes, and their long taproots will bust through hard-packed dirt and then expand, breaking up the soil and allowing air and water to pass through. In addition, the taproots can reach as deep as 16 inches into the soil and capture nitrogen that is inaccessible to shorter-rooted crops. The farmer will let the radish die over the winter or till it under, making the nitrogen available for the next crop. Because of their speedy growth, radishes are also good at squeezing out weeds.

In Oaxaca, Mexico, the radish has, in fact, become a superstar to the extent that there is an entire festival dedicated to it. *Noche de Rábanos* or "Night of the Radish" is celebrated December 23. Farmers let their radishes grow to 2 feet in length and use these enormous roots to sculpt scenes depicting the Nativity or important moments in Oaxacan history. The competition is held in the main square with elaborate displays and prizes. Noche de Rábanos might not improve the radish's culinary reputation, but let's review: soil improver, potential biofuel, medium for divine inspiration. A little respect for the garnish, please.

RUTABAGA

I didn't grow up eating rutabagas or turnips, and as a new cook, my small exposure to supermarket varieties had been mostly unpleasant. In my first year as a grower, my bias led me to plant a very short row of turnips for diversity rather than out of conviction. I harvested them young, as recommended in the seed catalog. To my surprise, they quickly sold out. Deciding to see what the fuss was about, I picked a few young turnips and roasted them alongside some carrots and potatoes. Ambrosia. They were tangy and sweet and complemented roasted meats perfectly, especially duck. Consequently, the next year I planted a longer row of turnips and added a small patch of rutabagas, thinking they were nearly the same thing. Not so, I learned. The turnips continued to sell and the rutabagas just made round trips in the market truck, barely enticing a single customer. The flavor is sweeter than the turnip, so I have to ask: What's wrong with the rutabaga?

The rutabaga is actually a cross between a turnip and a cabbage, with a flavor that leans pleasantly cabbage. It seems that they suffer from an image problem more than anything else. First there is the name, which is practically a punch line. Truthfully, the very sound of the word tells a child it is something he or she doesn't want to eat. We might take a lesson from Europe, where they are referred to as Swedish turnips or Swedes, which, at least, sounds attractive. They also suffer from stigma in that they were among the few food staples available during World War I and became a symbol of deprivation to a whole generation who passed their abhorrence down to their offspring. Perhaps a hotshot young chef wants to

champion them, and they can get some love like kale. I am not that chef, but I'm developing a real affection for them, albeit for reasons other than culinary.

I can thank rutabagas for the discovery of the Advanced Rutabaga Studies Institute (ARSI) on the web. Whether the site is partly or entirely a hoax is unclear, but it is thoroughly entertaining and, I would guess, authored by a true rutabaga lover. The purported institute, located in Forest Grove, Oregon, is headed by President-for-Life Obie MacAroon III, who champions the rutabaga's place in history as well as on the table. He is a great source for all things rutabaga if you have a free afternoon and some curiosity about brassica lore.

There is also the International Rutabaga Curling Competition, held every December in Ithaca, New York, where teams from up to 25 different countries "real and imagined" compete in a curling competition using rutabagas. Photos of contestants from the 2018 competition show them in costume, with themes ranging from rutabaga-tossing Vikings to the Notorious Rutabaga Ginsberg, complete with judicial robes (they came in third). Rutabagas may not be the current culinary trend, but what other vegetable is the source of so much fun?

Cooking with them is similar to turnips in that they are tangy and sweet. Roasting is always a good option and a timely one, seeing as how they are harvested just as cold weather comes along. Even if they have been harvested fresh, always peel them, since they are usually covered in wax to maintain their moisture. There are two very creative soup recipes in this book that include rutabaga. One takes advantage of rutabaga's talent for balancing the richness of roasted meats by pairing it with apples and pork belly (see pages 362–64). The other plays up its sweet and earthy nature by combining it with figs and spicy chickpeas (see pages 365–67).

SCALLIONS

Scallions may be as taken for granted as radish or parsley, considered little more than homely garnish. But, like dry towels, you'd miss them if they weren't around. Consider the classic dish of Peking duck. The traditional presentation is the roasted duck meat, wrapped in a thin pancake, topped with plum sauce and chopped scallions. The scallions may seem like they are thrown in for color, but if you took them out of the dish, it would not be half as good. Yellow onions would be too strong, and chives would not make themselves known. The middle ground of oniony flavor from scallions offers the perfect counterpart to the sweet sauce and fatty duck. There is no substitute.

Scallions are integral to salsas, nachos, salads, scallion pancakes, miso soup, yakitori, and too many Chinese and Korean dishes to count. There are so many culinary situations where an onion is too much, but you need a bit of onion flavor—scallions are the solution. I personally prefer nearly any cold salad—potato, pasta, or otherwise—with scallions rather than raw onions because they are not as harsh.

There is some confusion with the name, in that some people refer to scallions as shallots. To be clear, scallions are long, green shoots with a small white (sometimes purple) bulb that grows underground. They are grown in clusters and grow for a relatively short time until harvest (about 60 days). Shallots are a different plant, which creates a red bulb that is harvested like an onion and takes an entire season to reach maturity (over 100 days). Scallions are also called spring onions, green onions, table onions, salad onions, tubular onions, onion sticks, long onions, baby onions, precious onions, yard onions, gibbons, and syboes. I don't think sybo, the Scottish name for the vegetable, is going to catch on, but I like "precious onion" and may start using that myself.

Good-quality scallions are available year-round. Look for bunches that have dark green tops and firm, white tips. If you are lucky, you may run across the purple variety at a farmers market; the flavor is the same as white, they are just extra-pretty. When ready to use them, cut off the roots as close to the end as possible and rinse well under cold water, pulling off any wilted or yellowing leaves. You can use practically the whole plant from white tips to the tops of the greens, trimming off only the very last inch.

SEAWEED

If you feel like all of the veggies in the produce section shelf are same old, same old, perhaps you should consider expanding your culinary repertoire to include seaweed. Though many coastal communities feature seaweed in their diets, it is still not part of mainstream fare in most of the States outside of Japanese restaurants. This may be changing, as cooks are learning of the versatility of both fresh and dried versions. There is also a nutritional and environmental benefit to consuming seaweed. Seaweed advocates are trying to give it an image makeover and rebrand it as "sea vegetables," but if enough people give it a try and discover how good it is, that may not be necessary.

Nearly all of the seaweed varieties that are edible come from the ocean, not freshwater sources. The most common types to end up on a plate are kelp, dulse, wakame, kombu, nori, Irish moss, sea palm, hijiki, and arame. Obviously, finding the dried versions, especially of kombu, nori, wakame, arame, or hijiki, is easier than fresh unless you live near a coast.

Nori is the flat, black sheet of seaweed used for rolling sushi and wrapping the Japanese rice balls called onigiri. You can also slice it and add it as a garnish to a salad. Kombu is most commonly used to make dashi, a Japanese broth. Wakame comes as dried black slivers that are often used in miso soup. When using them, be aware that a few dried strands will expand considerably, so go easy unless you want an all-seaweed soup. Hijiki and arame are used in everything from soups to salads.

Fresh seaweed is gaining traction as a commercial crop and may tick a lot of boxes that concern today's consumers, including sustainability and nutrition. There has been a movement to start farming kelp along the Eastern seaboard as a hedge against dwindling fish stocks. It is among the most sustainable agricultural projects in existence. Seaweed farmers put out lines planted with kelp seedlings in late fall, when recreational boating and commercial fishing is mostly done. The kelp grows quickly and is ready to harvest in April. Not only does it not require inputs (fertilizer, pesticides) or take up any land, but it absorbs excess nutrients like nitrogen and carbon that are causing problems in our coastal regions and effectively cleans the water. The kelp itself (*Sacharima latisima*) is delicious and very versatile to cook with.

Suzie Flores Douglas of Stonington Kelp Co. is one such kelp farmer who sets her lines off the coast of Connecticut. Her operation is only two years old and she is still learning, but in her first year she harvested 2,500 pounds of kelp and expects to expand her site. Seaweed is used in a variety of applications, and when I asked her where the kelp may end up, she offered a list of potential clients that would make a land farmer green with envy. Her yield goes direct to chefs; is used as animal feed and fertilizer; and is also used in the cosmetics and biofuel industries. Ideally, though, she would like to see it used primarily for food.

When I asked her how she cooks with it, she said she puts it in everything, as one can consume it both cooked and raw. Raw kelp has a briny flavor and a crunchy-chewy texture. The taste of cooked kelp is very mild, so you can integrate it into a dish like lasagna and it won't change the flavor, but it adds loads of nutrients. Since Suzie has young children, she sneaks it into many of their meals. She also dries and pulverizes it, then uses it as a salt substitute.

At this point, marketing is everything. Getting chefs to incorporate it into their menus and encouraging broader awareness in the general public is essential to launching seaweed as the next big thing. Introducing a new food to the public is often more about psychology than appealing to taste buds; consumers need to change their perception of seaweed from

"slimy stuff you step on" to "delicious food." The taste is all there—we just need an attitude adjustment. A nonprofit group called Green-Wave exists to help those already involved with the fishing industry start kelp operations and find markets, as well as promote the new food. "Aqua farmers" know that public education will be key to their success. "We are very much at Step 1 in the process," says Douglas.

Finding edible seaweed is a matter of location. Dried seaweed is available in most supermarkets in the section with Asian food, and you can also order a wide variety online. Fresh seaweed is harder to come by; not only is its dis-

tribution limited but it is also highly seasonal. Frozen kelp can be found online under the name of Ocean Approved, which sells pureed kelp frozen into cubes meant for smoothies, sauces, soups, or anywhere you'd like a nutritional boost. They also sell frozen strips of kelp to be used for seaweed salad. The aqua farmers are doing their best to get their product to influential chefs, so if you see it on a menu, give it a try, knowing that you are in the hands of an expert who has experimented with it and is presenting it in a dish that he or she feels highlights its best qualities.

SEITAN

Seitan is made from wheat gluten. Known to have existed since the sixth century in China, it is a common ingredient and source of protein in cultures across Asia. Used most often in China, Japan, Vietnam, and North America, it has a texture similar to meat and has several different monikers in English, including "wheat meat." Like tofu, it has a very mild flavor that makes it a good platform for bold sauces and spices.

Seitan is made by adding water to wheat flour to activate the gluten. The mixture is then rinsed repeatedly to remove any starch, leaving behind a mass that is pure gluten. It has a satisfying, chewy texture that makes for a good replication of meat, if that is the effect you are going for. My philosophy about food is that it is better to eat with intention and enjoy the ingredients that are in front of you than to try to fool yourself that you are eating whatever you'd rather be having. Seitan has a character and taste of its own that is mild but quite good. That said, if you are trying to coax carnivores into cutting back on animal consumption, seitan is a good option for a meat-like component. Mock duck, for instance, is seitan hopped up on flavoring agents like soy sauce and MSG.

While other vegetarian processed foods like tofu come in standard blocks, seitan comes in a variety of forms, which may explain why it is not more commonly used: cooks are baffled by it (I was in this camp before I experimented with it for this book). In China, it is sold fried, steamed, and baked, with each iteration used in a different way. Fried seitan is put in soups, whereas steamed seitan is often shaped like a sausage, dyed pink, and referred to as "mock ham." Baked seitan, *kao fu*, is spongy in texture and is prized for soaking up savory sauces in stir-fry. In Japan, it is sold raw, formed into different shapes such as maple leaves, and steamed. It is also available "dry baked," taking on the appearance of bread.

In the States, it is sold mostly precooked with flavoring added. In my local market, I found "chicken style" seitan, which came in a plastic tub but was in large strips rather than a solid block. The "chicken style" meant it had poultry seasoning added and was surrounded by a chicken-tasting broth. I rinsed off the broth and used it to make Buddha Seitan (see page 657), which is now a family favorite. Other forms I have found are cubes and tube-shaped "sausages." Some brands, like Tofurkey, combine wheat gluten with tofu to make an amalgam meat-like substance that simulates deli meats, bacon, patties, and steaks. You can also make seitan yourself using vital wheat gluten, which comes in powder form, combined with umami-rich seasonings like garlic powder and yeast. Once you have created a dough, it can be shaped into any form you like and cooked, making for many recipes that pose as meatloaf, meatballs, sausages, and cuts of meat. Personally, the only shape I would be inclined to create would be a wheat stalk.

Seitan is low in calories and very high in protein (21 grams per 3 oz. serving) making it a healthy muscle-builder. I make no health claims regarding my favorite preparation for it, which involves deep-frying it and slathering it in a sugar- and sodium-heavy sauce. It should be noted that it is pure gluten, so is not a good option for the gluten-intolerant. But if soy is your allergy, then this one is for you. Asian markets and health food stores will likely have the widest variety of premade seitan, as well as vital wheat gluten, but I found several brands in my local supermarket as well.

HOMEMADE SEITAN

YIELD: APPROXIMATELY ½ LB. / **ACTIVE TIME:** 15 MINUTES / **TOTAL TIME:** 45 MINUTES

If you can't find premade seitan or don't care for the options in your local market, it is easy to make at home with the purchase of some unusual ingredients. You will need to find vital wheat gluten, which is wheat flour that has been stripped of any starch and dried. Health food stores or stores that specialize in baking will likely carry it, but you can also order online from King Arthur Flour or Bob's Red Mill. Nutritional yeast is the same species of yeast used for making bread and beer but has been deactivated. In other words, it is not "alive" and cannot be used for leavening or fermenting; rather, it is meant to be used as a seasoning. It has a cheesy, nutty taste that is terrific on popcorn and other savory dishes. You can look for it in the bulk spice section at your local supermarket or order it online. Once you have made a batch of seitan, you can cut it to suit your recipe and cook as you would meat or tofu.

1. In a mixing bowl, mix the gluten, yeast, and garlic powder until blended.

2. Incorporate the stock or water and soy sauce a little at a time until a dough forms. If it is too dry, add extra stock or water. Knead the dough for a few minutes until it feels elastic and all of the ingredients are thoroughly incorporated. Divide into two pieces and shape into round disks.

3. Bring a pot of stock, water, or a combination of the two, deep enough to cover the dough, to a boil. Put the disks in the pot and reduce heat to a simmer. Poach for 30 minutes. Turn off the heat and let cool in the pot.

INGREDIENTS:

1   CUP VITAL WHEAT GLUTEN

¼   CUP NUTRITIONAL YEAST

1   TEASPOON GARLIC POWDER

½   CUP VEGETABLE STOCK (SEE PAGE 755 FOR HOMEMADE) OR WATER, PLUS MORE FOR POACHING

1   TEASPOON SOY SAUCE

SHALLOTS

Shallots are first cousins to onions but they are sweeter, with a hint more garlic flavor and less bite when consumed raw. Indigenous to the Middle East, they are enjoyed worldwide but particularly beloved in France and Southeast Asia. The French use them in delicate sauces such as beurre blanc and béarnaise. They also show up in hearty salads such as Herbed Potato Salad (see page 539) and green lentil salads (see page 461). Thai cuisine also prefers shallots to onions, finding they offer greater depth of flavor in chili pastes and curries. The Vietnamese and Burmese use them fried as a topping for fried rice or noodles, as well as raw in zingy cold salads.

You may have wondered why a shallot is more expensive than an onion (in U.S. supermarkets, at least) and assumed it was because farmers were charging more for a highfalutin gourmet item. While they do have more of an "elite" status, it really comes down to bang for your buck. Shallots are smaller in size and weight than an onion. A farmer would have to devote the same amount of time, seed, fertilizer, and field space for something that results in lower yields. Like any other business, the farmer needs to price according to time and costs. Just a little agronomics to chew on with your Green Lentil Salad.

I always enjoyed growing shallots on my farm. If I could manage to keep them weed-free and give them some good soil, they were trouble-free and very rewarding. Not only do I love how they taste, but they store better than most onions. I have eaten them as late as 10 months after harvest and they were still perfectly firm. If you know of a local farm that grows them, I recommend stocking up when they are available. I keep mine in an unheated part of our basement, and just seeing the bin of rose-purple bulbs in mid-January makes me feel like I'm going to get through the winter just fine.

SHELL PEAS

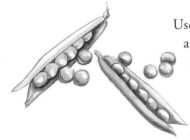

Used in soup, salads, and as a side, the shell pea is a sweet little nugget of protein and sugar that has mass appeal worldwide. It is one of the few legumes that is consumed as a fresh bean unto itself (unlike a green bean or sugar snap that is eaten in its casing), but timing for eating the perfect fresh pea is tricky.

Unless you have access to a garden, the shell pea is one vegetable that should be bought frozen. Immediately after picking them, the sugars in peas start to break down into starch and are only halted by the process of parboiling. Companies that harvest them process them right away, preserving the rich, sweet flavor with a quick treatment in hot water and then flash freezing. Even chefs acknowledge that frozen peas are the best option, and if you order a dish with peas in a restaurant, a previously frozen pea is likely what is on your plate. Not to worry. Peas freeze very well, and you will get excellent quality. I'm not as much of a fan of canned peas, mostly because the texture and color suffer from sitting in brine, but if you don't have access to frozen peas, canned work well in soups and casseroles.

While green peas are thought to have originated in the Mediterranean area, China is now the largest producer, but sugar snap peas and snow peas (see page 144) are included in that statistic. India is the next largest producer, and peas are often seen in Indian cuisine, from samosas to curries. The U.S. is third in production, but the green pea is well loved in the States, especially as a simple side combined with carrots. It also makes an appearance in two popular dishes: chicken pot pie and shepherd's pie. Peas do well in cream sauces with pasta in Italian cooking and in salads in French and Russian recipes.

If you have access to garden space and do not live in the tropics, I highly recommend planting some garden peas in spring for an early summer treat. We plant them in the kitchen garden every year and, aside from the edamame, they are the most anticipated vegetable. My children and I monitor the plants from sprout to flower and pounce on them as soon as they are ready. I have never once cooked our homegrown peas because they don't ever make it into the kitchen.

Peas are a cool-weather crop and will become leathery when the temperature gets too hot; they are a spring and fall crop exclusively, and only in temperate regions. We may not get to grow a whole list of tropical foods up here in the north, but being able to grow peas just may compensate.

As stated, frozen peas are great, so practically speaking, peas are available year-round. If you live near a farmers market, you might be able to find fresh peas in late spring or early summer. Ask the farmer when they were harvested, and if you purchase them, shell and eat them that day. You will need a pile of them to produce enough for a side dish for four. Or you can do like my kids and I and just eat them raw as a snack right then and there.

SPINACH

Spinach is the go-to green because it tastes great raw and stands up well to both short- and long-term cooking. The only frustrating part of spinach is how much it reduces in size when you cook it fresh. For this reason, if you are making a dish that requires a large portion of cooked spinach, such as Saag Aloo (see page 662), I suggest starting with frozen spinach so you don't look on in horror as the two large bags of fresh spinach you thought were going to feed a crowd reduce to a small lump in the pan.

For those who are stubborn about only eating fresh veggies, spinach may change your mind. Not only do you have the serious reduction in mass mentioned above but there just may be more nutritional value in cooked, frozen spinach. The nutrients in uncooked leafy greens degrade very quickly, so unless you acquire just-picked spinach, the frozen spinach will result in higher vitamin content. Also, if the spinach is raw, the massive amounts of iron and calcium that Popeye found so enriching are absorbed by another compound, oxalic acid, making it unavailable for your muscles. The iron in these green leaves becomes available to you only after cooking them. This is not to say that raw spinach is worthless. It is definitely good for you and has plenty of nutritional benefits, including worthy amounts of fiber, folate, vitamin C, and niacin, among other compounds.

China is the world's largest producer of spinach, accounting for over 85 percent of the global supply. The U.S. is the next largest contributor, and most of that is grown in California. We love our spinach here in the States, as is reflected in the value of the 2016 fresh crop: $281.8 million.

Spinach prefers cool weather and is best in the spring, winter, and fall months, but consistent demand has ensured that it is available fresh year-round. The crop is vulnerable to mold and pests so, unfortunately, conventionally grown crops are sprayed regularly. In the Environmental Working Group's "Dirty Dozen" list (the 12 most chemically laden fruits and vegetables), spinach was listed second in 2016. In the USDA report that examined 642 samples for spinach, they found, on average, seven different fungicides and insecticides. If you are buying conventionally grown fresh spinach, rinse it well under cold water. And if you are able, it is worth seeking out an organic option. For optimum nutrients and taste, buy it from your local farmer and ask if they sprayed it. Just because they are not certified organic does not mean it is covered in chemicals (see pages 707–11). With someone local, you get the highest possible nutrient content from just-picked greens and the opportunity to ask how it is grown.

Spinach was a regular crop on my farm, and I could never grow enough of it for the CSA. I'll never forget the year I seeded a late-fall crop in one of the greenhouses and was disappointed when it didn't pop up before the short days of winter halted all production. A few months later, around February, I poked my head in that greenhouse to make a list for bed preparation and was delighted to see an entire section of dark green poking up from the ground. Despite the fact the greenhouse was unheated, a warm spell had stimulated the seed to grow, and I had an unexpected, lush crop of baby spinach just when I needed it most.

SUGAR SNAP PEAS AND SNOW PEAS

Who doesn't love a sugar snap pea and its flat cousin, the snow pea? They are crunchy and sweet when raw, tender and mild when cooked. They are one of the few vegetables one can reliably get a kid to eat. I particularly love the French word for them, *mangetout*, which translates to "eat it all," distinguishing them from English or shell peas (see page 140), of which you only eat the peas. Sugar snap and snow peas have an edible shell that is arguably as delicious as the jewels inside, and one of the great delights of June is heading out to the garden to eat them right off the vine.

Sugar snap peas are popular in the States today but almost disappeared a century ago. There were a few strains of peas with an edible pod as early as the 1880s, but the quality must not have impressed, because by the 1970s there was such low demand that they were no longer commercially available. In 1979, plant breeders Dr. Calvin Lamborn and Dr. M. C. Parker of Twin Falls, Idaho, working to improve the snow pea, crossed it with a mutant shell pea and the sugar snap was born. The tender, sweet casing with equally delicious peas inside was an instant hit and became an All-America Selections winner—like the Oscars of the plant-breeding world. Now sugar snap seed is in such high demand that a farmer is wise to get his or her order in early because seed companies often sell out.

Like shell peas, sugar snap and snow peas are cool-weather crops. In the heat of midsummer, they make leathery pods or simply stop producing. For this reason they are readily available in North America in most months, save July and August. When you buy them, look for those that are stiff and bright green and always keep them cool. They will lose their flavor fairly quickly, so don't purchase them too far in advance of using them and keep them in a plastic bag to retain moisture. Some sugar snaps have a string along the edge of the pod that is too tough to eat but is easy to manage. Just grab the stem, break it off as close to the top as possible, and pull down on the attached stringy part.

Many Americans are introduced to snow peas via their local Chinese restaurant. China is, in fact, the largest producer of peas, a stat that includes shell, snap, and snow peas. Their mild flavor takes well to a zesty ginger-soy sauce, so they are common in stir-fries. I would also recommend using them raw in any salad, but particularly grain salads; they add moisture and crunch without making the salad watery, and they play well with almost all other flavors.

SUNCHOKES

Sunchokes, or Jerusalem artichokes, are native to North America. Neither related to the artichoke nor from Jerusalem, they are the tuberous part of a specific type of sunflower, *Helianthus tuberosus*, and have a nutty artichoke-like flavor. Once a part of the Native American diet, they were brought to Europe by explorers and remain a popular vegetable there. In the States, chefs in the know use them, but they are still not a part of the regular American diet.

Sunchokes taste like a cross between an artichoke and a potato. They can be fried, roasted, boiled, pureed, or put in gratins. High in potassium, iron, and fiber, there is plenty to like about their nutrient content. They also have high levels of inulin, which, though not bad for you, can cause gas. Even people who love them affectionately call them "fartichokes." Sources say that cooking or eating them with an acid, such as lemon, breaks down the inulin, making them acceptable to eat before first dates and long meetings. This is rather handy since they go very well with lemon, whether as a glaze or dip. My favorite way of eating them is to simply chop them, roast them, and then put out a lemon mayonnaise for dipping. They taste exactly like artichoke hearts without all the fuss.

The plant is extremely hardy and in some areas considered invasive. Their tubers multiply and spread underground unless you keep a close eye on them. A report put out by the Ministry of Farming in Ontario, Canada, described them as both a "specialty vegetable" and "nuisance" in the same sentence. When I first started my farm, I was determined to grow everything that was possible in my zone 4 climate, so I picked up a few pounds of sunchokes for fun. Aware of their tenacious nature, I put them away from other crops in the "wild thing" corner, along with horseradish and mint. These three plants are notorious for taking over whatever area you put them in, and given I was not very invested in the success of any of them, it was mostly an experiment to see which one would win the turf war (for the record, it was mint). I did have a few years of sunchoke harvests before they succumbed, though, and enjoyed them thoroughly.

When cooking them, you do not have to peel them, but be sure to scrub them well. They can be tossed in any stir-fry or curry with multiple other vegetables since they are mild enough to get along with most everyone in the vegetable bin. If you are a sunchoke novice, I recommend roasting them, as it's the best way to get a sense of their flavor and texture.

SWEET POTATOES

Although this is not the most important aspect about this vegetable, let's start with a correction that is 150 years overdue: a sweet potato is not a yam. For centuries, the produce industry has been mislabeling sweet potatoes as yams when they are not even closely related. Food historians have postulated that the mix-up began around the Civil War, when all sweet potatoes were white-fleshed. When the orange variety was introduced, merchants distinguished them by calling the new variety "yams," based on the African word *nyami*, meaning "to eat." A yam is an entirely different root vegetable from Africa that is dry and starchy. Never mind it not being in the same species or genus—it isn't even in the same family or order. The only thing the two vegetables have in common is that they are both plants. Your aunt's Thanksgiving candied yams? Those are sweet potatoes. The bin of red colored roots in the market labeled "yams"? Sweet potatoes. Yams are hardly ever imported to the States, though they are a staple in Africa, so it is time to drop the misnomer. If it isn't already clear, this mislabeling has been a pebble in my shoe for years.

Sweet potatoes are from the morning glory family (*Ipomoea*) and are indigenous to Central America. They are very popular in Asia and became an important crop in Japan and China to ensure food security in years of poor rice harvest. They are very high in nutrients, including fiber and vitamins A, B6, and C. China grows 67 percent of the world's supply, followed at a distant second by Nigeria. They are also enjoyed in South America, Australia, and New Zealand as well as the United States. Though they can be grown in northern regions, the southeastern United States grows the bulk of the American crop due to a longer frost-free growing period.

Sweet potatoes are strongly associated with Thanksgiving in forms that range from sweet potato puree to the previously mentioned candied yams (candied sweet potatoes!). For some reason, we feel the need to take one of the sweeter vegetables in existence and make them even sweeter by putting things like marshmallows and syrup on them. I prefer the opposite tack by using them in concert with something very spicy, like in the recipe for Jerk Chicken on page 661, or adding something acidic like lime juice to a simple roasted half. The roasted flesh also makes for a flavorful addition to dough, making a sweet potato bread or gnocchi recipe very easy. In any case, it is my personal preference to use their sugars to balance contrasting flavors instead of adding more sugar, but I mean no offense to Aunt Hilary's sweet potato pie; it's all good.

The largest harvest period of sweet potatoes in the U.S. will be in late summer into the fall, but they store very well and are now available year-round. Though the orange-fleshed varieties are the most popular, you can now find equally delicious types with white and purple flesh.

SWISS CHARD

When it comes to trendy vegetables in the States, poor Swiss chard never seems to make it onto the A-list. It has not garnered the popularity of spinach or taken on trend-of-the-decade status like kale. This is a mystery to me, since it doesn't reduce tenfold when cooked like spinach and has jewel-toned stems of red, yellow, and orange that make kale look like a Plain Jane. The taste can be described as hearty but approachable, and it can add a nice herbal note when incorporated into pasta dough, like in the spätzle recipe on page 668. It is a close relative of beets, and if you can't find chard for a specific recipe, you can always use beet greens, the taste being nearly identical. Plus you can use both the stems and the leaves of chard, though they should be cooked separately.

Chard is native to the Mediterranean area and is more commonly used in southern Europe and North Africa. How it picked up the Swiss part of its name is not clear, though some speculate it was to differentiate it from French spinach. Others attribute its name to Swiss botanist Gaspard Bauhin, who wrote about it.

One of the reasons it does not show up in large supermarkets as much as other greens is its propensity to wilt quickly. Once harvested it needs to be kept cool and moist (but not wet), and even then, it has a short shelf life. Look for it at farmers markets and use it within a few days for optimal freshness.

Though we all assume that young greens are more tender than full-grown, for chard it is the other way around. If you use baby chard for mesclun (which means "mixture" in French), make sure it is very young or it will be a little tough. The mature leaves, on the other hand, are nice and tender, though they should always be cooked because they are slightly bitter when raw.

Chard grows in both hot and cold weather, so it is available year-round. Along with the mystery as to why it doesn't have a cheering section in the kitchen, I've also wondered why ornamental horticulturists haven't developed it for flower gardens. The orange, yellow, red, and white stems are stunning against dark green leaves and it grows easily, even in average soil. Perhaps chard will soon have its day. Until then, the included recipes in this book are a good start toward building its fan base.

TARO

Taro is a root, or corm, of the colocasia plant and is a staple food in many parts of the world, though not so much in the continental United States. Native to India, its popularity spread worldwide, particularly to Africa and the South Pacific. It became an important part of the Hawaiian diet, where it is referred to as kalo. Hawaiians boil kalo in water and mash it to create a puree called poi, which is then served as a starchy base for other dishes, much like Southern grits. Poi is considered sacred food, and Hawaiian custom dictates that no fighting is allowed when a bowl of it is on the table.

Nigeria is the world's number-one producer of taro, followed by China. It is a wetland plant, grown under conditions similar to rice, and it requires clean, oxygenated water and tropical temperatures. Though it has its natural enemies like any other plant, it is fairly easy to grow and in fact, has become an invasive species in the southeastern U.S. Both Texas and Florida list it as a wetland invasive species, which outcompetes local flora for space and nutrients. A simple solution to their problem would be to promote taro as food that happens to be free for the taking should anyone care to harvest it themselves, but for some reason that concept has yet to catch on.

Though taro is not commonly seen in mainland American cooking, it is starting to make appearances, namely in the form of chips, which are delicious. It has a very straightforward, mild flavor and a starchy texture, which means it substitutes well for potatoes and is a nice base on which to place bolder flavors. A good example of this is a dish popular in Egypt in which boiled cubes of taro (known there by its plant name of colocasia) is combined with a zippy puree of chard, cilantro, and lemon (see page 547). The recipe was my first introduction to cooking taro, and I immediately took to it. I also found a great recipe from blogger Priscilla McDonald, who fried it and doused the batons with lime, chili, and salt (see page 265).

You can serve taro boiled, fried, steamed, or mashed, but it should not be served raw. Raw taro root and the plant's leaves contain calcium oxalate, which can cause numbing of the mouth and throat and may also cause kidney stones. Cooking the corm breaks down the calcium oxalate into benign compounds. I wouldn't want to scare you away from trying taro, but I would be remiss in not mentioning it. A great deal of the world's population consumes taro daily without harm, but it is not for the raw-food vegan.

Another consideration for cooking it is its color. Often (but not always) there are purple veins that run through the tuber's white flesh. This makes for a beautiful kaleidoscope when you slice it crosswise and fry it. If you mash it, however, as the Hawaiians would for poi, the resulting color is a purplish-gray. The appearance of food matters in how you perceive taste, especially color. For example, one night, when I was young, my mother made a dinner of swordfish, boiled cauliflower, and rice; the whole plate was going to be white and very dull. She must have been in a punchy mood because she decided the way to remedy the situation was to add blue food coloring to the rice. The periwinkle hue of the rice was so bright that it cast a blue-gray aura over the whole plate and none of us wanted to eat any of it. If we had closed our eyes, the taste would have been exactly what it should have been, but the blue color was telling our senses that this was not something to eat. There are natural colors in Western food that are not objectively appealing (black bean dip, split pea soup), but we have become accustomed to them. All of this is to say that for those who did not grow up with mashed taro, the color may be off-putting. Start with a fried or sautéed version to give it a try. If you like the flavor, tell your brain it is the same pureed and move on to a recipe like poi.

TOFU

Tofu is most commonly described as being devoid of flavor, but that is its most useful attribute. True, it is not going to alight great culinary passions on its own, but consider it a platform for the flavor you are really craving, such as soy sauce, sriracha, or curry. It is the boneless chicken breast of the vegetarian world: a nice substrate on which to show off the character of bolder players around it. Don't think of tofu as bland—think of it as a flavor train.

Tofu has been in the Chinese diet for 2,000 years and is also commonly used in the rest of East and Southeast Asia. In China, it is called *doufu*, which means "beans that are fermented," but Americans adopted the Japanese pronunciation. Benjamin Franklin was among the first Americans to take an interest in tofu, which is revealed in his letters to his dear friend John Bartram in the 1700s. In their correspondence, he mentions a "cheese" made from "Chinese garavances (soybeans)" and is clearly fascinated by the process. Franklin was a trendsetter, but it would take another 200 years for tofu to break into the culinary scene in the New World. It wasn't until the late 1900s that it began to become familiar to Western cooks, both in Asian and vegetarian dishes.

Franklin likely referred to it as cheese because the method of making tofu is similar to dairy-based cheese. To create tofu, a coagulant, either a salt or acid, is added to boiled soymilk, and the liquid binds into curds. The curds are pressed into a cake, which can vary in firmness depending upon how one wants to use it. Unpressed tofu, called *sun dubu*, is served like a porridge and is not commonly seen outside of Asian communities. The slightly firmer silken tofu comes in a block but is very soft and is often used for smoothies, in pastries, or as a substitute for eggs. The types most commonly seen in the West are firm or extra-firm tofu, which have had most of the moisture pressed out of them. These two types are easier to cut into cubes that hold their shape in a stir-fry or soup. Due to their lower moisture content, they are also good candidates for baking and frying. There are several other iterations such as processed tofu, thousand-layer tofu, stinky tofu (its real name), fermented tofu, and freeze-dried tofu if you are inclined to take a deep dive into the topic.

Tofu is an important source of protein for vegetarians. Unlike many other vegetable-sourced proteins, it is a complete protein, meaning it contains all nine essential amino acids. One cup of boiled soybeans contains about 29 grams of protein, which would make Popeye chuck his can of spinach and grab a bowl of mapo tofu for lunch. It is also gluten-free, which makes it the best option for vegetarians with an allergy to wheat products.

Its mild flavor makes it adaptable for a variety of dishes. One can embrace its mild nature and use it in a classic miso soup, allowing the tofu cubes to highlight the complex but delicate taste of white miso. It is also a good filler for dumplings, giving a springy texture to mix in with the vegetables of Tofu Momo Dumplings (see pages 234–35). Tofu may also be a an oasis in spicy dishes, giving your palate a refuge from fiery peppers.

TOMATILLOS

The tomatillo is a little gem native to Central America that adds a sweet-sour taste to any dish. It is a distant relative of the tomato but is closer genetically to the gooseberry. Most people are familiar with them through salsa verde (see page 266), a piquant Mexican sauce. But you can also use them raw if you want a little punch in your guacamole or succotash.

When I went looking for unusual ways to use tomatillos, I found that cooks tend to make a basic salsa verde with it to start and then use the salsa in creative ways, like under fried eggs, as a base for braising pork, or over enchiladas. A salsa verde is also nice on its own served with tortilla chips. But it also works well with other veggies, like corn and peppers. Just be aware that tomatillos lose their shape when cooked and will melt into more of a sauce—if you roast them, be sure to use the released juices.

Though they prefer warm weather, tomatillos are not finicky plants and grow prolifically in the Vermont summer. When I grew on a commercial scale, I found that they are one of the few vegetables you can neglect and still be overwhelmed with the harvest. One plant can produce up to 200 fruits, a fact I always seem to forget when considering how many to put in my now-small garden. My son, Henry, can't bear the thought of anything in our garden going to waste, so he is diligent about harvesting them. But after we have made a big vat of salsa verde and preserved some in jars for the winter months, even we run out of ideas of what to do, and the rest often go unharvested. It is almost unnecessary to plant them the following year because volunteers pop up from the dropped fruit of the previous summer. I'm told that a similar pattern happens in Mexico, so one can find them growing wild everywhere and they are treated with laissez-faire, much like blackberries in Seattle.

Locally grown tomatillos are available mid-to-late summer until the first frost. If they are harvested when green, they will be tarter than those harvested yellow. The longer they sit on the plant, the sweeter they get. Which ones you choose determines how much tartness you want for your dish. To prepare them, remove the husks and rinse them well under cold water because they have a sticky film on their skins.

Lycopersicon Galeni. Ang. 217. — *J.R.H.* 150. — *Ital.* Pomidoro. — *Gall.* Pomme d'amour

Magdalena Bouchard sculpsit

TOMATOES

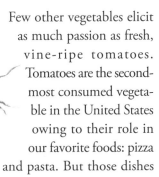

Few other vegetables elicit as much passion as fresh, vine-ripe tomatoes. Tomatoes are the second-most consumed vegetable in the United States owing to their role in our favorite foods: pizza and pasta. But those dishes use a tomato sauce where the tomato's flavor is part of a group that makes up a delicious whole. For the real aficionados, it is the raw, just-sliced tomato that draws deep sighs, and the best time of the year for these folks is August, when loads of perfect tomatoes show up at the market or, if you are lucky, in your backyard. All they need is a sprinkle of salt and perhaps a dash of extra virgin olive oil and balsamic vinegar and they taste of summer itself.

The largest producer of tomatoes in the world is China, followed by India and the United States. In recent years the U.S. has produced around 300,000 acres of processed tomatoes valued at $700 million and 130,000 acres of fresh-market tomatoes worth between $1.4 to $1.6 billion. The majority of America's tomatoes come from California and Florida year-round, but in late summer, you can find locally grown tomatoes in farmers markets across the country.

Originally from South America, tomatoes were initially treated with suspicion by Europeans when explorers brought them back from the New World. Though their reaction may seem amusing now, it is not entirely unfounded since many relatives of the tomato, including belladonna and mandrake, are poisonous. Tomatoes were eventually accepted and then wholeheartedly embraced, particularly in Italy, and now it is difficult to fathom many European cuisines without them. Portuguese explorers brought them to India in the 16th century, and from there they continued to spread to all corners of the earth.

There is always heated debate among tomato lovers as to what makes for a great 'mater. Purists contend that a greenhouse tomato is always inferior to a field tomato, but the issue is more complicated than it may seem. It is fair to say that the tomatoes sold in northern supermarkets in winter are subpar. Because they need to be shipped great distances from warm climates, they are often harvested before fully ripe and sprayed with ethylene gas that causes the skin to turn red whether they are ready or not. Plenty of these are field-grown. I cannot defend these tomatoes.

Then there are the summer tomatoes that are grown in greenhouses or grow tunnels that are allowed to fully ripen on the vine before they are picked. They get the same sun, perhaps a little more warmth, and are grown in the same soil as those in the field next to it. Most growers also roll up the sides of the house for airflow when they can, which means they are basically field tomatoes grown with a clear umbrella overhead. What the farmer is then controlling is water. Water is one of the most critical factors in a tomato's character. Most farmers who are paying attention will

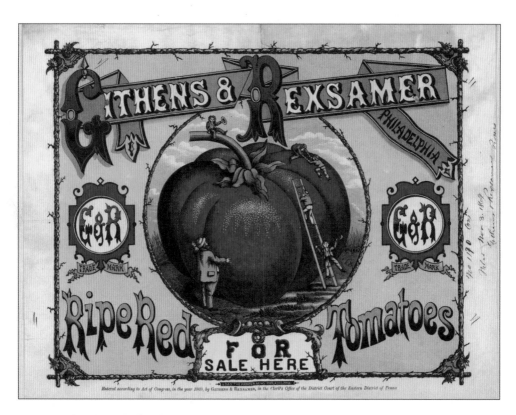

stop watering the plants before harvest to concentrate the flavors and then give them a nice long drink after. Tomatoes grown in the field are subject to the whims of nature, which include rain. After a heavy rain, a tomato will draw up the extra water, sometimes to the point of cracking, sometimes creating a watered-down version of itself. For any greenhouse doubters, I challenge you to try a tomato grown in a house versus one grown in a field harvested after a heavy rain and then render your opinion.

Heirloom tomatoes have made a big comeback thanks to farmers markets. Heirlooms are older varieties that have rich flavor and come in all kinds of shapes and sizes but have lower yields and are often prone to disease. When I first started my farm, I vowed to grow only heirloom tomatoes; after all, I had started the farm to grow great-tasting food, not commodities. My good intentions were often frustrated by diseases and plants that would churn out just a few gorgeous tomatoes before the killing frost came. Over the years, I opened my mind to the possibility that heirlooms weren't the only tomatoes with flavor and trialed hundreds of varieties, both old and new. In the end, I chose about 10 varieties that did well in my soil; they turned out to be a mix of hybrids and heirlooms. The most popular by a mile were the Sungold cherry tomatoes, which are a hybrid orange tomato that are unbelievably sweet and rich in flavor.

Supermarkets are making more of an effort to stock specialty heirloom and vine-ripened tomatoes, but if you live near a farmers market, that is where you will find the best for any dish that calls for raw tomatoes. When it comes to a slow-cooked tomato sauce, canned tomatoes are the way to go; they are more economical and have a very good, concentrated tomato flavor. I could fill volumes with how many dishes utilize the great taste of tomatoes but had to narrow it down to some classics. The following cover all of the seasons of the year: for spring when you just can't wait any longer for that summer tomato taste; a BLT with a twist (see page 698) and classic gazpacho (see page 384) for summer; an excellent Green Tomato Chutney (see page 270) for fall; a baked tomato recipe (see page 269); and a good basic tomato sauce for winter (see page 793).

TURNIPS

When Vermont announced it had chosen a state vegetable, I thought, "Perhaps it will be a locally bred tomato or a funky purple carrot." But no, it was announced, without a shred of irony, that the vegetable that best represents us is a turnip. The Gilfeather turnip, to be precise, originating from Wardsboro, circa 1902.

Turnips are not exactly a culinary darling. The young ones are delicious, but many in the supermarket have been sitting there for a while, and their flavor is something like a blaring tuba when it should be more like a trilling French horn. No child has ever yelled, "Yay!" upon hearing turnips are on the menu. They also carry with them connotations of ignorance, as seen in the phrase, "I didn't just fall off the turnip cart." And the Gilfeather, it must be said, is not going to win any beauty contests. What does this say about my state?

Turnips are consumed worldwide and are thought to come from central and eastern Asia. They were common in the European diet before being replaced with the potato from the New World. Though they are not exactly celebrated, they pop up in European culture in interesting places. During the celebration of the Scottish poet Robert Burns, revelers enjoy pureed turnips ("neeps") and a shot of whisky along with their haggis. Turnips and rutabagas are also thought to be the original jack-o'-lantern. During the traditional Celtic festival of Samhain, a precursor to Halloween, turnips, not pumpkins, were outfitted with grotesque faces and candles. In the 18th century, Charles Townshend, 2nd Viscount, aka "Turnip" Townshend, created a crop rotation that included turnips, allowing for fodder throughout the winter to feed livestock. It has been theorized that the subsequent improvement in the year-round diet led to a stronger workforce and the advent of the Industrial Revolution.

The history is entertaining, but it doesn't help with what to do with the humdrum turnip. Given that it is in the brassica family, take a tip from the Brussels sprouts and cauliflower trends and roast them. When brushed with a little oil and given some dry heat, they are delicious. The assertive tanginess mellows to a sweet nuttiness that can be addictive. They are also very conducive to glazes such as the miso-maple glaze in the recipe on page 546.

Turnip greens are also edible but are usually cooked. Though the leaves can feel fuzzy, that texture will diminish when heated. You can use them in places you might use kale, collards, or

mustard greens, and they are especially good in soup.

Salad turnips are varieties that are harvested very young and small. They have a flavor similar to their cousin the radish and are a crisp and tangy addition to summer salads. Some varieties, like Scarlet Queen, also add beautiful color. You are likely to find these in specialty markets in spring.

I learned to enjoy turnips when I started growing them, but I had never grown the Gilfeather. A few years ago, I found some at the local market and now I get it. They are really special; sweet and earthy in the best way. And after giving it some thought, I decided the state chose the right vegetable. The cold brings out their sweetest nature, just like Vermonters. Also, we tend to exceed expectations despite having a sour reputation and prove to be really delightful underneath a sometimes-rough exterior.

When looking for tasty turnips at the store, the smaller the better. The very best will be the bunched baby purple-tops that you might find at the farmers market. And if you want to know just how good the Gilfeather is, you'll have to visit Vermont during the fall when they are harvested.

Tab.39.

Rapa sativa, rotonda, radice candida. J.R.H. 228.
Ital. Rapa vsuale. Gall. Rave.

WATERCRESS

Watercress and its upland cousin, creasy greens, are feral versions of gourmet lettuces. While the product you buy in the market today is likely grown on a farm, cresses have been harvested wild in streams and meadows in many areas of the U.S. and Europe for centuries. Full of vitamins and minerals, they could literally be lifesavers since they are among the first edible greens to pop up after winter. In fact, in equal quantities, watercress contains more vitamin C than an orange, more iron than spinach, and more folate than bananas. In addition to saving lives, it can also save any dish from being bland.

Watercress (*Nasturtium officinale*) is peppery like arugula but more tender. It is an aquatic plant with a hollow stem that keeps the tops afloat in the water, but the roots grow submerged. Today's commercial production is done in hydroponic grow houses, but there used to be a thriving industry both here and in the UK that relied on natural streams and ponds. In England, the vegetable was so popular in the 19th century that a railroad called the Watercress Line was built to transport the green from Alresford, where it thrived in chalky, wet soils, to London. In the States, Madison County, Alabama, was the epicenter of production, earning the name "Watercress Capital of the World" during its heyday in the early 20th century.

Creasy greens (*Barbarea verna*) grow in the states south of Massachusetts. They have a very similar flavor to watercress and also grow wild, but are not aquatic. Southern journals often mention how welcome the greens are in late winter; just when you've had your fill of heavy comfort food, a zingy green emerges to cleanse the palate and maybe clear away a little of the gut that has formed. Their high vitamin C levels lent them another name, "scurvy grass" (not to be confused with a different green with the same name found in Europe, *Cochlearia spp.*), and their importance in recovering from winter malnourishment in olden days was no joke.

Both watercress and creasy greens are of the mustard family and have that radish bite to them, which makes them excellent with milder ingredients like pasta or cheese. You can add them to any salad, particularly if they are balanced with dried fruit or sliced apples. Like arugula, they are also treated like an herb and used in pesto or sauces, though cooking tames their fiery nature a little.

Watercress is highly perishable and should be eaten within a few days of purchase. You can keep it in the fridge with the roots submerged in a cup of water or wrap it well in plastic to keep in moisture.

WINTER SQUASH

Of all the plant breeders, it is very clear to me that those working with winter squash have the most fun. Cross a pink, banana-shaped Georgia Candy Roaster with a warty, green, pumpkin-like Kogigu and what do you get? I have no idea, but let's try it and find out. Crossbreeding winter squash is easy, and every year there are new shapes, both elegant and grotesque. And the color and pattern options—red, orange, green, blue, and all manner of stripes, dots, and streaks—are dazzling. The breeders also aim for

superior taste and texture, and we, the consumers, are the beneficiaries.

Roundish squashes, such as acorn or buttercup, are good for baking. Simply cut in half and scrape out the seeds, then bake in the oven with a bit of salt and butter. They are also good candidates for being converted into a whole meal when filled with sausage, grains, mushrooms, or other types of stuffing.

Other larger types, such as red kuri or hubbard, are less sweet and are ideal for soups or

Pepo fructu parvo, Pyriformi. Cucurbita aspera Pyriformis, parva. Ital. Zucca. — Gall. Citrouille.

stews, where you can augment their flavor with onions and other aromatics.

Perhaps the most unusual of the bunch is the spaghetti squash, which has flesh that resembles glassy strands of pasta. Its flavor is mild, and the strands can hold up to cooking, so folks looking for gluten-free pasta options can substitute spaghetti squash to pretty good results. I like to cut spaghetti squash in half, remove the seeds, and steam them. All they need when cooked is a little butter and a squirt of Tabasco.

The king of the kitchen is the butternut because, of all the winter squashes, it is easiest to peel and offers a nice big chunk of flesh that you can slice, cube, spiralize, or turn into batons for "squash fries." Supermarkets now offer pre-peeled, diced butternut, which is a nice convenience since all winter squash are challenging to cut. If you consider your knife skills subpar, I recommend the precut version. It may save you time and Band-Aids.

While I look forward to the new varieties every year, there are plenty of heirlooms that hold their own. My favorite is called Long Pie Pumpkin, which looks like an overgrown zucchini. Its dull appearance belies one of the sweetest winter squashes I've ever tried. I grew it on my farm for several years and it is still my top choice for pumpkin pie, not only because of its high sugar content but also for its depth of flavor.

When looking to purchase winter squash, look for firm fruits that don't have any soft spots. Most varieties benefit from curing after being picked, so no need to get excited about freshly picked butternut. Leaving them to sit for a month or two develops their sugars and flavor. Thinner-skinned varieties, such as Delicata, can be eaten just after harvest.

YU CHOY

Yu choy is life-saving. Just when you've had your umpteenth panfried dumpling or forked another plate full of dough-crusted General Tso's chicken into your mouth, a beautiful plate of simple greens comes out of the kitchen and is placed on the middle of the table. You have no idea what to call these greens other than "Chinese vegetables," but their cleansing taste is a miracle. They have that subtle mustard-green tang, though they are somewhat sweeter, and the leafy parts taste like spinach. It doesn't really matter what they are called, they are the perfect antidote to the indulgent meal you just consumed too much of.

Yu choy is part of the brassica (cabbage) family and is a close cousin to gai lan, also known as Chinese broccoli. Their appearance is nearly identical. The only differences are that yu choy has yellow flowers whereas gai lan has white ones, and yu choy is sweeter than gai lan with more tender stalks. If you cannot name the delicious dish that shows up on your table at the Chinese restaurant, don't feel too bad, because no one else seems to have settled on a name either. When delving into yu choy, I discovered it is also referred to as green choy sum, cai xin, choisum, you cai, cai hua, yai tsoi, flowering white cabbage, mock pak-choi, or false pak-choi. This may be because yu choy is used widely throughout Asia and has adopted different names depending on where it is being eaten.

Yu choy is native to China but is now shipped around the world to cater to Asian communities. Like others in the cabbage family, it prefers cool but not cold weather. Only taking about 40 days to maturity, it is one of the few greens that is harvested while it is flowering. (Most vegetables are too tough once they start flowering and are harvested in the bud stage, like broccoli or asparagus, or before flowering, like kale.)

This particular green cooks up quickly and is best served with a simple preparation. It has also bucked the trend of roasting by being so tasty when simply steamed. Though I have never seen it available in a chain supermarket, you can readily find it in the produce aisle of Asian markets. Ask for yu choy, and if that doesn't work, consult the list of alternative names above.

YUCA

Yuca, also known as cassava, is a root vegetable native to South America. It has a rough brown exterior and can reach several pounds in heft and grow as much as 4 feet deep. Though not used very much in American cooking, it is the third-largest source of carbohydrates in the world and is a food staple for millions. Most Americans have tried yuca without realizing it. Yuca root is where tapioca starch comes from, so if you have had tapioca pudding, you have tried yuca.

Being such a prominent staple in so many areas, there are myriad ways of preparing it. In Colombia, it is parboiled and then turned into fries. Caribbean cultures use it to make something called bollitos de yuca (see page 273), which are balls made of mashed yuca filled with meat or cheese and then fried. In Africa, the root is more commonly called cassava and is used as a starchy porridge that can be steamed into a bread-like form and eaten with stews and curries. Though it must be cooked in some way, it can be boiled, roasted, or fried. If you think of it as a potato with extra starch, you'll have no problem finding ways to prepare it.

Though it needs to grow in tropical regions, it is a fairly drought-resistant crop that can thrive in poor soils, making it a reliable staple for many cultures. Brazil, Nigeria, Indonesia, and Thailand are the largest producers in the world, growing 268 million tons in 2014. It is not only a good commodity crop for many regions, it also serves as a reliable subsistence crop for small farms.

Yuca is now more readily available in supermarkets in the States. Look for firm roots with no marks or dents. You must peel them down to the white interior before cooking, but then you can cook it any way you would a potato.

CULTIVATING A PATCH OF CASSAVA ON THE AGRICULTURAL EXPERIMENT PLOT

ZUCCHINI

Here's an embarrassing fact: I can't grow a zucchini. That's right, the vegetable that grows so prolifically under any conditions that there are jokes about it. "Why do people from [pick a state] lock their cars in August? So gardeners don't leave zucchini in the back seat." I've tried different varieties and different spots in my field, but every year it was a struggle to get any sort of fruit from those wretched plants. I had excellent crops of the notoriously finicky eggplant and could trick an artichoke plant into thinking it was in California, but zucchini eluded me. And unlike those who would cower from the sight of them after the umpteenth loaf of zucchini bread, I adore zucchini and find no end of uses for it in recipes.

Zucchini and its siblings, summer squash and pattypan squash, can be grilled, sautéed, used in soup, or turned into noodles for a refreshing change from pasta. It caramelizes really nicely if one is patient with it and gives it plenty of time and room to brown. It is also mild enough to be a foundation for bolder flavors like garlic and lemon.

All squash is indigenous to the Americas, but zucchini is thought to have been bred in northern Italy in the mid-19th century, a few hundred years after squash arrived in Europe. It was brought to the States in the early 20th century, most likely by Italian immigrants. Because it is so versatile and easy to grow, it is now planted worldwide. In 2017, it is estimated that 27.4 million metric tons of squash (this includes pumpkins) were produced on this planet. Just not in my backyard.

When choosing them, pick ones that are smaller, since they will be more tender and have smaller seeds. You can also pick a variety of colors, from dark emerald to bright yellow, since they all have relatively similar cooking times within the summer squash family. The Italian heirloom varieties, such as Constata Romanesco, have excellent flavor and beautiful striped skins. Middle Eastern types, like Magda, are buttery and have a nice bulbous shape that is great for producing thick slices for the grill. And the pop of yellow from summer squash adds nice color to ratatouille and light, hot-weather pastas. They can all be used interchangeably for all of these dishes.

Zucchini never did take in the field. But when I scaled down to a kitchen garden, I thought I would be victorious. The soil in that garden was so lush, there wasn't anything that didn't thrive. The zucchini plants did indeed do well and that first year of harvest I was ecstatic with the bountiful crop . . . until we tried it. All of the fruit that came off of those plants tasted like fish. The flavor was unmistakable, and all my family members noticed it. The second year was the same and the reason why remains a mystery. I've resigned myself to the fact that my farm does not want to produce zucchini. That's why I leave my car windows open in August.

SNACKS *and* APPETIZERS

Vegetable-centric snacks and appetizers can be much more exciting than crudité. Whether you're looking for a healthy go-to afternoon snack or something surprising to put out before a dinner party, the globetrotting recipes that follow include decadent dips, delicious dumplings, and deep-fried delights (just because these recipes are centered around vegetables doesn't mean they're all healthy). And if you are looking to put together a menu of small bites with big flavors, mix and match some of these preparations. No one will be disappointed, or hungry.

NOTE: For all recipes the ⓥ icon indicates a vegetarian preparation; the vegetable illustrations call out the featured vegetable.

ROASTED ARTICHOKE & GARLIC SPREAD

YIELD: 1 CUP / ACTIVE TIME: 5 MINUTES / TOTAL TIME: 10 TO 20 MINUTES

Pairing the nutty flavor of artichokes with the sweetness of roasted garlic makes for an incredibly versatile spread.

1. Preheat the broiler to low. Spread the artichoke hearts and garlic on a cookie sheet and broil, turning occasionally, for 5 to 15 minutes, until browned.

2. Place the artichoke hearts and garlic in a blender or food processor, add the remaining ingredients, and puree until the desired texture is achieved.

3. The spread can be served warm or chilled. Use as a filling for a sandwich or wrap, or use as a dip and serve with crusty bread.

INGREDIENTS:

1   (12 OZ.) BAG FROZEN ARTICHOKE HEARTS, THAWED AND HALVED OR QUARTERED

4   GARLIC CLOVES

2   TABLESPOONS WHITE VINEGAR OR APPLE CIDER VINEGAR

¼   TEASPOON KOSHER SALT

¼   CUP OLIVE OIL

    PINCH OF ONION POWDER (OPTIONAL)

ROMAN-STYLE ARTICHOKES

YIELD: 2 TO 4 SERVINGS / ACTIVE TIME: 20 MINUTES / TOTAL TIME: 30 MINUTES

My family and I had the good fortune to travel to Rome recently, and one of the highlights was a food tour through the Trastevere neighborhood. A poll revealed that the Roman-style artichokes were among the favorite things we tried that night. In Rome, fresh artichokes are stripped down to the heart, fried, and served very simply on their own, or sometimes with a little lemon. Here, we substitute some Lemon-Pepper Mayonnaise.

1. Prepare the artichokes by using a serrated knife to cut off the top half with the leaves and all but the last inch of the stem; continue whittling away the outer leaves until you see the hairy-looking choke within.

2. Using a paring knife, peel the outer layer of the remaining part of the stem; cut the remaining artichoke in quarters and remove the hairy part in the middle. You should have the heart with a little bit of lower leaves left. Place in a bowl of water, add a squeeze of lemon juice, and set aside.

3. Bring water to a boil in a small saucepan. Add the artichokes and parboil until they begin to feel tender, about 3 to 5 minutes. Remove from the water and drain.

4. Place another small pot on the stove and fill with enough oil that the artichoke hearts will be submerged. Warm the oil over medium heat until it starts to sizzle.

5. Place the artichokes in the oil and fry until they are brown all over, turning occasionally, 8 to 10 minutes.

6. Transfer to a paper towel–lined plate and let cool. Sprinkle with salt and serve with the lemon wedges and the Lemon-Pepper Mayonnaise.

INGREDIENTS:

- 2 LARGE ARTICHOKES
- 1 LEMON, QUARTERED
- VEGETABLE OIL, FOR FRYING
- SALT, TO TASTE
- LEMON-PEPPER MAYONNAISE (SEE RECIPE), FOR SERVING

LEMON-PEPPER MAYONNAISE

- 1 CUP MAYONNAISE
- 3 TABLESPOONS GRATED PARMESAN CHEESE
- 1 TABLESPOON LEMON ZEST
- 3 TABLESPOONS FRESH LEMON JUICE
- ½ TABLESPOON BLACK PEPPER
- 2 TEASPOONS KOSHER SALT

LEMON-PEPPER MAYONNAISE

1. Place all of the ingredients in a mixing bowl and whisk to combine.

ROASTED BEET SPREAD

YIELD: 2 CUPS / ACTIVE TIME: 20 MINUTES / TOTAL TIME: 1 HOUR AND 30 MINUTES

This earthy spread is best served with goat cheese and crusty bread.

1. Preheat the oven to 400°F.

2. Line a baking sheet with parchment paper. Place the beets in a bowl with 2 tablespoons of the oil and ¼ teaspoon of the salt. Toss to coat.

3. Arrange the beets on the baking sheet in a single layer and roast for about 1 hour, tossing periodically, until the beets are tender. You should have about 2 cups. Set the beets aside to cool.

4. Warm the cumin and coriander seeds in a dry skillet over medium-high heat for about 2 minutes, stirring constantly, until they release their fragrance and change color slightly. Be careful not to burn them or they will become bitter.

5. Grind the seeds in a spice grinder or crush with a mortar and pestle.

6. Place the beets in a food processor and add the remaining oil and salt, the ground seeds, garlic, chili, and lemon juice. Puree until well combined.

7. Taste and adjust the seasoning as needed. Transfer the dip to a bowl, stir in the cilantro, and serve.

INGREDIENTS:

- 4 BEETS, PEELED AND CUBED
- ¼ CUP OLIVE OIL
- ½ TEASPOON SEA SALT, PLUS MORE TO TASTE
- ¾ TEASPOON CUMIN SEEDS
- ¾ TEASPOON CORIANDER SEEDS
- 2 GARLIC CLOVES, MINCED, PLUS MORE TO TASTE
- 2 TEASPOONS SEEDED AND MINCED GREEN CHILI PEPPER
- 2 TEASPOONS FRESH LEMON JUICE, PLUS MORE TO TASTE
- ⅓ CUP MINCED CILANTRO LEAVES

ARUGULA PESTO

YIELD: 1 CUP / ACTIVE TIME: 10 MINUTES / TOTAL TIME: 10 MINUTES

This version of arugula pesto does not contain any cheese, though you could always add some. Since the greens aren't cooked, they maintain their spiciness, making this a good condiment for mild foods such as grilled zucchini or chicken kebabs. It also makes a terrific sauce for burrata cheese with roasted red peppers on the side.

1. Place the arugula, garlic, salt, walnuts, and lemon zest in a blender or food processor and pulse until fully pureed, scraping down the sides as needed.

2. With the machine running, slowly drizzle in the oil until it is fully incorporated. Add the lemon juice and pulse again to incorporate.

3. Taste, adjust the seasoning as needed, and serve.

INGREDIENTS:

2	CUPS ARUGULA
1	GARLIC CLOVE
½	TEASPOON KOSHER SALT
¼	CUP WALNUTS
1	TEASPOON LEMON ZEST
⅓	CUP OLIVE OIL
1	TEASPOON FRESH LEMON JUICE

CALIFORNIA GUACAMOLE

YIELD: 2 CUPS / ACTIVE TIME: 10 MINUTES / TOTAL TIME: 10 MINUTES

Everyone should have a basic guacamole recipe on hand, as it is one of the finest things to do with an avocado. This recipe is a bona fide California classic.

1. Place the avocados in a small bowl and mash roughly.

2. Add the lime juice, tomatoes, onion, garlic, salt, pepper, and Old Bay seasoning. Fold until everything is incorporated and the mixture has reached the desired consistency. While a chunkier guacamole is easier for dipping, pureeing the mixture in a food processor gives it a smoother finish.

3. Garnish with cilantro, top with a final splash of lime juice, and serve.

INGREDIENTS:

3   AVOCADOS, HALVED, SEEDED, AND PEELED

    JUICE OF 2 TO 3 LIMES, PLUS MORE FOR GARNISH

2   ROMA TOMATOES, SEEDED AND DICED

1   RED ONION, DICED

1-2 GARLIC CLOVES, MINCED

½   TEASPOON KOSHER SALT

    BLACK PEPPER, TO TASTE

    OLD BAY SEASONING, TO TASTE

1   TABLESPOON CHOPPED FRESH CILANTRO, FOR GARNISH

CAULIFLOWER HUMMUS

YIELD: 12 SERVINGS / ACTIVE TIME: 5 MINUTES / TOTAL TIME: 20 MINUTES

Apart from being the new potato and the new rice, cauliflower is also the new chickpea—softened, boiled cauliflower, when pureed, makes a rich and creamy hummus. This is so close to the real thing you'll be surprised.

1. Clean and cut the cauliflower and separate the florets. Place them in a bowl and microwave them for 10 minutes, or steam or boil them until tender.

2. Place the tender cauliflower and all of the remaining ingredients, except for the garnishes, in a food processor or blender and blitz until it reaches a nice, smooth consistency.

3. Taste, adjust the seasoning as necessary, and transfer to a serving bowl. Garnish with the parsley and the olive and serve.

INGREDIENTS:

- 1 LB. CAULIFLOWER
- ¼ CUP TAHINI
- 2 GARLIC CLOVES
- ½ CUP OLIVE OIL
- ½ CUP PITTED KALAMATA OLIVES
- 1 TEASPOON PAPRIKA
- 1 TEASPOON CUMIN
- JUICE OF 1 LEMON
- SALT AND PEPPER, TO TASTE
- 1 TABLESPOON CHOPPED PARSLEY, FOR GARNISH
- 1 OLIVE, FOR GARNISH

BEET CHIPS

YIELD: **4 TO 6 SERVINGS** / ACTIVE TIME: **5 MINUTES** / TOTAL TIME: **20 MINUTES**

You may have tried a commercial brand of beet chips from the supermarket, but they are quite easy to make at home. In this recipe, you don't even have to enlist a deep fryer to get crispy, addictive chips.

1. Preheat the oven to 400°F.

2. Place the beets and oil in a bowl and toss until the slices are evenly coated. Place on a baking sheet in a single layer. Bake for 12 to 15 minutes, or until crispy.

3. Remove from the oven, transfer to a bowl, add the salt, and toss. Serve warm or store in an airtight container.

INGREDIENTS:

5   BEETS, PEELED AND SLICED VERY THIN

¼   CUP OLIVE OIL

2   TEASPOONS SEA SALT

HOT & SPICY CARROTS

YIELD: 4 SERVINGS / ACTIVE TIME: 15 MINUTES / TOTAL TIME: 1 HOUR AND 30 MINUTES

This is a quick pickle recipe that can be used with other vegetables. You can marinate them for up to 5 days, but they will have plenty of flavor in just an hour.

1. Wash the daikon and carrots and cut into matchsticks or rounds that are about the size of a quarter. Pat dry.

2. Place the vinegar, salt, sugar, and water in a bowl and stir until the sugar dissolves. Add the carrots and daikon to the mixture and marinate for at least 1 hour before serving.

3. For the best flavor, store the pickles in an airtight mason jar in the refrigerator for up to 5 days. If you are interested in canning these pickled carrots, follow the instructions on page 716.

INGREDIENTS:

½   LB. DAIKON RADISH, PEELED

½   LB. LARGE CARROTS, PEELED

1   CUP UNSEASONED RICE VINEGAR

1   TEASPOON KOSHER OR SEA SALT

2   TABLESPOONS SUGAR, PLUS 2 TEASPOONS

1   CUP WATER

QUICK PICKLES

YIELD: 2 PINTS / ACTIVE TIME: 15 MINUTES / TOTAL TIME: 12 HOURS TO 2 DAYS

This is a go-to recipe for pickles. It will produce classic cucumber pickles but also works well for carrots, green beans, or cauliflower.

1. Wash two wide-mouth pint jars, lids, and bands in warm soapy water and rinse well. Set aside to dry or dry by hand.

2. Wash and dry the vegetables. Peel the carrots and the ends of the green beans (if using). Cut vegetables into desired shapes and sizes.

3. Divide whatever fresh herbs, spices, dried herbs, and/or garlic you are using between the jars.

4. Pack the vegetables into the jars, making sure there is ½ inch of space remaining at the top. Pack them in as tightly as you can without damaging the vegetables.

5. Combine the vinegar, water, and salt in a small saucepan and cook over high heat. If using, add the sugar. Bring to a boil, stirring to dissolve the salt and sugar. Pour the brine over the vegetables, filling each jar to within ½ inch of the top. You may not use all the brine.

6. Gently tap the jars against the counter a few times to remove all the air bubbles. Top off with more pickling brine if necessary.

7. Place the lids on the jars and screw on the bands until tight.

8. Let the jars cool to room temperature. Store the pickles in the refrigerator. The pickles will improve with flavor as they age, so try to wait at least 2 days before serving. If you are interested in canning these pickles, follow the instructions on page 716.

INGREDIENTS:

1   LB. FRESH VEGETABLES (CUCUMBERS, CARROTS, GREEN BEANS, SUMMER SQUASH, OR CHERRY TOMATOES)

2   SPRIGS FRESH HERBS, SUCH AS THYME, DILL, OR ROSEMARY (OPTIONAL)

1-2   TEASPOONS WHOLE SPICES, SUCH AS BLACK PEPPERCORNS, CORIANDER, OR MUSTARD SEEDS (OPTIONAL)

1   TEASPOON DRIED HERBS OR GROUND SPICES (OPTIONAL)

2   GARLIC CLOVES, SMASHED OR SLICED (OPTIONAL)

1   CUP PREFERRED VINEGAR

1   CUP WATER

1   TABLESPOON KOSHER SALT OR 2 TEASPOONS PICKLING SALT

1   TABLESPOON SUGAR (OPTIONAL)

SPICY PICKLES

YIELD: 12 CUPS / ACTIVE TIME: 20 MINUTES / TOTAL TIME: 5 TO 8 HOURS

This is the perfect recipe to have on hand when cucumbers show up in the spring. With a little preparation, you can make sure you have enough of these delicious pickles to last all year.

1. Place the cucumbers, onions, peppers, and garlic in a large bowl. Bring water to a boil in a canning pot.

2. Place the sugar, vinegar, mustard seeds, turmeric, and peppercorns in a large pot and bring to a boil over medium-high heat, stirring to dissolve the sugar.

3. Add the vegetables and the salt and return to a boil. Remove the pot from heat and let it cool slightly.

4. Fill sterilized mason jars with the vegetables and cover with the brine. Place the lids on the jars and secure the bands tightly. Place the jars in the boiling water for 40 minutes.

5. Use the tongs to remove the jars from the boiling water and let them cool. As they are cooling, you should hear the classic "ping and pop" sound of the lids creating a seal.

6. After 4 to 6 hours, check the lids. There should be no give in them, and they should be suctioned onto the jars. Discard any lids and food that did not seal properly. The pickles will keep in a cool, dark place for up to 1 year.

INGREDIENTS:

- 3   LBS. PICKLING CUCUMBERS, SLICED THIN
- 3   SMALL YELLOW ONIONS, SLICED THIN
- 1   RED BELL PEPPER, STEMMED, SEEDED, AND SLICED THIN
- 2   HABANERO PEPPERS, STEMMED, SEEDED, AND SLICED THIN
- 3   GARLIC CLOVES, SLICED
- 3   CUPS SUGAR
- 3   CUPS APPLE CIDER VINEGAR
- 2   TABLESPOONS MUSTARD SEEDS
- 2   TEASPOONS TURMERIC
- 1   TEASPOON BLACK PEPPERCORNS
- ⅓   CUP CANNING AND PICKLING SALT

TZATZIKI

YIELD: 2 CUPS / ACTIVE TIME: 5 MINUTES / TOTAL TIME: 1 HOUR

An excellent sauce to have on hand for nearly anything that comes off the grill. It is widely used from Greece to Eastern Europe and the Middle East, though it is given a different name in each region. I love it with any type of kebab or roasted potatoes.

1. Place the yogurt, cucumber, garlic, and lemon juice in a mixing bowl and stir to combine. Taste and add salt and pepper as needed. Stir in the parsley or dill (if using).

2. Place in the refrigerator and chill for 1 hour before serving.

INGREDIENTS:

1   CUP PLAIN FULL-FAT YOGURT

¾   CUP SEEDED AND MINCED CUCUMBER

1   GARLIC CLOVE, MINCED

JUICE FROM ¼ LEMON

SALT AND WHITE PEPPER, TO TASTE

FRESH PARSLEY OR DILL, CHOPPED, TO TASTE (OPTIONAL)

BLACK BEAN HUMMUS

YIELD: 4 CUPS / ACTIVE TIME: 10 MINUTES / TOTAL TIME: 10 MINUTES

A new take on hummus that blends black beans with the usual suspects (tahini) plus a few unusual ones (anchovy paste). This flavorful dip works with crudité or warm pita bread.

1. Place all of the ingredients, except for those designated for garnish or for serving, in a food processor and blend until the desired consistency is achieved. If too thick, add a tablespoon of water. If too thin, add more black beans.

2. Place in a serving bowl, garnish with the cilantro, and serve with warm pita bread and crudité.

INGREDIENTS:

2   (14 OZ.) CANS BLACK BEANS, DRAINED, PLUS MORE AS NEEDED

¼   CUP TAHINI

¾   CUP FRESH LIME JUICE

¾   CUP OLIVE OIL

2   TEASPOONS SEA SALT

1   TABLESPOON BLACK PEPPER

1   TEASPOON TABASCO™

1   TEASPOON ANCHOVY PASTE

WATER, AS NEEDED

FRESH CILANTRO LEAVES, CHOPPED, FOR GARNISH

PITA BREAD, WARMED, FOR SERVING

CRUDITÉ, FOR SERVING

EGGPLANT DIP

YIELD: 4 SERVINGS / ACTIVE TIME: 20 MINUTES / TOTAL TIME: 1 HOUR AND 30 MINUTES

This is a straightforward eggplant dip, much like baba ganoush but without the tahini. It is somewhat mild and is therefore a great opportunity to top with interesting spice blends. Here I've used dukkah, an Egyptian seasoning made from coriander, cumin, sesame, and nuts; it will add a bit of crunch and plenty of flavor.

1. Preheat oven to 350°F. Place the eggplant, cut-side down, on a greased baking sheet. Roast in the oven until the eggplant is very soft, about 30 minutes. Remove from the oven and let cool.

2. Place the oil and onion in a skillet and cook over medium heat until the onion is just beginning to brown, about 5 minutes. Add the garlic and cook 2 minutes more.

3. Remove the skin from the cooled eggplant and add the flesh to the pan. Cook the eggplant until it breaks down further and becomes extremely tender, about 5 minutes.

4. Remove from heat and add the maple syrup, lemon juice, salt, and pepper. For a smoother dip, puree the mixture. Otherwise, leave chunky. Let the mixture cool.

5. When cool, place it in a small bowl and top with the tomato and parsley or cilantro. Sprinkle the dukkah on top and serve with pita chips.

INGREDIENTS:

1   LARGE ITALIAN EGGPLANT, HALVED LENGTHWISE

1   TABLESPOON OLIVE OIL, PLUS MORE AS NEEDED

1   ONION, DICED

2   GARLIC CLOVES, CHOPPED

1   TABLESPOON MAPLE SYRUP

    FRESH LEMON JUICE, TO TASTE

    SALT AND PEPPER, TO TASTE

2   TABLESPOONS CHOPPED TOMATO

1   TABLESPOON CHOPPED FRESH PARSLEY OR CILANTRO

1   TABLESPOON DUKKAH

    PITA CHIPS, FOR SERVING

SCAPE NACHOS

YIELD: 4 SERVINGS / ACTIVE TIME: 15 MINUTES / TOTAL TIME: 15 MINUTES

Too often, nachos are reduced to a soggy mess that only tastes like melted cheese. This isn't necessarily a bad thing, but the best nachos comprise layered flavors that hold their own while working in harmony with one another. Quickly panfrying scapes insures that you'll taste their garlicky goodness through the cheese and salsa.

1. Preheat the oven to 400°F. As the oven comes up to temperature, place the oil in a small saucepan over medium heat and add the scapes. Cook for a few minutes, until they just start to brown. Remove from heat.

2. Spread the tortilla chips in one even layer on a baking sheet. Sprinkle the scapes evenly over the chips and then repeat with the cheese.

3. Put the baking sheet in the oven and bake until the cheese has melted and started to brown, 5 to 10 minutes.

4. Remove from the oven and serve immediately with salsa and sour cream on the side.

INGREDIENTS:

1   TABLESPOON OLIVE OIL

4   GARLIC SCAPES, CUT INTO 1-INCH PIECES, DISCARDING THE TIP ABOVE THE FLOWER

1   BAG PLAIN TORTILLA CHIPS

½   LB. SHARP CHEDDAR CHEESE, GRATED

     SALSA (SEE PAGES 798–802 FOR HOMEMADE OPTIONS), FOR SERVING

     SOUR CREAM, FOR SERVING

GARLIC SCAPES

There are two types of garlic: hardneck and softneck, the difference being pretty self-explanatory. A scape is the hardneck's attempt at shooting up a flower in the middle of its growth cycle. Growers will prune out the scape so the plant does not waste energy making a flower but instead devotes its energy to the bulb underground. It just so happens that scapes are delicious, and what might otherwise be considered a nuisance is actually great food.

Scapes look like green stems with a curlicue end and an unopened flower bud on the tip. The whole thing is edible except the very tip (which is too tough), and usually one cuts them into 1- to 2-inch segments to add to any dish. They have a mild, garlicky flavor that is terrific in a stir-fry or any salsa or sauce that jibes with garlic. Scape-lovers find all kinds of uses for them. The only problem is that there are not enough scape-lovers.

I have been promoting garlic scapes since I started scaling up the size of my crop, but so far they remain a footnote to garlic production. They make a brief appearance in fancy food blogs and at farmers markets, but I have yet to see them break into mainstream supermarkets. Ever since I became a food writer, I have been shouting their merits in whatever publication I can. Chefs, friends in the know, and other food writers also sing their praises, but the markets reveal that they have yet to really catch on. I used to sell some, but there was never enough demand for all of the scapes I could potentially harvest, and eventually I would just cut them and leave them on the ground. (My friends who run a farm down the road often toss them off their Fourth of July parade float instead of candy. Agriculture humor.) This is a shame, because they are truly great and could be a way for all hardneck garlic farmers to make extra income on a crop they are already growing.

Most of the garlic grown commercially on large farms in California is of the softneck variety, so scapes will only be found in late June near smaller farms that tend to have more diverse crops. Scape pesto and stir-fry are the go-to uses for them, but my absolute favorite is scape nachos, so I am including this very simple recipe in hopes of starting the mainstream scape revolution. Viva la scape!

DILLY BEANS

YIELD: 5 PINTS / ACTIVE TIME: 10 MINUTES / TOTAL TIME: 1 WEEK

This is a classic preparation for green beans—perfect for when they come in all at once in mid-summer.

1. Prepare a boiling water bath and 5 pint jars. Place the lids and bands in a small saucepan and simmer over low heat while you prepare the beans.

2. Wash and trim the beans so that they will fit in the jars. If the beans are particularly long, cut them in half. Place the vinegar, water, and salt in a medium saucepan and bring to a boil.

3. While the pickling liquid heats, pack your beans into the jars, leaving ½ inch of space free at the top.

4. Place a clove of garlic, 1 teaspoon dill seeds, and 1 teaspoon red pepper flakes in each jar.

5. Slowly pour the hot brine over the beans, leaving ½ inch free at the top. After the jars are full, tap them on the counter to remove the air bubbles. Add more brine if necessary.

6. Wipe the rims, apply the lids and bands, and process in the boiling water for 30 minutes. Use the tongs to remove the jars from the boiling water and let them cool. As they are cooling, you should hear the classic "ping and pop" sound of the lids creating a seal.

7. After 4 to 6 hours, check the lids. There should be no give in them, and they should be suctioned onto the jars. Discard any lids and food that did not seal properly. Let the beans sit for at least 1 week before serving.

INGREDIENTS:

3	LBS. GREEN BEANS
2½	CUPS WHITE VINEGAR
2½	CUPS WATER
¼	CUP PICKLING SALT
5	GARLIC CLOVES
5	TEASPOONS DILL SEEDS (NOT DILL WEED)
5	TEASPOONS RED PEPPER FLAKES

KALE CHIPS

YIELD: 4 SERVINGS / ACTIVE TIME: 5 MINUTES / TOTAL TIME: 15 MINUTES

Kale chips are quick and easy to make and a nice way to ease non-kale eaters into the leaf's vegetal flavor. It is best to use large, wide leaves for these, since that will allow some surface area for the oil and Parmesan. Once you have tried this basic recipe, you can switch it up and sprinkle on your favorite seasonings and flavors. Chili powder, cumin, honey, and curry are all good options.

1. Preheat oven to 400°F. Place the kale on a baking sheet and lightly coat with oil. Sprinkle the Parmesan and salt on top.

2. Put the baking sheet in the oven and roast for 5 to 8 minutes, until kale is crispy but not burnt.

3. Remove, let cool to room temperature, and serve.

INGREDIENTS:

10 KALE LEAVES, STEMS REMOVED (LACINATO OR RED RUSSIAN WORKS WELL)

OLIVE OIL, TO TASTE

PARMESAN CHEESE, GRATED, TO TASTE

SALT, TO TASTE

LEEK BOLANI

YIELD: 4 SERVINGS / ACTIVE TIME: 25 MINUTES / TOTAL TIME: 1 HOUR

Bolani is a traditional panfried flatbread from Afghanistan that is stuffed with various fillings, including leeks. It would make a nice addition to a meal of curry and rice. Or you can serve it with yogurt or chimichurri on the side. Given that it is cooked in a pan, when forming the pastry, you want to make it as flat as possible. In other words, don't mound the filling in the middle like you would a dumpling, but spread it out over the dough evenly and crimp the sides. If it is too bulbous, the dough that doesn't touch the pan won't cook as well.

1. To prepare the dough, place the flours and salt in a wide bowl, whisk to combine, then add the water and oil and gently mix together until it forms a ball. Dust a work surface with flour, place the dough on it, and knead until it is smooth, about 5 minutes. Return the dough to the bowl, cover, and let rest for 30 minutes.

2. To begin preparations for the filling, place the butter in a medium saucepan and melt over medium heat. Add the leeks and sauté until wilted and just beginning to brown, about 5 minutes. Add the chili, if using, and cook a few minutes more. Remove from heat and add the coriander and the cilantro or parsley.

3. Divide the dough into six pieces. Roll them out, one at a time, into a rectangular shape and place about ⅓ cup of the leek mixture on top. Spread the mixture over one half of each piece of dough and fold the other side up over the top, ensuring that the pastries are as flat as possible. Using the back of a fork, crimp the edges to seal.

4. Coat the bottom of a wide pan with a few tablespoons of oil and warm over medium heat. Gently place as many pastries in the pan as will fit and cook over medium heat for 2 to 3 minutes per side. The bolani should be lightly browned and cooked all the way through.

5. Place the cooked bolani on a paper towel–lined baking sheet to soak up excess oil. Season with salt and pepper and serve with yogurt or Chimichurri Redux.

INGREDIENTS:

FOR THE DOUGH

1   CUP ALL-PURPOSE FLOUR, PLUS MORE FOR DUSTING

1   CUP WHOLE WHEAT PASTRY FLOUR

1   TEASPOON KOSHER SALT

¾   CUPS WATER

1   TABLESPOON OLIVE OIL

FOR THE FILLING

1   TABLESPOON UNSALTED BUTTER

3   CUPS SLICED LEEKS

1   GREEN CHILI PEPPER, STEMMED, SEEDED, AND CHOPPED (OPTIONAL)

½   TEASPOON CORIANDER

½   CUP FRESH CILANTRO OR PARSLEY, CHOPPED

OLIVE OIL, AS NEEDED

SALT AND PEPPER, TO TASTE

YOGURT, FOR SERVING (OPTIONAL)

CHIMICHURRI REDUX (SEE PAGE 805), FOR SERVING

SHIITAKE DUXELLES PÂTÉ

YIELD: 4 SERVINGS / **ACTIVE TIME:** 20 MINUTES / **TOTAL TIME:** 30 MINUTES

A duxelles is a traditional French preparation of sautéed chopped mushrooms and shallots that can be used in anything from sauces to stuffing. Here I have turned it into a pâté to be served with crackers or bread as an hors d'oeuvre. Aside from shallots, there is no better pairing with mushrooms than cream and sherry, so all are included as supporting players to the main character: the spotlight-hogging shiitake. To give it an extra-creamy texture, you can add softened cream cheese at the end or leave the mushrooms to take the final bow by themselves.

1. Place a wide sauté pan over medium heat and add the oil. When it starts to shimmer, add the shallot and garlic and cook until slightly browned, about 5 to 7 minutes.

2. Add the mushrooms and a pinch of salt and continue to cook. When the mushrooms have released most of their liquid and are starting to brown, add the Sherry and stir, scraping the browned bits off the bottom of the pan.

3. Add the cream and thyme and continue to cook until the mixture has thickened and is almost a paste. Remove from heat.

4. Add the Parmesan, taste, and adjust the seasoning as needed. If adding cream cheese, let the mixture cool a little and then fold in the cream cheese until thoroughly combined.

5. Serve with crackers or bread.

INGREDIENTS:

- 1 TABLESPOON OLIVE OIL
- ½ CUP MINCED SHALLOT
- 1 SMALL GARLIC CLOVE, MINCED
- ¾ LB. SHIITAKE MUSHROOM CAPS, CHOPPED

  SALT, TO TASTE
- 1 TABLESPOON SHERRY
- ¼ CUP HEAVY CREAM

  LEAVES FROM 2 SPRIGS FRESH THYME OR ½ TEASPOON DRIED THYME
- 3 TABLESPOONS GRATED PARMESAN CHEESE
- ¼ CUP CREAM CHEESE (OPTIONAL)

  CRACKERS OR BREAD, FOR SERVING

MUSHROOM TOAST
with WHIPPED GOAT CHEESE

YIELD: **4 SERVINGS** / ACTIVE TIME: 10 MINUTES / TOTAL TIME: 30 MINUTES

Toast is as basic as it gets, but you'd be surprised by how well it cleans up. The deep, nutty flavor of the chestnut mushrooms adds a new layer to this dish, but you can always substitute your favorite mushrooms if chestnuts are unavailable.

1. Preheat the oven to 400°F.

2. Place the mushrooms on a baking sheet, drizzle with half of the oil, and sprinkle with salt. Place the mushrooms in the oven and roast until they begin to darken, about 10 to 15 minutes.

3. While the mushrooms are roasting, place the slices of bread on another baking sheet, brush the tops with the remaining oil, and sprinkle with salt. Place the slices of bread in the oven and bake until golden brown, about 10 minutes.

4. Place the cream in a mixing bowl and beat until stiff peaks begin to form. Add the goat cheese and beat until well combined.

5. Remove the mushrooms and bread from the oven and let cool for 5 minutes. Spread the cream-and-goat cheese mixture on the bread, top with the mushrooms, sunflower seeds, and rosemary, and drizzle with honey.

INGREDIENTS:

½   LB. CHESTNUT MUSHROOMS (OR MUSHROOM OF YOUR CHOICE), SLICED

2   TABLESPOONS OLIVE OIL

    SALT, TO TASTE

4   THICK SLICES SOURDOUGH BREAD

½   CUP HEAVY CREAM

½   CUP GOAT CHEESE, AT ROOM TEMPERATURE

2   OZ. SUNFLOWER SEEDS

2   TABLESPOONS FRESH ROSEMARY LEAVES

1   TABLESPOON HONEY

FRIED OKRA

YIELD: 4 SERVINGS / ACTIVE TIME: 25 MINUTES / TOTAL TIME: 26 HOURS

If you have reservations about trying a new food, there is a proven way to ease into it: fry it. Okra pairs very well with peppers of all kinds. Though the fried nuggets are good on their own, I recommend Jalapeño Pepper Jam for dipping.

1. Spread the okra on a baking sheet and sprinkle them with the flavored salt.

2. Place the cornmeal and flour in a bowl and whisk to combine. In another bowl, beat the egg until scrambled.

3. Add peanut oil to a Dutch oven until it is 2 to 3 inches deep. Heat to 350°F over high heat.

4. Dip the chunks of okra in the egg, transfer to the cornmeal mixture, and toss to coat.

5. When the oil is hot enough that a crumb of cornmeal sizzles, add all of the okra that will fit and fry. Keep an eye on them, turning them gently as they brown. When brown on all sides (about 5 minutes), use a slotted spoon to remove them from the oil and place on a paper towel–lined plate. Season with salt, let cool a few minutes, and serve with the Jalapeño Pepper Jam.

JALAPEÑO PEPPER JAM

1. Place peppers, sugar, and vinegar in a large nonreactive saucepan. Bring to a boil and cook for 5 minutes. Remove from heat and let cool for 1 hour.

2. Add the pectin and the food coloring, if desired. Bring to a rolling boil and cook for 1 minute. Pour into hot, sterilized half-pint canning jars, filling to within ½ inch of the top.

3. Wipe tops of the jars. Center lids on top and make sure to screw the bands on firmly.

4. Fill a canning pot or a large pot with a bottom rack with water and bring to a boil. Gently lower jars into water. The water should cover the jars by at least 1 inch.

5. Bring water to a full boil. Reduce heat to a gentle boil, cover, and cook for 5 minutes.

6. Carefully remove the jars from the water using tongs or a jar lifter.

7. Place upside-down on a rack or thick towels and let cool without moving for 12 to 24 hours.

8. The jars will make popping sounds if sealed properly. Once cool, check the seal on each jar by pressing down on lid. If it doesn't push down, it's sealed. If it does push down, store in refrigerator. Otherwise, store in a cool, dark place for up to 1 year.

INGREDIENTS:

- ½ LB. FRESH OKRA, TRIMMED AND CUT INTO 2-INCH PIECES
- JANE'S KRAZY MIXED-UP SALT, TO TASTE
- ¼ CUP CORNMEAL
- ¼ CUP ALL-PURPOSE FLOUR
- 1 EGG
- PEANUT OIL, FOR FRYING
- SALT, TO TASTE
- JALAPEÑO PEPPER JAM (SEE RECIPE), FOR SERVING

JALAPEÑO PEPPER JAM

- 1 CUP GREEN BELL PEPPER, STEMMED, SEEDED, AND MINCED OR GROUND
- ¼ CUP JALAPEÑO PEPPER, STEMMED, SEEDED TO TASTE, AND MINCED OR GROUND
- 4 CUPS SUGAR
- 1 CUP APPLE CIDER VINEGAR
- 1 (6 OZ.) PACKET LIQUID FRUIT PECTIN
- 3-5 DROPS GREEN FOOD COLORING (OPTIONAL)

PICKLED OKRA

YIELD: 2 PINTS / ACTIVE TIME: 15 MINUTES / TOTAL TIME: 5 TO 7 HOURS

Okra pickles beautifully, and it looks incredibly appealing in an appetizer spread.

1. In a large saucepan, bring 6 cups of water to a boil. This will serve as your bath once the jars have been filled.

2. Pack the okra, chilies, bay leaves, and garlic cloves into two sterilized 1-pint canning jars. Divide the dill seeds, coriander seeds, and peppercorns evenly between the jars.

3. In a medium saucepan, combine the water, vinegar, and salt and bring to a boil over high heat, stirring to dissolve the salt.

4. Pour the brine into the jars, leaving ½ inch of space free at the top. Apply the lids and bands.

5. Place the jars in the boiling water and boil for 10 minutes. Use tongs to remove the jars from the boiling water and let them cool. As they are cooling, you should hear the classic "ping and pop" sound of the lids creating a seal.

6. After 4 to 6 hours, check the lids. There should be no give in them, and they should be suctioned onto the jars. Discard any lids and food that did not seal properly. The okra can be served immediately or stored in a cool, dark place for up to 1 year. Refrigerate after opening.

INGREDIENTS:

1	LB. OKRA, TRIMMED
4	SMALL DRIED RED CHILI PEPPERS
2	BAY LEAVES
2	GARLIC CLOVES, HALVED
1	TEASPOON DILL SEEDS
1	TEASPOON CORIANDER SEEDS
1	TEASPOON BLACK PEPPERCORNS
1½	CUPS WATER
1½	CUPS APPLE CIDER VINEGAR
1½	TABLESPOONS KOSHER SALT

DAIKON, CARROT, AVOCADO
& SQUID INK PASTA SPRING ROLLS

YIELD: 4 SERVINGS / ACTIVE TIME: 20 MINUTES / TOTAL TIME: 30 MINUTES

This spring roll has a contrast of colors and flavors that makes it a perfect bite-sized appetizer. The tangy radish counters the sweet carrot and buttery avocado. The squid ink pasta adds unexpected color and briny umami. Unless you don't care for cilantro, do not leave it out, as it ties everything together with an herbal-citrus kick. Prepare all of your ingredients and have them ready, because you have to work fairly quickly with the spring roll wrappers.

1. Bring water to a boil in a saucepan. Take the squid ink spaghetti or rice vermicelli and break it in half. Drop it in the water and let cook until just al dente, 6 to 8 minutes. Rinse under cold water and set aside.

2. Place the soy sauce, vinegar, ginger, and scallion in a small bowl and stir to combine. Set the dipping sauce aside.

3. Find a cake pan or other vessel that will fit the spring roll sheets and fill it with hot water. Dip the wrappers in the hot water and let them soften for about 30 seconds. Remove them from the water and lay them on a plate. Take some of the carrot and daikon and lay it crosswise in the middle of a wrapper. Add a line of sliced avocado and some of the pasta. Top with some of the cilantro. Fold the edge of the wrapper over the vegetables and then roll the whole thing up as tightly as you can manage without breaking the delicate wrapper. Repeat until you have used all of the ingredients.

4. When ready to serve, slice the rolls into 2-inch pieces and arrange them on a plate around the dipping sauce.

INGREDIENTS:

¼ LB. SQUID INK SPAGHETTI OR RICE VERMICELLI

2 TABLESPOONS SOY SAUCE

1 TABLESPOON RICE WINE VINEGAR

1 TEASPOON GRATED GINGER

1 TEASPOON CHOPPED SCALLION

1 PACKAGE SPRING ROLL WRAPPERS (MADE WITH RICE FLOUR)

1 LARGE CARROT, PEELED AND JULIENNED

1 SMALL DAIKON RADISH, JULIENNED

FLESH FROM 1 AVOCADO, SLICED

¼ CUP CHOPPED FRESH CILANTRO

CARAMELIZED ONION & LEEK FOCACCIA

YIELD: 4 TO 6 SERVINGS / ACTIVE TIME: 1 HOUR / TOTAL TIME: 2 HOURS AND 45 MINUTES

The sweetness of caramelized onions is simply divine. This combination of leek and onion makes for a subtle (and slightly sweeter) topping.

1. Place the butter and 2 tablespoons of the oil in a skillet and warm over medium-low heat. When the butter has melted, add the onion and leek. Increase heat to medium-high and cook, stirring, until the onion and leek start to soften, about 5 minutes. Reduce heat to low and cook, stirring occasionally, until well browned, about 10 to 15 minutes. Set aside.

2. Proof the yeast by mixing it with the warm water in a large bowl. Let sit until foamy, about 10 minutes.

3. Combine the flour, salt, and pepper in a mixing bowl, and stir the mixture into the yeast mix. The dough will be sticky. Transfer to a flour-dusted surface and knead the dough until it loses its stickiness, about 10 minutes, incorporating more flour as needed.

4. Coat the bottom and sides of a large mixing bowl with oil. Place the ball of dough in the bowl, cover loosely with plastic wrap, put in a naturally warm, draft-free location, and let rise until doubled in size, about 45 minutes to 1 hour.

5. Preheat the oven to 450°F.

6. Put the remaining tablespoon of oil in a cast-iron skillet and press the dough into it. Top with the caramelized onion-and-leek mixture. Season generously with salt and pepper, then with the Parmesan. Cover loosely with plastic wrap and let rise for about 20 minutes.

7. Put in the oven and bake for 25 to 30 minutes, until golden brown and hot. Remove from oven and let rest for 5 minutes before removing from skillet to cool further.

INGREDIENTS:

1	STICK UNSALTED BUTTER
3	TABLESPOONS OLIVE OIL, PLUS MORE AS NEEDED
1	YELLOW ONION, PEELED AND SLICED THIN
1	LARGE LEEK, WHITE AND LIGHT GREEN PART ONLY, RINSED WELL AND SLICED THIN
1	TEASPOON ACTIVE DRY YEAST
1	CUP WARM WATER (110 TO 115°F)
2-2½	CUPS ALL-PURPOSE FLOUR, PLUS MORE FOR DUSTING
1	TEASPOON KOSHER SALT, PLUS MORE TO TASTE
1	TEASPOON BLACK PEPPER, PLUS MORE TO TASTE
	PARMESAN CHEESE, GRATED, FOR TOPPING

ONION RINGS

YIELD: 4 SERVINGS / ACTIVE TIME: 15 MINUTES / TOTAL TIME: 20 MINUTES

Onion rings are among my favorite fried foods. While we can all admit the crunchy fried bits are the best part, I don't care for the battered kind where you usually end up biting into it and pulling out a half-cooked onion. I prefer when the onion itself gets a bit crispy and crunchy. To ensure that, don't put too much batter on, so what you do have adheres well. For the coating I tried plain and panko bread crumbs. Panko is a style of bread crumbs from Japan that are a little bit bigger and lighter than traditional bread crumbs. They were both good in their own way, so my husband had the bright idea of combining the two. The plain bread crumbs adhered better to the onion, while the larger panko created those extra-crunchy bits that we all search out when looking for the perfect ring. We then cranked it up one more notch and added some Parmesan cheese. For this recipe, skip the kosher salt and use fine-grained so it will stick to the onion.

1. Place the flour in a shallow bowl, the beaten egg, milk, and paprika in another, and the bread crumbs and Parmesan in another.

2. Place a Dutch oven on the stove and add oil until it is 2 to 3 inches deep. Heat the oil until a few bread crumbs sizzle immediately when dropped in.

3. Dip the onion rings in the flour, then in the egg mixture, and lastly in the bread crumb mixture. Make sure the rings are fully covered by the bread crumb mixture. Carefully drop into the hot oil and fry for several minutes, until brown.

4. Using tongs, turn over to brown the other side (if necessary) and then transfer to a paper towel–lined plate.

5. Sprinkle with fine-grained salt, let cool briefly, and serve with the Creamy Adobo Dip.

CREAMY ADOBO DIP

1. Place all of the ingredients in a bowl, stir to combine, and serve.

INGREDIENTS:

- ½ CUP ALL-PURPOSE FLOUR
- 1 EGG, BEATEN
- ⅓ CUP WHOLE MILK
- ½ TEASPOON PAPRIKA
- ½ CUP PLAIN BREAD CRUMBS
- ½ CUP PANKO BREAD CRUMBS
- 1 TABLESPOON GRATED PARMESAN CHEESE
- VEGETABLE OIL, FOR FRYING
- 2 LARGE YELLOW ONIONS, SLICED INTO THICK RINGS
- FINE-GRAINED SALT, TO TASTE
- CREAMY ADOBO DIP (SEE RECIPE), FOR SERVING

CREAMY ADOBO DIP

- 2 TABLESPOONS MAYONNAISE
- 2 TABLESPOONS SOUR CREAM
- 1 TEASPOON ADOBO SAUCE (FROM A CAN OF CHIPOTLES IN ADOBO SAUCE)

PIEROGI *with* POTATO, ONION *&*
FARMER'S CHEESE FILLING

YIELD: 4 SERVINGS / ACTIVE TIME: 1 HOUR AND 30 MINUTES / TOTAL TIME: 3 HOURS AND 30 MINUTES

These dumplings, known as pierogi in Poland and varenyky in Ukraine, are endlessly versatile and seriously comforting. In addition to potatoes, onions, and cheese, they can be filled with mushrooms, sauerkraut, meat, or even fruit.

1. To begin preparations for the dough, place the cream cheese, egg, and salt in the bowl of a stand mixer fitted with the paddle attachment. Beat on medium until smooth. Add the water and beat until smooth. Replace the paddle attachment with the dough hook. With the mixer running, slowly add the all-purpose flour and mix until you have a dough that pulls away from the side of the bowl.

2. Transfer the dough to a work surface dusted with all-purpose flour and knead until it has a smooth and elastic texture, about 10 minutes. If it feels sticky, dust with additional all-purpose flour and knead to incorporate. If it feels too dry, wet your hands and continue kneading.

3. Wrap the dough tightly in plastic wrap and let rest for 1 hour at room temperature.

4. To begin preparations for the filling, bring a large pot of water to a boil and add the potatoes. Cook until a knife can be easily inserted into the thickest part, 30 to 40 minutes. Drain and, once cool enough to handle, remove the skins. While still warm, pass the potatoes through a potato ricer into a large bowl or mash until smooth. Add the egg and stir until well combined.

5. Warm a large skillet over medium-low heat for 2 to 3 minutes and then add the butter. Once the butter is foaming, add the onions and a couple pinches of salt and cook, stirring occasionally, until softened, about 10 minutes. Raise heat to medium and cook until the onions have browned, stirring occasionally, about 12 minutes. Remove from heat and let cool for 15 minutes.

6. Add the onions, farmer's cheese, and paprika to the potato mixture, season with salt and pepper, and stir to combine. Let cool to room temperature.

7. Cut the dough into four pieces. Set one piece on a lightly floured work surface and cover the others to prevent drying. Using a lightly floured rolling pin, flatten the dough to ½ inch thick. Continue

INGREDIENTS:

FOR THE DOUGH

- 5 OZ. CREAM CHEESE, AT ROOM TEMPERATURE
- 1 LARGE EGG, AT ROOM TEMPERATURE
- 1 TEASPOON KOSHER SALT
- 2 TABLESPOONS WARM WATER (110 TO 115°F)
- 1¼ CUPS ALL-PURPOSE FLOUR, PLUS MORE AS NEEDED

  SEMOLINA FLOUR, FOR DUSTING

FOR THE FILLING

- 3 YUKON GOLD POTATOES (ABOUT 1¼ LBS.)
- 1 LARGE EGG, AT ROOM TEMPERATURE, LIGHTLY BEATEN
- 4 TABLESPOONS UNSALTED BUTTER
- 3 YELLOW ONIONS, DICED

  SALT AND PEPPER, TO TASTE
- 4 OZ. FARMER'S CHEESE OR SMALL-CURD COTTAGE CHEESE
- 1¼ TEASPOONS SWEET PAPRIKA

FOR THE TOPPING

- 2 TABLESPOONS UNSALTED BUTTER
- 1 LARGE ONION, CHOPPED

  SALT, TO TASTE
- 3 SLICES BACON, CHOPPED
- ½ CUP SOUR CREAM

rolling the dough, turning occasionally, until it is ⅛ inch thick. Alternatively, flatten the dough to ½ inch thick, then run it through a pasta machine until you reach the third-to-thinnest setting.

8. Lightly dust each sheet of dough with flour and lay it on a surface lined with parchment paper or paper towels. Repeat until all the dough has been rolled out, stacking and separating the sheets with parchment paper or paper towels.

9. Working with one sheet of dough at a time, lay it on a lightly floured work surface and, using a 3-inch cookie cutter, cut out as many rounds as possible.

10. Spoon 2 teaspoons of filling into the center of each round. Lightly moisten the edge of the pierogi. Fold one edge of the pasta round over the filling, to create a half-moon, and press down to remove any air.

11. Prick each pierogi once in the center with a toothpick. Lightly dust the pierogis with flour, then arrange in a single layer on parchment paper–lined baking sheets heavily dusted with semolina flour. Let air-dry for 1 hour, turning them over halfway through.

12. To prepare the topping, warm a skillet over medium-low heat for 2 minutes, then add the butter. Once it is foaming, add the onion and a couple pinches of salt and cook, stirring, until softened, about 10 minutes. Raise heat to medium and cook until the onion has browned, about 12 minutes. Remove from heat and cover to keep warm.

13. Heat a separate medium skillet over medium-low heat for 2 minutes, then add the bacon. Cook, stirring frequently, until crispy. Transfer the bacon to a paper towel–lined plate to drain.

14. Bring a large pot of water to a boil, add salt (1 tablespoon for every 4 cups water) and stir. Using a large slotted spoon, carefully lower the pierogi, a few at a time, into the boiling water. Stir for the first minute to prevent any sticking. Reduce heat to medium. Cook until the pierogis float to the surface, 3 to 4 minutes. Remove a pierogi and slice in half to see if cooked through, then transfer the cooked pierogi to a colander to drain.

15. Arrange the pierogis on a warmed serving platter and top with the onion, bacon bits, and sour cream. Alternatively, the sour cream can be served on the side.

TIP: Once air-dried, you can place the pierogis in a bowl, cover with a kitchen towel, and refrigerate for up to 3 days. Or you can freeze them on the baking sheets, transfer to freezer bags, and store in the freezer for up to 2 months. Do not thaw them prior to cooking (they will become mushy), and add an extra minute or two to their cooking time.

PURPLE POTATO CHIPS

YIELD: 4 TO 6 SERVINGS / ACTIVE TIME: 5 MINUTES / TOTAL TIME: 20 MINUTES

Take advantage of the purple potato's striking color to make a different kind of chip.

1. Preheat the oven to 400°F.

2. Place the potatoes and the oil in a bowl and toss until the potatoes are evenly coated. Place the potatoes on a baking sheet in a single layer. Bake for 12 to 15 minutes, until crispy.

3. Remove from the oven, transfer to a bowl, add the salt, and toss lightly. Serve warm or store in an airtight container.

INGREDIENTS:

3   LARGE PURPLE POTATOES, SLICED THIN

¼   CUP OLIVE OIL

2   TEASPOONS SEA SALT

REALLY RADISH DIP

YIELD: 2 CUPS / ACTIVE TIME: 10 MINUTES / TOTAL TIME: 10 MINUTES

Though this is a simple dip to make using basic ingredients, the combination somehow tastes like a refined shrimp dip. While you might know it's a radish dip, go ahead and tell your guests it is shrimp dip, and see if the power of suggestion can turn a simple radish into a succulent shrimp.

1. Chop the radishes to the desired chunkiness of the dip and set aside.

2. Place the cream cheese and sour cream in a bowl and stir until smooth.

3. Fold in the chives and radishes and season with salt, pepper, and hot sauce.

4. Serve with crudité or crackers.

INGREDIENTS:

1   LB. RADISHES

½   CUP CREAM CHEESE, AT
      ROOM TEMPERATURE

⅓   CUP SOUR CREAM

2   TABLESPOONS CHOPPED
      FRESH CHIVES

      SALT AND PEPPER, TO TASTE

      HOT SAUCE, TO TASTE

      CRUDITÉ, FOR SERVING
      (OPTIONAL)

      CRACKERS, FOR SERVING
      (OPTIONAL)

AVOCADO TOAST
with QUICK-PICKLED WATERMELON RADISH

YIELD: 4 SERVINGS / ACTIVE TIME: 15 MINUTES / TOTAL TIME: 30 MINUTES

Avocado toast has already become a hipster cliché, but there is no denying it is really good. I like to spread it on a hearty whole grain or pumpernickel-type bread. Topping it with something zesty, like pickled watermelon radishes, makes for a perfect lunch.

1. Place the vinegar, sugar, and teaspoon of salt in a bowl, stir until the sugar dissolves, and then add the radish. Let sit for at least 20 minutes and up to a day.

2. Halve the avocados and remove the pits. Scoop out the flesh and place in a bowl. Add the lemon juice and Tabasco™ and mash until combined.

3. Spread some of the avocado mixture over a slice of bread and top with the pickled radishes. Season with salt and pepper, garnish with cilantro (if desired), and serve.

INGREDIENTS:

½ CUP WHITE VINEGAR

½ TEASPOON SUGAR

1 TEASPOON KOSHER SALT, PLUS MORE TO TASTE

1 WATERMELON RADISH, PEELED AND SLICED THIN

2 AVOCADOS

1 TEASPOON FRESH LEMON JUICE

TABASCO™, TO TASTE

BLACK PEPPER, TO TASTE

4 SLICES WHOLE GRAIN OR PUMPERNICKEL BREAD

FRESH CILANTRO, FOR GARNISH (OPTIONAL)

OKONOMIYAKI

YIELD: **4 TO 6 SERVINGS** / ACTIVE TIME: **20 MINUTES** / TOTAL TIME: **30 MINUTES**

Okonomiyaki is a popular street food in Japan, especially in Osaka. There is no official recipe since the ingredients vary depending upon the establishment, but basically it is a savory pancake filled with cabbage and topped with a sweet BBQ sauce, a hot sauce, or both. Some recipes include pork belly (aka bacon) and others add different veggies along with the cabbage. Since there are so many different variations, it felt like the perfect opportunity to fold in some seaweed.

1. Place the flour, stock, salt, eggs, and soy sauce in a large bowl and stir until combined. Add the cabbage and stir to incorporate.

2. In a separate bowl, combine the mayonnaise and sriracha and set aside.

3. Place a small pan over medium heat and add 1 tablespoon of oil. Add the seaweed and sauté until crisp, 1 to 2 minutes. Turn over and cook another minute, then transfer to a paper towel–lined plate to drain.

4. Warm a skillet over medium-high heat. Add the remaining oil and coat the bottom. Put roughly a cup of the cabbage mixture in the middle of the pan and, using a spatula, spread it into a thick pancake. If desired, cut two slices of bacon in half and place on top of the pancake. Let cook until the bottom has a nice, golden color, about 4 minutes. Turn over and repeat on the other side.

5. When fully cooked and brown on both sides, transfer to a plate. Put four or five dots of gochujang and sriracha mayonnaise on each pancake, then draw a fork through the sauces to make artful streaks. Top with the crisp seaweed and serve. Repeat with the remaining cabbage mixture and bacon slices, if using.

TIP: This recipe will make roughly four large pancakes. If you want to serve them all at once, place finished pancakes on a baking sheet and keep warm in a 325°F oven until the rest are finished.

INGREDIENTS:

- 1 CUP ALL-PURPOSE FLOUR
- ¾ CUP DASHI STOCK, VEGETABLE STOCK, OR CHICKEN STOCK (SEE PAGES 751, 755, AND 748, RESPECTIVELY, FOR HOMEMADE)
- PINCH OF KOSHER SALT
- 4 EGGS, BEATEN
- 2 TABLESPOONS SOY SAUCE
- 4 CUPS GRATED GREEN CABBAGE
- 3 TABLESPOONS JAPANESE MAYONNAISE
- 1 TABLESPOON SRIRACHA
- 2 TABLESPOONS OLIVE OIL
- SEVERAL LARGE PIECES OF DULSE SEAWEED
- 8 SLICES BACON (OPTIONAL)
- GOCHUJANG, TO TASTE

ROASTED SEAWEED SNACKS

YIELD: 4 SERVINGS / ACTIVE TIME: 5 MINUTES / TOTAL TIME: 15 MINUTES

Prepackaged roasted seaweed is a popular snack, but it is easy to make at home. Plus, there is the added advantage of seasoning the seaweed exactly to your liking, not to mention saving the world from more excessive packaging. Toasted sesame oil is an excellent, complementary flavor for the briny taste of the seaweed, but you can experiment with anything that sparks your curiosity, such as curry, wasabi, and garlic powders.

1. Preheat the oven to 400°F. Take a nori sheet and brush both sides liberally with sesame oil. Sprinkle with salt and any other seasonings and place on a baking sheet. Repeat with as many sheets as will fit on the baking sheet.

2. Put the baking sheet in the oven and bake for 5 minutes, then flip the seaweed over and bake for another 5 minutes.

3. Remove from the oven and enjoy.

INGREDIENTS:

4-6 NORI SEAWEED SHEETS

TOASTED SESAME OIL, AS NEEDED

SALT, TO TASTE

PREFERRED SEASONINGS, TO TASTE

TOFU MOMO DUMPLINGS

YIELD: 4 TO 6 SERVINGS / ACTIVE TIME: 1 HOUR AND 30 MINUTES / TOTAL TIME: 2 HOURS

Tofu gives body to the filling in these classic vegetarian dumplings.

1. Put the shiitake mushrooms in a heatproof bowl and add just enough hot water to cover them by a few inches. Soak until the caps soften, at least 30 minutes. Drain, then gently squeeze each mushroom to remove excess water. Remove the stems, discard, and mince the caps. Put the caps in a food processor, add a pinch of salt, then pulse 3 or 4 times. Add the tofu, spinach, scallions, cilantro, and another pinch of salt and pulse until minced. Add the garlic and ginger and pulse a few times to incorporate.

2. Transfer the mixture to a medium bowl. Add the carrots and soy sauce and mix until well combined. Take a small bit of the mixture, form into a patty, and fry in a small skillet. Taste and adjust the seasoning as needed.

3. Place a damp paper towel over the stack of dumpling wrappers to keep them from drying out. Line a baking sheet with parchment paper and set aside a small bowl of water for sealing.

4. Place a wrapper in a cupped hand and put about 1 tablespoon of filling in the center, leaving about ¾ inch of the wrapper clear all the way around. Lightly moisten that edge, fold one edge of the wrapper over the filling to form a half-moon, and tightly press the edges together to seal, pushing down to remove as much air as you can as you do it. To pleat the sealed edges, start at one end of the half-moon and make small folds in the wrapper, pressing them flat as you work your way along the edge, making 7 to 8 folds per dumpling. Repeat with the remaining wrappers and filling.

5. Bring 3 cups water to a boil in a large pot. Line a steaming tray with cabbage leaves or parchment paper cut to the size and shape of your steaming tray with lots of small incisions. Working in batches, set the momos in the steaming tray, leaving ½ inch between the momos and between the momos and the sides of the steaming tray. Place the steaming tray in the pot over the boiling water, cover, and steam until the momos have puffed out slightly and become slightly translucent, about 12 minutes. Transfer to a warmed plate and cover loosely with aluminum foil to keep warm. Repeat with the remaining momos.

6. Serve alongside the Tomato & Sesame Dipping Sauce.

INGREDIENTS:

- 7 DRIED SHIITAKE MUSHROOMS
- SALT, TO TASTE
- ½ LB. PRESSED TOFU, CUBED
- 1 LB. BABY SPINACH
- 5-6 SCALLIONS, WHITE AND LIGHT GREEN PARTS ONLY, TRIMMED AND SLICED THIN
- 2 HANDFULS FRESH CILANTRO LEAVES
- 3 GARLIC CLOVES, GRATED OR MINCED
- 2-INCH PIECE GINGER, PEELED AND MINCED
- 2 CARROTS, PEELED AND COARSELY GRATED
- 3 TABLESPOONS SOY SAUCE
- 1 BATCH BASIC DUMPLING WRAPPERS (SEE PAGE 783) OR 36 (3-INCH) ROUND WRAPPERS
- CABBAGE LEAVES, FOR STEAMING (OPTIONAL)
- TOMATO & SESAME DIPPING SAUCE (SEE RECIPE), FOR SERVING

TOMATO & SESAME DIPPING SAUCE

1. Warm a small saucepan over medium-low heat for 2 to 3 minutes. Add the oils and let them warm up for a minute. Add the onion, garlic, red pepper flakes, chili powder, and a pinch of salt. Cook until the onion starts to soften, about 5 minutes. Add the tomatoes, water, and soy sauce and bring to a boil. Reduce heat to medium-low and simmer until the pieces of tomato start to break down and the sauce has thickened, about 15 minutes.

2. Stir in the vinegar and season with pepper. Puree the mixture with an immersion blender, food processor, or blender. Transfer to a serving bowl and serve at room temperature.

> **TIP:** You can place the dumplings in the refrigerator on a baking sheet covered with a kitchen towel and refrigerate for up to 3 days. Or you can freeze them on the baking sheets, transfer to freezer bags, and store in the freezer for up to 2 months. Do not thaw them prior to cooking (they will become mushy), and add an extra minute or two to their cooking time.

INGREDIENTS:

TOMATO & SESAME DIPPING SAUCE

1   TABLESPOON TOASTED SESAME OIL

1   TABLESPOON PEANUT OIL

1   SMALL RED ONION, DICED

2   GARLIC CLOVES, ROUGHLY CHOPPED

½   TEASPOON RED PEPPER FLAKES

¼   TEASPOON CHILI POWDER

    SALT AND PEPPER, TO TASTE

3   VERY RIPE PLUM TOMATOES, CONCASSE (SEE PAGE 808)

¼   CUP WATER

1½ TABLESPOONS SOY SAUCE

2   TABLESPOONS RICE VINEGAR

ROASTED SUNCHOKES
with LEMON MAYONNAISE

YIELD: 4 SERVINGS / ACTIVE TIME: 10 MINUTES / TOTAL TIME: 30 MINUTES

My family's favorite way to eat freshly steamed artichokes is to dip the leaves and hearts in mayonnaise. I figured that since sunchokes were so close in flavor, they could be served in this way, too, and that hunch was spot on. The combination is delicious. I find that a squeeze of fresh lemon juice in some mayonnaise is pretty good, but if you have a favorite recipe for homemade mayo or a lemony aioli, that would be just as excellent.

1. Preheat the oven to 375°F. Place the sunchokes and oil in a bowl, toss to coat, and sprinkle with salt.

2. Place the sunchokes on a baking sheet in a single layer and put it in the oven. Roast for about 10 minutes, or until they start to brown. Remove the tray, turn the sunchokes over, and put back in the oven for 10 to 15 minutes longer, or until the sunchokes are fully browned around the edges.

3. Remove from the oven and transfer them to a serving plate.

4. Put the mayonnaise and lemon juice in a small bowl, stir to combine, and serve alongside the sunchokes.

INGREDIENTS:

1   LB. SUNCHOKES, SCRUBBED CLEAN AND CHOPPED, WITH ANY DARK SPOTS TRIMMED

1   TABLESPOON OLIVE OIL

1   TABLESPOON KOSHER SALT

½   CUP MAYONNAISE

    FRESH LEMON JUICE, TO TASTE

PICKLED TURNIPS

YIELD: 4 SERVINGS / ACTIVE TIME: 10 MINUTES / TOTAL TIME: 24 HOURS

Pickled turnips are popular in the Middle East to pep up grilled meats or stewed vegetables. This easy recipe is perfect for a tapas-style meal.

1. Remove the stem from the turnip and run the bulb under cold water until clean. Cut into even quarters and place in a container that can accommodate hot liquids.

2. Place the remaining ingredients in a medium saucepan and stir to combine. Bring the contents of the pot to a steady boil and then pour it over the turnips.

3. Cover the container with an airtight lid and let cool to room temperature. Once cooled, store in the refrigerator overnight before serving. If you are interested in canning these pickled turnips, follow the instructions on page 716.

INGREDIENTS:

1	LB. JAPANESE TURNIPS
4	CUPS RICE WINE VINEGAR
2	CUPS WATER
½	CUP FISH SAUCE
1¼	CUPS SUGAR
¼	CUP FRESH LIME JUICE

PORK & ROASTED SQUASH POT STICKERS

YIELD: 6 SERVINGS / ACTIVE TIME: 1 HOUR AND 30 MINUTES / TOTAL TIME: 1 HOUR AND 45 MINUTES

Pork and squash pair well together, so why not combine them for a different take on this Chinese dumpling? The butternut squash adds welcome sweetness and texture to the filling.

1. Place all of the aromatics in a small skillet over medium heat and toast, stirring, until fragrant, 2 to 3 minutes. Transfer to a spice grinder or food processor and grind into a fine powder.

2. Preheat the oven to 350°F. Toss the squash with the olive oil and 1 tablespoon of the spice mix until well coated. Place on a parchment–lined baking sheet, place it in the oven, and roast, turning the squash over after about 15 minutes, until lightly caramelized and soft, about 30 minutes. Transfer the squash to a large bowl and mash with a fork until smooth. Add the pork, ginger, rice wine or dry Sherry, soy sauce, sesame oil, 3 of the scallions, the egg white, and 1 tablespoon of the spice mix and mix well until thoroughly combined.

3. Place a damp paper towel over the stack of dumpling wrappers to keep them from drying out. Line a baking sheet with parchment paper and prepare a small bowl of water for sealing.

4. Lay a wrapper in front of you and place a heaping teaspoon of filling in the middle of it. Dip your finger in the water and run it along the edges of the square. Fold one of the corners over the filling to create a triangle and tightly press the edges together to seal, pushing down to remove as much air as you can. Repeat with the remaining wrappers and filling.

5. Place 1 tablespoon of the peanut oil in a large skillet and warm over medium-high heat. When it starts to shimmer, add the dumplings in batches and cook, without turning, until they are golden brown on the bottom. Add 2 tablespoons water, cover, and steam until cooked through, about 4 minutes. Transfer the cooked dumplings to a warmed platter and tent with foil to keep warm. Dry the skillet with a paper towel and repeat until all of the pot stickers have been cooked. Sprinkle with the remaining scallions and serve piping hot with the Dipping Sauce.

TIP: You can place the pot stickers in the refrigerator on a baking sheet covered with a kitchen towel and refrigerate for up to 3 days. Or you can freeze them on the baking sheets, transfer to freezer

INGREDIENTS:

1 TEASPOON CORIANDER SEEDS

8 WHOLE CLOVES

½ TEASPOON SZECHUAN PEPPERCORNS

½ TEASPOON BLACK PEPPERCORNS

1 STAR ANISE POD

2 CARDAMOM PODS, CRUSHED

2 BAY LEAVES

2 CINNAMON STICKS, BROKEN INTO BITS

2½ LBS. BUTTERNUT SQUASH, PEELED, SEEDED, AND CUT INTO ½-INCH CUBES

2 TABLESPOONS OLIVE OIL

½ LB. GROUND PORK

3 TABLESPOONS MINCED GINGER

3 TABLESPOONS SHAOXING RICE WINE OR DRY SHERRY

5 TABLESPOONS SOY SAUCE

1 TABLESPOON TOASTED SESAME OIL

5 SCALLIONS, TRIMMED AND MINCED

1 EGG WHITE, LIGHTLY BEATEN

1 RECIPE BASIC DUMPLING WRAPPERS (SEE PAGE 783) OR 40 (3-INCH) ROUND WRAPPERS

Continued . . .

bags, and store in the freezer for up to 2 months. Do not thaw them prior to cooking (they will become mushy), and add an extra minute or two to their cooking time.

DIPPING SAUCE

1. Place all of the ingredients in a small bowl, whisk to combine, and serve.

INGREDIENTS:

2 TABLESPOONS PEANUT OIL

   WATER, AS NEEDED

   DIPPING SAUCE (SEE RECIPE), FOR SERVING

DIPPING SAUCE

2 TABLESPOONS CHINESE BLACK VINEGAR OR BALSAMIC VINEGAR

2 TABLESPOONS LIGHT SOY SAUCE

2 TEASPOONS SUGAR

2 TEASPOONS HOT CHILI OIL

OYSTER MUSHROOMS *with* MIGNONETTE SAUCE

YIELD: 4 SERVINGS / ACTIVE TIME: 15 MINUTES / TOTAL TIME: 15 MINUTES

Mignonette sauce is a very traditional accompaniment to raw oysters. It is very simple to make, consisting of minced shallots, vinegar, black pepper, and salt. The zing and tang of the sauce is the perfect complement to mild oysters. Vermont is a landlocked state, so fresh oysters are not common fare around here, but mushrooms are. Oyster mushrooms are so named because some find them to have an oyster-like taste, so I browned a pile of oyster mushrooms in butter, lightly salted them, and served them up next to a ramekin of mignonette sauce. It was a winner.

1. If the mushrooms are still in a cluster, cut them into individual pieces. Warm a pan that will hold all of the mushrooms in one layer over medium heat. Melt the butter, add the mushrooms, sprinkle lightly with salt, and cook until they brown, about 6 minutes. Turn and brown on the other side.

2. When fully cooked, transfer to a plate and serve with the Mignonette Sauce.

MIGNONETTE SAUCE

1. Place all of the ingredients in a ramekin or small bowl, stir to combine, and serve.

INGREDIENTS:

½   LB. FRESH OYSTER
     MUSHROOMS

1   TABLESPOON UNSALTED
     BUTTER

     SALT, TO TASTE

     MIGNONETTE SAUCE (SEE
     RECIPE), FOR SERVING

MIGNONETTE SAUCE

1   TABLESPOON MINCED
     SHALLOT

2   TABLESPOONS WHITE OR
     RED WINE VINEGAR

     BLACK PEPPER, TO TASTE

½   TEASPOON KOSHER SALT

SWEET POTATO & TAHINI DIP *with* SPICED HONEY

YIELD: 1 CUP / ACTIVE TIME: 15 MINUTES / TOTAL TIME: 45 MINUTES

Sweet potatoes pair well with earthy tahini. A little lemon juice balances the dip with acidity and brightness. Serve this when you've had enough of hummus and want something a little different.

1. Preheat the oven to 400°F. Place the sweet potato cut-side down on a greased baking sheet. At the same time, pour a little oil on the onion and put that on the baking sheet as well. Place the garlic cloves on a small square of aluminum foil, place a few drops of oil on them, wrap them in the foil, and place the pouch on the baking sheet. Put the baking sheet in the oven and roast for approximately 20 minutes, then remove the garlic. Roast the sweet potato and onion for another 10 minutes, or until the potato is very tender and the onion is nicely roasted and soft. Remove from the oven and let cool.

2. Scoop the flesh from the sweet potato into a food processor or blender. Add the roasted onion and garlic, tahini, lemon juice, and salt. Pulse until it becomes a smooth paste. Taste and adjust seasoning as necessary.

3. Place the honey in a very small pot and heat gently. Add the ancho chili powder, remove from heat, and let sit for a few minutes to infuse the honey.

4. Put the puree in a shallow dish and make a well in the center. Pour some spiced honey in the well and then garnish with the chopped pistachios. Serve with pita chips or crackers.

INGREDIENTS:

1	SWEET POTATO, HALVED
1	TABLESPOON OLIVE OIL
1	YELLOW ONION, PEELED AND QUARTERED
2	LARGE GARLIC CLOVES, PEELED
¼	CUP TAHINI
1	TEASPOON FRESH LEMON JUICE
½	TEASPOON KOSHER SALT
2	TABLESPOONS HONEY
½	TEASPOON ANCHO CHILI POWDER
1	TABLESPOON CHOPPED PISTACHIOS, FOR GARNISH
	PITA CHIPS OR CRACKERS, FOR SERVING

ZUCCHINI ROLLS

YIELD: 4 SERVINGS / ACTIVE TIME: 20 MINUTES / TOTAL TIME: 30 MINUTES

Grilled zucchini takes very well to tangy flavors like goat cheese. This simple blend of cheese, herbs, and vegetables makes for a colorful and delicious appetizer.

1. Preheat your gas or charcoal grill to medium heat.

2. Brush the zucchini slices with oil and season with a bit of salt and pepper.

3. When the grill reaches about 400°F, place the zucchini on the grill and cook until tender, about 8 minutes, flipping them over halfway through. Leave the grill on.

4. In a medium bowl, mix together the goat cheese, parsley, and lemon juice.

5. Evenly spread the goat cheese mixture over the grilled zucchini slices. Add spinach leaves and as much or as little basil as desired and then roll the slices up. Secure the rolls with toothpicks.

6. Place the rolls seam-side down on the grill and cook for about 1 minute. Remove from heat and serve immediately.

INGREDIENTS:

3 SMALL ZUCCHINI, SLICED LENGTHWISE INTO ¼-INCH-WIDE SLICES

2 TABLESPOONS OLIVE OIL

SALT AND PEPPER, TO TASTE

1½ OZ. GOAT CHEESE, AT ROOM TEMPERATURE

1 TABLESPOON CHOPPED FRESH PARSLEY

½ TEASPOON FRESH LEMON JUICE

2 OZ. BABY SPINACH

FRESH BASIL, CHOPPED, TO TASTE

SAUTÉED SWISS CHARD, BLUE CHEESE & HONEY TOAST CRISPS

YIELD: 4 SERVINGS / ACTIVE TIME: 10 MINUTES / TOTAL TIME: 15 MINUTES

Lightly cooked Swiss chard is piled on a cracker or toast point with sharp blue cheese and a drizzle of honey for this quick appetizer. The mineral taste of the leaves balances the salty, tangy cheese and sweet honey. Not only is the combination unique but the presentation, with its contrast of emerald green, creamy white, and blue, is gorgeous.

1. Place the oil in a medium skillet, warm over medium heat, and add the chard. Sauté until the leaves are fully wilted and the excess water has cooked off, 3 to 5 minutes. Season with salt and lemon juice, remove from heat, and let cool.

2. Arrange the crackers or toast points on a plate and top with a spoonful of the cooked chard. Place a small piece of blue cheese on top of each mound of chard and then drizzle the entire plate with honey.

INGREDIENTS:

½ TABLESPOON OLIVE OIL

8 LARGE LEAVES OF CHARD, STEMS REMOVED, CHOPPED

SALT, TO TASTE

FRESH LEMON JUICE, TO TASTE

WHEAT CRACKERS OR TOAST POINTS, FOR SERVING

1 OZ. BLUE CHEESE

HONEY, FOR GARNISH

ZUCCHINI, SHIITAKE & EGG JIAOZI

YIELD: 4 TO 6 SERVINGS / ACTIVE TIME: 1 HOUR AND 30 MINUTES / TOTAL TIME: 4 TO 5 HOURS

Zucchini and shiitakes partner well in this vegetarian version of a traditional Chinese dumpling.

1. Toss the zucchini and 1½ teaspoons of the salt in a mixing bowl. Place the zucchini in a fine sieve and let stand for an hour.

2. Transfer the zucchini to a kitchen towel and twist the towel to remove as much moisture as possible. Transfer to a large bowl and set aside.

3. Warm a large nonstick skillet over low heat for a minute. Add the peanut oil and raise heat to medium-high. When the oil begins to shimmer, add the eggs and cook, stirring continuously, until just set. Transfer the eggs to a plate and cut into very small pieces, then add to the bowl with the zucchini along with the mushrooms, ginger, soy sauce, rice wine (or Sherry), sesame oil, pepper, sugar, and remaining salt and stir until thoroughly combined. Cover the bowl with clear plastic wrap and refrigerate for 2 to 3 hours.

4. Stir the scallions into the mixture. Take a small amount of the mixture, flatten into a patty, and fry it in a small skillet. Taste and adjust the seasoning of the mixture as needed.

5. Place a damp paper towel over the stack of dumpling wrappers to keep them from drying out. Line a baking sheet with parchment paper and fill a small bowl with water for sealing.

6. Place a wrapper in a cupped hand and put about 1 tablespoon of filling in the center, leaving about ¾ inch of the wrapper clear all the way around it. Lightly moisten the edge with water. Fold one edge of the wrapper over the filling to form a half-moon and seal the the edges together, pushing down to remove as much air as possible. Repeat with the remaining wrappers and filling.

7. Bring 3 cups of water to a boil in a large pot. Line a steaming tray with cabbage leaves, or parchment paper cut to the size and shape of your steaming tray with lots of small incisions to allow steam to circulate. Set the jiaozi in the steaming tray, leaving ½ inch between each jiaozi and between the jiaozi and the sides of the steaming tray. Place the steaming tray over the boiling water, cover, and steam until the dumplings are tender but still chewy, about 8 minutes.

8. Garnish with the cilantro and serve with the Sweet & Spicy Dipping Sauce.

INGREDIENTS:

- 4 ZUCCHINI, GRATED
- 2½ TEASPOONS KOSHER SALT
- 2 TABLESPOONS PEANUT OIL
- 4 LARGE EGGS, LIGHTLY BEATEN
- 8 SHIITAKE MUSHROOM CAPS, MINCED
- 2-INCH PIECE GINGER, PEELED AND MINCED
- 3 TABLESPOONS SOY SAUCE
- 3 TABLESPOONS SHAOXING RICE WINE OR DRY SHERRY
- 2 TABLESPOONS TOASTED SESAME OIL
- 1 TEASPOON BLACK PEPPER
- ½ TABLESPOON SUGAR
- 5-6 SCALLIONS, TRIMMED AND SLICED THIN
- 2 BATCHES BASIC DUMPLING WRAPPERS (SEE PAGE 783) OR 40 (3-INCH) ROUND WRAPPERS
- CABBAGE LEAVES, FOR STEAMING (OPTIONAL)
- FRESH CILANTRO, MINCED, FOR GARNISH
- SWEET & SPICY DIPPING SAUCE (SEE RECIPE), FOR SERVING

SWEET & SPICY DIPPING SAUCE

1. Place all of the ingredients in a small bowl, whisk to combine, and serve.

> **TIP:** You can place the jiaozi in the refrigerator on a baking sheet covered with a kitchen towel and refrigerate for up to 3 days. Or you can freeze them on the baking sheets, transfer to freezer bags, and store in the freezer for up to 2 months. Do not thaw them prior to cooking (they will become mushy), just add an extra minute or so to their cooking time.

SWEET & SPICY DIPPING SAUCE

2   GARLIC CLOVES, MINCED

⅓   CUP SOY SAUCE

2½   TABLESPOONS SHAOXING RICE WINE OR DRY SHERRY

1   TEASPOON CHILI OIL

PUNJABI SAMOSA

YIELD: 4 SERVINGS / ACTIVE TIME: 45 MINUTES / TOTAL TIME: 1 HOUR AND 30 MINUTES

The Cilantro Chutney is a beautiful counterbalance to the delicate spice of the filling.

1. Place the potatoes in a saucepan and cover with water. Bring the water to a boil and cook until the potatoes are fork-tender, about 20 minutes. Transfer to a bowl, mash until smooth, and set aside.

2. Place the oil in a skillet and warm over medium heat. Add the crushed seeds and cook, stirring continuously, until fragrant, about 1 minute. Add the ginger, garlic, and jalapeño, stir-fry for 2 minutes, and then add the chili powder, ground coriander, turmeric, amchoor powder, and garam masala and cook for another minute before adding the mashed potatoes and the curry leaves. Stir to combine, season with salt, transfer the mixture to a bowl, and let it cool.

3. When the mixture has cooled, add oil to a Dutch oven and heat it to 325°F over medium heat. Brush the flat edge of each Samosa Wrapper with water. Fold one corner of the flat edge toward the other to make a cone and then pinch to seal. Fill each cone one-third of the way with the potato mixture, brush the opening with water, and pinch until sealed. Place the sealed samosas on a parchment–lined baking sheet.

4. When all of the wrappers have been filled, add them to the hot oil in batches and fry, turning them as they cook, until they are golden brown, about 5 minutes. Transfer the cooked samosas to a paper towel–lined plate to drain and serve with the Cilantro Chutney once they have all been cooked.

CILANTRO CHUTNEY

1. Place all of the ingredients, except for the water and salt, in a food processor and puree until smooth, adding water as needed to get the desired consistency. Season with salt and refrigerate until ready to serve.

INGREDIENTS:

2 RUSSET POTATOES, PEELED AND CHOPPED

2 TABLESPOONS VEGETABLE OIL, PLUS MORE FOR FRYING

1 TEASPOON CORIANDER SEEDS, CRUSHED

½ TEASPOON FENNEL SEEDS, CRUSHED

PINCH OF FENUGREEK SEEDS, CRUSHED

1 TABLESPOON MINCED GINGER

1 TEASPOON MINCED GARLIC

1 TEASPOON SEEDED AND MINCED JALAPEÑO PEPPER

2 TEASPOONS CHILI POWDER

2 TABLESPOONS GROUND CORIANDER

¾ TEASPOON TURMERIC

1 TABLESPOON AMCHOOR POWDER

½ TEASPOON GARAM MASALA

6 CURRY LEAVES, MINCED

SALT, TO TASTE

1 BATCH SAMOSA WRAPPERS (SEE PAGE 788)

CILANTRO CHUTNEY (SEE RECIPE), FOR SERVING

CILANTRO CHUTNEY

1 BUNCH FRESH CILANTRO

¼ CUP GRATED FRESH COCONUT

15 MINT LEAVES

1 TABLESPOON SEEDED AND MINCED JALAPEÑO PEPPER

1 GARLIC CLOVE

1 TEASPOON MINCED GINGER

1 PLUM TOMATO, CONCASSE (SEE PAGE 808)

1 TABLESPOON FRESH LEMON JUICE

WATER, AS NEEDED

SALT, TO TASTE

DAL FARA

YIELD: 4 SERVINGS / ACTIVE TIME: 30 MINUTES / TOTAL TIME: 24 HOURS

This popular snack in India is typically made with split peas, but this version capitalizes on the wonderful nutty flavor of chickpeas.

1. To begin preparations for the filling, place the chickpeas in a mixing bowl, cover with water, and soak overnight.

2. The next day, drain the chickpeas and place in a food processor with all of the remaining filling ingredients. Puree until smooth and set aside.

3. To prepare the dough, place the rice flour and a pinch of salt in a mixing bowl, stir to combine, and then add the oil. Stir to incorporate and gradually add water until the dough just holds together. Take care not to overwork the mixture. Cover the bowl with a damp cloth and let rest for 20 minutes.

4. Place the dough on a flour-dusted work surface and divide it into 16 pieces. Roll the pieces into balls. Lightly moisten your hands, place a ball of dough in one hand, and flatten it into a 3-inch round that is ⅛ inch thick. Place 1 tablespoon of filling in the center of the round, fold into a half-moon, and pinch the edge to seal the dumpling. Repeat with the remaining balls of dough and filling.

5. Bring a large pot of salted water to a boil. Working in batches of four to six dumplings, place them in the water and stir to ensure they don't stick to the bottom. Once they rise to the surface, cook for another 2 minutes. Remove with a slotted spoon, transfer to a warm platter, and tent with foil to keep warm. When all of the dumplings have been cooked, serve with the Herb Chutney.

HERB CHUTNEY

1. Place the herbs, garlic, jalapeño, onion, and tamarind pulp in a food processor and puree until smooth, adding water if the mixture is too thick. Season with salt and refrigerate until ready to serve.

INGREDIENTS:

FOR THE FILLING

1½ CUPS DRIED CHICKPEAS

2 TABLESPOONS WATER, PLUS MORE FOR SOAKING THE CHICKPEAS

2-INCH PIECE GINGER, PEELED AND CHOPPED

½ CUP FRESH CILANTRO LEAVES

½ JALAPEÑO PEPPER, SEEDED AND MINCED

1 TEASPOON CUMIN SEEDS

PINCH OF HING POWDER (OPTIONAL)

SALT, TO TASTE

FOR THE DOUGH

3 CUPS RICE FLOUR, PLUS MORE AS NEEDED

SALT, TO TASTE

4 TEASPOONS OLIVE OIL

WARM WATER (110°F), AS NEEDED

HERB CHUTNEY (SEE RECIPE), FOR SERVING

HERB CHUTNEY

1 CUP FRESH CILANTRO LEAVES, CHOPPED, PLUS MORE FOR GARNISH

½ CUP FRESH MINT LEAVES, PLUS MORE FOR GARNISH

4 GARLIC CLOVES

1 TEASPOON SEEDED AND MINCED JALAPEÑO PEPPER

1 SMALL YELLOW ONION, CHOPPED

¼ CUP TAMARIND PULP

WATER, AS NEEDED

SALT, TO TASTE

CHAI KUIH

YIELD: 4 SERVINGS / ACTIVE TIME: 35 MINUTES / TOTAL TIME: 1 HOUR

These "vegetable cakes" are a popular street food in a number of Chinese cities.

1. Place the oil in a wok or large skillet and warm over low heat. When the oil begins to shimmer, add the jicama, mushrooms, and carrot and cook, stirring frequently, until the jicama is tender but still crunchy, about 15 minutes. Add the soy sauce and sugar, season with salt and pepper, and stir to combine. Remove from heat and let the mixture cool.

2. Line a baking sheet with parchment paper. Place 1 tablespoon of the filling in the center of a dumpling wrapper. Moisten the wrapper's edge with a wet finger and take the far edge of the wrapper and gently fold it over the filling to meet the other edge. Using your thumb and index finger, pinch both edges together to create a tight seal, pressing down to remove as much air as possible. Place the filled dumplings on the baking sheet and repeat with the remaining wrappers and filling.

3. Place 1 inch of water in a large pot and bring it to a boil. Line a steaming tray with the cabbage leaves and place the dumplings in the tray, leaving ½ inch between each of the dumplings and also between the dumplings and the edge of the tray. Place the tray over the boiling water, cover, and steam until the dumplings are tender but still chewy, about 10 minutes. Transfer the dumplings to a warmed platter and serve immediately, accompanied by chili sauce or the Szechuan Peppercorn Oil.

SZECHUAN PEPPERCORN OIL

1. Place the oil, star anise, cinnamon stick, bay leaves, and Szechuan peppercorns in a skillet. Cook over the lowest-possible heat for 20 minutes, taking care not to let the spices burn.

2. Place the red pepper flakes in a small bowl. Strain the warm oil over the flakes. Let cool, season with salt, and reserve until ready to serve.

INGREDIENTS:

2	TABLESPOONS PEANUT OR GRAPESEED OIL
1	LB. JICAMA, PEELED AND GRATED
¼	CUP MINCED SHIITAKE MUSHROOM CAPS
1	CARROT, PEELED AND FINELY GRATED
2	TABLESPOONS SOY SAUCE
1	TEASPOON SUGAR
	SALT AND PEPPER, TO TASTE
	CRYSTAL DUMPLING WRAPPERS (SEE PAGE 784)
	CABBAGE LEAVES, FOR STEAMING
	CHILI SAUCE OR SZECHUAN PEPPERCORN OIL (SEE RECIPE), FOR SERVING

SZECHUAN PEPPERCORN OIL

1½	CUPS VEGETABLE OIL
5	STAR ANISE PODS
1	CINNAMON STICK
2	BAY LEAVES
3	TABLESPOONS SZECHUAN PEPPERCORNS
⅓	CUP RED PEPPER FLAKES
1	TEASPOON KOSHER SALT

SHIITAKE SIU MAI

YIELD: 6 TO 8 SERVINGS / ACTIVE TIME: 35 MINUTES / TOTAL TIME: 45 MINUTES

This sweet-and-savory filling will even satisfy the dim sum purist who feels the flavor provided by the pork in the traditional offering is essential.

1. Place all of the ingredients, except for the wrappers, cabbage leaves, and carrots, in a mixing bowl and stir until well combined.

2. Place a wrapper in a cupped hand and fill with enough of the mixture to fill the wrapper to the top. Flatten the filling with a butter knife and gently tighten the wrapper around the filling, forming a rough cylindrical shape with a flat bottom. Place the filled dumplings on a parchment–lined baking sheet and repeat with the remaining wrappers and filling.

3. Place 1 inch of water in a large pot and bring it to a boil. Line a steaming tray with the cabbage leaves and then add the siu mai, leaving ½ inch between each of the dumplings and also between the dumplings and the edge of the tray. Place the steaming tray over the boiling water, cover, and steam until the dumplings are cooked through, tender, and still chewy, about 10 minutes. Transfer the cooked dumplings to a warmed platter, garnish with the carrots, and serve with additional soy sauce.

INGREDIENTS:

- 8 SHIITAKE MUSHROOM CAPS, MINCED
- 4 SCALLIONS, TRIMMED AND SLICED THIN
- ¼ RED BELL PEPPER, SEEDED AND MINCED
- ¼ CUP RAISINS
- ¼ CUP PINE NUTS, TOASTED
- ¼ CUP CANNED CORN
- 1 TABLESPOON SOY SAUCE, PLUS MORE FOR SERVING
- 1 TABLESPOON SHAOXING RICE WINE OR DRY SHERRY
- 1 TEASPOON FISH SAUCE
- 1 TEASPOON TOASTED SESAME OIL
- 2 TEASPOONS CORNSTARCH
- ½ TEASPOON SUGAR
- ½ TEASPOON WHITE PEPPER
- 36 ROUND WONTON WRAPPERS (SEE PAGE 791)

  CABBAGE LEAVES, FOR STEAMING

  CARROTS, PEELED AND MINCED, FOR GARNISH

KIMCHI MANDU

YIELD: 4 SERVINGS / ACTIVE TIME: 1 HOUR / TOTAL TIME: 1 HOUR AND 30 MINUTES

Each bite of these delicious dumplings proves salty, sour, savory, spicy, crunchy, and creamy.

1. Place the tofu in a single layer on a paper towel–lined baking sheet. Cover with paper towels and pat dry. Let the pieces sit for 30 minutes, changing the paper towels halfway through. After 30 minutes, mince the tofu and place it in a large mixing bowl.

2. While the tofu drains, bring water to a boil in a saucepan. Place the bean sprouts in a bowl of cold water, discard the hulls that float to the top, and rinse under cold water. Add the sprouts to the boiling water and cook for 2 minutes. Remove with a strainer and run them under cold water. Drain, mince, and place in the mixing bowl with the minced tofu.

3. Place the Kimchi in a kitchen towel and wring the towel to remove as much liquid as possible. Mince and add to the mixing bowl. Add the garlic, shallots, egg, sesame oil, salt, and pepper and stir until combined.

4. Place a generous tablespoon of filling in the middle of a dumpling wrapper. Moisten the wrapper's edge with a wet finger, fold into a half-moon, and press down on the edge to seal the dumpling, removing as much air as possible. Place the filled mandu on a parchment–lined baking sheet and repeat with the remaining wrappers and filling.

5. Place a large skillet over medium-high heat and add enough oil to coat the bottom. When the oil starts to shimmer, add the mandu in batches and cook until the bottoms are crisp and golden brown, 2 to 3 minutes. Reduce heat to medium-low, add 2 tablespoons of water, cover the skillet, and cook until the water has evaporated. Transfer the mandu to a warmed platter and tent loosely with foil to keep warm. Repeat with the remaining mandu. When all of the dumplings have been cooked, serve alongside the Sweet & Spicy Dipping Sauce.

INGREDIENTS:

- 1 LB. EXTRA-FIRM TOFU, DRAINED AND CUBED
- 1½ CUPS MUNG BEAN SPROUTS, PICKED OVER
- 1½ CUPS KIMCHI (SEE PAGE 470)
- 5 GARLIC CLOVES, MINCED
- 2 LARGE SHALLOTS, MINCED
- 1 LARGE EGG
- 1½ TEASPOONS TOASTED SESAME OIL
- 2 TEASPOONS KOSHER SALT
  BLACK PEPPER, TO TASTE
- 1 BATCH BASIC DUMPLING WRAPPERS (SEE PAGE 783)
  PEANUT OIL, FOR FRYING
  WATER, AS NEEDED
  SWEET & SPICY DIPPING SAUCE (SEE PAGE 249), FOR SERVING

TIROPITAKIA

YIELD: 4 TO 6 SERVINGS / ACTIVE TIME: 45 MINUTES / TOTAL TIME: 1 HOUR AND 15 MINUTES

You can make the dough for this Greek delicacy yourself, but the number of quality phyllo options at the store make it okay to take the easy road.

1. Place the feta in a mixing bowl and break it up with a fork. Add the kefalotyri, parsley, eggs, and pepper and stir to combine. Set the mixture aside.

2. Place 1 sheet of the phyllo dough on a large sheet of parchment paper. Gently brush the sheet with some of the melted butter, place another sheet on top, and brush this with more of the butter. Cut the phyllo dough into 2-inch strips, place 1 teaspoon of the filling at the end of the strip closest to you, and fold over one corner to make a triangle. Fold the strip up until the filling is completely covered. Repeat with the remaining sheets of phyllo dough and filling.

3. Preheat the oven to 350°F. Place the filled triangles on a buttered baking sheet and bake in the oven until golden brown, about 15 minutes. Remove and let cool briefly before serving.

INGREDIENTS:

½ LB. FETA CHEESE

1 CUP GRATED KEFALOTYRI CHEESE

¼ CUP CHOPPED FRESH PARSLEY

2 EGGS, BEATEN

BLACK PEPPER, TO TASTE

1 (1 LB.) PACKAGE FROZEN PHYLLO DOUGH, THAWED

2 STICKS UNSALTED BUTTER, MELTED

VEGETARIAN EMPANADAS

YIELD: 4 SERVINGS / ACTIVE TIME: 45 MINUTES / TOTAL TIME: 1 HOUR AND 15 MINUTES

Achiote is a vibrant orange-red spice that is made from ground annatto seeds, and its nutty, sweet, and earthy flavor is the key to these delectable pockets.

1. Place the 2 teaspoons of vegetable oil in a skillet and warm over medium heat. Add the onion, cabbage, and carrots and cook until soft, about 10 minutes. Add the garlic, cook for 2 minutes, and then transfer the mixture to a mixing bowl. Add the tomatoes and seasonings, stir to combine, and let the mixture cool completely.

2. Add oil to a Dutch oven until it is 3 inches deep and bring it to 350°F. Preheat the oven to 200°F and place a a baking sheet in the oven. Place the dough on a flour-dusted work surface and roll each piece into a 5-inch circle. Place 3 tablespoons of the filling in the center of a circle, brush the edge with water, and fold into a half-moon. Press down on the edge to seal the empanada tight, trying to remove as much air as possible. Repeat with the remaining pieces of dough and filling.

3. Working in two batches, place the empanadas in the hot oil and fry until golden brown, about 5 minutes. Drain on paper towels and place them in the warm oven while you cook the next batch. Serve warm.

INGREDIENTS:

- 2 TEASPOONS VEGETABLE OIL, PLUS MORE FOR FRYING
- 1 YELLOW ONION, MINCED
- 1 CUP GRATED NAPA CABBAGE
- 2 CARROTS, PEELED AND GRATED
- 1 GARLIC CLOVE, MINCED
- 1 (14 OZ.) CAN DICED TOMATOES
- ½ TEASPOON KOSHER SALT
- ¼ TEASPOON BLACK PEPPER
- ½ TEASPOON ACHIOTE
- ½ TEASPOON CUMIN
- CHILI POWDER, TO TASTE
- 1 BATCH EMPANADA DOUGH (SEE PAGE 787), MADE WITH BUTTER

CHILI-LIME TARO FRIES

YIELD: 4 SERVINGS / ACTIVE TIME: 15 MINUTES / TOTAL TIME: 20 MINUTES

Priscilla McDonald writes the blog *Red Shallot Kitchen*. Her recipes, encompassing flavors from across the planet, feature everything from chicken biryani to sausages with sauerkraut. This one for taro fries caught my eye because it includes two of my favorite seasonings: ancho chili powder and fresh lime juice. If you are new to taro, this recipe is a delicious introduction, and you'll soon see why fried taro is a popular street food in Thailand.

1. Add oil to a Dutch oven until it is 2 or 3 inches deep. Warm to 350°F over medium-high heat. Add the taro root strips and fry until golden brown, about 5 minutes. Make sure not to crowd the pot, working in batches if necessary.

2. Transfer the fries to a large bowl. Sprinkle immediately with the salt and chili powder and drizzle with lime juice.

3. Toss until the seasonings are evenly distributed and serve.

INGREDIENTS:

VEGETABLE OIL, FOR FRYING

1 LARGE TARO ROOT, PEELED AND CUT INTO FRENCH FRY-LENGTH STRIPS

SALT, TO TASTE

ANCHO CHILI POWDER, TO TASTE

2 TABLESPOONS FRESH LIME JUICE

SALSA VERDE

A basic recipe for salsa verde, this can be used as a dip or as a sauce for many Mexican dishes.

1. Turn the broiler to high. Place the onion, garlic, tomatillos, and jalapeño, if using, on a baking sheet. Drizzle with the oil and then place the baking sheet under the broiler. Broil for 7 minutes, or until vegetables begin to blacken.

2. Remove from oven and let cool. Once vegetables are cool enough to handle, peel the garlic and then add the vegetables to a blender or food processor. Be sure to pour in all the juices from the tomatillos. Add the cumin, lime juice, and cilantro.

3. Puree until the salsa achieves the desired consistency. Season to taste and serve.

INGREDIENTS:

1 ONION, PEELED AND QUARTERED

2 GARLIC CLOVES, UNPEELED

¾ LB. TOMATILLOS, HUSKED AND RINSED

1 SMALL JALAPEÑO PEPPER (OPTIONAL)

1 TABLESPOON OLIVE OIL

1 TEASPOON CUMIN

FRESH LIME JUICE, TO TASTE

½ CUP FRESH CILANTRO, CHOPPED

SALT, TO TASTE

BAKED TOMATOES
with MOZZARELLA *&* CHIVE OIL

YIELD: 4 SERVINGS / ACTIVE TIME: 10 MINUTES / TOTAL TIME: 30 MINUTES

Everyone knows a caprese salad is made with fresh tomatoes and mozzarella with basil, olive oil, and balsamic. It is a summer classic that celebrates the best time of year for tomatoes. But what if you are craving a tomato salad in late winter and only have the supermarket varieties at your disposal? My friend Jones concocted this recipe, which concentrates the flavor of a less-than-perfect tomato by baking it in the oven. The mozzarella counters the acidity of the fruit with its mild creaminess and the chive oil gives the dish a little zing. The combination of the three baked in the oven offers a result that is both distinct from the caprese salad and reminiscent of the summer that will eventually come.

1. Preheat the oven to 400°F. Place 2 tablespoons of the oil on a baking sheet and place the tomato slices on top, using them to spread out the oil while also getting oil on both sides of the slices. Sprinkle with salt, pepper, and thyme. Place in the oven and roast for 15 minutes.

2. Place the chives and the remaining oil in a blender and pulse until smooth. Set aside.

3. Remove the pan from the oven. Slice the mozzarella and put the slices on top of the slices of tomato. Return the pan to the oven and roast for another 10 minutes, or until the mozzarella has begun to melt. Remove from the oven and transfer to a plate.

4. Drizzle the chive oil on top and serve hot or at room temperature.

INGREDIENTS:

6   TABLESPOONS OLIVE OIL

2   LARGE TOMATOES, CUT INTO THICK SLICES

SALT AND PEPPER, TO TASTE

1   TEASPOON FRESH OR DRIED THYME

¼   CUP CHOPPED FRESH CHIVES

1   BALL FRESH MOZZARELLA CHEESE

GREEN TOMATO CHUTNEY

YIELD: 4 TO 6 PINTS / ACTIVE TIME: 35 MINUTES / TOTAL TIME: 5 TO 7 HOURS

Green tomato chutney was likely invented to use up the last of the tomatoes before the first frost. At our house the chutney is not just for making the best of the leftovers but also one of the reasons I grow tomatoes. We use it all winter on pork and lamb chops and it is also very nice as a condiment for a grilled cheese sandwich made with sharp cheddar.

1. Bring water to a boil in a canning pot.

2. Place all of the ingredients in a large saucepan and bring to a boil. Reduce to a simmer and cook, stirring occasionally, until the onions and tomatoes are tender and the juices have thickened, 20 to 30 minutes.

3. Transfer to sterilized mason jars. Place the lids on the jars and secure the bands tightly. Place the jars in the boiling water for 40 minutes.

4. Use tongs to remove the jars from the boiling water and let them cool. As they are cooling, you should hear the classic "ping and pop" sound of the lids creating a seal.

5. After 4 to 6 hours, check the lids. There should be no give in them, and they should be suctioned onto the jars. Discard any lids and food that did not seal properly.

INGREDIENTS:

3	LBS. GREEN TOMATOES, DICED
1	LARGE ONION, DICED
2	TABLESPOONS MINCED GINGER
2	GARLIC CLOVES, CHOPPED
1	TEASPOON MUSTARD SEEDS
1	TEASPOON CUMIN
1	TEASPOON GROUND CORIANDER
2	TEASPOONS KOSHER SALT
½	CUP HONEY OR MAPLE SYRUP
1	CUP APPLE CIDER VINEGAR
1	CUP RAISINS

BOLLITOS DE YUCA

YIELD: 4 SERVINGS / ACTIVE TIME: 20 MINUTES / TOTAL TIME: 3 TO 5 HOURS

This is a recipe from the Dominican Republic. The yuca is very mild, so I recommend pairing these with a zesty dipping sauce like Citrus Salsa. Just be sure to dice the fruit and vegetables into very small pieces so the salsa can adhere to the *bollitos*.

1. Place the yuca and salt in a large saucepan filled with water. Bring to a boil and cook until the yuca is tender, about 20 minutes. Drain, place the yuca in a food processor, and puree. Transfer the puree to a mixing bowl.

2. Add the butter, parsley, and milk to the yuca and mix well. Season with salt and let cool to room temperature.

3. Put 1 tablespoon of the mixture in the palm of one hand. Flatten it, put a cheese cube in the center, and close the dough around the cube. Place the balls on a baking sheet and repeat with the remaining puree and cheese.

4. Place in the refrigerator, uncovered, for 2 to 4 hours.

5. Add vegetable oil to a Dutch oven until it is 3 inches deep and heat to 350°F. Place the egg in a small bowl and whisk until scrambled. Place the flour in another bowl. Dip a ball into the egg, then into the flour, coating it entirely, and then shake to remove the excess. Place the coated balls in the oil and fry, turning as they brown, until they are golden brown all over. Transfer the cooked balls to a paper towel–lined plate to drain. When all of the balls have been cooked, serve with the Citrus Salsa.

CITRUS SALSA

1. Place all of the ingredients in a small bowl, whisk until combined, and serve.

INGREDIENTS:

1 LB. YUCA, PEELED

1 TABLESPOON KOSHER SALT, PLUS MORE TO TASTE

2 TABLESPOONS UNSALTED BUTTER

1 TEASPOON MINCED FRESH PARSLEY

¼ CUP MILK

½ LB. CHEDDAR CHEESE, CUT INTO 1-INCH CUBES

VEGETABLE OIL, FOR FRYING

1 EGG

¼ CUP ALL-PURPOSE FLOUR

CITRUS SALSA (SEE RECIPE), FOR SERVING

CITRUS SALSA

1 CUP DICED PINEAPPLE

¼ CUCUMBER, DICED

¼ CUP DICED MANGO

1 SMALL SHALLOT, MINCED

2 TABLESPOONS DICED RED BELL PEPPER

1 TABLESPOON MINCED FRESH CILANTRO

2 TABLESPOONS FRESH LIME JUICE

2-3 DASHES OF HOT SAUCE

1 TEASPOON BLACK PEPPER

1 TEASPOON KOSHER SALT

CORN & ZUCCHINI FRITTERS *with* BASIL MAYO

YIELD: 4 TO 6 SERVINGS / ACTIVE TIME: 45 MINUTES / TOTAL TIME: 1 HOUR

There is a secret ingredient in these fritters that makes them above average. I add a dollop of Thai green curry paste to the mix and the result is divine. The spices and fragrant lime leaf from the curry paste are the perfect match for the sweet corn. Make these as finger food for a party or just as a snack.

1. Place the zucchini in a colander over the sink, generously sprinkle with salt, and stir to combine. Let sit while you prepare the rest.

2. In a large bowl, combine the corn, scallion, egg, flour, curry paste, and the 1 teaspoon of salt.

3. After the zucchini has had a few minutes to sit, take a handful and squeeze hard to wring out excess water. Continue with all of the zucchini until you can't squeeze anymore. You can also bundle the zucchini in a clean kitchen towel and wring the towel to remove excess moisture.

4. Once drained, add the zucchini to the corn mixture and stir to combine.

5. Place the oil in a sauté pan and warm over medium-high heat. When the oil starts to shimmer, add four to five spoonfuls of the zucchini-and-corn mixture to the pan, gently pressing down to flatten each one into a patty. Cook, turning, until browned on both sides and cooked through, about 8 minutes. Transfer the cooked fritters to a paper towel–lined plate and repeat with the rest of the mixture.

6. Combine the mayonnaise and basil in a bowl and serve alongside the fritters.

INGREDIENTS:

- 1 LB. ZUCCHINI, GRATED
- 1 TEASPOON KOSHER SALT, PLUS MORE TO TASTE
- 2 CUPS CORN KERNELS (PREFERABLY FRESH)
- 1 TABLESPOON MINCED SCALLION
- 1 EGG
- ⅓ CUP ALL-PURPOSE FLOUR
- 1 TABLESPOON GREEN CURRY PASTE
- 1 TABLESPOON OLIVE OIL
- 1 CUP MAYONNAISE
- ½ CUP CHOPPED FRESH BASIL

SOUPS *and* STEWS

Soups and stews are great ways to convert humble ingredients into filling, tasty meals. They are often cost-effective and great for entertaining because they can be prepared beforehand (and often taste better if they've spent a night in the fridge before being reheated the next day). The vegetable-centric recipes in this chapter range from bright bowls of the freshest spring and summer produce to toothsome, slow-cooked beans sure to warm you up on a cold winter day.

WHITE BEAN SOUP *with* FRIED ARTICHOKES & PROSCIUTTO

YIELD: 2 SERVINGS / ACTIVE TIME: 35 MINUTES / TOTAL TIME: 1 HOUR

Some of my favorite Italian ingredients are found in this soup. This recipe uses canned white beans, but if you want to take the time to soak some dried beans, it will be even better. I do insist on a fresh artichoke, however, because you only have to fuss with one and the results will be so much better for it.

1. Bring water to a boil in a small saucepan and add the artichoke. Cover, reduce heat to medium-low, and cook until the stem is just tender, about 10 minutes. Remove from the water and let cool.

2. Place a medium saucepan over medium heat and add enough oil to coat the bottom. Add the onion to the pot and sauté until just starting to brown, about 5 minutes. Add the garlic and cook until it begins to brown, about 2 minutes.

3. Add the beans and stock to the pot and cook for about 10 minutes. Then puree the mixture using a blender or an immersion blender.

4. Place the prosciutto in a small pan and cook over medium heat until just starting to brown, about 5 minutes. Transfer to a plate and set aside.

5. When the artichoke is cool enough to handle, remove all of the leaves until you have just the core left. Carefully cut out the fibrous center, or "choke," leaving the heart. Chop the heart into bite-sized pieces.

6. Coat the bottom of the pan that had the prosciutto in it with oil and warm over medium heat. Add the artichoke heart and cook, stirring occasionally, until browned on all sides, about 5 minutes. Transfer to the plate with the prosciutto.

7. To serve, warm the white bean puree over medium heat and season with salt and pepper. Ladle into two soup bowls and divide the prosciutto, artichoke heart, chopped parsley, lemon juice, and lemon zest between them.

INGREDIENTS:

- 1 LARGE ARTICHOKE
- OLIVE OIL, AS NEEDED
- 1 SMALL YELLOW ONION, DICED
- 2 GARLIC CLOVES, MINCED
- 1 (14 OZ.) CAN GREAT NORTHERN BEANS, DRAINED AND RINSED
- 2 CUPS CHICKEN STOCK (SEE PAGE 748 FOR HOMEMADE)
- 2 SLICES PROSCIUTTO, TORN INTO PIECES
- SALT AND PEPPER, TO TASTE
- 2 TABLESPOONS CHOPPED FRESH PARSLEY
- 2 TEASPOONS FRESH LEMON JUICE
- 1 TEASPOON LEMON ZEST

GREEN ASPARAGUS SOUP *with* CURED LEMON SLICES

YIELD: 4 SERVINGS / ACTIVE TIME: 30 MINUTES / TOTAL TIME: 1 HOUR

Adelicious and simple soup prepared with one of the best ingredients Mother Nature blessed us with.

1. In a medium saucepan, add the butter and melt over medium heat. Add the onion, leeks, and celery and cook until they start to soften, about 5 minutes.

2. Add the potato and bay leaf and cook, stirring occasionally, for 5 minutes. Add the stock, bring to a boil, and then reduce heat so that the soup simmers. Cook until the potatoes are tender, about 15 minutes.

3. Place the oil in a large sauté pan and warm over medium-high heat. Add the asparagus and cook until bright green and firm, about 4 minutes. Reserve 12 of the asparagus tips for garnish.

4. Add the asparagus to the soup and simmer until tender, about 5 minutes.

5. Transfer the soup to a blender or food processor, puree until smooth, and then strain through a fine sieve.

6. Return soup to the pan, add the cream, and season with salt and pepper. Ladle into warmed bowls and garnish with the asparagus tips and Cured Lemon Slices.

CURED LEMON SLICES

1. Place the lemon slices on a baking sheet.

2. Combine the salt and sugar in a bowl and sprinkle half of the mixture over the lemon slices. Let stand for 15 minutes.

3. Flip the lemon slices over, sprinkle the remaining mixture over them, and let stand for 15 minutes.

4. Bring a medium saucepan of water to a boil and prepare an ice water bath. Add the lemon slices and boil for 30 seconds. Remove them, submerge in the ice water bath, pat dry with paper towels, and set aside until ready to serve.

INGREDIENTS:

2   TABLESPOONS UNSALTED BUTTER

1   ONION, CHOPPED

2   CUPS CHOPPED LEEKS, WHITE PARTS ONLY

2   CELERY STALKS, CHOPPED

1   LARGE POTATO, PEELED AND CHOPPED

1   BAY LEAF

4   CUPS CHICKEN STOCK (FOR HOMEMADE, SEE PAGE 748)

2   TABLESPOONS OLIVE OIL

3   CUPS GREEN ASPARAGUS, TRIMMED AND QUARTERED

¾   CUP HEAVY CREAM

    SALT AND PEPPER, TO TASTE

    CURED LEMON SLICES (SEE RECIPE), FOR GARNISH

CURED LEMON SLICES

1   LEMON, SEEDED AND SLICED THIN

1   TABLESPOON KOSHER SALT

3   TABLESPOONS SUGAR

CREAMED ASPARAGUS SOUP
with BUTTERMILK *&* GARLIC CHIPS

YIELD: 4 TO 6 SERVINGS / ACTIVE TIME: 30 MINUTES / TOTAL TIME: 1 HOUR

Asparagus is typically freshest in late April, making it the perfect vegetable to welcome the warmer weather.

1. Cut off the tips of the asparagus and set them aside. Cut off the woody ends of the asparagus and discard. Cut what remains of the stalks into 2-inch pieces.

2. Melt the butter in a saucepan over medium-low heat. Add the onion and sauté until it is soft and translucent, about 6 minutes.

3. Add the stock and 2-inch pieces of asparagus to the saucepan, raise heat to medium, and simmer for 20 minutes.

4. Place the oil in a Dutch oven and bring it to 350°F over medium-high heat. Place the garlic in the oil, cook until golden brown, and then place on a paper towel–lined plate to drain.

5. Bring a small pot of salted water to a boil and then add the asparagus tips. Cook for approximately 2 minutes, drain, and set aside.

6. Once the soup has simmered for 20 minutes, transfer it to a food processor or blender and puree until smooth. Pour into warmed bowls, season with salt, and garnish each bowl with a drizzle of buttermilk, the asparagus tips, and the garlic chips.

TIP: Make sure to vent the blender when pureeing this soup and other hot liquids. Otherwise, pressure can build and leave a real mess.

INGREDIENTS:

2	BUNCHES ASPARAGUS
4	TABLESPOONS UNSALTED BUTTER
1	SMALL ONION, DICED
4	CUPS CHICKEN STOCK (SEE PAGE 748 FOR HOMEMADE)
1	CUP CANOLA OIL
4	GARLIC CLOVES, SLICED VERY THIN USING A MANDOLINE
	SALT, TO TASTE
½	CUP BUTTERMILK, FOR GARNISH

CHILLED AVOCADO SOUP
with CRAB & MANGO SALAD

YIELD: 6 SERVINGS / ACTIVE TIME: 25 MINUTES / TOTAL TIME: 1 HOUR AND 30 MINUTES

This is a great summer soup. The fat from the avocados gives a very creamy mouthfeel. Paired with the crab and mango salsa, it's a wonderfully balanced dish. If you feel like splurging, change the crab to lobster.

1. Place all of the ingredients in a food processor or blender and puree until smooth. Strain through a fine sieve and chill in the refrigerator for a minimum of 1 hour.

2. Place the towers of Crab & Mango Salad on chilled plates and remove the ring cutter.

3. Pour the soup around the towers of salsa and garnish with a dollop of crème fraîche and the chives.

CRAB & MANGO SALAD

1. Place the mango, pepper, onion, chives, vinegar, and oil in a bowl and stir gently until combined. Season with salt and chill in refrigerator until ready to serve.

2. Just before serving, use a ring cutter to make six towers out of the salad. Top each with the crabmeat.

INGREDIENTS:

FLESH FROM 3 AVOCADOS, CHOPPED

5 CUPS VEGETABLE STOCK (SEE PAGE 755 FOR HOMEMADE)

JUICE OF 2 LIMES

1 TEASPOON CUMIN

2 TEASPOONS KOSHER SALT

¼ TEASPOON CAYENNE PEPPER

CRAB & MANGO SALSA (SEE RECIPE)

FRESH CHIVES, FOR GARNISH

CRÈME FRAÎCHE, FOR GARNISH

CRAB & MANGO SALAD

½ CUP PEELED AND CHOPPED MANGO

½ RED BELL PEPPER, STEMMED, SEEDED, AND FINELY CHOPPED

3 TABLESPOONS MINCED RED ONION

1 TEASPOON MINCED FRESH CHIVES

1 TEASPOON RICE VINEGAR

2 TABLESPOONS OLIVE OIL

SALT, TO TASTE

½ LB. PEEKYTOE CRABMEAT, CLEANED, COOKED, AND FREE OF SHELL

KARELIAN BORSCHT

YIELD: 4 SERVINGS / ACTIVE TIME: 35 MINUTES / TOTAL TIME: 1 HOUR

Karelia is an area that used to belong to Finland but was ceded to Russia after World War II. This recipe is inspired by one from a Finnish-American cook, Beatrice Ojakangas. Many versions of borscht puree the vegetables, but I prefer this version, in which the vegetables are grated and bits of sausage are added for oomph. I've included sour cream as a garnish because that is traditional for borscht, but I hardly ever add it myself since the soup is plenty satisfying without it.

1. Place a large pot on the stove and turn the heat to medium. Drop bite-sized chunks of the sausage meat into the pot. Continue until all of the meat is in the pot. Cook, turning occasionally, until fully browned, then use a slotted spoon to transfer the sausage to a bowl lined with paper towels. Pour all but a tablespoon of the rendered fat into a small bowl and set aside.

2. Place the beets in the pot and cook, stirring occasionally, until they start to soften, about 8 minutes. Add some of the reserved fat if the pan starts to look dry.

3. Add the onion and garlic to the pot and cook until the onion turns translucent, about 3 minutes. Add the cabbage, celery, carrots, and fennel seeds and cook until the vegetables start to soften, about 10 minutes.

4. Add the stock, vinegar, sugar, bay leaf, and reserved sausage. Make sure there is enough liquid to cover all of the ingredients; add more stock if needed. Simmer until all of the vegetables are tender, about 15 minutes. Season with salt and pepper, discard the bay leaf, and ladle into warmed bowls. Top each portion with a dollop of sour cream and serve with warm rolls.

INGREDIENTS:

½   LB. GROUND PORK SAUSAGE

1   LB. BEETS, PEELED AND GRATED

1   ONION, GRATED

2   GARLIC CLOVES, MINCED

1   LB. RED CABBAGE, GRATED

1   LARGE CELERY STALK, GRATED

2   CARROTS, PEELED AND GRATED

1   TEASPOON FENNEL SEEDS

4   CUPS BEEF STOCK (SEE PAGE 747 FOR HOMEMADE), PLUS MORE AS NEEDED

2   TABLESPOONS APPLE CIDER VINEGAR

1   TABLESPOON SUGAR

1   BAY LEAF

    SALT AND PEPPER, TO TASTE

    SOUR CREAM (OPTIONAL), FOR GARNISH

    WARM ROLLS, FOR SERVING

ASPARAGUS & PEA SOUP

YIELD: 6 SERVINGS / ACTIVE TIME: 25 MINUTES / TOTAL TIME: 1 HOUR AND 20 MINUTES

Spring is a big tease; just when you think the cold weather is past, a raw, rainy day swoops in. This soup is not too heavy but still chases away a chill, and it is fresh enough to remind you that summer is just around the corner.

1. Remove the woody ends of the asparagus and discard. Separate the spears, remove the tips and reserve them for garnish, and chop what remains into bite-sized pieces.

2. In a medium saucepan, add the butter and cook over medium heat until melted. Add the leek and cook until it starts to soften, about 5 minutes.

3. Add the chopped asparagus, the cup of peas, and the parsley. Cook for 3 minutes, add the stock, and bring to a boil. Reduce heat so that the soup simmers and cook until the vegetables are tender, 6 to 8 minutes.

4. Transfer the soup to a food processor, puree until smooth, and strain through a fine sieve.

5. Place the soup in a clean saucepan. Add the cream and lemon zest, season with salt and pepper, and bring to a simmer.

6. Bring a small pan of salted water to a boil and prepare an ice water bath. Place the asparagus tips in the pan and cook for 3 to 4 minutes, or until tender. Remove the tips, submerge in the ice-water bath, pat dry with paper towels, and set aside.

7. Ladle the soup into warmed bowls, garnish with the asparagus tips, reserved peas, mint leaves, reserved lemon zest, and Parmesan, and serve with the Parmesan Crisps.

PARMESAN CRISPS

1. Preheat the oven to 400°F.

2. Place the cheeses in a mixing bowl and stir to combine.

3. Sprinkle the cheese mixture on a parchment-lined baking sheet. Use a ring cutter to make eight circles.

4. Sprinkle a pinch of cayenne over each circle. Place the tray in the oven and bake for 7 minutes, or until crispy.

INGREDIENTS:

- ¾ LB. ASPARAGUS
- 2 TABLESPOONS UNSALTED BUTTER
- 1 LEEK, TRIMMED, RINSED WELL, AND CHOPPED
- 1¼ CUPS PEAS, ¼ CUP RESERVED FOR GARNISH
- 1 TABLESPOON CHOPPED FRESH PARSLEY
- 5 CUPS VEGETABLE STOCK (SEE PAGE 755 FOR HOMEMADE)
- ½ CUP HEAVY CREAM
- ZEST OF 2 LEMONS, HALF RESERVED FOR GARNISH
- SALT AND PEPPER, TO TASTE
- FRESH MINT LEAVES, FOR GARNISH
- PARMESAN CHEESE, SHAVED, FOR GARNISH
- PARMESAN CRISPS (SEE RECIPE), FOR SERVING

PARMESAN CRISPS

- 1 CUP GRATED PARMESAN CHEESE
- 1 CUP GRATED SHARP CHEDDAR CHEESE
- CAYENNE PEPPER, TO TASTE

MISO RAMEN SOUP FOR ONE,
with ALL THE GOOD STUFF

YIELD: 1 SERVING / ACTIVE TIME: 20 MINUTES / TOTAL TIME: 30 MINUTES

This soup is warming but not heavy. The base is a very typical miso-based broth. I chose these vegetables to provide a good balance: meaty shiitakes, mild bok choy, tangy radishes, and sweet asparagus. But you can substitute nearly anything you like. The recipe is designed to make one big bowl of soup to please no one but yourself, so put your favorites in. If using store-bought stock, be conservative with the soy sauce. Canned and boxed stocks, no matter the kind, are often very high in sodium, so choose the low-sodium type if it is available. Of course, homemade stock is even better; see pages 748 for chicken, 755 for vegetable, 756 for mushroom, and 751 for dashi.

1. Place the oil in a medium saucepan and warm over medium heat. Add the shiitakes and cook, turning occasionally, until browned all over, about 8 minutes. Remove the mushrooms from the pot and set them aside.

2. Add the stock and ginger and bring to a simmer. Remove the ginger, or keep it in the pot if a spicier soup is desired.

3. Add the remaining ingredients, stir to combine, and simmer until the noodles and vegetables are cooked through, 5 to 8 minutes.

4. Taste, adjust seasoning as needed, and ladle into a large bowl.

INGREDIENTS:

- 1 TABLESPOON OLIVE OIL
- 4 OZ. FRESH SHIITAKE MUSHROOMS, STEMS REMOVED, CHOPPED
- 2 CUPS VEGETABLE STOCK (SEE PAGE 755 FOR HOMEMADE)
- ½ TABLESPOON PEELED AND CHOPPED GINGER
- 2 OZ. BOK CHOY, TRIMMED AND SLICED
- 1 OZ. ASPARAGUS, CUT INTO 2-INCH PIECES
- 1-2 OZ. RAMEN NOODLES
- 2 RADISHES, SLICED
- ½ TABLESPOON WHITE MISO
- 1 TABLESPOON WAKAME SEAWEED (OPTIONAL)
- 1 TABLESPOON SOY SAUCE
- 1 TABLESPOON MIRIN

PHO *with* STRIP STEAK

YIELD: 4 TO 6 SERVINGS / **ACTIVE TIME:** 15 MINUTES / **TOTAL TIME:** 4½ TO 8½ HOURS

Bok choy is the perfect mild and sweet element to balance a spicy Vietnamese pho.

1. To prepare the broth, place all of the ingredients in a slow cooker. Cover and cook on low for at least 4 hours. For a stronger tasting broth, cook for 8 hours.

2. Strain the broth through a fine sieve. Discard the solids and return the broth to the slow cooker.

3. To begin preparations for the noodles and strip steak, place the noodles and bok choy in the broth, cover, and cook on low for approximately 30 minutes, until the noodles are tender and the bok choy is al dente.

4. Slice the steak into ¼-inch-thick pieces. Ladle the broth, noodles, and baby bok choy into bowls and top with the steak. The broth will cook the steak to rare. If you prefer the steak to be cooked more, add it to the slow cooker and cook for 2 to 3 minutes for medium rare, 3 to 5 minutes for medium. Season with sriracha. If desired, serve with bean sprouts, chili peppers, lime wedges, cilantro, Thai basil, and scallions.

TIP: If you don't want to have to strain the broth, place the spices, garlic, and ginger in two large coffee filters. Tie the filters closed with kitchen twine and place the pouch in the broth. When the broth is finished cooking, remove the spice pouch and the lemongrass stalks and discard.

INGREDIENTS:

FOR THE BROTH

8	CUPS BEEF STOCK (SEE PAGE 747 FOR HOMEMADE)
1	LARGE CINNAMON STICK
4	BAY LEAVES
6	STAR ANISE PODS
2	TEASPOONS KOSHER SALT
2	TEASPOONS BLACK PEPPERCORNS (FOR MORE FLAVOR, SUBSTITUTE SZECHUAN PEPPERCORNS FOR 1 TEASPOON BLACK PEPPERCORNS)
2	TEASPOONS CORIANDER SEEDS
1	TEASPOON ALLSPICE BERRIES
1	TEASPOON FENNEL SEEDS
¼	CUP PEELED AND SMASHED FRESH GINGER
6	GARLIC CLOVES, SMASHED
4	LEMONGRASS STALKS, CRACKED OPEN
1	YELLOW ONION, CUT INTO 6 WEDGES
2	TABLESPOONS LIQUID AMINOS OR DARK SOY SAUCE
2	TABLESPOONS RICE VINEGAR
2	TABLESPOONS FISH SAUCE

FOR THE NOODLES AND STRIP STEAK

½	LB. DRIED CHINESE YELLOW NOODLES
4	BABY BOK CHOY, WASHED AND QUARTERED
1	(1 LB.) N.Y. STRIP STEAK
	SRIRACHA OR OTHER HOT SAUCE, TO TASTE
1	CUP BEAN SPROUTS (OPTIONAL), FOR SERVING
2	CHILI PEPPERS, SLICED (OPTIONAL), FOR SERVING
	LIME WEDGES (OPTIONAL), FOR SERVING
	FRESH CILANTRO, CHOPPED (OPTIONAL), FOR SERVING
	THAI BASIL LEAVES, CHOPPED (OPTIONAL), FOR SERVING
	SCALLIONS, CHOPPED (OPTIONAL), FOR SERVING

BEEF & BRAISED CABBAGE SOUP
with HORSERADISH CREAM

YIELD: 6 SERVINGS / ACTIVE TIME: 30 MINUTES / TOTAL TIME: 2 HOURS AND 30 MINUTES

Consider bringing this to your next potluck dinner, as it's great with or without the steak. It also pairs well with game meats.

1. Preheat the oven to 300°F.

2. Place the cabbage, onions, apple, brown sugar, garlic, nutmeg, caraway seeds, vinegar, and ½ cup of the stock in a large mixing bowl and stir until thoroughly combined.

3. Season with salt and pepper and transfer to a large, buttered casserole dish. Cover and place in the oven. Cook for 1 hour and 30 minutes, removing occasionally to stir the contents of the casserole dish.

4. Turn off the oven and open the oven door slightly. When the dish has cooled slightly, remove it from the oven and set aside. Preheat oven to 450°F.

5. In a medium sauté pan, add the oil and warm over medium heat. Season the steak with salt and pepper and then add it to the pan. Cook until seared on both sides, about 3 minutes per side. Remove from the pan and set aside.

6. Spoon the cabbage mixture into a large saucepan. Add the remaining stock and bring to a boil. Reduce heat so that the soup simmers and cook for 10 minutes.

7. Place the sirloin in the oven and cook until it is the desired level of doneness. Remove from the oven and let stand for 5 minutes.

8. Ladle the soup into warmed bowls. Slice the steak thin and place some on top of each portion. Garnish with the Horseradish Cream and watercress.

HORSERADISH CREAM

1. Place the horseradish, vinegar, mustard, and 4 tablespoons of the cream in a mixing bowl and stir to combine.

2. Lightly whip the remaining cream and then fold this into the horseradish mixture. Season with salt and pepper and refrigerate until ready to serve.

INGREDIENTS:

2	LBS. RED CABBAGE, CORED AND SHREDDED
2	ONIONS, SLICED THIN
1	LARGE APPLE, PEELED, CORED, AND CHOPPED
3	TABLESPOONS BROWN SUGAR
2	GARLIC CLOVES, MINCED
¼	TEASPOON GRATED NUTMEG
½	TEASPOON CARAWAY SEEDS
3	TABLESPOONS APPLE CIDER VINEGAR
4	CUPS BEEF STOCK (SEE PAGE 747 FOR HOMEMADE)
	SALT AND PEPPER, TO TASTE
2	TABLESPOONS OLIVE OIL
1½	LBS. SIRLOIN STEAK, TRIMMED
	HORSERADISH CREAM (SEE RECIPE), FOR GARNISH
	WATERCRESS, FOR GARNISH

HORSERADISH CREAM

2	TABLESPOONS PEELED AND GRATED FRESH HORSERADISH
2	TEASPOONS WHITE WINE VINEGAR
½	TEASPOON DIJON MUSTARD
1	CUP HEAVY CREAM
	SALT AND PEPPER, TO TASTE

SMOKED CHORIZO & CABBAGE SOUP

YIELD: 4 SERVINGS / ACTIVE TIME: 15 MINUTES / TOTAL TIME: 30 MINUTES

This soup is a great use of European ingredients and techniques.

1. Place the oil in a medium saucepan and warm over medium heat.

2. When the oil starts to shimmer, add the onion and cook until soft, about 5 minutes.

3. Add the thyme, chorizo, cabbage, cumin seeds, and cinnamon stick, cover, and cook for 5 minutes, stirring occasionally.

4. Add the stock and bring to a boil. Reduce heat so that the soup simmers and cook for an additional 10 minutes.

5. Season with salt and pepper and ladle into warmed bowls.

INGREDIENTS:

2 TABLESPOONS OLIVE OIL

1 ONION, CHOPPED

   LEAVES FROM 4 SPRIGS FRESH THYME, CHOPPED

1 LB. DRIED SMOKED CHORIZO, SLICED INTO ¼-INCH PIECES

1 GREEN CABBAGE, CORED AND SLICED

1 TABLESPOON CUMIN SEEDS

1 CINNAMON STICK

6 CUPS CHICKEN STOCK (SEE PAGE 748 FOR HOMEMADE)

   SALT AND PEPPER, TO TASTE

CARROT & GINGER SOUP *with* TURMERIC CREAM

YIELD: 4 TO 6 SERVINGS / ACTIVE TIME: 25 MINUTES / TOTAL TIME: 1 HOUR

This soup does not hold back on the ginger. The carrots can more than handle that amount of spice, though the turmeric cream is really what balances the whole dish.

1. In a medium saucepan, add the butter and melt over medium heat. Add the onions and cook, stirring often, until soft, about 5 minutes.

2. Add the carrots, ginger, and orange zest. Cook until the carrots start to soften, about 5 minutes.

3. Add the orange juice and white wine and cook until the liquid has evaporated. Add the stock, bring to a boil, and season with salt and pepper. Reduce heat so that the soup simmers and cook until the vegetables are tender, 10 to 15 minutes.

4. Transfer the soup to a food processor, puree until smooth, and strain through a fine sieve.

5. Place the soup in a clean pan and season with salt and pepper. If it is too thick, add more stock. Cook over medium heat until warmed through.

6. Ladle into warmed bowls and garnish with the Turmeric Cream and dill.

TURMERIC CREAM

1. Place the cream in a bowl and whip until soft peaks begin to form.

2. Add the turmeric and salt. Stir to combine and refrigerate until ready to use.

INGREDIENTS:

- 4 TABLESPOONS UNSALTED BUTTER
- 2 ONIONS, DICED
- 6 CUPS PEELED AND CHOPPED CARROTS
- ¼ CUP PEELED AND MINCED GINGER
- ZEST AND JUICE OF 2 ORANGES
- 1 CUP WHITE WINE
- 8 CUPS VEGETABLE STOCK (SEE PAGE 755 FOR HOMEMADE), PLUS MORE AS NEEDED
- SALT AND PEPPER, TO TASTE
- TURMERIC CREAM (SEE RECIPE), FOR GARNISH
- FRESH DILL, CHOPPED, FOR GARNISH

TURMERIC CREAM

- ½ CUP HEAVY CREAM
- ½ TEASPOON TURMERIC
- PINCH OF KOSHER SALT

CURRIED CARROT, SPINACH & TOFU BROTH

YIELD: 4 SERVINGS / ACTIVE TIME: 20 MINUTES / TOTAL TIME: 45 MINUTES

A very simple and very soothing soup that is both sweet and spicy. If you use vegetable stock in place of the chicken stock, this is a perfect vegan dinner.

1. Place the oil in a medium saucepan and warm over medium heat.

2. Add the onion, garlic, and curry powder and cook until the onion softens, about 5 minutes.

3. Add the stock, chili pepper, lime zest and juice, soy sauce, jaggery, and lime leaves. Bring to a boil, then reduce heat so that the soup simmers and cook for 10 minutes.

4. Add the carrot and continue to simmer for 5 minutes.

5. Just before serving, add the spinach and tofu. Cook until warmed through, season with salt and pepper, and ladle into warmed bowls.

INGREDIENTS:

1   TABLESPOON OLIVE OIL

1   ONION, CHOPPED

1   GARLIC CLOVE, MINCED

2   TABLESPOONS CURRY POWDER

6   CUPS CHICKEN OR VEGETABLE STOCK (SEE PAGE 748 OR 755, RESPECTIVELY, FOR HOMEMADE)

1   BIRD'S EYE CHILI PEPPER, STEMMED, SEEDED, AND SLICED

  ZEST AND JUICE OF 1 LIME

2   TABLESPOONS SOY SAUCE

4   TABLESPOONS JAGGERY

2   MAKRUT LIME LEAVES

1   CARROT, PEELED AND CUT INTO MATCHSTICKS

2   CUPS SPINACH

¾   LB. TOFU, CUT INTO ½-INCH CUBES

  SALT AND PEPPER, TO TASTE

VEGAN CAULIFLOWER & BLACK BEAN CHILI

YIELD: 4 TO 6 SERVINGS / ACTIVE TIME: 15 MINUTES / TOTAL TIME: 45 MINUTES

This recipe is vegan but it's sure to be a hit with everyone, especially if you dress it up with guacamole and tortilla chips on the side.

1. Place the oil in a saucepan and warm over medium heat.

2. Add the onions, peppers, and garlic and cook until soft, about 7 minutes.

3. Add the cauliflower and cook until the florets are lightly browned, about 5 minutes.

4. Add the tomatoes, stock, and chili powder and bring to a boil. Reduce heat so that the soup simmers, cover, and cook for 15 minutes.

5. Remove the cover and cook until the soup starts to thicken and the cauliflower is tender, about 15 minutes.

6. Add the beans, cook for another 3 minutes, and season with salt and pepper. Ladle into warmed bowls and garnish with the parsley.

INGREDIENTS:

2 TABLESPOONS OLIVE OIL

2 RED ONIONS, MINCED

1 RED BELL PEPPER, STEMMED, SEEDED, AND MINCED

1 YELLOW BELL PEPPER, FINELY CHOPPED

2 GARLIC CLOVES, MINCED

2 HEADS CAULIFLOWER, FLORETS REMOVED AND MINCED

2 (28 OZ.) CANS STEWED TOMATOES

2 CUPS VEGETABLE STOCK (SEE PAGE 755 FOR HOMEMADE)

1 TABLESPOON CHILI POWDER, OR TO TASTE

2 (14 OZ.) CANS BLACK BEANS, RINSED AND DRAINED

SALT AND PEPPER, TO TASTE

FRESH PARSLEY, CHOPPED, FOR GARNISH

CELERIAC & ROASTED GARLIC SOUP
with PICKLED TOMATOES *and* FUNNEL CAKE

YIELD: 4 SERVINGS / **ACTIVE TIME:** 45 MINUTES / **TOTAL TIME:** 13 HOURS AND 30 MINUTES

This soup combines old and new. The base consists of a creamy, garlicky celeriac puree that would be at home in a traditional bistro. But then it takes a turn toward a Midwestern fair with pickled tomatoes and peppery funnel cakes to liven up the whole dish.

1. Preheat the oven to 350°F.

2. Place the head of garlic on a baking sheet and drizzle the oil over the top. Place in the oven and roast for 30 minutes, or until golden brown. Remove from the oven and let stand until cool. When cool, slice off top and remove individual cloves. Set aside.

3. Place the butter in a medium saucepan and melt over medium heat. Add the onion and celeriac and cook until the onion starts to soften, about 5 minutes.

4. Add the herbs, cover the pan, and cook for 5 minutes, stirring often.

5. Add the wine, stock, and roasted garlic and bring to a boil.

6. Reduce heat so that the soup simmers, add the cream, and cook until the celeriac is tender, about 15 minutes.

7. Transfer the soup to a food processor or blender, puree until smooth, and strain through a fine sieve.

8. Place in a clean pan, and bring to a boil. Season with salt and pepper and ladle into warmed bowls. Garnish with the scallion greens and serve with the Pickled Tomatoes and the Pepper & Onion Funnel Cake.

INGREDIENTS:

1	HEAD GARLIC
1	TABLESPOON OLIVE OIL
2	TABLESPOONS UNSALTED BUTTER
½	ONION, DICED
8	CUPS DICED CELERIAC
	LEAVES FROM 1 SPRIG FRESH THYME, CHOPPED
	LEAVES FROM 1 SPRIG ROSEMARY, CHOPPED
1	CUP WHITE WINE
2	CUPS VEGETABLE STOCK (SEE PAGE 755 FOR HOMEMADE)
4	CUPS HEAVY CREAM
	SALT AND PEPPER, TO TASTE
	SCALLION GREENS, CHOPPED, FOR GARNISH
	PICKLED TOMATOES (SEE RECIPE), FOR SERVING
	PEPPER & ONION FUNNEL CAKE (SEE RECIPE), FOR SERVING

Continued . . .

PICKLED TOMATOES

1. Place all of the ingredients, except for the tomato, in a small saucepan, stir to combine, and bring to a simmer over medium heat. Remove from heat and let cool.

2. Once cool, add the tomatoes and refrigerate for 12 hours or overnight.

PEPPER & ONION FUNNEL CAKE

1. Place the oil in a Dutch oven and heat to 375°F.

2. Place the eggs, vinegar, Tabasco™, and Worcestershire sauce in a bowl and whisk to combine.

3. While whisking constantly, slowly add the flour and baking powder. Add the scallion whites, pepper, and red onion and stir until incorporated.

4. Drop spoonfuls of the mixture into the hot oil and fry until golden brown.

5. Remove with a slotted spoon, place on a paper towel–lined plate to drain, and season with salt. Serve immediately.

INGREDIENTS:

PICKLED TOMATOES
- ¼ CUP WHITE WINE VINEGAR
- 1½ TABLESPOONS BROWN SUGAR
- 2 TEASPOONS KOSHER SALT
- ½ TEASPOON MINCED GARLIC
- 2 TEASPOONS MUSTARD SEEDS
- ¼ TEASPOON BLACK PEPPER
- 1 TEASPOON CUMIN
- ¼ TEASPOON CAYENNE PEPPER
- ¼ TEASPOON TURMERIC
- 1½ TABLESPOONS OLIVE OIL
- 1 TOMATO, CONCASSE (SEE PAGE 808) AND CHOPPED

PEPPER & ONION FUNNEL CAKE
- 4 CUPS VEGETABLE OIL
- 2 EGGS
- 1 TEASPOON RICE WINE VINEGAR
- ½ TEASPOON TABASCO™
- ½ TEASPOON WORCESTERSHIRE SAUCE
- ⅓ CUP ALL-PURPOSE FLOUR
- ¼ TEASPOON BAKING POWDER
- 2 SCALLION WHITES, CHOPPED
- 2 TABLESPOONS CHOPPED GREEN BELL PEPPER
- 2 TABLESPOONS DICED RED ONION
- SALT, TO TASTE

CELERIAC & TRUFFLE SOUP

YIELD: 4 SERVINGS / ACTIVE TIME: 25 MINUTES / TOTAL TIME: 1 HOUR

Celeriac, along with eggs and creamy pasta, is among those elements ordained to be paired with the jewels of the earth otherwise known as truffles. The flavor of celeriac is mild enough to act as support for the assertive truffle without being overwhelmed. If you have access to fresh truffles, feel free to shave a few slices onto the top of the finished soup.

1. Place the butter in a medium saucepan and melt over medium heat. Add the onion and celeriac and cook until onion is soft, about 5 minutes.

2. Add the herbs, cover the pan, reduce heat to medium-low, and cook, stirring often, for 5 minutes.

3. Add the stock, white wine, and truffle paste and bring to a boil. Add the cream and cook for 2 minutes. Reduce heat so that the soup simmers and cook until the celeriac is tender, about 15 minutes.

4. Transfer the soup to a food processor or blender, puree until smooth, and strain through a fine sieve.

5. Season with salt and pepper, place in a clean pan, and bring to a boil. Add the truffle paste and whisk until it is emulsified, about 1 minute.

6. Ladle into warmed bowls, garnish with additional truffle paste, the truffle oil, and celery leaves, and serve with the Truffle Croutons.

TRUFFLE CROUTONS

1. Place the vegetable oil and truffle oil in a mixing bowl and whisk to combine.

2. In a sauté pan, add the oil mixture and warm over low heat. Add the cubes of brioche, raise heat to medium, and cook until the brioche has browned.

3. Add the truffle paste and cook for 1 minute.

4. Remove the brioche and place on paper towels to drain. Season with salt and pepper and serve.

INGREDIENTS:

- 2 TABLESPOONS UNSALTED BUTTER
- ½ ONION, DICED
- 8 CUPS PEELED AND DICED CELERIAC
- LEAVES FROM 1 SPRIG FRESH THYME, CHOPPED
- LEAVES FROM 1 SPRIG FRESH ROSEMARY, CHOPPED
- 2 CUPS VEGETABLE STOCK (SEE PAGE 755 FOR HOMEMADE)
- 1 CUP WHITE WINE
- ¼ CUP BLACK TRUFFLE PASTE, PLUS MORE FOR GARNISH
- 4 CUPS HEAVY CREAM
- SALT AND PEPPER, TO TASTE
- TRUFFLE CROUTONS (SEE RECIPE), FOR SERVING
- WHITE TRUFFLE OIL, FOR GARNISH
- CELERY LEAVES, FOR GARNISH

TRUFFLE CROUTONS

- ¼ CUP VEGETABLE OIL
- 2 TABLESPOONS TRUFFLE OIL
- 1 CUP BRIOCHE CUBES
- 1 TEASPOON BLACK TRUFFLE PASTE
- SALT AND PEPPER, TO TASTE

CELERIAC BISQUE
with POACHED CLAMS & PARSLEY OIL

YIELD: 4 TO 6 SERVINGS / ACTIVE TIME: 40 MINUTES / TOTAL TIME: 3 HOURS AND 15 MINUTES

Clams, which become sweeter in the late fall and early winter, are a natural match for this rich, creamy bisque that celeriac forms the base of. The key to this dish is using the poaching liquid in the soup, as it bridges the gap between the flavors.

1. Place the clams and 1 tablespoon of the salt in a large pot and cover with cold water. Soak for 2 hours to remove some of the sand from the clams, making sure to change the water every 30 minutes.

2. Drain the clams, place them in a large pot, and add the white wine, the shallots, the crushed garlic cloves, 4 sprigs of the thyme, and 1 of the bay leaves. Cover and cook over high heat until the majority of the clams have opened. Discard any clams that do not open. Strain and reserve 1½ cups of the cooking liquid. Remove the clam meat from the shells and set aside.

3. Place the butter, onion, celery, and sliced garlic in a large pot and cook over medium-high heat until the onion is translucent, about 3 minutes. Add the celeriac, cream, milk, remaining salt, remaining thyme, remaining bay leaf, and the reserved cooking liquid and simmer over low heat until the celeriac is tender, about 20 minutes.

4. Remove the sprigs of thyme and bay leaf, transfer the bisque to a blender, and puree until smooth. Return to the saucepan, season to taste, and add the clam meat. Simmer over low heat until the clam meat is warmed through, about 2 minutes.

5. Place the parsley and oil in a blender and puree on high for about 1 minute. Strain the oil through a piece of cheesecloth or a coffee filter and discard the solids. This oil can be stored in the refrigerator for up to 1 week.

6. Ladle the soup into warmed bowls and garnish with the parsley oil.

INGREDIENTS:

18   LITTLENECK CLAMS

2½   TABLESPOONS KOSHER SALT, PLUS MORE TO TASTE

1   CUP WHITE WINE

2   SHALLOTS, SLICED

6   GARLIC CLOVES, 3 CRUSHED, 3 SLICED

6   SPRIGS FRESH THYME

2   BAY LEAVES

4   TABLESPOONS UNSALTED BUTTER

1   YELLOW ONION, SLICED

1   CUP SLICED CELERY

8   CUPS PEELED AND DICED CELERIAC

2   CUPS HEAVY CREAM

6   CUPS WHOLE MILK

1   CUP FRESH PARSLEY LEAVES

⅓   CUP OLIVE OIL

SOUPS AND STEWS | 305

CELERY BISQUE *with* CRISPY CELERY HEARTS

YIELD: 6 SERVINGS / ACTIVE TIME: 15 MINUTES / TOTAL TIME: 1 HOUR

Celery soup sounds rather austere, but it is actually very rich and hearty. This creamy bisque is a lovely winter warmer that gets a crispy topper with beer-battered celery hearts.

1. Place the butter in a medium saucepan and melt over medium heat. Add the onion, leek, and celery and cook until tender, about 5 minutes. Add the bay leaf, potato, and celeriac and cook for another 5 minutes.

2. Add the stock and cinnamon stick and bring to a boil. Reduce heat so that the soup simmers and cook until the potatoes and celeriac are tender, about 15 minutes.

3. Remove the cinnamon stick and transfer the soup to a blender or food processor. Puree until smooth and creamy and pass through a fine sieve.

4. Return the soup to the pan and bring it to a simmer. Add the cream and season with nutmeg, salt, and pepper. Simmer until warmed through, ladle into warmed bowls, and serve with the Crispy Celery Hearts.

CRISPY CELERY HEARTS

1. Place the oil in a Dutch oven and heat to 350°F.

2. Combine 1 cup of the flour, the cornstarch, and baking powder in a bowl. Sift the mixture through a fine sieve. Add the beer and whisk until smooth.

3. In a small bowl, add the remaining flour and the celery hearts and toss until the celery hearts are evenly coated. Dip each celery heart in the batter and then place them in the hot oil. Fry until golden brown. Use a slotted spoon or tongs to remove from oil and set on a paper towel–lined plate to drain. Season with salt and pepper and serve immediately.

INGREDIENTS:

4	TABLESPOONS UNSALTED BUTTER
1	SMALL ONION, CHOPPED
½	LEEK, WHITE PART ONLY, CUT INTO ¾-INCH PIECES
2	CELERY STALKS, CHOPPED
1	BAY LEAF
1	POTATO, PEELED AND CHOPPED
1	CELERIAC, PEELED AND CHOPPED
4	CUPS CHICKEN STOCK (SEE PAGE 748 FOR HOMEMADE)
1	CINNAMON STICK
½	CUP HEAVY CREAM
	GROUND NUTMEG, TO TASTE
	SALT AND PEPPER, TO TASTE
	CRISPY CELERY HEARTS (SEE RECIPE), FOR SERVING

CRISPY CELERY HEARTS

4	CUPS VEGETABLE OIL
1½	CUPS ALL-PURPOSE FLOUR
½	CUP CORNSTARCH
1	TEASPOON BAKING POWDER
1½	CUPS BEER (ALE PREFERRED)
18	CELERY HEARTS
	SALT AND PEPPER, TO TASTE

HAM HOCK & COLLARD GREEN SOUP

YIELD: 4 SERVINGS / ACTIVE TIME: 30 MINUTES / TOTAL TIME: 1 HOUR AND 35 MINUTES

Since collard greens are not always easy to come by, this preparation gives the option for kale instead, and it is equally (if not more) delicious. When choosing ham hocks, ask your butcher for nice, meaty ones.

1. Prepare an ice water bath. Place the water and salt in a large saucepan and bring to a boil. Add the greens and cook until soft, about 4 minutes. Remove with a slotted spoon and submerge in the ice water bath. Place on kitchen towels to dry. Drain the water from the pot.

2. Place the oil and the salt pork in the saucepan and warm over medium heat until the salt pork has melted. Add the onion and celery and cook until they have softened, about 5 minutes. Add the flour slowly, stirring constantly, and cook for 4 minutes.

3. Gradually add the stock, whisking constantly to prevent any lumps from forming. Bring to a boil, reduce heat so that the soup simmers, and add the ham hocks and Sachet d'Épices. Simmer for 1 hour, stirring occasionally.

4. Remove ham hocks and Sachet d'Épices and return the collard greens to the saucepan.

5. Remove the meat from the ham hocks, mince, and return the meat to the soup.

6. Add the cream, season with salt and pepper, and ladle into warmed bowls.

INGREDIENTS:

16 CUPS WATER

1 TEASPOON KOSHER SALT, PLUS MORE TO TASTE

1 LB. COLLARD GREENS OR KALE, CHOPPED

1 TABLESPOON OLIVE OIL

2 OZ. SALT PORK

½ CUP MINCED ONION

¼ CUP MINCED CELERY

½ CUP ALL-PURPOSE FLOUR

8 CUPS CHICKEN STOCK (SEE PAGE 748 FOR HOMEMADE)

2 SMOKED HAM HOCKS

1 SACHET D'ÉPICES (SEE PAGE 809)

½ CUP HEAVY CREAM

BLACK PEPPER, TO TASTE

CAULIFLOWER SOUP

YIELD: 4 SERVINGS / ACTIVE TIME: 25 MINUTES / TOTAL TIME: 40 MINUTES

Crème du Barry is a traditional French cream of cauliflower soup. The ingredients are very simple: stock, cauliflower, cream, and potato, which works as a thickener. I learned how to make it at culinary school and was enamored by its thick, rich flavor. Like most pureed soups, however, it needs a boost from garnishes. As cauliflower can easily be overwhelmed by other flavors and I really wanted its essence to come through, I decided the best garnish would be more cauliflower. Instead of using the poached cauliflower from the soup, I took a quarter of the head, cut it into small pieces, and browned it in a pan to get that roasted cauliflower taste that we have all fallen for. For even more texture, I finished the roasted bits with some bread crumbs, parsley, and lemon zest.

1. Place the butter in a large stockpot and melt over medium heat. Add the onion, celery, and potato and sweat the vegetables for a few minutes, but don't let them brown.

2. Add three-quarters of the cauliflower and the flour to the pot and cook, stirring constantly, for 2 minutes.

3. Add the stock and simmer until the cauliflower is tender, about 15 minutes.

4. Use a blender or an immersion blender to puree the soup. If using a blender, return the soup to the pot. Add the cream and season with salt and white pepper.

5. Chop the remaining cauliflower into small pieces. Place the oil in a saucepan, add the chopped cauliflower, and sauté over medium heat until the cauliflower is fully browned, about 10 minutes.

6. Add the bread crumbs and cook until they are toasted, about 2 minutes. Remove from heat and add the parsley and lemon zest. Ladle the soup into bowls and top with the sautéed cauliflower mixture.

INGREDIENTS:

- 1 TABLESPOON UNSALTED BUTTER
- 1 ONION, DICED
- 1 CELERY STALK, DICED
- 1 SMALL POTATO, PEELED AND DICED
- 1 HEAD CAULIFLOWER, QUARTERED
- 1 TABLESPOON ALL-PURPOSE FLOUR
- 4 CUPS CHICKEN OR VEGETABLE STOCK (SEE PAGES 748 OR 755, RESPECTIVELY, FOR HOMEMADE)
- ¼ CUP HEAVY CREAM
- SALT AND WHITE PEPPER, TO TASTE
- 1 TABLESPOON OLIVE OIL
- 2 TABLESPOONS PANKO BREAD CRUMBS
- 2 TABLESPOONS CHOPPED FRESH PARSLEY
- ½ TEASPOON LEMON ZEST

CALDO VERDE

YIELD: 4 SERVINGS / ACTIVE TIME: 25 MINUTES / TOTAL TIME: 40 MINUTES

A very simple soup that is perfect for a cold winter day. It starts with simmering onion, garlic, and potatoes in stock and then, once everything is nice and tender, pureeing it to create a creamy base without adding any cream. The collard greens and sausage are added at the end. Unlike many recipes for collard greens, this one cooks them for only a few minutes, so you want to make sure they are cut into thin ribbons so they soften up enough.

1. Place the oil in a large stockpot and warm over medium heat. Once the oil is shimmering, add the onion and garlic and sauté until they begin to brown, about 5 minutes.

2. Add the potatoes and stock and bring to a boil. Reduce heat so that the soup simmers and cook until potatoes are fork-tender, about 15 minutes.

3. Use a blender, immersion blender, or potato masher to achieve the consistency that you want the soup to be.

4. If using a blender, return the soup to the pot and warm over medium heat. Add the collards and sausage to the pot and cook until warmed through, about 5 minutes. Remove from heat, season with salt and pepper, and ladle into warmed bowls.

INGREDIENTS:

1 TABLESPOON OLIVE OIL

1 LARGE ONION, DICED

2 GARLIC CLOVES, CHOPPED

2 LARGE YUKON GOLD POTATOES, PEELED AND DICED

4 CUPS CHICKEN STOCK (SEE PAGE 748 FOR HOMEMADE)

1 BUNCH (ABOUT 7 LARGE LEAVES) COLLARD GREENS, STEMMED AND SLICED VERY THIN

1 LB. LINGUICA OR OTHER SPICY COOKED SAUSAGE, DICED

SALT AND PEPPER, TO TASTE

DRIED FAVA BEAN SOUP *with* GRILLED HALLOUMI CHEESE *and* PARSLEY & LEMON OIL

YIELD: 4 SERVINGS / ACTIVE TIME: 30 MINUTES / TOTAL TIME: 24 HOURS

The Parsley & Lemon Oil is a delicious counterpart to the earthy fava beans and salty halloumi cheese.

1. Place the fava beans, stock, and garlic in a saucepan and bring to a boil. Reduce heat so that the soup simmers, cover, and cook until the beans are falling apart, about 1 hour. If the liquid level starts to get too low, add water as needed.

2. Transfer the soup to a food processor and puree until smooth.

3. Place the soup in a clean pan, season with salt and pepper, and cook over medium heat until warmed through. Ladle into warmed bowls and serve with the Parsley & Lemon Oil, Grilled Halloumi Cheese, and lemon wedges.

PARSLEY & LEMON OIL

1. Place the oil in a saucepan and warm over medium heat. Add the shallot and cook until soft, about 5 minutes.

2. Remove the pan from heat and add the lemon zest. Let stand for 1 hour.

3. Whisk in the lemon juice and then fold in the parsley. Set aside until ready to serve.

GRILLED HALLOUMI CHEESE

1. Preheat a gas or charcoal grill to 350°F. If cooking indoors, warm a grill or sauté pan over medium-high heat.

2. Place the oil in a small bowl and then add the cheese. Toss until the cheese is evenly coated.

3. Place the cheese in a nonstick frying pan and cook until browned on each side, about 2 minutes per side. Serve immediately.

INGREDIENTS:

1½ CUPS DRIED FAVA BEANS, SOAKED OVERNIGHT

6 CUPS VEAL STOCK (SEE PAGE 747 FOR HOMEMADE)

4 GARLIC CLOVES, MINCED

WATER, AS NEEDED

SALT AND PEPPER, TO TASTE

PARSLEY & LEMON OIL (SEE RECIPE), FOR SERVING

GRILLED HALLOUMI CHEESE (SEE RECIPE), FOR SERVING

LEMON WEDGES, FOR SERVING

PARSLEY & LEMON OIL

¼ CUP OLIVE OIL

1 SHALLOT, MINCED

ZEST AND JUICE OF 1 LEMON

2 TABLESPOONS CHOPPED FRESH PARSLEY

GRILLED HALLOUMI CHEESE

1 TABLESPOON OLIVE OIL

½ LB. HALLOUMI, SLICED INTO 4 PIECES

FRENCH LENTIL SOUP

YIELD: 4 TO 6 SERVINGS / ACTIVE TIME: 25 MINUTES / TOTAL TIME: 1 HOUR AND 15 MINUTES

This classic gets its backbone from caraway seeds, wine, and vinegar. Make it with the Caraway Water Biscuits and it is more than hearty enough for dinner.

1. Place the oil in a medium saucepan and warm over medium heat. Add the onion and garlic and cook until the onion starts to soften, about 5 minutes.

2. Add the carrot, leek, and celery and cook until soft, about 5 minutes. Add the tomato paste and cook, stirring constantly, for 2 minutes.

3. Add the lentils, stock, Sachet d'Épices, bay leaf, thyme, caraway seeds, and lemon. Bring to a boil, then reduce heat so that the soup simmers and cook until the lentils are tender, about 30 minutes.

4. Remove the Sachet d'Épices and lemon slices. Add the vinegar and Riesling and season with salt and pepper. Ladle into warmed bowls and serve with the Caraway Water Biscuits.

CARAWAY WATER BISCUITS

1. Preheat the oven to 350°F.

2. Place the flour and water in a mixing bowl and whisk until combined. Add the salt and stir to incorporate.

3. Use a pastry brush to transfer the batter to a parchment–lined baking sheet, taking care to make nice, long crackers.

4. Sprinkle caraway seeds on the crackers and place the sheet in the oven. Bake for 8 minutes or until golden brown, then remove and let the crackers cool.

INGREDIENTS:

2	TABLESPOONS OLIVE OIL
1	ONION, PEELED AND CHOPPED
1	GARLIC CLOVE, MINCED
1	CARROT, PEELED AND MINCED
1	LEEK, WHITE PART ONLY, MINCED
1	CELERY STALK, MINCED
1	TABLESPOON TOMATO PASTE
1½	CUPS FRENCH LENTILS
6	CUPS CHICKEN STOCK (SEE PAGE 748 FOR HOMEMADE)
1	SACHET D'ÉPICES (SEE PAGE 809)
1	BAY LEAF
	LEAVES FROM 2 SPRIGS THYME, CHOPPED
¼	TEASPOON CARAWAY SEEDS
½	LEMON, SLICED
1	TABLESPOON APPLE CIDER VINEGAR
¼	CUP RIESLING
	SALT AND PEPPER, TO TASTE
	CARAWAY WATER BISCUITS (SEE RECIPE), FOR SERVING

CARAWAY WATER BISCUITS

½	CUP ALL-PURPOSE FLOUR
10	TABLESPOONS WATER
	PINCH OF KOSHER SALT
2	TABLESPOONS CARAWAY SEEDS

MOROCCAN LEGUME SOUP *with* HONEY BUNS

YIELD: 4 SERVINGS / ACTIVE TIME: 45 MINUTES / TOTAL TIME: 24 HOURS

This authentic Moroccan soup is served with warmed honey buns, but biscuits or pita bread are good options as well.

1. Place the oil in a medium saucepan and warm over medium heat. Add the onion and cook until soft, about 5 minutes.

2. Add the ginger, turmeric, cinnamon, saffron, tomatoes, sugar, chickpeas, and stock, stir to combine, and bring to a boil. Reduce heat so that the soup simmers, cover, and cook for 10 minutes.

3. Add the lentils and fava beans and cook until all of the legumes are tender, about 15 minutes. Add the cilantro and parsley, season with salt and pepper, ladle into warmed bowls, and serve with the Honey Buns.

HONEY BUNS

1. Combine the yeast and the water in a bowl and let stand until the mixture starts to foam.

2. Sift the flour and salt into a mixing bowl. Add the yeast mixture, honey, and fennel seeds, and then add the cup of milk in a slow stream. Stir until thoroughly combined.

3. Place the dough on a floured work surface and knead until it is smooth and elastic, about 5 minutes.

4. Cover the dough with a damp kitchen towel and let stand until it has doubled in size, about 30 minutes.

5. Preheat the oven to 450°F.

6. Divide the dough into 12 pieces and shape each piece into a ball.

7. Place on a baking sheet and let stand for 10 minutes.

8. Place the egg yolk and remaining milk in a small bowl and whisk to combine. Brush the top of each bun with the mixture, sprinkle the poppy seeds on top, if using, and place the sheet in the oven. Bake for 15 minutes, or until golden brown on top and bottom.

9. Remove the buns from the tray and place on a wire rack to cool slightly before serving.

INGREDIENTS:

- 1½ TABLESPOONS OLIVE OIL
- 1 ONION, SLICED
- ¼ TEASPOON GROUND GINGER
- ¼ TEASPOON TURMERIC
- ½ TEASPOON CINNAMON
  PINCH OF SAFFRON
- 1 (14 OZ.) CAN DICED TOMATOES
- 1 TEASPOON SUGAR
- ½ CUP CHICKPEAS, SOAKED OVERNIGHT AND DRAINED
- 4 CUPS VEAL STOCK (SEE PAGE 747 FOR HOMEMADE)
- ⅓ CUP BROWN LENTILS, SOAKED OVERNIGHT AND DRAINED
- ½ CUP DRIED FAVA BEANS, SOAKED OVERNIGHT AND DRAINED
- 1 TABLESPOON CHOPPED FRESH CILANTRO
- 1 TABLESPOON CHOPPED FRESH PARSLEY
  SALT AND PEPPER, TO TASTE
  HONEY BUNS (SEE RECIPE), FOR SERVING

HONEY BUNS
- ½ TEASPOON ACTIVE DRY YEAST
- 1 TABLESPOON LUKEWARM WATER (90°F)
- 1¾ CUPS BREAD FLOUR, PLUS MORE FOR DUSTING
- ½ TEASPOON KOSHER SALT
- 2 TABLESPOONS HONEY
- 1 TEASPOON FENNEL SEEDS
- 1 CUP WHOLE MILK, PLUS 1 TABLESPOON
- 1 EGG YOLK
- 1 TEASPOON POPPY SEEDS (OPTIONAL)

DAL

YIELD: 4 SERVINGS / ACTIVE TIME: 20 MINUTES / TOTAL TIME: 1 HOUR AND 30 MINUTES

This is an everyday staple in most parts of India, appearing in myriad guises. It's a simple stew of yellow peas, orange lentils, or mung beans that should be slightly soupy so that its deliciousness can seep down into the basmati rice.

1. Place the oil in a large Dutch oven and warm over medium-high heat.

2. Add the onion, garlic, red pepper flakes, curry leaves (if using), and salt and sauté until the onion is slightly translucent, about 3 minutes.

3. Add the yellow split peas, water, and turmeric and bring to a simmer. Cover and gently simmer for 1 hour, removing the lid to stir occasionally.

4. Remove the lid and simmer, stirring occasionally, until the dal has thickened, about 30 minutes. When the dal has the consistency of porridge, stir in the peas and cook until they are warmed through.

5. To serve, ladle the dal over the rice.

INGREDIENTS:

- 2 TABLESPOONS VEGETABLE OIL
- 1 YELLOW ONION, DICED
- 2 GARLIC CLOVES, MINCED
- 2 TEASPOONS RED PEPPER FLAKES, OR TO TASTE
- 2 CURRY LEAVES (OPTIONAL)
- 1 TEASPOON SALT
- 1½ CUPS YELLOW SPLIT PEAS, SORTED AND RINSED
- 4 CUPS WATER
- 1 TEASPOON TURMERIC
- 1 CUP FRESH PEAS
- 2 CUPS COOKED BASMATI RICE

PORK & BEAN STEW

YIELD: 4 TO 6 SERVINGS / ACTIVE TIME: 1 HOUR / TOTAL TIME: 24 HOURS

Stews are a great way to showcase braised meats without overpowering the senses with their savory flavors. The long cooking time allows the meat to become melt-in-your-mouth delicious and is well worth the wait. This iconic stew is perfect for large gatherings, and it tastes even better the next day (if you have any leftovers, that is).

1. Drain the beans, place them in a saucepan, and cover with water. Bring to a boil, reduce heat so that the beans simmer, and cook until tender, about 1 hour. Strain and reserve the cooking liquid. Set the beans aside.

2. Place the pork in a mixing bowl, add the salt and pepper, and toss to coat. Add the flour and toss to coat.

3. Place the oil in a Dutch oven and warm over high heat. When the oil starts to shimmer, add half of the pork pieces in a single layer and cook, turning, until they are browned on all sides, about 10 minutes. Transfer the browned pieces to a plate, add the remaining pork, and cook until browned all over. Transfer to the plate with the other pork.

4. Place the onions, celery, carrots, mushrooms, and garlic in the pot and cook until the onions are translucent, about 5 minutes. Add the tomato paste and the beans and stir to coat. Return the pork back in the pot and deglaze with the stock.

5. Add the tomato sauce, thyme, and bay leaf and bring to a boil. Reduce heat so that the stew simmers, cover, and cook, stirring occasionally, until the stew has thickened to the desired consistency, 35 to 45 minutes. Season to taste, remove the thyme and bay leaf, ladle into warmed bowls, and garnish with the parsley.

INGREDIENTS:

- 1 CUP CANNELLINI BEANS, SOAKED OVERNIGHT
- 1½ LBS. PORK SHOULDER, CUT INTO 1-INCH CUBES
- 1½ TABLESPOONS KOSHER SALT
- 2 TEASPOONS BLACK PEPPER
- ¼ CUP ALL-PURPOSE FLOUR
- ¼ CUP OLIVE OIL
- 2 LARGE ONIONS, DICED
- 3 CELERY STALKS, DICED
- 3 CARROTS, PEELED AND DICED
- 2 CUPS OYSTER MUSHROOMS
- 4 LARGE GARLIC CLOVES, MINCED
- 3 TABLESPOONS TOMATO PASTE
- 2 CUPS CHICKEN STOCK (SEE PAGE 748 FOR HOMEMADE)
- 2 CUPS TOMATO SAUCE (SEE PAGE 793 FOR HOMEMADE)
- 4 SPRIGS THYME
- 1 BAY LEAF
- ¼ CUP CHOPPED FRESH PARSLEY LEAVES, FOR GARNISH

SARDINIAN SPINACH, CANNELLINI & FREGOLA SOUP

YIELD: 4 SERVINGS / ACTIVE TIME: 45 MINUTES / TOTAL TIME: 1 HOUR AND 30 MINUTES

This is a classic bean-and-vegetable soup using fregola, which is a toasted pasta with a nutty, earthy flavor. If you can't find it, you can substitute a differently shaped small pasta.

1. Prepare the leeks by trimming away the root ends and dark green leaves, keeping only the white and light green parts. With a sharp knife, cut each leek in half lengthwise and remove the two outer layers. Place the leeks in a large bowl of water and swish them around to remove any dirt. Drain well, then mince and transfer to a kitchen towel. Set aside.

2. Warm a Dutch oven over medium-low heat for 2 to 3 minutes. Add the oil and garlic and raise heat to medium-high. When the surface of the oil begins to shimmer, remove the garlic and discard it. Add the onion, celery, leeks, and a couple pinches of salt and stir to combine. When the mixture begins to sizzle, reduce heat to low, cover, and cook, stirring occasionally, until the vegetables are very tender, about 15 minutes.

3. Raise heat to medium-high and add the cannellini beans and tomato paste. Season with salt and pepper and cook, stirring frequently, until the cannellini beans begin to look slightly toasted, about 8 minutes.

4. Add the tomatoes and stock and bring to a boil. Reduce heat to low, cover, and simmer for 30 minutes. Taste and adjust the seasoning as needed.

5. Add the fregola and cook until it is tender but still chewy, about 15 minutes. A few minutes before the fregola is done cooking, add the spinach and stir.

6. Ladle the soup into four warmed soup bowls and garnish with the Pecorino Sardo and additional olive oil.

INGREDIENTS:

- 2 LEEKS
- ¼ CUP OLIVE OIL, PLUS MORE FOR GARNISH
- 2 GARLIC CLOVES, CRUSHED
- 1 SMALL RED ONION, MINCED
- 4 CELERY STALKS, MINCED
-    SALT AND PEPPER, TO TASTE
- 1 (14 OZ.) CAN CANNELLINI BEANS, RINSED AND DRAINED
- 1 TABLESPOON TOMATO PASTE
- 4 VERY RIPE PLUM TOMATOES, CONCASSE (SEE PAGE 808)
- 6 CUPS CHICKEN OR VEGETABLE STOCK (SEE PAGES 748 OR 755, RESPECTIVELY, FOR HOMEMADE)
- ⅔ CUP FREGOLA
- ½ LB. FRESH BABY SPINACH
-    PECORINO SARDO CHEESE, GRATED, FOR GARNISH

CARIBBEAN-STYLE STEWED PIGEON PEAS

YIELD: 2 TO 4 SERVINGS / ACTIVE TIME: 30 MINUTES / TOTAL TIME: 1 HOUR

This is a dish from Joanne Rappos, author of the food blog *Olive and Mango*. Joanne is of Greek heritage, though Canadian by birth, and she lived in Trinidad with her husband for many years. Her cooking is heavily influenced by both Caribbean and Mediterranean flavors, as you can taste in this complex dish. This is one of Joanne and her husband's favorite dishes, and she went through many versions before she got the taste just right.

1. Place the oil in a large pot or Dutch oven and warm over medium heat. Once the oil is shimmering, add the brown sugar and allow it to caramelize to the point that it's bubbling and starting to smoke, about 3 minutes. Add the molasses to achieve desired color and consistency, if desired.

2. Add the pigeon peas, being careful not to splatter the caramel. Cover and let simmer for a few minutes, stirring and checking on the pigeon peas every so often. If using, add more molasses as needed to darken the peas.

3. Uncover the pot, raise heat to high, and cook, stirring constantly, until a majority of the moisture has evaporated, 1 to 2 minutes.

4. Add the onion, garlic, pimiento peppers, tomato, pumpkin, scallions, thyme, and cilantro and sauté for a minute.

5. Add the coconut milk, water, and Scotch bonnet pepper (if using) and stir to combine. Bring the soup to a boil, then reduce heat so that it simmers. Simmer until the peas are tender and the pumpkin can be mashed easily, 20 to 30 minutes.

6. Season with salt and pepper and ladle into warmed bowls.

INGREDIENTS:

- 2 TABLESPOONS COCONUT OIL
- 2 TABLESPOONS BROWN SUGAR
- 1-2 TEASPOONS MOLASSES, PLUS MORE AS NEEDED (OPTIONAL)
- 2 CUPS PIGEON PEAS
- 1 ONION, DICED
- 2 GARLIC CLOVES, MINCED
- 2-3 PIMIENTO PEPPERS, DICED
- 1 TOMATO, DICED
- 1 CUP PEELED AND CHOPPED PUMPKIN
- 2 SCALLIONS, CHOPPED
- 1 TEASPOON CHOPPED THYME LEAVES
- ¼ CUP CHOPPED CILANTRO
- 1 CUP COCONUT MILK
- 1 CUP WATER
- 1 WHOLE SCOTCH BONNET PEPPER (OPTIONAL)
- SALT AND PEPPER, TO TASTE

EGGPLANT SOUP *with* EGGPLANT SCHNITZEL

YIELD: 4 SERVINGS / ACTIVE TIME: 30 MINUTES / TOTAL TIME: 1 HOUR AND 20 MINUTES

The crunchy texture of the Eggplant Schnitzel helps emphasize the creaminess of the soup. Be sure to salt the eggplant before frying, as it tempers the naturally bitter flavor.

1. Place the oil, shallots, and garlic in a large saucepan and cook until the shallots are soft, about 5 minutes.

2. Add the eggplant and cook, stirring occasionally, until it starts to break down, about 10 minutes. Add the stock, bring to a simmer, and cook for 10 minutes.

3. Transfer the soup to a food processor, puree until smooth, and strain through a fine sieve.

4. Place the soup in a clean pan, add the cream and parsley, and bring to a simmer over medium-low heat.

5. Season with salt and pepper and ladle into warmed bowls. Serve with the Gremolata and Eggplant Schnitzel and garnish with the mozzarella pearls.

GREMOLATA

1. Place all of the ingredients in a small bowl, stir to combine, and set aside until ready to serve.

EGGPLANT SCHNITZEL

1. Place the eggplant on a plate. Lightly salt on both sides and let stand for 30 minutes.

2. Place the flour and bread crumbs on two separate plates. Dredge the eggplant in the flour so that both sides are coated.

3. Dip the floured eggplant into the beaten eggs until coated. Gently remove the eggplant and roll it in the bread crumbs until evenly coated.

4. Add oil to a large sauté pan until it is about ¼ inch deep and warm over medium heat. Working in batches, add the breaded eggplant and fry until golden brown, about 5 minutes. Remove and set on a paper towel–lined plate to drain and cool slightly before serving.

INGREDIENTS:

1   TABLESPOON OLIVE OIL

2   SHALLOTS, MINCED

1   GARLIC CLOVE, MINCED

1   EGGPLANT, PEELED AND CHOPPED

4   CUPS CHICKEN STOCK (SEE PAGE 748 FOR HOMEMADE)

½   CUP HEAVY CREAM

2   TABLESPOONS CHOPPED FRESH PARSLEY

     SALT AND PEPPER, TO TASTE

     GREMOLATA (SEE RECIPE), FOR SERVING

     EGGPLANT SCHNITZEL (SEE RECIPE), FOR SERVING

     MOZZARELLA CHEESE PEARLS, FOR GARNISH

GREMOLATA

2   GARLIC CLOVES, MINCED

     ZEST OF 2 LEMONS

1   TABLESPOON CHOPPED FRESH PARSLEY

EGGPLANT SCHNITZEL

4   SLICES EGGPLANT, ¼-INCH THICK

     SALT, TO TASTE

⅓   CUP ALL-PURPOSE FLOUR

⅔   CUP BREAD CRUMBS

2   EGGS, BEATEN

¼   CUP VEGETABLE OIL, PLUS MORE AS NEEDED

BOUILLABAISSE

YIELD: 8 SERVINGS / ACTIVE TIME: 30 MINUTES / TOTAL TIME: 45 MINUTES

There are as many versions of this famous French stew as there are of American chili, but the basic template is a fish stock laced with saffron and loaded with seafood and vegetables. Usually it is topped with a large, buttered crouton that may also have aioli or a garlicky rouille on top. It is robust, luscious, and complex. While fennel is often meant to be a contributing player in soups, it is front and center here, augmented by Pernod, a liqueur that tastes of licorice.

1. Place the oil in a large stockpot and warm over medium heat. Add the leek, onion, and garlic and cook until the onion is translucent, about 3 minutes. Add the carrot and fennel and cook until the vegetables have softened, about 5 minutes.

2. Add the stock, thyme, tarragon, and Pernod and bring to a gentle boil. Reduce heat so that the soup simmers and cook until the vegetables are just tender, about 10 minutes.

3. Add the tomatoes and cook another 5 minutes.

4. Remove a ladleful of liquid from the soup and add the saffron to it, crushing it with your fingers a little before putting in. Add the orange zest and then add the saffron infusion back in to the soup. Turn off heat and let sit.

5. Approximately 10 minutes before serving, butter the baguette slices and toast them under the broiler for a few minutes until browned. Set aside.

6. Bring the soup to a simmer and season with salt and pepper. Add the monkfish, bass, and red snapper and poach until cooked through, 2 to 3 minutes. Add the shrimp and cook for another 2 minutes. Ladle the soup into warmed soup bowls, making sure to equally distribute the fish in each. Top each portion with a slice of the toasted baguette and serve the rest on the side.

INGREDIENTS:

- 1 TABLESPOON OLIVE OIL
- 1 LEEK, TRIMMED, RINSED WELL, AND SLICED
- 1 LARGE ONION, DICED
- 4 GARLIC CLOVES, DICED
- 1 CARROT, PEELED AND DICED
- 1 BULB FENNEL, SLICED THIN
- 12 CUPS FISH STOCK (SEE PAGE 752 FOR HOMEMADE)
- 1 TEASPOON CHOPPED THYME LEAVES
- 1 TEASPOON CHOPPED TARRAGON
- ¼ CUP PERNOD
- 1 (14 OZ.) CAN DICED TOMATOES
- 2 PINCHES OF SAFFRON
- 1 TEASPOON ORANGE ZEST
- 1 BAGUETTE, SLICED
-    UNSALTED BUTTER, AS NEEDED
-    SALT AND PEPPER, TO TASTE
- 2 LBS. MONKFISH
- 4 LBS. BASS
- 4 LBS. RED SNAPPER
- 1 LB. SHRIMP, SHELLED AND DEVEINED

MEXICAN SWEET ROASTED GARLIC SOUP

YIELD: 4 SERVINGS / ACTIVE TIME: 20 MINUTES / TOTAL TIME: 1 HOUR

This soup, when poured tableside, will really blow your guests away.

1. Place the stock and Confit Garlic in a medium saucepan and simmer for 20 minutes.

2. Transfer to a food processor or blender, puree until smooth, and strain through a fine sieve.

3. Place in a clean pan, bring to a simmer, and season with salt and pepper.

4. Remove from heat and whisk in the eggs.

5. Pour the soup into bowls tableside and serve with the Garlic Croutons, Garlic-Roasted Scallions, avocado, queso fresco or feta, tomato, chipotles, and cilantro leaves.

INGREDIENTS:

5 CUPS CHICKEN STOCK (SEE PAGE 748 FOR HOMEMADE)

CONFIT GARLIC (SEE RECIPE)

SALT AND PEPPER, TO TASTE

2 EGGS, LIGHTLY BEATEN

GARLIC CROUTONS (SEE RECIPE), FOR SERVING

GARLIC-ROASTED SCALLIONS (SEE RECIPE), FOR SERVING

FLESH FROM 1 AVOCADO, CHOPPED, FOR SERVING

3 OZ. QUESO FRESCO OR FETA CHEESE, FOR SERVING

1 LARGE TOMATO, CONCASSE (SEE PAGE 808), FOR SERVING

4 CHIPOTLES IN ADOBO, SEEDED AND SLICED THIN, FOR SERVING

CILANTRO LEAVES, FOR SERVING

Continued . . .

CONFIT GARLIC

1. Place the oil in a small saucepan and warm over medium heat. Reduce heat to lowest setting, add the garlic, and cook, stirring frequently, until soft and golden brown, about 15 minutes.

2. Strain and set the garlic aside. Reserve the oil.

GARLIC CROUTONS

1. Place the oil in a small sauté pan and warm over medium heat.

2. Add the bread cubes and cook, stirring frequently, until browned on all sides, about 7 minutes.

3. Season with salt and pepper and transfer to a paper towel to drain and cool slightly.

GARLIC-ROASTED SCALLIONS

1. Preheat oven to 350°F.

2. Place the scallions on a baking sheet, drizzle the reserved oil over them, and season with salt and pepper.

3. Place in the oven and roast for 8 minutes, or until the scallions are soft and lightly colored. Remove and let cool slightly before serving.

INGREDIENTS:

CONFIT GARLIC

½ CUP OLIVE OIL

1 HEAD GARLIC, CLOVES REMOVED AND MINCED

GARLIC CROUTONS

3 TABLESPOONS OIL RESERVED FROM CONFIT GARLIC

4 SLICES BREAD, CRUSTS REMOVED, CUT INTO CUBES

SALT AND PEPPER, TO TASTE

GARLIC-ROASTED SCALLIONS

4 SCALLIONS, TRIMMED

3 TEASPOONS OIL RESERVED FROM CONFIT GARLIC

SALT AND PEPPER, TO TASTE

LEEK & FISH SOUP

YIELD: 4 TO 6 SERVINGS / ACTIVE TIME: 30 MINUTES / TOTAL TIME: 1 HOUR

A soup so filling, it's nearly a stew. This is a perfect example of *fruits de mer*.

1. Place the oil in a medium saucepan and warm over medium heat. Add the leeks, crushed coriander seeds, and red pepper flakes and cook until the leeks start to soften, about 5 minutes.

2. Add the potatoes, tomatoes, stock, wine, bay leaves, star anise, orange zest, and saffron and bring to a boil. Reduce heat so that the soup simmers and cook until the potatoes are tender, about 15 minutes.

3. Taste and adjust the seasoning as needed. Add the cod and the squid to the soup and cook until cooked through, 3 to 4 minutes. Add the shrimp and cook for 2 minutes. Season with salt and pepper.

4. Ladle into warmed bowls and serve with the Garlic Mayonnaise and Parsley Grilled Baguette.

INGREDIENTS:

2 TABLESPOONS OLIVE OIL

   WHITES FROM 2 LEEKS, TRIMMED, RINSED WELL, AND SLICED THIN

2 TEASPOONS CORIANDER SEEDS, CRUSHED

   PINCH OF RED PEPPER FLAKES

3 CUPS MULTI-COLORED LITTLE CREAMER POTATOES, CUT INTO ¼-INCH SLICES

1 (14 OZ.) CAN DICED TOMATOES

4 CUPS FISH STOCK (SEE PAGE 752 FOR HOMEMADE)

1 CUP WHITE WINE

2 BAY LEAVES

1 STAR ANISE POD

   ZEST OF 1 ORANGE

   PINCH OF SAFFRON

1 LB. COD FILLETS, CUT INTO ½-INCH PIECES

1 LB. SMALL SQUID, BODIES HALVED AND SCORED, TENTACLES LEFT WHOLE

10 OZ. SHRIMP, SHELLED AND DEVEINED

   SALT AND PEPPER, TO TASTE

   GARLIC MAYONNAISE (SEE RECIPE), FOR SERVING

   PARSLEY GRILLED BAGUETTE (SEE RECIPE), FOR SERVING

Continued . . .

GARLIC MAYONNAISE

1. Place the egg yolk, garlic, vinegar, water, and mustard powder in a stainless steel bowl and whisk until foamy.

2. Gradually add the oils in a thin stream, whisking constantly, until the oils have been incorporated and the mayonnaise is thick.

3. Add the lemon juice, season with salt and pepper, and refrigerate immediately.

PARSLEY GRILLED BAGUETTE

1. Place 2 tablespoons of the butter in a medium sauté pan and melt over medium heat.

2. Add 4 slices of the baguette, cook for 1 minute, flip, sprinkle half of the chopped parsley on top, and cook for another minute.

3. Flip the pieces of bread over and cook on the sides with the parsley for 30 seconds.

4. Repeat with the remaining 4 slices of baguette, adding butter as needed.

INGREDIENTS:

GARLIC MAYONNAISE

1	EGG YOLK
4	GARLIC CLOVES, MASHED
1	TABLESPOON WHITE VINEGAR
1	TABLESPOON WATER
½	TEASPOON MUSTARD POWDER
1	CUP VEGETABLE OIL
½	CUP OLIVE OIL
1	TEASPOON FRESH LEMON JUICE
	SALT AND PEPPER, TO TASTE

PARSLEY GRILLED BAGUETTE

4	TABLESPOONS UNSALTED BUTTER
8	SLICES BAGUETTE
1	TABLESPOON CHOPPED FRESH PARSLEY

SWEET & SOUR EGG DROP SOUP
with BLACK RICE NOODLES, MUSHROOMS & TOFU

YIELD: 6 SERVINGS / ACTIVE TIME: 30 MINUTES / TOTAL TIME: 45 MINUTES

This soup brings together big flavors like chili oil, ginger, and vinegar. The mushrooms and tofu provide the perfect counterpoints to soak up the spice and heat. Something to keep in mind if you're looking for a dinner that you can make ahead of time: this soup is even more delicious the following day.

1. Drain the tofu and cut it into ½-inch cubes. Arrange in a single layer on a paper towel–lined baking sheet. Cover with paper towels and pat dry. Let sit for 30 minutes, changing the paper towels after 15 minutes.

2. While the tofu drains, bring a large pot of water to a boil and add the noodles. Cook until tender but still chewy, about 5 minutes. Drain and rinse under cold water. Drain again, transfer to a medium bowl, and toss with ½ tablespoon of the sesame oil to prevent sticking.

3. Warm a large skillet over low heat for 2 to 3 minutes. Add 1 tablespoon of the sesame oil and raise heat to medium. When the oil begins to shimmer, add the garlic, ginger, thinly sliced scallions, and a pinch of salt and cook, stirring occasionally, until the vegetables start to soften, about 5 minutes. Add the pork and cook, breaking it up with a wooden spoon, until it is cooked through, 8 to 10 minutes. Add the stock and bring to a gentle boil. Add the tofu, mushrooms, vinegar, soy sauce, sugar, the remaining sesame oil, and the chili oil (if using) and return to a gentle boil. Reduce heat so that the soup simmers, taste, and season with salt, sugar, or vinegar if necessary.

4. Place the eggs in a small bowl and whisk until scrambled. Slowly whisk them into the soup and bring it back to a simmer.

5. Divide the noodles between six warmed bowls and ladle the soup over them. Garnish with the chopped scallions and toasted sesame seeds and serve immediately.

INGREDIENTS:

- 1 LB. EXTRA-FIRM TOFU
- 10 OZ. BLACK RICE RAMEN NOODLES
- 2½ TABLESPOONS TOASTED SESAME OIL
- 3 GARLIC CLOVES, MINCED
- 2-INCH PIECE GINGER, PEELED AND MINCED
- 9 SCALLIONS, TRIMMED, 6 SLICED THIN, 3 CHOPPED AND RESERVED FOR GARNISH
- SALT, TO TASTE
- ½ LB. GROUND PORK
- 8 CUPS CHICKEN STOCK (SEE PAGE 748 FOR HOMEMADE)
- 8 CREMINI MUSHROOMS, SLICED
- ¼ CUP RICE OR APPLE CIDER VINEGAR, PLUS MORE TO TASTE
- 3 TABLESPOONS SOY SAUCE
- 2 TEASPOONS SUGAR, PLUS MORE TO TASTE
- 1 TABLESPOON CHILI OIL (OPTIONAL)
- 2 LARGE EGGS
- TOASTED SESAME SEEDS, FOR GARNISH

CREAM OF MUSHROOM SOUP

YIELD: 4 SERVINGS / ACTIVE TIME: 20 MINUTES / TOTAL TIME: 45 MINUTES

This soup is quick, but rich. I prefer the texture of fusilli for this preparation, but feel free to use your favorite pasta, or whatever's in the cupboard.

1. Place the butter in a medium saucepan and melt over medium heat. Add the onion and garlic and cook until the onion has softened, about 5 minutes.

2. Add the Madeira and cook until it evaporates. Add the mushrooms and cook until all of their liquid has been released.

3. Add the stock and bring to a boil. Reduce heat so that the soup simmers and cook for 10 minutes.

4. Transfer the soup to a food processor or blender, puree until smooth and creamy, and then strain through a fine sieve.

5. Place the soup in a clean pan and bring to a simmer. Add the fusili and cook until it is tender.

6. Add the cream and simmer for 2 minutes. Season with salt and pepper, ladle into warmed bowls, and garnish with parsley.

INGREDIENTS:

4	TABLESPOONS UNSALTED BUTTER
1	ONION, CHOPPED
2	GARLIC CLOVES, CHOPPED
⅓	CUP MADEIRA
¾	LB. WILD MUSHROOMS
4	CUPS MUSHROOM STOCK (SEE PAGE 756 FOR HOMEMADE)
1½	CUPS FUSILLI PASTA
1	CUP HEAVY CREAM
	SALT AND PEPPER, TO TASTE
	PARSLEY, CHOPPED, FOR GARNISH

TRUFFLED MUSHROOM CONSOMMÉ

YIELD: 4 SERVINGS / ACTIVE TIME: 25 MINUTES / TOTAL TIME: 1 HOUR AND 15 MINUTES

If you are looking for a little more flavor out of the Duxelles, try adding a dash of Sherry or Madeira.

1. Place all of the ingredients, except for the salt and pepper and garnishes, in a large stockpot, stir to combine, and slowly bring the soup to a simmer. Cook for 45 minutes, with the egg whites creating a raft that will clarify the stock.

2. Ladle the stock through cheesecloth, place in a clean pan, and bring to a boil. Season with salt and pepper, ladle into warmed bowls, and garnish with the Duxelles, parsley, truffle oil, and truffle paste.

DUXELLES

1. Place the butter in a medium saucepan and melt over medium heat. Add the shallot and garlic and cook until they start to soften, about 5 minutes.

2. Add the mushrooms and a pinch of salt and cook until the mushrooms start to release their liquid, about 5 minutes.

3. Cook until all the liquid has evaporated. Season with salt and pepper, fold in the chopped parsley, and serve immediately.

INGREDIENTS:

- 2 CARROTS, PEELED AND CHOPPED
- 1 ONION, CHOPPED
- 2 CELERY STALKS, CHOPPED
- ½ LB. LEAN GROUND CHICKEN
- ¾ CUP CHOPPED TOMATOES
- 6 CUPS MUSHROOM STOCK (SEE PAGE 756 FOR HOMEMADE)
- 1 SACHET D'ÉPICES, 1 CLOVE AND 1 ALLSPICE BERRY ADDED (SEE PAGE 809)
- 5 EGG WHITES, BEATEN

  SALT AND PEPPER, TO TASTE

  DUXELLES (SEE RECIPE), FOR GARNISH

  PARSLEY, FOR GARNISH

  TRUFFLE OIL, FOR GARNISH

  TRUFFLE PASTE, FOR GARNISH

DUXELLES

- 1 TABLESPOON UNSALTED BUTTER
- 1 SHALLOT, MINCED
- ½ GARLIC CLOVE, MINCED
- 1 CUP ASSORTED MUSHROOMS, TRIMMED AND MINCED

  SALT AND PEPPER, TO TASTE
- 1 TEASPOON CHOPPED FRESH PARSLEY

FOREST MUSHROOM SOUP
with TRUFFLED MADEIRA CREAM

YIELD: 4 SERVINGS / ACTIVE TIME: 20 MINUTES / TOTAL TIME: 1 HOUR AND 15 MINUTES

This is one of my all-time favorite soups. The secret is to cook as much moisture as possible out of the mushrooms, which really concentrates the flavor.

1. Add the butter, onion, and garlic to a medium saucepan and cook until soft, about 5 minutes.

2. Add the Madeira and cook until it evaporates. Add the mushrooms and cook until they have released all of their liquid.

3. Add the stock and bring to a boil. Reduce heat so that the soup simmers and cook for 10 minutes.

4. Transfer the soup to a food processor or blender, puree until smooth and creamy, and strain through a fine sieve.

5. Place the soup in a clean pan, add the cream and Worcestershire sauce, and season with salt and pepper. Bring to a simmer over medium-low heat.

6. Ladle into warmed bowls and garnish with the sautéed mushrooms, a dollop of Truffled Madeira Cream, and parsley.

TRUFFLED MADEIRA CREAM

1. Place the Madeira in a small saucepan and simmer over medium heat until it has reduced to a syrup, about 15 minutes. Remove from heat and let cool.

2. Place the cream in a bowl and whip until soft peaks begin to form.

3. Add the Madeira reduction and whip until stiff peaks form.

4. Add the parsley and truffle paste and fold to combine. Season with salt and pepper and refrigerate until ready to use.

INGREDIENTS:

4   TABLESPOONS UNSALTED BUTTER

1   ONION, CHOPPED

2   GARLIC CLOVES, CHOPPED

⅓   CUP MADEIRA

½   LB. WILD MUSHROOMS

5   OZ. PORTOBELLO MUSHROOMS

4   CUPS MUSHROOM STOCK (SEE PAGE 756 FOR HOMEMADE)

1   CUP HEAVY CREAM

1   TABLESPOON WORCESTERSHIRE SAUCE

   SALT AND PEPPER, TO TASTE

   SAUTÉED MUSHROOMS, FOR GARNISH

   TRUFFLED MADEIRA CREAM (SEE RECIPE), FOR GARNISH

   PARSLEY, CHOPPED, FOR GARNISH

TRUFFLED MADEIRA CREAM

1   CUP MADEIRA

½   CUP HEAVY CREAM

1   TEASPOON CHOPPED FRESH PARSLEY

1   TABLESPOON TRUFFLE PASTE

   SALT AND PEPPER, TO TASTE

CARAMELIZED ONION SOUP
with BAKED HERB CROUTONS

YIELD: 4 SERVINGS / ACTIVE TIME: 30 MINUTES / TOTAL TIME: 1 HOUR

Is there anything better than onion soup on a cold winter day?

1. Place the butter in a medium saucepan and melt over low heat. Add the onions and cook over the lowest possible heat until caramelized, about 30 minutes. Stir the onions every few minutes and add small amounts of water when they begin to stick to the pan.

2. Add the garlic, thyme, Riesling, and Madeira and cook until the liquid has reduced by half. Add the cream and simmer for 10 minutes.

3. Transfer the soup to a food processor or blender and puree until smooth. Season with salt and pepper and serve with the Baked Herb Croutons.

BAKED HERB CROUTONS

1. Preheat the oven to 350°F.

2. Place the herbs and oil in a small bowl and stir to combine. Place the slices of baguette on a baking sheet and drizzle the herb-infused oil over them.

3. Season with salt and pepper, place in the oven, and bake for 10 minutes, or until golden brown.

INGREDIENTS:

- 4 TABLESPOONS UNSALTED BUTTER
- 6 SPANISH ONIONS, CHOPPED
- WATER, AS NEEDED
- 2 GARLIC CLOVES, MINCED
- LEAVES FROM 1 SPRIG THYME, CHOPPED
- ½ CUP RIESLING
- ½ CUP MADEIRA
- 4 CUPS HEAVY CREAM
- SALT AND PEPPER, TO TASTE
- BAKED HERB CROUTONS (SEE RECIPE), FOR SERVING

BAKED HERB CROUTONS

- 1 TABLESPOON CHOPPED PARSLEY
- 1 TABLESPOON CHOPPED TARRAGON
- 1 TABLESPOON CHOPPED FRESH CHIVES
- ¼ CUP OLIVE OIL
- 8 SLICES BAGUETTE
- SALT AND PEPPER, TO TASTE

CARAMELIZED ONIONS

If you have a few onions on hand, you have the potential for a great topper for so many dishes. Caramelized onions can elevate burgers, pork chops, grilled mushrooms, cheese, eggs—the list is endless, and all you need are onions and time. Keep in mind, the volume will decrease substantially after cooking, so start with a big pile. For reference, 4 cups of sliced yellow onions produces less than 1 cup of caramelized onions.

Another important factor is to keep your flame low. A high flame will burn the outside of the onion before it has a chance to brown and cook the interior. Burning even a few of them will impart a bitter flavor to the entire batch. It can take up to 30 minutes until they are all fully browned and limp. Have patience and leave it low and slow.

Lastly, once you have the onions perfectly caramelized, you can take them in many different directions by deglazing with a little liquid of your choice. Try a few tablespoons of orange juice and fresh chopped rosemary, or a teaspoon of maple syrup and a teaspoon of apple cider.

---

1. Warm the oil over medium-low heat in a large sauté pan. Once the oil is shimmering, add the onions and stir to coat. Reduce heat to low and let the onions brown before stirring again. Continue to cook the onions, checking on them every few minutes to make sure they are not burning and adding more oil if the pan becomes too dry.

2. When all of the onions are brown and limp, pour a few tablespoons of water in the pan to deglaze the bottom and retrieve all of the flavor that has accumulated there. You can also add the vinegar and thyme if you so choose.

3. Season with salt and pepper and serve.

INGREDIENTS:

- 3 TABLESPOONS OLIVE OIL, PLUS MORE AS NEEDED
- 2 LARGE ONIONS (RED OR YELLOW), SLICED
- WATER, AS NEEDED
- 1 TEASPOON BALSAMIC VINEGAR (OPTIONAL)
- ½ TEASPOON CHOPPED FRESH THYME LEAVES (OPTIONAL)
- SALT AND PEPPER, TO TASTE

PARSNIP & PEAR SOUP

YIELD: 4 TO 6 SERVINGS / **ACTIVE TIME:** 30 MINUTES / **TOTAL TIME:** 1 HOUR AND 15 MINUTES

In this soup, a sweet base is countered by wine-poached pears and tangy blue cheese. A perfect soup for a fall evening.

1. Place the butter in a medium saucepan and melt over medium heat. Add the parsnips, onion, pears, garlic, and thyme and cook, stirring frequently, until soft, about 10 minutes.

2. Add the white wine and cook until it has evaporated, about 10 minutes. Add the stock and simmer until the parsnip is tender, about 30 minutes.

3. Transfer the soup to a food processor or blender, puree until smooth, and strain through a fine sieve.

4. Taste and adjust the seasoning as needed. Ladle into warmed bowls, serve with the Poached Pears, and garnish with the blue cheese crumbles.

POACHED PEARS

1. Place all of the ingredients, except for the pear, in a medium saucepan and bring to a boil. Turn off heat and let stand.

2. Add the pear and return to a boil.

3. Remove from heat and let the pear cool in the mixture. For the best results, let the pear steep in the mixture in the refrigerator overnight. Remove the pear with a slotted spoon and serve with the soup.

INGREDIENTS:

2   TABLESPOONS UNSALTED BUTTER

4   CUPS PEELED AND DICED PARSNIPS

1   ONION, CHOPPED

1   CUP PEELED AND DICED PEARS

1   GARLIC CLOVE, MINCED

    LEAVES FROM 1 SPRIG THYME, CHOPPED

½   CUP WHITE WINE

8   CUPS CHICKEN STOCK (SEE PAGE 748 FOR HOMEMADE)

    POACHED PEARS (SEE RECIPE), FOR SERVING

    BLUE CHEESE CRUMBLES, FOR GARNISH

POACHED PEARS

1   CUP RED WINE

¼   CUP SUGAR

1   TEASPOON FRESH LEMON JUICE

1   CINNAMON STICK

1   STAR ANISE POD

1   PEAR, PEELED AND DICED

PORTOBELLO MUSHROOM RAVIOLI *in* BEET SOUP

YIELD: 4 SERVINGS / ACTIVE TIME: 1 HOUR / TOTAL TIME: 1 HOUR AND 30 MINUTES

A beautifully light and elegant meal to serve your guests. Once you get some practice with making ravioli, try making some into heart shapes to serve on Valentine's Day—they'll look great in the beet soup.

1. To begin preparations for the ravioli, combine the flour and salt on a clean work surface and make a well in the center. Place the egg yolks and the oil in the well and slowly incorporate the flour until the dough holds together. Knead the dough until smooth, about 5 minutes. Cover the dough in plastic wrap and let stand at room temperature for 30 minutes.

2. Place the butter in a medium saucepan and melt over medium heat. Add the mushrooms and cook until they start to release their liquid, about 5 minutes. Add the shallot, garlic, and thyme and cook until the shallot starts to soften, about 5 minutes. Remove the pan from the stove and strain to remove any excess liquid. Let the mixture cool. Once it is cool, place in a small bowl and add the mascarpone. Stir to combine, season with salt and pepper, and set the filling aside.

3. To begin forming the ravioli, separate the pasta dough into two pieces. Use a pasta maker to roll each piece into a long, thin rectangle. Place one of the rectangles over a floured ravioli tray and place a teaspoon of the filling into the depressions. Combine the beaten egg and water in a small bowl. Dip a pastry brush or a finger into it and run lightly over the edge of each ravioli.

4. Gently lay the other rectangle over the piece in the ravioli tray. Use a rolling pin to gently cut out the ravioli. Remove the cut ravioli and place them on a flour-dusted baking sheet.

5. To begin preparations for the soup, place the oil in a large saucepan and warm over medium heat. Add the onion, garlic, and fennel seeds and cook until the onion is soft, about 5 minutes. Add the beet and cook for 5 minutes. Add the stock and orange juice, bring to a boil, then reduce heat so that the soup simmers and cook until the beet is tender, about 15 minutes.

6. Season with salt and pepper and return to a boil. Once boiling, drop the ravioli into the pan and cook for 3 minutes. Ladle the soup into shallow bowls and garnish with fennel fronds.

INGREDIENTS:

FOR THE RAVIOLI

1 CUP "00" FLOUR, PLUS MORE FOR DUSTING

PINCH OF KOSHER SALT, PLUS MORE TO TASTE

1 CUP BEATEN EGG YOLKS

1 TEASPOON OLIVE OIL

1 TABLESPOON UNSALTED BUTTER

2 CUPS CHOPPED PORTOBELLO MUSHROOMS

1 SHALLOT, MINCED

1 GARLIC CLOVE, MINCED

LEAVES FROM 1 SPRIG THYME, CHOPPED

2 TABLESPOONS MASCARPONE CHEESE

BLACK PEPPER, TO TASTE

1 EGG, BEATEN

1 TABLESPOON WATER

FOR THE SOUP

1 TABLESPOON OLIVE OIL

1 ONION, CHOPPED

2 GARLIC CLOVES, MINCED

1 TEASPOON FENNEL SEEDS

1 LARGE BEET, PEELED AND MINCED

6 CUPS CHICKEN STOCK (SEE PAGE 748 FOR HOMEMADE)

¼ CUP ORANGE JUICE

SALT AND PEPPER, TO TASTE

FENNEL FRONDS, FOR GARNISH

PARSNIP SOUP
with BUTTERNUT SQUASH CROUTONS

YIELD: 6 SERVINGS / ACTIVE TIME: 30 MINUTES / TOTAL TIME: 2 HOURS

Making the Butternut Squash Bread for this soup may seem like extra work, but the result is worth the added effort.

1. Place the butter in a large saucepan and melt over medium heat. Add the parsnips, carrot, onion, and celery and cook for 5 minutes, or until soft, stirring often.

2. Add the stock and bay leaf, bring to a boil, and then reduce heat so that the soup simmers. Simmer until the vegetables are tender, about 20 minutes.

3. Remove the bay leaf and transfer the soup to a food processor or blender. Puree until smooth and strain through a fine sieve.

4. Return soup to the pan and add the cream, salt, pepper, and nutmeg. Bring it back to a simmer.

5. When everything is warmed through, ladle into warmed bowls and top with the Butternut Squash Croutons.

INGREDIENTS:

- 2 TABLESPOONS UNSALTED BUTTER
- 6 CUPS PEELED AND CHOPPED PARSNIPS
- 1 CARROT, PEELED AND CHOPPED
- ½ ONION, CHOPPED
- 1 CELERY STALK, CHOPPED
- 8 CUPS VEGETABLE STOCK (SEE PAGE 755 FOR HOMEMADE)
- 1 BAY LEAF
- 2 CUPS HEAVY CREAM

  SALT AND PEPPER, TO TASTE

  GRATED NUTMEG, TO TASTE

  BUTTERNUT SQUASH CROUTONS (SEE RECIPE), FOR SERVING

Continued . . .

BUTTERNUT SQUASH BREAD

1. Preheat oven to 350°F and line a 9 × 5-inch loaf pan with parchment paper.

2. Place the flour, baking powder, baking soda, salt, and cinnamon in a mixing bowl and stir to combine. Set aside.

3. Place the butter in the bowl of a stand mixer fitted with the paddle attachment and beat until creamy. Add the sugars and beat until fluffy.

4. Add the eggs one at a time and beat until smooth. Add the butternut squash and beat until incorporated.

5. Add the dry mixture and beat on low until everything is just combined. Be careful not to overmix.

6. Pour the batter into the loaf pan, place the pan in the oven, and bake for 50 minutes, or until a toothpick inserted into the bread comes out clean.

7. Remove from the oven, leave the bread in the pan, and let cool on a wire rack for 10 minutes. Remove bread from loaf pan and let it cool completely.

BUTTERNUT SQUASH CROUTONS

1. Preheat the oven to 350°F.

2. Place the bread cubes on a baking sheet, sprinkle the rosemary over the top, and drizzle with the oil.

3. Place in the oven and bake for 5 minutes. Remove, gently turn over, and bake for an additional 5 minutes, or until golden brown. Remove, let cool, and serve.

INGREDIENTS:

BUTTERNUT SQUASH BREAD

1½ CUPS ALL-PURPOSE FLOUR

1 TEASPOON BAKING POWDER

¼ TEASPOON BAKING SODA

¼ TEASPOON KOSHER SALT

¼ TEASPOON CINNAMON

1 STICK UNSALTED BUTTER, AT ROOM TEMPERATURE

½ CUP GRANULATED SUGAR

½ CUP FIRMLY PACKED LIGHT BROWN SUGAR

2 LARGE EGGS

1 CUP COOKED AND MASHED BUTTERNUT SQUASH, AT ROOM TEMPERATURE

BUTTERNUT SQUASH CROUTONS

1 CUP BUTTERNUT SQUASH BREAD CUBES

1 TABLESPOON FRESH ROSEMARY LEAVES, CHOPPED

1 TABLESPOON OLIVE OIL

CREAMED PARSNIP SOUP
with ARUGULA PESTO

YIELD: 4 SERVINGS / ACTIVE TIME: 15 MINUTES / TOTAL TIME: 50 MINUTES

Grating the parsnips speeds up the cooking time dramatically. If they're going to be sitting around for a bit, leave them in cold water with a splash of lemon juice so that they don't oxidize.

1. Place the butter in a medium saucepan and melt over medium heat. Add the onion, garlic, and thyme and cook until the onion is soft, about 5 minutes.

2. Add the parsnips and cook for 5 minutes. Add the stock, bring to a boil, and then reduce heat so that the soup simmers. Cook until the parsnips are tender, about 10 minutes.

3. Remove the pan from heat and the soup transfer to a food processor or a blender. Puree the soup until it is smooth and then strain through a fine sieve.

4. Place the soup in a clean pan, bring to a simmer, and add the cream. Simmer for 5 minutes.

5. Season with salt and pepper, ladle into warmed bowls, garnish with the parsley, and serve with Arugula Pesto.

INGREDIENTS:

2 TABLESPOONS UNSALTED BUTTER

1 ONION, CHOPPED

1 GARLIC CLOVE, MINCED

LEAVES FROM 2 SPRIGS THYME, CHOPPED

5 PARSNIPS, PEELED AND GRATED

6 CUPS VEGETABLE STOCK (SEE PAGE 755 FOR HOMEMADE)

2 CUPS HEAVY CREAM

SALT AND PEPPER, TO TASTE

PARSLEY, CHOPPED, FOR GARNISH

ARUGULA PESTO (SEE PAGE 184), FOR SERVING

PARSNIP & BARLEY SOUP

YIELD: 6 SERVINGS / ACTIVE TIME: 20 MINUTES / TOTAL TIME: 45 MINUTES

The barley contributes a lovely texture to this creamy soup.

1. Place the butter in a medium saucepan and melt over medium heat. Add the onion, leek, and parsnips and cook until they start to soften, about 5 minutes.

2. Add the bay leaf and potato and cook for 5 minutes. Add the stock, cinnamon stick, and barley and bring to a boil. Reduce heat so that the soup simmers and cook until the barley is tender, about 20 minutes.

3. Remove the bay leaf and cinnamon stick and transfer the soup to a food processor or blender. Puree until smooth and creamy and strain through a fine sieve.

4. Return the soup to the pan and bring to a simmer. Add the cream and season with salt and pepper. When everything is warmed through, ladle into warmed bowls and garnish with the celery hearts and nutmeg.

INGREDIENTS:

4   TABLESPOONS UNSALTED BUTTER

1   SMALL ONION, CHOPPED

½   LEEK, WHITE PART ONLY, CUT INTO ¾-INCH PIECES

6   PARSNIPS, PEELED AND CHOPPED

1   BAY LEAF

1   POTATO, PEELED AND CHOPPED

6   CUPS CHICKEN STOCK (SEE PAGE 748 FOR HOMEMADE)

1   CINNAMON STICK

½   CUP BARLEY

½   CUP HEAVY CREAM

SALT AND PEPPER, TO TASTE

CELERY HEARTS, FOR GARNISH

FRESH NUTMEG, GRATED, FOR GARNISH

PEA SOUP *with* PASTA & RICOTTA SALATA

YIELD: 4 SERVINGS / ACTIVE TIME: 25 MINUTES / TOTAL TIME: 45 MINUTES

A rustic and warming soup topped with ricotta salata, a medium-firm cheese that has just a little bit of tang. Since the ingredients are very simple, make sure they are of the best quality, including a flavorful stock and fully ripe tomatoes.

1. Warm a Dutch oven over medium-low heat for 2 to 3 minutes. Add the oil and raise heat to medium-high. When the oil begins to shimmer, add the onion and a couple pinches of salt and stir to combine well. When the onion begins to sizzle, reduce heat to low, cover the pot, and cook, stirring occasionally, until the onion becomes very soft, about 15 minutes.

2. Add the peas and a couple pinches of salt, raise heat to medium-high, and cook, stirring frequently, for about 3 minutes. Add the tomatoes and any juices that have accumulated in the bowl, the sugar, and the stock, and bring to a boil. Taste and season with salt and pepper as needed. Add the pasta and cook until the pasta is tender but pleasantly chewy, 6 to 8 minutes.

3. Ladle the soup into four warmed bowls and sprinkle the cheese and basil on top.

INGREDIENTS:

- 3 **TABLESPOONS OLIVE OIL**
- 1 **LARGE YELLOW ONION, CHOPPED**
- **SALT AND BLACK PEPPER, TO TASTE**
- 3 **CUPS FRESH PEAS**
- 8 **VERY RIPE PLUM TOMATOES, CONCASSE (SEE PAGE 808)**
- ¼ **TEASPOON SUGAR**
- 4 **CUPS CHICKEN OR VEGETABLE STOCK (SEE PAGES 748 OR 755, RESPECTIVELY, FOR HOMEMADE)**
- 1½ **CUPS SHORT PASTA OF CHOICE**
- ½ **CUP CRUMBLED RICOTTA SALATA OR FETA CHEESE, FOR GARNISH**
- **FRESH BASIL LEAVES, SLICED THIN, FOR GARNISH**

SPRING PEA SOUP *with* LEMON RICOTTA

YIELD: 4 SERVINGS / ACTIVE TIME: 15 MINUTES / TOTAL TIME: 25 MINUTES

Early in the spring, peas are absolutely perfect—tender enough that they don't require a long cook time and bursting with country-fresh flavor. Pair them with mint and creamy, zesty ricotta, and you've got a dish that positively sings.

1. Place the ricotta, cream, grated lemon zest, and the 2 teaspoons of salt in a food processor and puree until smooth. Taste, adjust the seasoning as needed, and set aside.

2. Place the water and remaining salt in a medium saucepan and bring to a boil over medium heat. Place the strips of lemon zest in the saucepan with the peas and shallots. Cook until the peas are just cooked through, 2 to 3 minutes. Drain, reserve 2 cups of the cooking liquid, and immediately transfer the peas, strips of lemon zest, and shallots to a blender. Add the mint leaves and half of the reserved cooking liquid and puree until the desired consistency is achieved, adding more cooking liquid as needed.

3. Season to taste, ladle into warmed bowls, and place a spoonful of the lemon ricotta in each bowl. Garnish with additional mint and serve immediately, as the soup's brilliant green color starts to fade as it cools.

INGREDIENTS:

1	CUP RICOTTA CHEESE
¼	CUP HEAVY CREAM
2	TABLESPOONS GRATED LEMON ZEST, PLUS 6 STRIPS
2	TABLESPOONS KOSHER SALT, PLUS 2 TEASPOONS
12	CUPS WATER
3	CUPS FRESH PEAS
3	SMALL SHALLOTS, DICED
6	MINT LEAVES, PLUS MORE FOR GARNISH

CHICKEN GOULASH

YIELD: 4 SERVINGS / ACTIVE TIME: 20 MINUTES / TOTAL TIME: 1 HOUR

What better way to show off peppers than a pepper stew with pepper seasoning? Goulash is a traditional Hungarian dish often made with beef, but chicken thighs also work. Use the highest quality paprika you can track down, as it is the main flavoring agent. I serve this over buttered noodles with a big dollop of sour cream on top.

1. Cut the chicken thighs into bite-sized chunks. Warm a Dutch oven over high heat. Place the chicken in the pot in one layer and add oil as needed. Reduce heat to medium-high and cook, stirring occasionally, until the chicken is browned all over, about 8 minutes.

2. Add the onion and garlic and cook until they start to soften, about 5 minutes. Add the peppers, flour, and paprika and stir to incorporate. Cook for 3 minutes and then add the stock, tomatoes, bay leaf, and salt. Stir gently to combine, reduce heat so that the goulash simmers, and cover the pot. Cook the goulash until the chicken is tender, 30 to 40 minutes. Stir the goulash occasionally and make sure there is enough liquid in the pot. If the liquid level looks low, add more stock.

3. Remove from heat, taste, and adjust the seasoning as needed. Serve over buttered noodles or rice and garnish each serving with some parsley and a dollop of sour cream.

INGREDIENTS:

1½ LBS. BONELESS, SKINLESS CHICKEN THIGHS

OLIVE OIL, AS NEEDED

1 ONION, DICED

2 GARLIC CLOVES, MINCED

1 LB. SWEET PEPPERS, STEMMED, SEEDED, AND DICED

1 TABLESPOON ALL-PURPOSE FLOUR

2 TABLESPOONS PAPRIKA

1 CUP CHICKEN STOCK (SEE PAGE 748 FOR HOMEMADE), PLUS MORE AS NEEDED

1 CUP DICED TOMATOES

1 BAY LEAF

1 TEASPOON KOSHER SALT

BUTTERED NOODLES OR RICE, FOR SERVING

1 BUNCH PARSLEY, CHOPPED, FOR GARNISH

SOUR CREAM, FOR GARNISH

APPLE & RUTABAGA SOUP *with* PORK BELLY

YIELD: 6 SERVINGS / ACTIVE TIME: 25 MINUTES / TOTAL TIME: 24 HOURS

This is a great soup for the fall, with the acidity and lightness balancing out the richness of the pork belly.

1. Place the butter in a large saucepan and melt over medium heat. Add the onion, apple, rutabaga, butternut squash, carrots, and sweet potato and cook until they start to soften, about 10 minutes.

2. Add the stock and bring to a boil. Reduce heat so that the soup simmers and cook until everything is cooked through and tender, about 20 minutes.

3. Transfer the soup to a food processor or blender, puree until smooth, and strain through a fine sieve.

4. Return the soup to the pan and bring to a simmer. Add the cream and season with salt and cayenne. Ladle into bowls, garnish with the rosemary, and serve with Roasted Pork Belly.

INGREDIENTS:

- 4 TABLESPOONS UNSALTED BUTTER
- 1 CUP CHOPPED ONION
- 1 CUP PEELED AND CHOPPED TART APPLE
- 1 CUP PEELED AND CHOPPED RUTABAGA
- 1 CUP PEELED AND CHOPPED BUTTERNUT SQUASH
- 1 CUP PEELED AND CHOPPED CARROTS
- 1 CUP PEELED AND CHOPPED SWEET POTATO
- 4 CUPS VEGETABLE STOCK (SEE PAGE 755 FOR HOMEMADE)
- 3 CUPS HEAVY CREAM
  SALT AND CAYENNE PEPPER, TO TASTE
  ROSEMARY LEAVES, CHOPPED, FOR GARNISH
  ROASTED PORK BELLY (SEE RECIPE), FOR SERVING

Continued . . .

ROASTED PORK BELLY

1. Place the pork belly fat-side up on the counter and score a crosshatch pattern across it with a sharp knife. The cut should be approximately ¼ inch deep (see diagram below). Set the pork belly aside.

2. Place the remaining ingredients in a medium saucepan, stir to combine, and bring to a boil. Remove from heat and let cool completely.

3. When cool, place the pork belly and the contents of the saucepan in a roasting pan. Place in refrigerator and marinate overnight.

4. Preheat oven to 450°F. Remove the roasting pan from the refrigerator and let it come to room temperature.

5. Rinse the marinated pork belly and set on a rack in a rimmed baking sheet, fat-side up.

6. Place in the oven and roast for 30 minutes. Lower the temperature to 275°F and roast until the pork belly is tender but not mushy, about 1 hour.

7. Remove from the oven, cut the pork belly into 6 pieces, and serve.

INGREDIENTS:

ROASTED PORK BELLY

1½	LBS. PORK BELLY
6	CUPS WATER
1	TEASPOON FENNEL SEEDS
2	STAR ANISE PODS
1	CINNAMON STICK
1	TEASPOON BLACK PEPPERCORNS
6	WHOLE CLOVES
1	BAY LEAF
¼	CUP KOSHER SALT

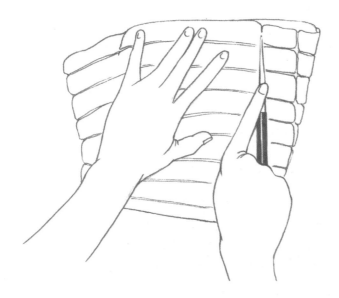

RUTABAGA & FIG SOUP
with HONEY-ROASTED FIGS
& BARBECUED CHICKPEAS

YIELD: 4 SERVINGS / ACTIVE TIME: 30 MINUTES / TOTAL TIME: 24 HOURS

Due to its slightly sour finish, I decided to add some honey-roasted figs to balance out this soup.

---

1. Place the oil in a medium saucepan and warm over medium heat. Add the onion and rutabaga and cook until they start to soften, about 10 minutes. Add the honey, stock, thyme, and figs and bring to a boil.

2. Reduce heat so that the soup simmers and cook until the rutabaga is tender, about 20 minutes.

3. Transfer the soup to a food processor or blender and puree until smooth. Place in a clean pan, add the buttermilk, and bring to a simmer.

4. Season with salt and pepper, ladle into warmed bowls, and serve with the Honey-Roasted Figs and Barbecued Chickpeas.

INGREDIENTS:

2   TABLESPOONS OLIVE OIL

1   ONION, CHOPPED

4   CUPS PEELED AND CHOPPED RUTABAGA

1   TABLESPOON HONEY

4   CUPS VEGETABLE STOCK (SEE PAGE 755 FOR HOMEMADE)

1   TEASPOON CHOPPED FRESH THYME

16 BLACK MISSION FIGS

1   CUP BUTTERMILK

    SALT AND PEPPER, TO TASTE

    HONEY-ROASTED FIGS (SEE RECIPE), FOR SERVING

    BARBECUED CHICKPEAS (SEE RECIPE), FOR SERVING

Continued . . .

HONEY-ROASTED FIGS

1. Place the honey in a nonstick sauté pan and warm over medium heat.

2. Place the figs in the pan, cut-side down, and cook until the flesh turns golden brown, about 5 minutes.

3. Sprinkle the cinnamon over the figs and gently stir to coat. Remove the figs from the pan and serve.

BARBECUED CHICKPEAS

1. Bring 4 cups of water to a boil in a saucepan. Add the chickpeas, reduce heat so that the water simmers, and cook until the chickpeas are tender, about 20 minutes. Drain the chickpeas and place on a paper towel to dry.

2. Place the oil in a Dutch oven and heat to 350°F.

3. Combine the remaining ingredients in a bowl, sift the mixture through a fine sieve, and set it aside.

4. Place the chickpeas in the hot oil and fry until golden brown, about 3 minutes. Remove and place in the bowl with the seasoning mixture. Toss to coat and serve.

INGREDIENTS:

HONEY-ROASTED FIGS

2   TABLESPOONS HONEY

4   BLACK MISSION FIGS, HALVED

    PINCH OF CINNAMON

BARBECUED CHICKPEAS

¼   CUP DRIED CHICKPEAS, SOAKED OVERNIGHT AND DRAINED

2   CUPS VEGETABLE OIL

1   TEASPOON SMOKED PAPRIKA

½   TEASPOON ONION POWDER

½   TEASPOON BROWN SUGAR

¼   TEASPOON GARLIC POWDER

¼   TEASPOON KOSHER SALT

    PINCH OF CHILI POWDER

VERMONT POTATO CHEDDAR SOUP

YIELD: 4 SERVINGS / ACTIVE TIME: 25 MINUTES / TOTAL TIME: 45 MINUTES

This soup is often called Canadian Cheddar Soup but being from the land of Cabot (home of the "World's Best Cheddar"), I take exception. This soup will leave you patting your stomach and asking yourself if you really have it in you to take on anything else for the day. The sharpest cheddar you can find will result in the best soup.

1. Place the oil in a Dutch oven and warm over medium heat. Once the oil is shimmering, add the onion and carrots and cook until they start to soften, about 5 minutes. Add the garlic, cook until fragrant, and then add the potatoes, stock, and white wine. Bring to a boil and then reduce heat so that the soup simmers. Simmer until the vegetables are tender, about 20 minutes.

2. Transfer the soup to a blender or food processor and puree until it is just slightly chunky.

3. Return the soup to the pan and warm over low heat. Add the cheddar, dill, and a few dashes of Worcestershire sauce. Season with salt and pepper, cook until warmed through, and serve.

INGREDIENTS:

1 TABLESPOON OLIVE OIL

1 LARGE YELLOW ONION, DICED

2 CARROTS, PEELED AND DICED

2 GARLIC CLOVES, MINCED

2 LBS. YELLOW POTATOES, WASHED AND DICED

4 CUPS CHICKEN STOCK (SEE PAGE 748 FOR HOMEMADE)

⅓ CUP WHITE WINE

¾ LB. SHARP CHEDDAR CHEESE, GRATED

2 TEASPOONS CHOPPED FRESH DILL

WORCESTERSHIRE SAUCE, TO TASTE

SALT AND PEPPER, TO TASTE

BABY SPINACH & YOGURT SOUP

YIELD: 4 SERVINGS / ACTIVE TIME: 20 MINUTES / TOTAL TIME: 1 HOUR

This very simple and quick vegetarian soup is transformed by the Turmeric Oil.

1. Place the oil in a large saucepan and warm over medium heat. When the oil starts to shimmer, add the onion and cook until it starts to soften, about 5 minutes.

2. Add 8 cups of the spinach, cover the pan, and cook until all the spinach is wilted, about 5 minutes.

3. Add the scallions, rice, and stock and simmer until the rice is tender, about 18 minutes.

4. Transfer the soup to a food processor or blender, add the garlic and remaining spinach, and puree until smooth. Strain through a fine sieve, place in a clean pan, bring to a simmer, and add the yogurt.

5. Season with salt and pepper, ladle into warmed bowls, and serve with the Shallots & Wilted Spinach and Turmeric Oil.

SHALLOTS & WILTED SPINACH

1. Place the oil in a medium saucepan and warm over medium heat. When the oil starts to shimmer, add the shallots and cook until they start to soften, about 5 minutes.

2. Add the spinach and cook until wilted, about 5 minutes.

3. Season with salt and pepper and serve.

TURMERIC OIL

1. Place the oil and turmeric in a bowl and whisk vigorously to combine.

2. Season with salt and pepper, strain through a fine sieve, and reserve until ready to use.

INGREDIENTS:

- 2 TABLESPOONS OLIVE OIL
- 1 ONION, CHOPPED
- 12 CUPS PACKED BABY SPINACH
- 2 SCALLIONS, CHOPPED
- 3 TABLESPOONS LONG-GRAIN RICE
- 3 CUPS VEGETABLE STOCK (SEE PAGE 755 FOR HOMEMADE)
- 1 GARLIC CLOVE, MINCED
- 1½ CUPS WHOLE-MILK YOGURT
- SALT AND PEPPER, TO TASTE
- SHALLOTS & WILTED SPINACH (SEE RECIPE), FOR SERVING
- TURMERIC OIL (SEE RECIPE), FOR SERVING

SHALLOTS & WILTED SPINACH

- ¼ CUP OLIVE OIL
- 2 SHALLOTS, MINCED
- 4 CUPS FIRMLY PACKED BABY SPINACH
- SALT AND PEPPER, TO TASTE

TURMERIC OIL

- ½ CUP OLIVE OIL
- 2 TEASPOONS TURMERIC
- SALT AND PEPPER, TO TASTE

SPICY BABY SPINACH & RICE SOUP

YIELD: 4 SERVINGS / ACTIVE TIME: 15 MINUTES / TOTAL TIME: 45 MINUTES

This is a vegetarian delicacy, perfect for a spring or summer day. Feel free to toss in whatever other vegetables you like.

1. Place the water and spinach in a large saucepan and cook over medium-high heat until the spinach is wilted, about 5 minutes. Drain, allow the spinach to cool, and then mince it.

2. Place the oil in a large saucepan and warm over medium heat. When it starts to shimmer, add the onion, garlic, and chili pepper and cook until the onion starts to soften, about 5 minutes.

3. Add the stock and stir in the rice. Bring to a boil, reduce heat so that the soup simmers, and cook until the rice is almost tender, about 15 minutes.

4. Return the spinach to the pan and cook until the rice is completely tender, about 5 minutes. Season with salt and pepper, ladle into warmed bowls, and garnish with the Romano cheese.

INGREDIENTS:

2   TABLESPOONS WATER

12   CUPS PACKED BABY
     SPINACH

3   TABLESPOONS OLIVE OIL

1   SMALL ONION, DICED

2   GARLIC CLOVES, MINCED

1   SMALL RED CHILI PEPPER,
     STEMMED, SEEDED, AND
     MINCED

4   CUPS VEGETABLE STOCK
     (SEE PAGE 755 FOR
     HOMEMADE)

⅓   CUP ARBORIO RICE

     SALT AND PEPPER, TO TASTE

     ROMANO CHEESE, GRATED,
     FOR GARNISH

COCONUT & SPINACH SOUP
with TOASTED ALMONDS

YIELD: 4 SERVINGS / ACTIVE TIME: 20 MINUTES / TOTAL TIME: 30 MINUTES

Sweet coconut seems like an unlikely partner for spinach, but you'll be surprised how well they work together.

1. Place 2 tablespoons of the butter in a medium saucepan and melt over medium heat. Add the onion and cook until it starts to soften, about 5 minutes.

2. Add the spinach, cover, and cook until it is wilted, about 5 minutes. Add the stock and bring to a boil.

3. Transfer the soup to a food processor, blend until creamy, and strain through a fine sieve.

4. Add the remaining butter to a clean saucepan and melt over medium heat. Add the flour and cook, stirring constantly, for 2 minutes. Add the soup and coconut milk to the pan with the butter and flour and cook until warmed through, about 5 minutes. Season with salt and pepper and add the nutmeg.

5. Ladle the soup into warmed bowls and garnish with additional nutmeg, chives, toasted almonds, and shredded coconut.

INGREDIENTS:

3 TABLESPOONS UNSALTED BUTTER

1 ONION, CHOPPED

16 CUPS PACKED SPINACH, CHOPPED

4 CUPS VEGETABLE STOCK (SEE PAGE 755 FOR HOMEMADE)

1 TABLESPOON ALL-PURPOSE FLOUR

2 CUPS COCONUT MILK

SALT AND PEPPER, TO TASTE

¼ TEASPOON GRATED NUTMEG, PLUS MORE FOR GARNISH

FRESH CHIVES, CHOPPED, FOR GARNISH

SLIVERED ALMONDS, TOASTED, FOR GARNISH

UNSWEETENED SHREDDED COCONUT, FOR GARNISH

SAFFRON & SUNCHOKE SOUP

YIELD: 4 SERVINGS / ACTIVE TIME: 30 MINUTES / TOTAL TIME: 1 HOUR AND 45 MINUTES

This creamy soup is balanced by a pinch of saffron and a shot of lemon juice, meaning it will brighten even the dreariest day. After chopping the sunchokes, store them in a bowl with enough water to cover and a squeeze of lemon juice to keep them fresh.

1. Place the oil in a medium saucepan and warm over medium heat. When the oil starts to shimmer, add the onion and cook until it starts to soften, about 5 minutes.

2. Add the garlic and sunchokes and cook for 5 minutes. Add the stock and bring to a boil. Reduce heat so that the soup simmers and cook until the sunchokes are starting to soften, about 15 minutes.

3. Add the saffron and lemon juice and cook until the sunchokes are completely tender, about 15 minutes. Transfer the soup to a food processor or blender, puree, and then strain through a fine sieve.

4. Return the soup to the pan and bring to a simmer.

5. When everything is warmed through, ladle the soup into warmed bowls, garnish with the parsley, toasted almonds, and additional saffron, and serve with the Sunchoke Aioli with Crispy Skins.

SUNCHOKE AIOLI WITH CRISPY SKINS

1. Preheat the oven to 200°F and prepare an ice water bath.

2. Place the sunchokes in a small saucepan and cover with water. Bring to a boil and cook until they are very tender, 20 to 25 minutes.

3. Transfer the sunchokes to the ice water bath. Remove, cut them in half, and remove the flesh with a spoon. Set aside.

4. Place the skins on a baking sheet, place them in the oven, and roast until crispy, about 20 minutes. Remove and let cool.

5. While the skins are roasting, mash the sunchoke flesh until smooth. Add the egg yolks, garlic, mustard, and lemon juice and whisk vigorously until the mixture is smooth.

6. While whisking constantly, slowly drizzle in the oil. Season with salt and pepper and serve with the roasted skins.

INGREDIENTS:

- 2 TABLESPOONS OLIVE OIL
- 1 ONION, DICED
- 1 GARLIC CLOVE, MINCED
- 2 CUPS PEELED AND CHOPPED SUNCHOKES
- 4 CUPS CHICKEN STOCK (SEE PAGE 748 FOR HOMEMADE)
- PINCH OF SAFFRON, PLUS MORE FOR GARNISH
- JUICE OF ½ LEMON
- PARSLEY, CHOPPED, FOR GARNISH
- ALMONDS, TOASTED, FOR GARNISH
- SUNCHOKE AIOLI WITH CRISPY SKINS (SEE RECIPE), FOR SERVING

SUNCHOKE AIOLI WITH CRISPY SKINS

- 2 SUNCHOKES
- 2 EGG YOLKS
- ½ GARLIC CLOVE, MINCED
- ½ TEASPOON DIJON MUSTARD
- 1 TEASPOON FRESH LEMON JUICE
- ½ CUP OLIVE OIL
- SALT AND PEPPER, TO TASTE

SWEET POTATO SOUP

YIELD: 4 TO 6 SERVINGS / ACTIVE TIME: 25 MINUTES / TOTAL TIME: 55 MINUTES

Do you love sweet potatoes? Then you are certain to love this soup. The curry is very subtle, but it adds a nice bit of flavor.

1. Place the butter in a medium saucepan and melt over medium heat. Add the onion and cook until it starts to soften, about 5 minutes.

2. Add the stock, curry powder, sweet potatoes, maple syrup, thyme, and cayenne. Bring to a boil, reduce heat so that the soup simmers, and cook for 25 minutes, or until the sweet potatoes are tender.

3. Remove the sprigs of thyme and transfer the soup to a food processor or blender. Puree until smooth and creamy and then strain through a fine sieve.

4. Return the soup to the pan and bring to a simmer. Add the cream and nutmeg, season with salt and pepper, and ladle into warmed bowls. Garnish with a dollop of the Rum Cream, the cilantro, and additional curry powder.

RUM CREAM

1. Place the cream in a bowl and whip until soft peaks form.

2. Add the lemon juice, lemon zest, rum, and sugar. Stir to combine and refrigerate until ready to use.

INGREDIENTS:

- 1½ TABLESPOONS UNSALTED BUTTER
- 1 SMALL ONION, CHOPPED
- 5 CUPS CHICKEN STOCK (SEE PAGE 748 FOR HOMEMADE)
- ½ TEASPOON CURRY POWDER, PLUS MORE FOR GARNISH
- 4 SWEET POTATOES, PEELED AND CHOPPED
- 2 TABLESPOONS MAPLE SYRUP
- 2 SPRIGS THYME

  PINCH OF CAYENNE PEPPER
- 2 CUPS HEAVY CREAM
- 2 PINCHES OF GROUND NUTMEG

  SALT AND PEPPER, TO TASTE

  RUM CREAM (SEE RECIPE), FOR GARNISH

  CILANTRO, CHOPPED, FOR GARNISH

RUM CREAM

- ½ CUP HEAVY CREAM
- ¼ TEASPOON FRESH LEMON JUICE

  PINCH OF LEMON ZEST
- 2 TABLESPOONS MYERS'S RUM

  PINCH OF SUGAR

BUTTERNUT SQUASH & CHORIZO BISQUE

YIELD: 4 SERVINGS / ACTIVE TIME: 15 MINUTES / TOTAL TIME: 1 HOUR AND 30 MINUTES

This toothsome bisque is the result of pitting sweet against spicy, producing stunning results.

1. Preheat the oven to 400°F.

2. Place the squash, onion, 2 tablespoons of the oil, and a pinch of salt in a bowl and toss to combine. Place the mixture in a baking dish and roast until the onion is browned, about 15 to 25 minutes. Transfer the onion to a bowl, return the squash to the oven, and roast for another 20 to 30 minutes, until the squash is fork-tender. Remove from the oven and transfer to the bowl containing the onion.

3. Place the remaining oil in a skillet and warm over medium-high heat. When the oil starts to shimmer, add the chorizo and cook, turning occasionally, until it is browned all over, about 5 minutes. Transfer to a paper towel–lined plate to drain. When cool enough to handle, chop the chorizo into bite-sized pieces.

4. Place the squash, onion, chorizo, bay leaves, cream, stock, and milk in a large saucepan and bring to a boil over medium-high heat, stirring often. Reduce heat so that the soup simmers and cook until the flavor is to your liking, about 20 minutes.

5. Remove the bay leaves, transfer the soup to a food processor or blender, and puree until smooth. Return the soup to the saucepan and bring to a simmer. Add the butter, stir until it has melted, and ladle into warmed bowls.

INGREDIENTS:

1 LARGE BUTTERNUT SQUASH, PEELED AND SLICED

1 ONION, SLICED

3 TABLESPOONS OLIVE OIL

SALT AND PEPPER, TO TASTE

½ LB. CHORIZO, CASING REMOVED

2 BAY LEAVES

1 CUP HEAVY CREAM

1 CUP VEGETABLE STOCK (SEE PAGE 755 FOR HOMEMADE)

1 CUP WHOLE MILK

4 TABLESPOONS UNSALTED BUTTER

BUTTERNUT SQUASH, QUINOA & CHICKEN SOUP

YIELD: 4 SERVINGS / ACTIVE TIME: 20 MINUTES / TOTAL TIME: 2 HOURS

This is a great post-workout meal, thanks to the healthy carbs from the sweet potato, the nutrient-dense quinoa, and protein from the chicken. Plus, it just tastes good. Beats any protein shake.

1. Preheat the oven to 375°F.

2. Place the butternut squash on a baking sheet, drizzle 2 tablespoons of the oil over the top, and place in the oven. Roast for 50 minutes, or until the flesh is very tender. Remove from the oven and let cool.

3. Place the remaining oil in a Dutch oven and warm over medium heat. Add the chicken breasts and cook, turning occasionally, until evenly browned, about 8 minutes. Remove the chicken with a slotted spoon and set aside.

4. Add the onion and cook until it has softened, about 5 minutes. Add the garlic, cook for an additional 2 minutes, and then add 3 cups of the stock, the stewed tomatoes, and the oregano. Bring to a boil and then reduce heat so that the soup simmers.

5. Scoop the flesh of the butternut squash into a food processor or blender with the remaining stock. Puree until smooth.

6. Add the butternut squash puree, chicken, and quinoa to the simmering soup. Cook until the quinoa is tender, about 15 minutes.

7. Season with salt and pepper and ladle into warmed bowls.

INGREDIENTS:

1   BUTTERNUT SQUASH, HALVED AND SEEDED

3   TABLESPOONS OLIVE OIL

2   BONELESS, SKINLESS CHICKEN BREASTS, CUT INTO ½-INCH CUBES

1   ONION, CHOPPED

2   GARLIC CLOVES, MINCED

4   CUPS CHICKEN STOCK (SEE PAGE 748 FOR HOMEMADE)

1   (14 OZ.) CAN STEWED TOMATOES, CHOPPED

    LEAVES FROM 1 SPRIG OREGANO, CHOPPED

⅔   CUP QUINOA

    SALT AND PEPPER, TO TASTE

GAZPACHO

YIELD: 4 SERVINGS / ACTIVE TIME: 15 MINUTES / TOTAL TIME: 1 HOUR AND 15 MINUTES

Also known as "salad soup," gazpacho is one of the best ways to celebrate summer produce. Made with everything that is peaking in the garden in August, it is a delightful cold tomato soup from Spain that doesn't require so much as a single bit of heat applied to it (unless you want to add homemade croutons). You can vary the quantities of most of the vegetables to taste, but be very conservative with the onion and garlic so that they don't overwhelm everything else.

1. Place the onion, garlic, two-thirds of the tomatoes, half of the pepper, and half of the oil in a food processor or blender, puree until smooth, and pour into a large bowl.

2. Place half of the cucumber in the food processor or blender with the remaining oil, the vinegar, salt, half of the parsley, and croutons. Puree until smooth and add to the first puree. Stir to combine, taste, and adjust the seasoning as needed. Refrigerate for at least 1 hour.

3. Dice the remaining tomato, cucumber, and pepper. Ladle the cold soup into bowls and top with the diced vegetables and more croutons.

INGREDIENTS:

- ¼ ONION
- 1 SMALL GARLIC CLOVE
- 2 LBS. TOMATOES
- 1 ORANGE, YELLOW, OR RED BELL PEPPER
- ¼ CUP OLIVE OIL
- 1 CUCUMBER, PEELED AND SEEDED
- 1 TABLESPOON SHERRY VINEGAR
- SALT, TO TASTE
- ¼ CUP CHOPPED PARSLEY
- 4 CROUTONS (SEE PAGE 332 FOR HOMEMADE), PLUS MORE FOR GARNISH

COLD ZUCCHINI SOUP

YIELD: 4 SERVINGS / ACTIVE TIME: 10 MINUTES / TOTAL TIME: 1 HOUR AND 30 MINUTES

In this soup, zucchini is simmered in chicken stock until tender and then pureed in a blender. This is a great recipe for using the larger squash that can weigh several pounds. Once chilled, a touch of cream and lemon juice is all it needs to become the perfect summer lunch.

1. Place the zucchini, onion, and bay leaf in a saucepan and cover with the stock. Bring the soup to a boil, reduce heat so that the soup simmers, and cook until the vegetables are nearly falling apart, about 20 minutes. Remove from heat and let the soup cool slightly.

2. Remove the bay leaf and place the soup in a blender or a food processor. Puree until smooth and then refrigerate for at least 1 hour.

3. When ready to serve, add the cream and a squeeze of lemon juice and season with salt and pepper. Taste and adjust the seasoning as necessary.

4. Ladle into bowls and garnish with the parsley and slices of lemon.

TIP: If the zucchini is so large that it is difficult to pierce the skin with your fingernail and the interior seeds are large and very hard, then it is too mature to cook with.

INGREDIENTS:

2	LBS. ZUCCHINI, CHOPPED
1	YELLOW ONION, SLICED
1	BAY LEAF
	CHICKEN STOCK (SEE PAGE 748 FOR HOMEMADE), AS NEEDED
¼	CUP LIGHT CREAM
	FRESH LEMON JUICE, TO TASTE
	SALT AND PEPPER, TO TASTE
	FRESH PARSLEY, CHOPPED, FOR GARNISH
	LEMON SLICES, FOR GARNISH

SOUTHWESTERN CORN CHOWDER

YIELD: 4 TO 6 SERVINGS / ACTIVE TIME: 20 MINUTES / TOTAL TIME: 40 MINUTES

This chowder is a good example of how well frozen corn works in soups and stews, which is handy because you'll want to make this when the weather turns cold and fresh corn is nowhere to be found. The base is made with ingredients you may expect like stock and onion and one that is unusual: corn tortillas. They provide flavor but also act as a thickener for a hearty soup.

1. Place the oil in a medium saucepan and warm over medium heat. Add the onion and garlic and cook until the onion turns translucent, about 3 minutes.

2. Slice the tortillas into strips and add them to the pot. Cook, stirring occasionally, until they soften slightly, about 5 minutes.

3. Add the tomatoes, jalapeño (if using), stock, cumin, coriander, oregano, and ancho chili powder and bring to a boil. Reduce heat so that the soup simmers and cook for 10 minutes.

4. Remove from heat and let cool for 5 minutes. Use an immersion blender or a food processor to puree the soup.

5. If using a food processor, return the soup to the pan. Add the chicken or turkey, corn, bell pepper, and cream. Warm over medium heat until the corn is cooked through, about 5 minutes.

6. Season with salt and pepper, ladle into warmed bowls, and serve with the lime wedges and tortilla chips.

INGREDIENTS:

- 1 TABLESPOON OLIVE OIL
- 1 LARGE ONION, PEELED AND CHOPPED
- 2 GARLIC CLOVES, PEELED AND CHOPPED
- 3 CORN TORTILLAS (SEE PAGE 797 FOR HOMEMADE)
- 1 CUP DICED TOMATOES
- ½ JALAPEÑO PEPPER (OPTIONAL)
- 4 CUPS CHICKEN STOCK (SEE PAGE 748 FOR HOMEMADE)
- 1 TEASPOON CUMIN
- 1 TEASPOON DRIED CORIANDER
- 1 TEASPOON DRIED OREGANO
- 1 TEASPOON ANCHO CHILI POWDER
- 2 CUPS COOKED AND DICED CHICKEN OR TURKEY
- 1½ CUPS FROZEN CORN
- 1 RED BELL PEPPER, DICED
- ½ CUP HEAVY CREAM
- SALT AND PEPPER, TO TASTE
- LIME WEDGES, FOR SERVING
- TORTILLA CHIPS, FOR SERVING

CHILLED CORN SOUP *with* GARLIC CUSTARD

YIELD: 4 SERVINGS / ACTIVE TIME: 30 MINUTES / TOTAL TIME: 2 HOURS AND 30 MINUTES

This recipe is easily made the day before. Corncobs have a lot of nutrients and flavor, and the corn stock is the secret of this soup.

1. Remove the corn kernels from the cobs.

2. In a large stockpot, add the water, the corncobs, bay leaf, thyme, peppercorns, and one of the chopped onions and bring to a boil.

3. Reduce heat so that the soup simmers and cook for 1 hour.

4. Strain through a fine sieve and reserve the stock.

5. In a medium saucepan, melt the butter. Add the remaining onion and the garlic and cook over medium heat until the onion starts to soften, about 5 minutes.

6. Add the corn kernels, reserving 2 tablespoons for garnish, and reduce heat to low. Cook for 5 minutes.

7. Transfer the corn mixture to a food processor and combine with 4 cups of the corn stock. Puree, adding more stock if necessary to produce the desired consistency.

8. Add the lemon juice and season with salt and pepper. Chill in the refrigerator for at least 1 hour.

9. Place the Garlic Custard, reserved corn kernels, and cilantro leaves in the middle of chilled bowls. Pour the soup around the center and serve.

INGREDIENTS:

8	EARS SWEET CORN
10	CUPS WATER
1	BAY LEAF
12	FRESH THYME SPRIGS
6	PEPPERCORNS
2	ONIONS, PEELED AND CHOPPED
2	TABLESPOONS UNSALTED BUTTER
4	GARLIC CLOVES, MINCED
2	TABLESPOONS FRESH LEMON JUICE
	SALT AND PEPPER, TO TASTE
	GARLIC CUSTARD (SEE RECIPE), FOR GARNISH
	FRESH CILANTRO, FOR GARNISH

Continued . . .

GARLIC CUSTARD

1. Preheat oven to 325°F.

2. Grease four 4 oz. ramekins. Place them in a baking dish.

3. In a small saucepan, melt the butter. Add the garlic and cook over low heat until it is soft, about 5 minutes.

4. Add the cream and the salt. Increase heat to medium and bring to a simmer.

5. Remove from heat, let stand for 10 minutes, and strain through a fine sieve.

6. Add the eggs and the yolk to a medium-sized bowl and whisk until scrambled. Add the chives and whisk to incorporate.

7. Add the garlic mixture and whisk until combined. Season with salt and pepper.

8. Divide the mixture between the ramekins and place the dish in the oven. Before closing the door, pour enough hot water in the dish to go halfway up the ramekins.

9. Cook for 18 minutes, or until the custards are firm and a knife comes out clean when inserted.

10. Remove from the oven and chill the custards in the refrigerator for 1 hour.

11. When ready to serve, use a knife to remove each custard from the ramekin.

INGREDIENTS:

GARLIC CUSTARD

1	TABLESPOON UNSALTED BUTTER
3	GARLIC CLOVES, MINCED
1	CUP HEAVY CREAM
½	TEASPOON KOSHER SALT, PLUS MORE TO TASTE
	BLACK PEPPER, TO TASTE
2	EGGS
1	EGG YOLK
1½	TEASPOONS CHOPPED FRESH CHIVES

CORN *and* PLANTAIN SOUP

YIELD: 4 SERVINGS / ACTIVE TIME: 15 MINUTES / TOTAL TIME: 40 MINUTES

This is a traditional African soup that is both sweet and spicy. Feel free to substitute vegetable stock (see page 755) for the chicken stock to make this vegetarian. Or go full vegan by using coconut oil instead of butter.

1. In a medium saucepan, add the butter and cook over medium heat until melted. Add the onion and garlic and cook until they start to soften, about 5 minutes.

2. Add the plantains, tomatoes, corn kernels, and tarragon. Cook for 5 minutes.

3. Add the stock, jalapeño, and nutmeg and bring to a boil.

4. Reduce to a simmer and cook until the plantains are tender, about 10 minutes.

5. Season with salt and pepper and serve in warmed bowls.

INGREDIENTS:

4   TABLESPOONS UNSALTED BUTTER

1   ONION, CHOPPED

2   GARLIC CLOVES, MINCED

2   RIPE YELLOW PLANTAINS, PEELED AND SLICED

2   PLUM TOMATOES, CONCASSE (SEE PAGE 808)

2   CUPS CORN KERNELS

    LEAVES FROM 1 SPRIG TARRAGON, CHOPPED

4   CUPS CHICKEN STOCK (SEE PAGE 748 FOR HOMEMADE)

1   TABLESPOON MINCED JALAPEÑO PEPPER

⅛   TEASPOON GROUND NUTMEG

    SALT AND PEPPER, TO TASTE

CORN & SEAFOOD CHOWDER

YIELD: **4 TO 6 SERVINGS** / ACTIVE TIME: **1 HOUR** / TOTAL TIME: **3 HOURS AND 15 MINUTES**

For a dish that utilizes the famously light fruits of the sea, this is a very rich chowder.

1. In a blender, add the corn kernels and milk and puree until creamy.

2. In a medium saucepan, add the butter and cook over medium heat until melted. Add the garlic and bacon and cook for 5 minutes. Add the pepper and celery and sweat for 4 minutes, or until soft.

3. Add the rice and cook for 4 minutes. Add the flour and cook for 2 minutes, stirring constantly.

4. Gradually add the corn puree and stock to the saucepan. Bring to a simmer and cook for 20 minutes, or until the rice is tender.

5. Stir in the scallops, haddock, and lobster. Cook for 4 minutes, then add the parsley, cayenne, and tomatoes. Cook for a few more minutes, season with salt and pepper, and ladle into warmed bowls. Garnish with additional parsley and serve with the Salt Cod Beignets.

SALT COD BEIGNETS

1. In a small saucepan, add the milk and butter and bring to a boil.

2. Add the flour and stir until it forms a ball of dough.

3. Remove the saucepan from heat and let stand for 10 minutes.

4. Add the egg slowly and whisk until well-combined. Add the salt cod and cilantro, stir to incorporate, roll the dough into a log, wrap with plastic wrap, and place in the freezer for 2 hours.

5. Place the oil in a Dutch oven and warm over medium-high heat until it reaches 375°F.

6. Remove the log from the freezer and cut into ½-inch-thick slices.

7. Gently place each slice in the oil and fry until golden brown.

8. Use a slotted spoon to remove from the oil and set on a paper towel to drain.

9. Season with salt and pepper and serve.

INGREDIENTS:

- 1½ CUPS CORN KERNELS
- 2 CUPS MILK
- 2 TABLESPOONS UNSALTED BUTTER
- 1 GARLIC CLOVE, MINCED
- 4 STRIPS THICK-CUT BACON, CHOPPED
- 1 GREEN BELL PEPPER, STEMMED, SEEDED, AND CHOPPED
- ¾ CUP CHOPPED CELERY
- ½ CUP LONG-GRAIN RICE
- 1 TABLESPOON ALL-PURPOSE FLOUR
- 2 CUPS FISH STOCK (SEE PAGE 752 FOR HOMEMADE)
- 4 SCALLOPS, CUT INTO ¼-INCH PIECES
- 4 OZ. HADDOCK, CUT INTO ½-INCH PIECES
- 3 OZ. LOBSTER, CUT INTO ¼-INCH PIECES
- 2 TABLESPOONS PARSLEY, CHOPPED, PLUS MORE FOR GARNISH
- ⅛ TEASPOON CAYENNE PEPPER
- 1½ CUPS TOMATOES, CONCASSE (SEE PAGE 808)
  SALT AND PEPPER, TO TASTE
  SALT COD BEIGNETS (SEE RECIPE), FOR SERVING

SALT COD BEIGNETS
- ½ CUP MILK
- 3 TABLESPOONS UNSALTED BUTTER
- ¼ CUP ALL-PURPOSE FLOUR
- 1 EGG
- 4 OZ. SALT COD, CHOPPED
- 1 TABLESPOON CHOPPED FRESH CILANTRO
- 2 CUPS VEGETABLE OIL
  SALT AND PEPPER, TO TASTE

ROASTED CORN & RED PEPPER BISQUE
with BUTTER-POACHED LOBSTER

YIELD: 4 SERVINGS / ACTIVE TIME: 30 MINUTES / TOTAL TIME: 1 HOUR AND 30 MINUTES

During the dog days of summer in New England, you can find corn almost everywhere, and its sweetness is a perfect match for the famously fresh taste of Maine lobster. This dish proves that in New England we are spoiled by all of the great ingredients that the region makes available.

1. Preheat the oven to 375°F.

2. Place the corn in a single layer on a large baking sheet and drizzle with the oil. Season with salt, place in the oven, and roast until the corn starts to darken and caramelize, 12 to 18 minutes. Remove from the oven and raise the temperature to 425°F.

3. Place the peppers on a baking sheet and place them in the oven. Cook, turning occasionally, until the skin is blistered all over, about 30 minutes. Remove from the oven and let cool. When cool enough to handle, remove the skins and seeds and discard. Set the peppers aside.

4. Place the corn, peppers, 4 tablespoons of butter, cream, and milk in a saucepan and bring to a simmer, stirring, over medium heat. Simmer for 20 minutes, making sure that it does not come to a boil.

5. While the bisque is simmering, place the remaining butter in a small saucepan and melt over low heat. Add the lobster meat and cook for 7 to 10 minutes, spooning the butter over the lobster as it cooks. When the lobster is tender and warmed through, remove from heat and set aside.

6. After simmering for 20 minutes, remove the bisque from heat and let cool for 10 minutes.

7. Transfer the bisque to a blender and puree until smooth. If the mixture has cooled too much, return to the saucepan and cook until warmed through. If not, ladle into warmed bowls and top each one with pieces of the poached lobster.

INGREDIENTS:

3   CUPS FRESH CORN KERNELS

2   TABLESPOONS OLIVE OIL

    SALT AND PEPPER, TO TASTE

3   RED BELL PEPPERS

1½   STICKS UNSALTED BUTTER

½   CUP HEAVY CREAM

½   CUP MILK

    MEAT FROM 2 COOKED CHICKEN LOBSTERS

VEGETARIAN GREEN GUMBO

YIELD: 4 TO 6 SERVINGS / ACTIVE TIME: 25 MINUTES / TOTAL TIME: 40 MINUTES

This revitalizing and healthy gumbo will go great with a fresh baguette or toasted garlic bread.

1. In a large saucepan, add the oil and cook over medium heat until warm.

2. Add the onion, garlic, celery, and bell pepper and cook for 5 minutes, or until soft.

3. Add the cabbage, oregano, thyme, and bay leaf and cook for 5 minutes.

4. Add the stock and bring to a boil. Reduce heat so that the soup simmers and cook for 5 minutes.

5. Add the collard greens and cook for 5 minutes, then add the spinach, watercress, and tofu. Cook for 2 minutes before adding the parsley, allspice, and cayenne. Season with salt and pepper, simmer for 2 minutes, and then serve in warmed bowls.

INGREDIENTS:

1 TABLESPOON VEGETABLE OIL

1 ONION, CHOPPED

2 GARLIC CLOVES, MINCED

1 CELERY STALK, DICED

1 GREEN BELL PEPPER, CHOPPED

¼ GREEN CABBAGE, CORE REMOVED AND FINELY SLICED

½ TEASPOON OREGANO, LEAVES REMOVED AND CHOPPED

½ TEASPOON THYME, LEAVES REMOVED AND CHOPPED

1 BAY LEAF

6 CUPS VEGETABLE STOCK (SEE PAGE 755 FOR HOMEMADE)

2 CUPS COLLARD GREENS, FINELY GRATED

2 CUPS SPINACH, FINELY GRATED

1 BUNCH WATERCRESS

12 OZ. TOFU, CUT INTO ¼-INCH PIECES

¼ CUP PARSLEY, LEAVES REMOVED AND CHOPPED

½ TEASPOON ALLSPICE

PINCH OF CAYENNE PEPPER

SALT AND PEPPER, TO TASTE

SALADS

Salads should never be thought of as filler to make you feel better about yourself. Not only can they make for the perfect addition to a well-rounded meal or serve as a citric counterbalance to richer recipes, salads can be wonderful meals in their own right. Many of these salads utilize the best in seasonal ingredients. Others are bulked up with noodles and grains. What all these salads have in common, however, is the ability to conquer hunger with inventive flavor combinations that rely heavily on vegetables.

ARUGULA, NECTARINE, FARRO & GOAT CHEESE SALAD *with* WHITE BALSAMIC VINAIGRETTE

YIELD: 2 SERVINGS / ACTIVE TIME: 10 MINUTES / TOTAL TIME: 30 MINUTES

Arugula pairs beautifully with sweet fruit, and what better choice than a honey-sweet summer nectarine? I've topped this salad with a white balsamic dressing, which draws out the sweetness of the fruit. You can sub out the farro for wild rice with very good results.

1. In a medium-sized pot bring 2 cups of water to a boil, add the farro, and then lower the heat and simmer for 15 minutes, or until all the liquid has been absorbed. Set aside to cool.

2. Whisk the vinegar, mustard, salt, pepper, and honey together in a mixing bowl. Once mixed, slowly drizzle in the olive oil to emulsify the dressing. Set aside.

3. In a large bowl, gently toss the farro, nectarine, goat cheese, and cashews to combine. Add a few tablespoons of dressing to taste.

4. Put the arugula on a plate and top with the farro mixture. Add a little more vinaigrette to taste and serve.

INGREDIENTS:

1	CUP FARRO
3	TABLESPOONS WHITE BALSAMIC VINEGAR
1	TEASPOON DIJON MUSTARD
½	TEASPOON SALT
½	TEASPOON BLACK PEPPER
1	TEASPOON HONEY
½	CUP OLIVE OIL
1	RIPE NECTARINE, PITTED AND DICED
2	OZ. GOAT CHEESE, CRUMBLED
2	TABLESPOONS ROUGHLY CHOPPED CASHEWS
2	HANDFULS OF ARUGULA

AVOCADO HALVES FILLED *with* CRAB SALAD

YIELD: 2 SERVINGS / ACTIVE TIME: 15 MINUTES / TOTAL TIME: 15 MINUTES

This recipe is reminiscent of the time when avocados were a novelty, occasionally seen on country club menus. In some renditions, the half is topped with poached shrimp and a Thousand Island-type sauce. Sneer if you like, but the combination is excellent. This is a more refined preparation, topped with crab salad and chives. The lemon juice and mustard bring out the buttery nature of the avocado.

1. Slice the avocado lengthwise down to the pit and pull the halves apart. Remove the pit by gently prying it free with a knife or spoon.

2. Combine all of the remaining ingredients, except for the chives, in a bowl, folding as gently as possible to keep the crabmeat from breaking up too much. Taste and adjust the seasoning as necessary.

3. Place a large spoonful of the salad in the middle of each half of the avocado, top with the chives, and serve.

INGREDIENTS:

1	AVOCADO
4	OZ. LUMP CRABMEAT
1	TABLESPOON CHOPPED SCALLIONS
1	TABLESPOON MINCED CELERY
1	TABLESPOON MAYONNAISE
1	TEASPOON DIJON MUSTARD
1	TEASPOON FRESH LEMON JUICE
	SALT AND PEPPER, TO TASTE
1	TABLESPOON CHOPPED FRESH CHIVES

RAW BEET SALAD *with* BLOOD ORANGE, JALAPEÑO & BRIE

YIELD: 4 TO 6 SERVINGS / ACTIVE TIME: 20 TO 30 MINUTES / TOTAL TIME: 2½ TO 24 HOURS

This salad riffs on the traditional beet-and-goat cheese salad by switching out the goat cheese for creamy Brie. Leaving the beets raw and grating and marinating them both tenderizes and flavors the roots.

1. Place the beet greens and stems in a bowl of ice water to remove any dirt.

2. Place the shredded beets and the jalapeño in a salad bowl.

3. Remove the beet greens and stems from the ice water and dice the stems. Set the greens aside. Add the beet stems to the salad bowl. Add the salt and stir.

4. Take the blood orange segments and add to the salad bowl, being sure to remove any membranes from the fruit. Squeeze the juice from the remnants of the orange into the bowl.

5. In a separate small bowl, whisk the oil, honey, and vinegar together and pour over the beet mixture.

6. Cover the salad bowl and refrigerate for at least 2 hours. For best results, leave in the refrigerator overnight.

7. Combine the beet greens with the arugula and place them in the salad bowl. Toss to combine, top with the Brie, and serve.

TIP: Beets, while super delicious, stain everything they touch. Make sure that whatever bowl you grate the beets into is big enough to put a box grater inside. This will prevent the beets from spilling and staining everything. When cooking with beets, it is best to use stainless steel or glass cookware.

INGREDIENTS:

- 5-7 RED BEETS, PEELED AND GRATED, STEMS AND GREENS RESERVED
- 1 JALAPEÑO PEPPER, STEMMED, SEEDED TO TASTE, AND MINCED
- ½ TEASPOON KOSHER SALT
- ZEST, SEGMENTS, AND JUICE OF 1 BLOOD ORANGE
- 3 TABLESPOONS OLIVE OIL
- 3 TABLESPOONS HONEY
- 1 TABLESPOON RICE VINEGAR
- 2 LBS. ARUGULA
- ½ LB. BRIE CHEESE, SLICED AND AT ROOM TEMPERATURE

ROASTED BABY BEET, RADISH & APPLE SALAD
with BLUE CHEESE MOUSSE

YIELD: 4 TO 6 SERVINGS / **ACTIVE TIME:** 30 MINUTES / **TOTAL TIME:** 1 HOUR AND 20 MINUTES

Baby beets are picked in the spring to thin the field and leave room for other beets to grow, an early harvest that results in a rich and delicate flavor. When you're working with something so uniquely delicious, it's important to keep it simple, and roasting these beets with a few aromatics is all they require.

1. Preheat the oven to 400°F.

2. Form three sheets of aluminum foil into pouches. Group the beets according to color and place each group into a pouch. Drizzle each with the oil and sprinkle with salt. Divide the whole sprigs of thyme, garlic, and water between the pouches and seal them. Place the pouches on a baking sheet, place in the oven, and cook until fork-tender, 45 minutes to 1 hour depending on the size of the beets. Remove the pouches from the oven and let cool. When cool enough to handle, peel the beets, cut into bite-sized pieces, and set aside.

3. Bring a pot of salted water to a boil and prepare an ice water bath in a mixing bowl. Remove the greens from the radishes, wash them thoroughly, and set aside. Quarter the radishes.

4. Place the radishes in the boiling water, cook for 1 minute, and then transfer to the water bath until completely cool. Drain and set aside.

5. Place the blue cheese, heavy cream, ricotta, and thyme leaves in a food processor and puree until smooth. Set the mousse aside.

6. Place the beets, except for the red variety, in a salad bowl. Add the radishes, radish greens, and apples and toss to combine. Add half of the vinaigrette, season with salt and pepper, and toss to coat.

7. Spread the mousse on the serving dishes. Place the salad on top, sprinkle the red beets over the salad, drizzle with the remaining vinaigrette, and garnish with the honeycomb.

HONEY MUSTARD VINAIGRETTE

1. Place all of the ingredients, except for the oil, in a small mixing bowl and whisk to combine. Add the oil in a slow stream and whisk until incorporated.

INGREDIENTS:

9	BABY BEETS (3 EACH OF RED, GOLDEN, AND PINK)
3	TABLESPOONS OLIVE OIL
1	TABLESPOON KOSHER SALT, PLUS MORE TO TASTE
9	SPRIGS FRESH THYME, 6 LEFT WHOLE, LEAVES REMOVED FROM 3
6	GARLIC CLOVES
6	TABLESPOONS WATER
8	RADISHES WITH TOPS
¾	CUP BLUE CHEESE, AT ROOM TEMPERATURE
½	CUP HEAVY CREAM
½	CUP RICOTTA CHEESE, AT ROOM TEMPERATURE
2	APPLES, PEELED, CORED, AND DICED
¼	CUP HONEY MUSTARD VINAIGRETTE (SEE RECIPE)
	BLACK PEPPER, TO TASTE
2	OZ. HONEYCOMB, FOR GARNISH

HONEY MUSTARD VINAIGRETTE

¼	CUP HONEY
2	TABLESPOONS WHOLE GRAIN MUSTARD
3	TABLESPOONS APPLE CIDER VINEGAR
1	TEASPOON KOSHER SALT
½	TEASPOON BLACK PEPPER
⅓	CUP OLIVE OIL

RED & GREEN CABBAGE SALAD
with GINGER & TAHINI DRESSING

YIELD: 2 SERVINGS / ACTIVE TIME: 15 MINUTES / TOTAL TIME: 15 MINUTES

This is a great recipe for the weekend after Thanksgiving, but it is also delicious enough to make anytime with sliced turkey from the deli. The zesty dressing pairs wonderfully with the cabbage, and the ginger notes tie it all together.

1. Place all of the ingredients in a salad bowl, except for the dressing and turkey. Add the dressing and toss to coat. Taste and add more dressing if desired. Add the turkey, toss to evenly distribute, and serve.

GINGER & TAHINI DRESSING

1. Combine all of the ingredients in a bowl and whisk vigorously until combined.

INGREDIENTS:

- 2   CUPS THINLY SLICED GREEN CABBAGE
- 2   CUPS THINLY SLICED RED CABBAGE
- 3   TABLESPOONS CHOPPED PEANUTS
- 3   SCALLIONS, TRIMMED AND CHOPPED
- ½   CUP CHOPPED FRESH CILANTRO OR PARSLEY
- ¼   CUP GINGER & TAHINI DRESSING (SEE RECIPE), PLUS MORE TO TASTE
- ¼   LB. COOKED TURKEY, DICED

GINGER & TAHINI DRESSING

- 3   TABLESPOONS FRESH LEMON JUICE
- 2   TABLESPOONS SOY SAUCE
- 2   TABLESPOONS TAHINI
- 1   TEASPOON MAPLE SYRUP
- 1   TEASPOON GRATED GINGER
- 1   TEASPOON RICE VINEGAR
- 1   TEASPOON TOASTED SESAME OIL
- ½   CUP OLIVE OIL

THAI CHILI, SHRIMP & BASIL SALAD
with NAPA CABBAGE

YIELD: 6 SERVINGS / ACTIVE TIME: 20 MINUTES / TOTAL TIME: 25 MINUTES

In this recipe, napa cabbage acts as the referee for a riot of flavors. Sweet shrimp mingle with fiery chilies and sambal oelek, an Indonesian chili paste, as well as loads of basil, mint, and cilantro. This is the perfect dinner for a hot summer night.

1. Place all of the ingredients, except for the dressing and the cashews, in a mixing bowl and stir to combine.

2. Add the dressing, toss to combine, top with crushed cashews, and serve.

THAI CHILI DRESSING

1. Place all of the ingredients in a blender and puree until smooth.

TIP: If you've got time and you want even more flavor, prepare the salad the day before and reserve half of the dressing for the second day. Serve the reserved dressing on the side or pour it on top.

INGREDIENTS:

- ½   HEAD NAPA CABBAGE, CORED AND CHOPPED
- 1   CUP CHOPPED FRESH MINT LEAVES
- 2   CUPS FRESH BASIL LEAVES, CHOPPED
- 1   CUP FRESH CILANTRO, CHOPPED
- 1   RED ONION, SLICED THIN
- 3   SCALLIONS, TRIMMED AND SLICED THIN
- 1   CARROT, PEELED AND SLICED THIN ON A BIAS
- 1   LB. SHRIMP (16/20 PREFERRED), SHELLED AND DEVEINED, COOKED, AND CUT INTO LARGE PIECES

    THAI CHILI DRESSING (SEE RECIPE)

- ¼   CUP RAW CASHEWS, CRUSHED, FOR GARNISH

THAI CHILI DRESSING

- 2   RED BIRD'S EYE CHILI PEPPERS
- ½   CUP SOY SAUCE
- ½   CUP SAMBAL OELEK

    JUICE FROM 3 LIMES

- ¼   CUP BROWN SUGAR
- 1   TABLESPOON MINCED FRESH GINGER
- 2   TABLESPOONS CURRY POWDER

ROASTED BRASSICA SALAD *with* PICKLED RAMPS & BUTTERMILK CAESAR DRESSING

YIELD: 4 TO 6 SERVINGS / ACTIVE TIME: 20 MINUTES / TOTAL TIME: 35 MINUTES

Broccoli, Brussels sprouts, and cauliflower are only a few of the fine members of the brassica family. Charring them brings out their sweet side, which pairs wonderfully with the creamy and slightly acidic buttermilk dressing.

1. Bring a large pot of salted water to a boil. Add the cauliflower, cook for 1 minute, remove with a slotted spoon, and transfer to a paper towel–lined plate. Wait for the water to return to a boil, add the broccoli, and cook for 30 seconds. Use a slotted spoon to remove the broccoli and let the water drip off before transferring it to the paper towel–lined plate.

2. Place the oil and Brussels sprouts, cut-side down, in a large cast-iron skillet. Add the broccoli and cauliflower, season with salt and pepper, and cook over high heat without moving the vegetables. Cook until charred, turn over, and cook until charred on that side. Remove and transfer to a bowl.

3. Add the Pickled Ramps and Buttermilk Caesar Dressing to the bowl and toss to evenly coat. Garnish with Parmesan cheese and red pepper flakes and serve.

PICKLED RAMPS

1. Place all of the ingredients, except for the ramps, in a small saucepan and bring to a boil over medium heat.

2. Add the ramps, reduce heat, and simmer for 1 minute. Transfer to a mason jar, cover with aluminum foil, and let cool completely. Once cool, cover with a lid and store in the refrigerator for up to 1 week.

BUTTERMILK CAESAR DRESSING

1. Place all of the ingredients in a food processor and puree until combined. Season to taste and serve.

INGREDIENTS:

1	SMALL HEAD CAULIFLOWER, TRIMMED AND CUT INTO BITE-SIZED PIECES
1	HEAD BROCCOLI, CUT INTO FLORETS
¼	CUP OLIVE OIL
¼	LB. BRUSSELS SPROUTS, TRIMMED AND HALVED
	SALT AND PEPPER, TO TASTE
10	PICKLED RAMPS (SEE RECIPE)
	BUTTERMILK CAESAR DRESSING (SEE RECIPE)
	PARMESAN CHEESE, GRATED, FOR GARNISH
	RED PEPPER FLAKES, FOR GARNISH

PICKLED RAMPS

½	CUP CHAMPAGNE VINEGAR
½	CUP WATER
¼	CUP SUGAR
1½	TEASPOONS KOSHER SALT
¼	TEASPOON FENNEL SEEDS
¼	TEASPOON CORIANDER SEEDS
⅛	TEASPOON RED PEPPER FLAKES
10	SMALL RAMP BULBS

BUTTERMILK CAESAR DRESSING

1	LARGE GARLIC CLOVE, MINCED
2	ANCHOVY FILLETS
⅔	CUP MAYONNAISE
¼	CUP BUTTERMILK
¼	CUP GRATED PARMESAN CHEESE
	ZEST OF 1 LEMON
1	TEASPOON WORCESTERSHIRE SAUCE
1	TEASPOON KOSHER SALT, PLUS MORE TO TASTE
½	TEASPOON BLACK PEPPER, PLUS MORE TO TASTE

SHAVED BRUSSELS SPROUTS & KALE SALAD
with BLOOD ORANGE VINAIGRETTE

YIELD: 4 TO 6 SERVINGS / ACTIVE TIME: 10 MINUTES / TOTAL TIME: 25 MINUTES

Brussels sprouts are as delicious raw as they are cooked, and pairing their robust, savory flavor with bright citrus is the perfect way to play up that attribute.

1. Place the bacon in a sauté pan and cook over medium heat until crisp, about 8 minutes. Transfer to a paper towel–lined plate to drain. When cool enough to handle, chop into bite-sized pieces.

2. Remove the skin from the segments of blood orange and cut each segment in half. Place in a mixing bowl, add the Brussels sprouts and kale, season with salt and pepper, and toss to combine. Add the Blood Orange Vinaigrette, toss to evenly coat, and season to taste.

3. Plate the salad, top with the bacon, garnish with the toasted pecans and Parmesan cheese, and serve with the remaining vinaigrette on the side.

BLOOD ORANGE VINAIGRETTE

1. Place all of the ingredients, except for the oil, in a blender. Puree on high and add the oil in a slow stream. Puree until the mixture has emulsified and season to taste.

INGREDIENTS:

- ½   LB. BACON, SLICED
- 3   BLOOD ORANGES, PEELED
- 1   LB. BRUSSELS SPROUTS, TRIMMED AND SLICED VERY THIN WITH A MANDOLINE
- 2   CUPS PACKED BABY KALE

  SALT AND PEPPER, TO TASTE
- ⅔   CUP BLOOD ORANGE VINAIGRETTE (SEE RECIPE)
- ½   CUP TOASTED PECANS, FOR GARNISH

  PARMESAN CHEESE, SHAVED, FOR GARNISH

BLOOD ORANGE VINAIGRETTE

- ½   CUP BLOOD ORANGE JUICE (ABOUT 2 BLOOD ORANGES)
- ½   TEASPOON KOSHER SALT
- ¼   TEASPOON BLACK PEPPER
- 1½   TABLESPOONS APPLE CIDER VINEGAR
- 1   TABLESPOON HONEY
- 1   ICE CUBE
- 1   CUP OLIVE OIL

SLICED BRUSSELS SPROUTS
with LEMON, OLIVE OIL & HAZELNUTS

YIELD: 2 TO 4 SERVINGS / ACTIVE TIME: 15 MINUTES / TOTAL TIME: 20 MINUTES

This is an excellent salad to serve alongside milder elements such as poached eggs or mozzarella cheese. The hazelnuts create a nice bridge between the robust flavor of the raw Brussels sprouts and the tangy zip of lemon juice. Just a touch of maple syrup brings out the sweetness in everything.

1. Place the hazelnuts in a sauté pan and toast over medium heat until they just start to brown, about 5 minutes. Transfer the nuts to a clean, dry kitchen towel, fold the towel over the nuts, and rub them together until the skins have loosened. Remove the cleaned nuts and discard the skins. Roughly chop the hazelnuts.

2. Add the Brussels sprouts to a bowl and drizzle the oil, lemon juice, and maple syrup over the top. Season with salt, add the hazelnuts, toss to combine, and serve.

INGREDIENTS:

¼ CUP HAZELNUTS

½ LB. BRUSSELS SPROUTS, TRIMMED AND SLICED VERY THIN WITH A MANDOLINE

⅓ CUP OLIVE OIL

1 TABLESPOON FRESH LEMON JUICE

1 TEASPOON MAPLE SYRUP

SALT, TO TASTE

CELERY, APPLE & BLUE CHEESE SALAD

YIELD: 2 TO 4 SERVINGS / ACTIVE TIME: 10 MINUTES / TOTAL TIME: 10 MINUTES

Celery gets its aria in this winter salad. Easy to assemble, it is the perfect dish for a potluck or Christmas buffet. There are elements of sweetness from the apples, tanginess from the cranberries, earthiness from the walnuts, and savory creaminess from the blue cheese. And celery is the perfect base to tie all these notes together. For the best presentation, cut everything to a similar size.

1. Combine all of the ingredients in a salad bowl and toss gently to combine. Taste, adjust the seasoning as necessary, and serve.

INGREDIENTS:

4   CUPS DICED CELERY

2   APPLES, CORED, SEEDED, AND DICED

1   CUP TOASTED WALNUTS, CHOPPED

4   OZ. BLUE CHEESE, CRUMBLED

1   CUP DRIED CRANBERRIES

¼   CUP OLIVE OIL

3   TABLESPOONS FRESH LEMON JUICE

    SALT AND PEPPER, TO TASTE

GRILLED CAULIFLOWER SALAD

YIELD: 4 SERVINGS / ACTIVE TIME: 20 MINUTES / TOTAL TIME: 1 HOUR

Mixing grilled cauliflower with a tahini dressing is genius, as the flavor of each enhances the other wonderfully. For extra flavor, you could also brush oil on cauliflower steaks and put them directly on the grill.

1. Cook the kamut berries according to package directions, rinse with cold water, and drain. Set aside.

2. Preheat your grill to medium heat. Place the cauliflower and 1 tablespoon of the oil in a bowl and toss to coat. Then, place the cauliflower on a large piece of foil and fold the foil up along the edges, crimping to form a sealed packet.

3. When the grill is about 400°F, place the packet on the grill, cover the grill, and cook until the cauliflower is tender, 10 to 15 minutes. Remove from heat and let cool.

4. Place the remaining oil, the tahini, lemon juice, water, minced garlic, and a pinch of both salt and pepper in a large salad bowl. Stir to combine. Add 1 tablespoon of the dressing to the packet of cauliflower and toss to coat.

5. Place the arugula and kamut in the salad bowl and toss to coat. Divide between the serving plates and top each portion with some of the cauliflower and the slices of avocado.

INGREDIENTS:

½ CUP UNCOOKED KAMUT BERRIES

4 CUPS CAULIFLOWER FLORETS

3 TABLESPOONS OLIVE OIL

2 TABLESPOONS TAHINI

2 TABLESPOONS FRESH LEMON JUICE

2 TABLESPOONS WARM WATER (105°F)

1 GARLIC CLOVE, MINCED

SALT AND PEPPER, TO TASTE

2 CUPS BABY ARUGULA

FLESH FROM 1 AVOCADO, SLICED THIN

CHILI-DUSTED CAULIFLOWER & CHICKPEA SALAD

YIELD: 4 TO 6 SERVINGS / ACTIVE TIME: 25 MINUTES / TOTAL TIME: 45 MINUTES

Cauliflower takes on so many different flavors well. Here, it is paired with chickpeas and chili powder for a hearty salad.

1. Preheat the oven to 400°F.

2. Place all of the ingredients, except for the dressing, in a mixing bowl and toss to coat. Place the mixture in a 9 × 13-inch baking pan. Place the pan in the oven and roast for 30 minutes, or until the cauliflower is still crunchy and slightly charred.

3. Place the cauliflower-and-chickpea mixture in a bowl. Add the dressing, toss to coat, and serve.

CHILI SPICE BLEND

1. Place all of the ingredients in a small bowl and stir to combine.

RED WINE & CHILI DRESSING

1. Place all of the ingredients in a mixing bowl and whisk until the sugar has dissolved.

INGREDIENTS:

- ½ LB. CHICKPEAS, COOKED
- 1 HEAD PURPLE CAULIFLOWER, TRIMMED AND CUT INTO BITE-SIZED PIECES
- 1 HEAD WHITE CAULIFLOWER, TRIMMED AND CUT INTO BITE-SIZED PIECES
- 3 GARLIC CLOVES, SLICED THIN
- 1 SHALLOT, PEELED AND SLICED INTO THIN RINGS
- ⅓ CUP OLIVE OIL
- ½ BATCH CHILI SPICE BLEND (SEE RECIPE)
- ½ TABLESPOON KOSHER SALT
- RED WINE & CHILI DRESSING (SEE RECIPE)

CHILI SPICE BLEND
- 1 TEASPOON DARK CHILI POWDER
- 1 TEASPOON CHIPOTLE PEPPER POWDER
- 1 TEASPOON BLACK PEPPER
- 1 TEASPOON ONION POWDER
- 1 TEASPOON GARLIC POWDER
- ½ TEASPOON PAPRIKA
- 1 TABLESPOON KOSHER SALT

RED WINE & CHILI DRESSING
- 2 SCALLIONS, SLICED THIN
- 2 RED FRESNO PEPPERS, SEEDED AND SLICED INTO THIN RINGS
- 3 TABLESPOONS GRANULATED SUGAR
- ¼ CUP RED WINE VINEGAR
- ½ BATCH CHILI SPICE BLEND (SEE RECIPE)

CELERIAC REMOULADE *with* SMOKED TROUT

YIELD: 2 SERVINGS / ACTIVE TIME: 10 MINUTES / TOTAL TIME: 10 MINUTES

This is a classic means of preparing celery root, aka celeriac: the grated root is combined with a tangy sauce and used as a base for seafood or other cold appetizers. The addictive recipe was just one of the many eye-opening experiences I had at culinary school.

1. Bring a medium saucepan of water to a boil and add a generous spoonful of salt. Add the celeriac and cook for 1 minute. Drain, rinse with cold water, and let it drain completely.

2. Place the mayonnaise, Tabasco™, mustard, lemon juice, and capers in a bowl and stir to combine.

3. Add the celeriac to the mayonnaise mixture, fold to combine, and season with salt and pepper.

4. Place a few lettuce leaves on each serving plate, place a mound of the remoulade on top, and top with a few pieces of the smoked trout. Garnish with chives or parsley and serve with a lemon wedge on the side.

INGREDIENTS:

SALT AND WHITE PEPPER, TO TASTE

1 LARGE CELERIAC, PEELED AND GRATED

⅓ CUP MAYONNAISE

1 DASH TABASCO™

1 TEASPOON DIJON MUSTARD

2 TEASPOONS FRESH LEMON JUICE

1 TEASPOON CAPERS

BIBB LETTUCE, FOR SERVING

4 OZ. SMOKED TROUT, TORN INTO LARGE PIECES

FRESH CHIVES OR PARSLEY, CHOPPED, FOR GARNISH

LEMON WEDGES, FOR SERVING

MELON, CUCUMBER & PROSCIUTTO SALAD
with MINT VINAIGRETTE

YIELD: 4 TO 6 SERVINGS / ACTIVE TIME: 15 MINUTES / TOTAL TIME: 40 MINUTES

The versatile melon can comfortably straddle the sweet-savory divide. Here it pairs up with crispy, cured prosciutto and creamy feta to carry this dynamic salad.

1. Preheat the oven to 350°F.

2. Place the prosciutto on a parchment-lined baking sheet. Cover with another sheet of parchment and place another baking sheet that is the same size on top. Place in the oven and bake until the prosciutto is crisp, about 12 minutes. Remove from the oven and let cool. When the prosciutto is cool enough to handle, chop it into bite-sized pieces.

3. Place the cantaloupe, honeydew melon, and cucumber in a salad bowl, season with salt and pepper, and toss to combine. Add the jalapeño and vinaigrette and toss until evenly coated. Plate the salad, top with the chopped prosciutto and feta, and garnish with the mint leaves.

MINT VINAIGRETTE

1. Place all of the ingredients in a mixing bowl and whisk until thoroughly combined.

INGREDIENTS:

8   SLICES PROSCIUTTO

3   CUPS DICED CANTALOUPE

3   CUPS DICED HONEYDEW MELON

1   CUCUMBER, SLICED

    SALT AND PEPPER, TO TASTE

1   JALAPEÑO PEPPER, STEMMED, SEEDED TO TASTE, AND SLICED

    MINT VINAIGRETTE (SEE RECIPE), TO TASTE

⅔   CUP CRUMBLED FETA CHEESE

    FRESH MINT LEAVES, CHOPPED, FOR GARNISH

MINT VINAIGRETTE

3   TABLESPOONS CHOPPED FRESH MINT

¼   CUP OLIVE OIL

3   TABLESPOONS APPLE CIDER VINEGAR

1   TABLESPOON HONEY

2   TEASPOONS DICED SHALLOT

1   TEASPOON KOSHER SALT

¼   TEASPOON BLACK PEPPER

THAI BEEF & CUCUMBER SALAD

YIELD: 2 SERVINGS / ACTIVE TIME: 15 MINUTES / TOTAL TIME: 1 HOUR 30 MINUTES

When the weather is hot, even the grill seems too much to bear. This is a light but filling salad, and it is a perfect use for leftover roast beef or steak, or deli-sliced roast beef. The whole recipe requires no cooking save for boiling water for the noodles.

1. Bring 6 cups of water to a boil in a medium saucepan and place the noodles in a baking pan. Pour the water over the noodles and let sit until tender, about 20 minutes. Drain well and place them in a bowl.

2. Add the remaining ingredients, except for the sesame seeds, and toss to combine. Chill in the refrigerator for 1 hour, garnish with the sesame seeds, and serve.

INGREDIENTS:

- 2 OZ. PACKAGE MUNG BEAN OR THIN RICE NOODLES
- 1 CARROT, PEELED AND GRATED
- 1 SMALL CUCUMBER, SEEDED AND DICED
- ZEST AND JUICE OF 1 LIME
- 10 FRESH MINT LEAVES, CHOPPED
- 1-2 TABLESPOONS SOY SAUCE
- 1 TEASPOON PALM SUGAR OR MAPLE SYRUP
- ½ TEASPOON KOSHER SALT
- 1 TABLESPOON THAI FISH SAUCE
- 2-4 OZ. THINLY SLICED ROAST BEEF OR LEFTOVER STEAK, TORN INTO BITE-SIZED PIECES
- RICE VINEGAR, TO TASTE
- HOT SAUCE, TO TASTE
- SESAME SEEDS, FOR GARNISH

CUCUMBER NOODLES *with* COCONUT, LIME & CUMIN DRESSING

YIELD: 4 SERVINGS / ACTIVE TIME: 30 MINUTES / TOTAL TIME: 40 MINUTES TO 2 HOURS AND 25 MINUTES

The combination of warming, pungent cumin, sweet and soothing coconut, and crispy cucumber is endlessly satisfying. This salad is fairly easy to assemble as well, though it does require opening up a young Thai coconut. Thai coconuts are as large as melons, resemble a whitish yurt, and have a moist, aromatic pulp that is very different from the solid flesh of mature coconuts. They can be found at most well-stocked Asian markets.

1. Quarter each cucumber half and then cut the quarters into "noodles" that are ⅛ inch wide. Place the strands on paper towels to drain.

2. Place the coconut on a work surface and steady it by holding the bottom with one hand. Using a mallet and a very large, sharp knife, place the bottom corner of the knife blade about 1½ inches below the tip of the coconut. Gently strike the knife with a mallet to create a small indentation on the surface. Place the bottom corner of the blade in the indentation, strike down harder on the mallet to crack the outer shell and break through to the inner shell of the coconut.

3. Make your second cut, using the same technique, so that the two combined incisions create a 90-degree angle. Continue this process with the third cut, which will create a "U" shape and then the fourth cut, which will create a square shape at the top of the coconut.

4. Using the bottom corner of your knife blade, pry open the square at the top of the coconut. If the square doesn't release easily, go over the cuts made again, this time using more force.

5. Once pried open, invert the coconut and pour the coconut water into a glass or cup and set aside.

6. Open the coconut by turning it over so that its opening is now on the side. Place the bottom corner of the knife blade halfway along the length of the coconut. Gently strike the knife with a mallet to create a small indentation on the surface. Making sure the bottom corner of the blade is placed in the previous indentation, strike down harder on the mallet to split the coconut open. Using a spoon, scrape out the coconut flesh inside and transfer it to a small bowl.

Continued . . .

INGREDIENTS:

- 5   LARGE CUCUMBERS, PEELED, HALVED LENGTHWISE, AND SEEDED
- 1   YOUNG THAI COCONUT
-      ZEST AND JUICE FROM 2 LIMES
- ¼   CUP COCONUT WATER (RESERVED FROM THE YOUNG THAI COCONUT)
- 1   TEASPOON CHILI-GARLIC SAUCE, PLUS MORE AS NEEDED
- 1   TEASPOON GRATED GINGER
- 1   TEASPOON SUGAR
- 1   TEASPOON CUMIN
- 1   TEASPOON KOSHER SALT
- ½   CUP SALTED, ROASTED PEANUTS, CHOPPED, FOR GARNISH
- 5-6   SCALLIONS, TRIMMED AND SLICED THIN, FOR GARNISH

7. Put the coconut flesh, lime juice, coconut water, chili-garlic sauce, ginger, sugar, cumin, and salt in a small food processor or a blender and puree until smooth.

8. Transfer the cucumber noodles to a large serving bowl. Top with the coconut mixture and toss to coat. Chill for at least 15 minutes and up to 2 hours in the refrigerator.

9. Sprinkle the lime zest, peanuts, and scallions on top of the dressed noodles and serve.

RICE SALAD BOWL *with* ADZUKI BEANS, AVOCADO, SNAP PEAS, JICAMA & BENIHANA'S GINGER DRESSING

YIELD: **2 SERVINGS** / ACTIVE TIME: **15 MINUTES** / TOTAL TIME: **20 MINUTES**

Growing up we would occasionally have the good fortune to go to a Benihana Hibachi Restaurant. The theater of cooking on the open stovetop was always great, but I also loved the food. At the beginning of the meal, one was presented with an iceberg lettuce salad that was coated in an orange-colored ginger dressing. The dressing was so good, you didn't even notice the bland lettuce or wan cherry tomatoes. Any vegetable would have been acceptable as long as it had that dressing. It turns out that I wasn't the only one who pined for that dressing, and the secret is now out.

1. Drain the adzuki beans and rinse under cool water. Drain again and set aside.

2. Divide the rice between two bowls. In this order, artfully arrange the beans, carrot, jicama, snap peas, and avocado on top of each portion.

3. Top each portion with a pinch of salt and some of the dressing, garnish with the sesame seeds, and serve.

BENIHANA'S GINGER DRESSING

1. Place all of the ingredients in a blender or food processor and puree until smooth.

INGREDIENTS:

- ½ CUP CANNED ADZUKI BEANS
- ½ CUP COOKED WHITE RICE, AT ROOM TEMPERATURE
- 1 CARROT, PEELED AND GRATED
- ½ JICAMA, PEELED AND JULIENNED
- 4-6 SUGAR SNAP PEAS, SLICED
- FLESH FROM 1 AVOCADO, SLICED THIN
- SALT, TO TASTE
- BENIHANA'S GINGER DRESSING (SEE RECIPE)
- WHITE SESAME SEEDS, FOR GARNISH

BENIHANA'S GINGER DRESSING

- ¼ CUP CHOPPED WHITE ONION
- ¼ CUP PEANUT OIL
- 1 TABLESPOON RICE VINEGAR
- 1 TABLESPOON MINCED FRESH GINGER
- 1 TABLESPOON MINCED CELERY
- 1 TABLESPOON SOY SAUCE
- 1 TEASPOON TOMATO PASTE
- 1½ TEASPOONS SUGAR
- 1 TEASPOON FRESH LEMON JUICE
- ½ TEASPOON KOSHER SALT
- BLACK PEPPER, TO TASTE

FENNEL, GRAPEFRUIT & PISTACHIO SALAD

YIELD: 2 SERVINGS / ACTIVE TIME: 10 MINUTES / TOTAL TIME: 10 MINUTES

While this may seem like an odd combination, the individual flavors meld together into a simple salad that was made for those days when you just don't feel like cooking.

1. Place the fennel and grapefruit in a bowl, drizzle with the oil, add the salt, season with pepper, and then add the pistachios. Toss to combine and serve.

TIP: To supreme a citrus fruit, trim the top and bottom from a piece of citrus and place it cut-side up. Cut along the contour of the fruit to remove the pith and peel. Cut one segment, lengthwise, between the pulp and the membrane. Make a similar slice on the other side of the segment and then remove the pulp. Set aside and repeat with the remaining segments.

INGREDIENTS:

½ LARGE FENNEL BULB, TRIMMED, CORED, AND SLICED VERY THIN

1 RUBY RED GRAPEFRUIT, SUPREMED AND CHOPPED

1 TABLESPOON OLIVE OIL

¼ TEASPOON KOSHER SALT

BLACK PEPPER, TO TASTE

2 TABLESPOONS SHELLED AND CHOPPED PISTACHIOS

COLD GREEN BEAN SALAD
with BLUE CHEESE & WALNUTS

YIELD: 4 SERVINGS / ACTIVE TIME: 15 MINUTES / TOTAL TIME: 20 MINUTES

When the green beans are coming in strong midsummer and you are looking for new ways to utilize them, try this salad. It is a cinch to prepare, requiring only that you blanch the beans and then whip up a vinaigrette. This would be a good time to use a high-quality blue cheese such as Stilton or Roquefort. The Vermont cheese maker Jasper Hill makes a fabulous blue called Bayley Hazen Blue. Only the freshest beans are worthy of that award-winning stuff.

1. Bring water to a boil in a medium saucepan. Add the green beans and salt and cook until the beans are al dente, about 5 minutes.

2. Drain and run beans under cold water to stop the cooking process. Pat dry with a paper towel.

3. Place the mustard, shallot, vinegar, and oil in a bowl and whisk to combine.

4. Place the green beans and remaining ingredients in a bowl and toss to combine. Add the vinaigrette, toss to coat, and serve cold or at room temperature.

INGREDIENTS:

1   LB. GREEN BEANS, TRIMMED

     SALT, TO TASTE

1   TEASPOON DIJON MUSTARD

½   TABLESPOON MINCED SHALLOT

2   TABLESPOONS WHITE WINE VINEGAR

⅓   CUP OLIVE OIL

     BLACK PEPPER, TO TASTE

2-4 OZ. BLUE CHEESE, CRUMBLED

2   OZ. WALNUTS, ROUGHLY CHOPPED

FIVE-BEAN SALAD
with GOOSEBERRY VINAIGRETTE

YIELD: 6 SERVINGS / ACTIVE TIME: 30 MINUTES / TOTAL TIME: 2 DAYS

Slow cooking the beans in chicken stock and cooling them overnight provides a lovely counter to the sweet and tangy dressing. This salad features the all-stars of the bean world, but you can use any bean you find appealing.

1. Drain and rinse the beans and peas and transfer them to a slow cooker. Add the stock, granulated garlic, bay leaves, red pepper flakes, and salt and cook on low for 8 hours, or until the beans are tender. Turn off the slow cooker and let the beans come to room temperature. Place the beans in the refrigerator overnight.

2. Place all of the remaining ingredients, except for the dressing, in a large salad bowl. Stir until combined.

3. Drain the beans. Place the beans in the salad bowl, add half of the Gooseberry Vinaigrette, and toss to coat. Serve with the remaining dressing on the side.

GOOSEBERRY VINAIGRETTE

1. Place all of the ingredients in a blender and puree until the consistency is silky and the dressing is thick enough to coat a wooden spoon.

TIP: Slow cooking the beans for this recipe imparts a far more complex flavor than using canned beans and is well worth the additional time.

INGREDIENTS:

- ¼ LB. KIDNEY BEANS, SOAKED OVERNIGHT
- ¼ LB. CANNELLINI BEANS, SOAKED OVERNIGHT
- ¼ LB. PINK BEANS, SOAKED OVERNIGHT
- ¼ LB. PINTO BEANS, SOAKED OVERNIGHT
- ¼ LB. WHOLE DRIED GREEN PEAS, SOAKED OVERNIGHT
- 4-6 CUPS CHICKEN STOCK (SEE PAGE 748 FOR HOMEMADE)
- 2 TABLESPOONS GRANULATED GARLIC
- 2 BAY LEAVES
- PINCH OF RED PEPPER FLAKES
- 3 TABLESPOONS KOSHER SALT
- 2 CUPS MINCED CELERY
- 2 LARGE RED RADISHES, GRATED
- 1 PARSNIP, PEELED AND MINCED
- ½ CUP CHOPPED FRESH PARSLEY
- 1 CUP CHOPPED SCALLION GREENS
- JUICE OF ½ LEMON
- GOOSEBERRY VINAIGRETTE (SEE RECIPE)

GOOSEBERRY VINAIGRETTE
- 3½ OZ. GOOSEBERRIES, WASHED
- ¼ CUP RED WINE VINEGAR
- ¼ CUP HONEY
- ½ CUP OLIVE OIL
- 1 TABLESPOON KOSHER SALT

LATE SUMMER SALAD *with* WILD MUSHROOMS, PARMESAN & PINE NUTS

YIELD: 2 TO 4 SERVINGS / ACTIVE TIME: 25 MINUTES / TOTAL TIME: 35 MINUTES

The trick to searing mushrooms is to give them plenty of room in the pan and not disturb them. This gets them nice and brown. Adding a light sprinkling of salt will help them release excess moisture as well, which further concentrates the flavor.

1. Coat the bottom of a saucepan with some of the oil and warm over medium-high heat. When the oil starts to shimmer, add the mushrooms, taking care not to crowd the pan. Sprinkle a pinch of salt over the mushrooms and then let them cook undisturbed until they release their liquid and begin to brown. Gently turn them over to sear the other side. When they are done, remove from the pan and set aside.

2. Place the onion and garlic in the pan, adding an additional splash of oil if the pan looks dry. Cook over medium heat until the onion has softened, about 5 minutes. Turn off heat and deglaze the pan with the vinegar, scraping off any browned bits from the bottom of the pan. Remove from heat and let the pan cool to room temperature.

3. Place the pine nuts in a dry skillet and toast over medium heat for 2 minutes, shaking the pan frequently so as not to burn the pine nuts. Transfer to a bowl and let cool.

4. Place the cooled onion-and-garlic mixture in a bowl and add the remaining oil. Whisk until combined and season with salt.

5. Arrange the greens on plates and top with the mushrooms, pine nuts, and a light sprinkling of Parmesan and dill. Top with the dressing and serve.

INGREDIENTS:

½ CUP OLIVE OIL, PLUS MORE AS NEEDED

½ LB. WILD MUSHROOMS, SLICED

SALT, TO TASTE

¼ CUP DICED RED ONION

1 GARLIC CLOVE, CHOPPED

¼ CUP BALSAMIC VINEGAR

1 TABLESPOON PINE NUTS

MESCLUN GREENS, FOR SERVING

2 TABLESPOONS GRATED PARMESAN CHEESE

CHOPPED DILL, TO TASTE

RED ONION VINAIGRETTE

YIELD: ¾ CUP / **ACTIVE TIME:** 10 MINUTES / **TOTAL TIME:** 10 MINUTES

This dressing has such nice kick that it only needs some mild Boston Bibb lettuce and sliced avocado to make a lovely salad. Adding watermelon radish would lend that simple dish some wonderful color, however.

1. Soak the red onion in water for 5 to 7 minutes to diminish its sharp bite and then chop it.

2. Combine all of the ingredients in a jar and shake until thoroughly combined. Serve immediately or store in the refrigerator until ready to use.

INGREDIENTS:

1	RED ONION, SLICED THIN
½	CUP OLIVE OIL, PLUS 2 TEASPOONS
1	GARLIC CLOVE, MINCED
½	TEASPOON MINCED FRESH THYME
¼	CUP APPLE CIDER VINEGAR
2	TABLESPOONS WHITE BALSAMIC VINEGAR
4	TEASPOONS HONEY
1	TEASPOON KOSHER SALT
1	TEASPOON BLACK PEPPER

SWEET ONION SALAD

YIELD: 4 SERVINGS / ACTIVE TIME: 20 MINUTES / TOTAL TIME: 25 MINUTES

Give the traditional tomato salad a little extra twist with grilled onions.

1. Preheat a gas or charcoal grill to medium heat and skewer the onions so they are easy to turn while grilling. Brush both sides with oil and season with salt and pepper.

2. When the grill is about 400°F, place the skewered onions directly onto the grill. Cook for about 10 minutes, turning at least once, until the edges become slightly soft and the onions start to char.

3. Remove from heat and cut the onions in half. Place them in a bowl and toss to separate the layers.

4. Add the tomatoes, basil, the 2 tablespoons of oil, and vinegar, toss until coated, and serve.

INGREDIENTS:

2   SWEET ONIONS, CUT INTO ½-INCH-THICK SLICES

2   TABLESPOONS OLIVE OIL, PLUS MORE AS NEEDED

     SALT AND PEPPER, TO TASTE

1   PINT GRAPE TOMATOES, HALVED

12   FRESH BASIL LEAVES, SLICED THIN OR TORN

2   TEASPOONS BALSAMIC VINEGAR

TABBOULEH *with* FETA

YIELD: 4 CUPS / ACTIVE TIME: 15 MINUTES / TOTAL TIME: 45 MINUTES

I love having tabbouleh in the fridge in summer. It is easy to make and fills you up without making you feel too heavy, a major plus in the heat. This recipe includes traditional ingredients like tomato and cucumber, but feel free to add any raw vegetable you like. Look for bulgur wheat in the bulk aisle, as it is less expensive there than in the prepackaged blends.

1. Place the bulgur in a heatproof bowl and add the boiling water, salt, and half of the lemon juice. Cover and let sit for about 20 minutes, or until the bulgur has absorbed the majority of the liquid and is tender. Drain any excess water and let cool completely.

2. Add the parsley, cucumber, tomato, scallions, mint, oil, and the remaining lemon juice and season with pepper. Taste and adjust the seasoning as necessary.

3. When ready to serve, place mesclun greens on a plate, top with the tabbouleh, and garnish with the feta.

INGREDIENTS:

½ CUP MEDIUM-GRAIN BULGUR WHEAT

1½ CUPS BOILING WATER

½ TEASPOON KOSHER SALT, PLUS MORE TO TASTE

½ CUP FRESH LEMON JUICE

2 CUPS CHOPPED FRESH FLAT-LEAF PARSLEY

1 CUCUMBER, PEELED, SEEDED, AND DICED

1 TOMATO, DICED

¼ CUP SLICED SCALLIONS

1 CUP FRESH MINT LEAVES

2 TABLESPOONS OLIVE OIL

BLACK PEPPER, TO TASTE

MESCLUN GREENS, FOR SERVING

2 OZ. FETA CHEESE, CRUMBLED, FOR GARNISH

ROASTED RADICCHIO, PEAR & GORGONZOLA SALAD

YIELD: 4 SERVINGS / ACTIVE TIME: 15 MINUTES / TOTAL TIME: 40 MINUTES

Cooking radicchio mellows it considerably, and as long as you are roasting it, you may as well roast the pears, too. This recipe is really more of an outline, as you should assemble this salad to your taste.

1. Preheat the oven to 400°F. Place the radicchio and pear on a baking sheet and drizzle with oil. Place in the oven and roast until they start to brown, about 10 minutes. Remove from the oven and let cool.

2. Build the salad on individual plates by putting greens, arugula, radicchio, pear, and hazelnuts on each one. Top with gorgonzola and drizzle with balsamic vinegar and olive oil. Season with salt and pepper and serve.

INGREDIENTS:

1   SMALL HEAD RADICCHIO, CORED AND SLICED

1   RIPE, FIRM PEAR, CORED AND SLICED

    OLIVE OIL, AS NEEDED

    MESCLUN GREENS, AS NEEDED

    ARUGULA, TO TASTE

¼   CUP ROUGHLY CHOPPED HAZELNUTS

1-2   OZ. GORGONZOLA CHEESE

    BALSAMIC VINEGAR, TO TASTE

    SALT AND PEPPER, TO TASTE

RADICCHIO & RICOTTA SALATA SALAD
with APPLE CIDER VINAIGRETTE

YIELD: 4 SERVINGS / ACTIVE TIME: 10 MINUTES / TOTAL TIME: 10 MINUTES

This is a salad designed to wake up the palate. The bitter radicchio counters the sweet apple and fennel. The key is to slice everything very fine, so all of the flavors can fit on the fork. The vinaigrette is the perfect sweet-tart topper, cutting through the smokiness of the grilled chicken for an irresistible finish.

1. Arrange the greens on four plates and top with equal amounts of radicchio, fennel, apple, and the ricotta salata. Top with the chicken, if using, and serve with the Apple Cider Vinaigrette.

APPLE CIDER VINAIGRETTE

1. Place all of the ingredients in a jar, shake until thoroughly combined, and serve.

INGREDIENTS:

- 3½ CUPS MESCLUN GREENS
- ½ HEAD RADICCHIO, CORED AND SLICED VERY THIN
- ½ LARGE FENNEL, TRIMMED AND SLICED VERY THIN
- 1 APPLE, CORED, SEEDED, AND SLICED THIN
- 2-3 OZ. RICOTTA SALATA CHEESE
- 2 CHICKEN BREASTS, GRILLED AND SLICED (OPTIONAL)

  APPLE CIDER VINAIGRETTE (SEE RECIPE), FOR SERVING

APPLE CIDER VINAIGRETTE
- 3 TABLESPOONS APPLE CIDER VINEGAR
- ½ CUP OLIVE OIL
- ½ TEASPOON SEA SALT
- ½ TEASPOON BLACK PEPPER
- 1 TEASPOON HONEY

LARB GAI

YIELD: 4 SERVINGS / ACTIVE TIME: 20 MINUTES / TOTAL TIME: 35 MINUTES

This zippy chicken salad originated in Laos but is commonly found in Thailand, and it's a good example of ingredients common to the region's cuisine. The only one that may be unfamiliar to American cooks is toasted rice powder. It is very easy to make: just dry-roast some rice in a pan until light brown and grind it to a powder. It gives a subtle, toasty flavor to the whole dish.

1. Warm a skillet over medium heat and add the chicken and a little water. Cook, using a wooden spoon to break the chicken up, until the chicken starts to brown, about 5 minutes. Add the shallot and cook until the chicken is cooked through. Transfer the mixture to a bowl and let cool.

2. Once the mixture has cooled, add the lemongrass, lime leaves, chili peppers (if using), lime juice, fish sauce, soy sauce, Toasted Rice Powder, cilantro, and mint. Stir to combine, taste, and season with salt and pepper.

3. Serve with the lettuce leaves, using them to scoop the mixture.

TIP: Lemongrass and lime leaves can be very fibrous, so make sure they are both minced very fine. Use an electric herb chopper, if one is available.

TOASTED RICE POWDER

1. Warm a cast-iron skillet over medium-high heat. Add the rice and toast until it starts to brown.

2. Remove and grind into a fine powder with a mortar and pestle.

INGREDIENTS:

1 LB. GROUND CHICKEN

1 SHALLOT, DICED

1 LEMONGRASS STALK, MINCED

2 MAKRUT LIME LEAVES, MINCED

3 RED CHILI PEPPERS, SEEDED AND CHOPPED (OPTIONAL)

¼ CUP FRESH LIME JUICE

1 TABLESPOON FISH SAUCE

1 TABLESPOON SOY SAUCE

1 TABLESPOON TOASTED RICE POWDER (SEE RECIPE)

¼ CUP CHOPPED FRESH CILANTRO

12 FRESH MINT LEAVES, CHOPPED

SALT AND PEPPER, TO TASTE

BIBB LETTUCE LEAVES, FOR SERVING

TOASTED RICE POWDER

½ CUP JASMINE RICE

COLD RICE SALAD *with* SUGAR SNAP PEAS, CARROTS, KOHLRABI & SHRIMP

YIELD: **4 SERVINGS** / ACTIVE TIME: **10 MINUTES** / TOTAL TIME: **40 MINUTES**

This is a great salad for a hot night since the only thing you need to cook is the rice, which you make in advance to give it time to cool down. White rice works perfectly well, but don't be afraid to experiment with one of the many varieties available, such as bamboo rice or forbidden rice.

1. Prepare rice according to the directions on the package. Remove from heat but keep it covered so that it does not dry out.

2. Once rice is cool, divide it between four bowls. Top each portion with some of the vegetables and three shrimp. Serve with the Basil & Cilantro Vinaigrette on the side.

BASIL & CILANTRO VINAIGRETTE

1. Place all of the ingredients in a jar and shake until combined.

INGREDIENTS:

1   CUP RICE

      HANDFUL OF SUGAR SNAP PEAS, TRIMMED AND SLICED

3   CARROTS, PEELED AND GRATED

1   KOHLRABI, PEELED AND CUBED

12   COOKED SHRIMP, CHILLED

      BASIL & CILANTRO VINAIGRETTE (SEE RECIPE), FOR SERVING

BASIL & CILANTRO VINAIGRETTE

½   CUP CHOPPED FRESH CILANTRO

½   CUP CHOPPED FRESH BASIL

2   TABLESPOONS CHOPPED FRESH FLAT-LEAF PARSLEY

1   GARLIC CLOVE, MINCED

2   TABLESPOONS SEEDED AND MINCED JALAPEÑO PEPPER

2   TABLESPOONS FRESH LIME OR LEMON JUICE

⅓   CUP OLIVE OIL

1   TEASPOON BLACK PEPPER

1   TEASPOON KOSHER SALT

PEA, HEART OF PALM, ARUGULA & PINE NUT SALAD

YIELD: 2 SERVINGS / ACTIVE TIME: 15 MINUTES / TOTAL TIME: 30 MINUTES

If you are in a salad rut, this one will launch you out of it. My sister-in-law Jen first discovered this recipe and served it to my mother, who now makes it at least a few times a month. The sweet peas are the perfect contrast to the peppery arugula and the hearts of palm and pine nuts round out the flavors and textures perfectly. The Red Wine Vinaigrette adds just the right amount of zing, and some Parmesan cheese makes it hearty enough for a substantial lunch.

1. Place the pine nuts in a small skillet and toast over high heat for about 1 minute, shaking the pan frequently to make sure they do not burn. Remove from heat and let cool.

2. Bring water to a boil in a saucepan. Add the frozen peas. When the water returns to a boil, drain the peas and run under very cold water. Drain again and set aside.

3. Place the arugula, hearts of palm, Parmesan, pine nuts, and peas in a salad bowl and toss to combine.

4. Add half the vinaigrette, toss to coat, taste, and add more dressing as necessary. Serve immediately.

RED WINE VINAIGRETTE

1. Place all of the ingredients in a jar and shake until combined.

INGREDIENTS:

1	TABLESPOON PINE NUTS
1	CUP FROZEN PEAS
2	CUPS PACKED ARUGULA
2	HEARTS OF PALM, SLICED
2	TABLESPOONS GRATED PARMESAN CHEESE
	RED WINE VINAIGRETTE (SEE RECIPE)

RED WINE VINAIGRETTE

3	TABLESPOONS RED WINE VINEGAR
½	CUP OLIVE OIL
1	TEASPOON DIJON MUSTARD
1	SHALLOT, MINCED
½	TEASPOON KOSHER SALT
½	TEASPOON BLACK PEPPER

ZUCCHINI NOODLES *with* OVEN-ROASTED STILTON, RADICCHIO & PEACHES

YIELD: 4 SERVINGS / ACTIVE TIME: 30 MINUTES / TOTAL TIME: 40 MINUTES

This recipe turns the concept of a salad on its head. Each element is cooked separately and then assembled at room temperature for a light supper.

1. Bring a large pot of water to a boil. Once it's boiling, add salt (1 tablespoon of salt for every 4 cups of water). Trim both ends from each zucchini. Using the julienne attachment of a mandoline or a vegetable spiralizer, carefully slice the zucchini into thin "noodles." Add the zucchini to the boiling water and cook for 2 minutes. Drain, run under cold water until cool, drain again, and set aside.

2. Place the pine nuts in a small skillet and toast over medium heat, stirring continuously, until they start to brown, about 2 minutes. Remove from heat and let cool.

3. Preheat the oven to 500°F.

4. Place the pine nuts, basil, and lemon juice in a food processor and puree until smooth. Transfer the mixture to a large bowl, add the oil, season with salt and pepper, and whisk to combine. Add the zucchini and toss to coat.

5. Place the Stilton, lemon zest, and honey in a small bowl, season with salt and pepper, and toss to combine. Transfer the mixture to a parchment-lined baking sheet, place it in the oven, turn the broiler on high, and broil until the top of the mixture has browned, 2 to 3 minutes. Remove from the oven and let cool for 2 minutes.

6. Arrange the radicchio on a platter and top with the zucchini, peach wedges, toasted cheese mixture, and the cranberries. Serve at room temperature.

INGREDIENTS:

SALT AND PEPPER, TO TASTE

4 ZUCCHINI

⅓ CUP PINE NUTS

2 HANDFULS FRESH BASIL LEAVES

ZEST AND JUICE OF 1 LEMON

2 TABLESPOONS OLIVE OIL

4 OZ. STILTON CHEESE, CRUMBLED

1½ TABLESPOONS HONEY

2 CUPS SHREDDED RADICCHIO

1 PEACH, HALVED, PITTED, AND CUT INTO WEDGES

1 TABLESPOON DRIED CRANBERRIES

SPINACH, BACON, AVOCADO & ORANGE SALAD

YIELD: 4 SERVINGS / ACTIVE TIME: 15 MINUTES / TOTAL TIME: 15 MINUTES

Spinach-and-bacon salad is a classic preparation. In our house, we add segmented oranges, avocado, and sunflower seeds and toss it all in a moderately sweet dressing. If you want to make it vegetarian, switch out the bacon for sautéed shiitake mushrooms. There is enough going on in this salad to make a meal of it, perhaps with some fresh bread on the side.

1. Place the spinach in a large salad bowl. Halve the orange segments and add them to the salad bowl, reserving one piece.

2. Squeeze the reserved orange segment over the avocado slices to prevent browning and add the avocado to the salad bowl. Add the vinaigrette, toss to coat, and top the salad with the bacon and sunflower seeds before serving.

RED WINE & MAPLE VINAIGRETTE

1. Place all of the ingredients in a small jar and shake until combined.

INGREDIENTS:

5 OZ. BABY SPINACH

1 NAVEL ORANGE, SUPREMED (SEE PAGE 432)

   FLESH FROM 1 AVOCADO, SLICED

   RED WINE & MAPLE VINAIGRETTE (SEE RECIPE)

2-4 SLICES BACON, COOKED AND CRUMBLED

1 TABLESPOON SUNFLOWER SEEDS

RED WINE & MAPLE VINAIGRETTE

½ CUP OLIVE OIL

2 TABLESPOONS RED WINE VINEGAR

1 TEASPOON DIJON MUSTARD

1 TEASPOON MAPLE SYRUP

   SALT AND PEPPER, TO TASTE

CHILLED CORN SALAD

YIELD: 4 TO 6 SERVINGS / ACTIVE TIME: 15 MINUTES / TOTAL TIME: 4 TO 24 HOURS

This recipe is a riff on the classic Mexican dish known as *esquites*.

1. Preheat the oven to 400°F.

2. Place the corn on a baking sheet and roast in the oven until it turns a light golden brown, about 35 minutes.

3. Remove the corn from the oven, let cool slightly, and then transfer to a large mixing bowl. Add the remaining ingredients and stir to combine.

4. Place the salad in the refrigerator for at least 3 hours, although letting it chill overnight is highly recommended.

TIP: The amount of jalapeño suggested in the ingredients is a safe amount of heat to serve to a broad spectrum of tastes. If you and yours like things spicier, feel free to include the seeds or another jalapeño.

INGREDIENTS:

2   CUPS CORN KERNELS

2   TABLESPOONS UNSALTED BUTTER

1   JALAPEÑO PEPPER, SEEDED, RIBBED, AND DICED, PLUS MORE TO TASTE

½   TEASPOON KOSHER SALT, PLUS MORE TO TASTE

2   TABLESPOONS MAYONNAISE

2   TEASPOONS GARLIC POWDER

3   TABLESPOONS SOUR CREAM OR MEXICAN CREMA

¼   TEASPOON CAYENNE PEPPER

¼   TEASPOON CHILI POWDER

2   TABLESPOONS FETA CHEESE

2   TABLESPOONS COTIJA CHEESE

2   TEASPOONS FRESH LIME JUICE

½   CUP CHOPPED FRESH CILANTRO

    BLACK PEPPER, TO TASTE

MIDSUMMER CORN & BEAN SALAD

YIELD: 4 TO 6 SERVINGS / ACTIVE TIME: 15 MINUTES / TOTAL TIME: 24 HOURS

This is a great make-ahead recipe when the local corn is ripe. In fact, if it is really fresh with great flavor, you can skip the cooking part all together and use raw kernels. I had some lovely dried beans on hand, but if you are pressed for time, use canned white or black beans. The maple syrup is meant to accentuate the sweetness of the corn, so add according to your personal preference.

1. Place the oil in a wide sauté pan, add the corn, and cook over medium-high heat until slightly brown, about 5 minutes. Remove from heat and let cool.

2. Drain the beans and place in a saucepan. Cover with water. Bring to a boil, reduce heat to a simmer, and cook until the beans are tender, about 45 minutes. Drain and cool.

3. Place all of the ingredients in a salad bowl, toss to combine, and chill in the refrigerator for 2 hours.

4. Taste, adjust seasoning as needed, and serve.

INGREDIENTS:

1 TABLESPOON OLIVE OIL

4 CUPS CORN KERNELS (PREFERABLY FRESH)

½ CUP DRIED BEANS, SOAKED OVERNIGHT

1 SMALL RED BELL PEPPER, DICED

1 SMALL GREEN BELL PEPPER, DICED

½ RED ONION, DICED

JUICE OF ½ LIME

1 TEASPOON CUMIN

TABASCO™, TO TASTE

3 TABLESPOONS CHOPPED FRESH CILANTRO

1 TABLESPOON MAPLE SYRUP, PLUS MORE TO TASTE

SALT AND PEPPER, TO TASTE

VIETNAMESE NOODLE SALAD

YIELD: 4 SERVINGS / ACTIVE TIME: 30 MINUTES / TOTAL TIME: 1 HOUR

Cold noodle salad is just the thing on a hot day. Why not assemble this tangy dish with refreshing herbs, cucumbers, tofu, and a Vietnamese dressing the next time the thermometer starts to climb?

1. Drain and cut the tofu into ½-inch strips. Arrange them in a single layer on a paper towel–lined tray. Cover with paper towels and pat dry. Let sit for 30 minutes, changing the paper towels after 15 minutes. Cut the dried strips into ½-inch cubes and set aside.

2. Bring a large pot of water to a boil. As it heats up, pick over the bean sprouts, discarding any discolored or spoiled ones. Put the remaining sprouts in a bowl of cold water. Discard the hulls that float to the top, then rinse under cold water. Add the sprouts to the boiling water and cook for 1 minute. Remove with a strainer and immediately run under cold water to stop them from cooking further. Drain well and chop.

3. Add the noodles to the pot of boiling water and stir for the first minute to prevent any sticking. Cook until they are tender but chewy, 5 to 7 minutes. Drain, rinse under cold water, and drain again.

4. Warm a large, deep skillet over medium heat for 2 to 3 minutes. Add the oil, raise heat to medium-high, and let warm for about 2 minutes. As the oil heats up, gently pat the tofu pieces with paper towels one more time and lightly sprinkle them with salt. When the oil starts to shimmer, add the tofu to the skillet in a single layer, working in batches if necessary. Make sure there is plenty of room in the skillet, as the tofu pieces will cook better. Cook, turning occasionally, until browned on all sides, 4 to 6 minutes total. Transfer to a paper towel–lined plate to drain.

5. Divide the noodles between four shallow bowls. Arrange the lettuce, herbs, cucumber, and tofu on top. Drizzle the Nuoc Cham over each portion and garnish with peanuts.

NUOC CHAM

1. Place all of the ingredients in a small bowl and stir until the sugar has dissolved.

TIP: The Nuoc Cham can be prepared up to 3 to 4 hours in advance and refrigerated. Just be sure to bring it back to room temperature before using.

INGREDIENTS:

1	LB. EXTRA-FIRM TOFU
2	CUPS MUNG BEAN SPROUTS
½	LB. KOREAN ACORN NOODLES OR RICE STICK NOODLES
¼	CUP PEANUT OIL
	SALT, TO TASTE
2½	CUPS GRATED ROMAINE LETTUCE
2	HANDFULS SOFT FRESH HERB MIXTURE, COARSELY CHOPPED OR TORN (MINT, CILANTRO, BASIL, AND/OR VIETNAMESE CORIANDER)
2	CUCUMBERS, PEELED AND JULIENNED
	NUOC CHAM (SEE RECIPE)
2	TABLESPOONS CHOPPED ROASTED PEANUTS, FOR GARNISH

NUOC CHAM

⅓	CUP HOT WATER
¼	CUP FRESH LIME JUICE
¼	CUP FISH SAUCE
¼	CUP BROWN SUGAR
3	TABLESPOONS RICE VINEGAR
3	GARLIC CLOVES, MINCED
	1-INCH PIECE FRESH GINGER, PEELED AND GRATED
1	HOT CHILI PEPPER, STEMMED, SEEDED, AND CHOPPED

UNABASHEDLY FRENCH GREEN LENTIL SALAD
with SHALLOTS

YIELD: 2 SERVINGS / ACTIVE TIME: 15 MINUTES / TOTAL TIME: 30 MINUTES

Green lentils from France are different from red, yellow, and brown lentils in that they hold their shape when cooked, which makes them perfect for a cold salad. This salad makes for a hearty lunch when put over greens. You can also take any leftover roasted veggies, dice them up, and put them on top with some goat cheese. The shallots, Dijon, and a generous pour of olive oil all make for a classic French preparation, so I have named it accordingly,

1. Place the lentils in a saucepan and cover by a few inches with water. Bring to a boil and then reduce heat to a simmer. Simmer until just tender, about 15 minutes. Drain and let cool.

2. Place the shallot, vinegar, oil, and mustard in a bowl and stir to combine. Place the lentils in a serving dish and top them with the shallot mixture, the carrot, and tarragon. Season with salt and pepper and serve.

INGREDIENTS:

⅓   CUP FRENCH GREEN LENTILS

2   TABLESPOONS DICED SHALLOT

1   TABLESPOON RED WINE VINEGAR

2   TABLESPOONS OLIVE OIL

1   TEASPOON WHOLE GRAIN DIJON MUSTARD

1   CARROT, PEELED AND GRATED

1   TEASPOON CHOPPED FRESH TARRAGON

SALT AND PEPPER, TO TASTE

SIDES

A nutritionally balanced meal is important, but even more important is that the components of said meal play well together, both in terms of diet and taste. The side dishes collected here make good on both of these requirements, from hearty, assertively flavored roasted vegetables to creamy gratins and lighter steamed offerings. No matter the entrée at the center of a meal, you will find accompaniments here that are sure to be ideal complements.

ASPARAGUS THREE WAYS,
plus TWO SAUCES

YIELD: 4 SERVINGS / ACTIVE TIME: 10 MINUTES / TOTAL TIME: 10 MINUTES

Steamed or grilled asparagus is amenable to many different sauces and dressings. The most traditional would be hollandaise, which adds a rich, lemony accompaniment to the sweet spears. Another option is the nutty tang of tahini dressing. As there are so many options, I've given the basics for cooking asparagus three ways, each as delectable as the next.

1. To prepare any asparagus, rinse well under cold water.

2. Take a spear and bend it close to the end that is opposite the pointy tip; it will snap off at the point where it starts to be too fibrous and tough to eat. Discard any fibrous ends, or reserve them for another preparation.

3. To blanch asparagus, put the spears in salted, boiling water for about 3 minutes, or just tender. Transfer immediately to an ice water bath to retain the green color.

4. To steam asparagus, arrange the spears in a steaming tray, place the tray above 1 inch of boiling water, and steam for roughly 5 minutes. Transfer immediately to an ice water bath to retain the green color.

5. To grill asparagus, preheat your grill to medium-high heat. Put the asparagus in a bowl and drizzle on some oil and salt. Toss to coat. Put the asparagus on the grill and cook until it just starts to char, about 4 minutes. Turn, cook the other side for another 4 minutes, then transfer to a plate.

6. Serve any of these preparations with your sauce of choice and season to taste.

INGREDIENTS:

1½ LBS. ASPARAGUS

SALT, TO TASTE

OLIVE OIL, TO TASTE

BLENDER HOLLANDAISE
(SEE RECIPE), FOR SERVING
(OPTIONAL)

TAHINI DRESSING (SEE
RECIPE), FOR SERVING
(OPTIONAL)

Continued . . .

BLENDER HOLLANDAISE

1. Place the egg yolks, salt, and lemon juice in a blender and turn on high for a few seconds.

2. Melt the butter in a small saucepan over medium-low heat, being careful not to let it brown.

3. While the butter is hot, turn on the blender and, with the top off, slowly drizzle the hot butter into the eggs until fully emulsified.

4. Taste and adjust seasoning if necessary.

TAHINI DRESSING

1. Place the tahini, garlic, oil, and honey in a blender and puree until smooth.

2. Whisk in the lemon juice. If the sauce is too thick, add some water a spoonful at a time.

3. Place the sesame seeds in a small pan and toast over medium heat. Cook for about 3 minutes.

4. Season the dressing with salt and pepper, top with the toasted sesame seeds, and serve.

INGREDIENTS:

BLENDER HOLLANDAISE

3   LARGE EGG YOLKS

¼   TEASPOON KOSHER SALT

2   TABLESPOONS FRESH LEMON JUICE

1   STICK UNSALTED BUTTER

TAHINI DRESSING

¼   CUP TAHINI

1   GARLIC CLOVE, CRUSHED

2   TABLESPOONS OLIVE OIL

1   TEASPOON HONEY

    JUICE OF 1 LEMON

    WATER, AS NEEDED

1   TABLESPOON SESAME SEEDS, FOR GARNISH

    SALT AND BLACK PEPPER, TO TASTE

SIMPLE STIR-FRIED BOK CHOY

YIELD: 2 SERVINGS / ACTIVE TIME: 10 MINUTES / TOTAL TIME: 10 MINUTES

I have always considered bok choy to be the most elegant member of the cabbage family. It is sweet and delicate; the perfect accompaniment to any main dish. When I want a simple side, I'll make this stir-fry. Adding a splash of mirin at the end of cooking brings out the sweetness of the vegetable without overwhelming it.

1. Place the oil in a small pan and warm over medium-high heat. When it starts to shimmer, add the bok choy and sauté until the green part of the cabbage has wilted, about 5 minutes.

2. Add garlic and cook for 2 minutes, then add the mirin and soy sauce, stir to combine, and cook for 1 more minute.

3. Season with salt and serve.

INGREDIENTS:

1   TABLESPOON OLIVE OIL

½   LB. BOK CHOY, SLICED

2   GARLIC CLOVES, MINCED

1   TABLESPOON MIRIN

1   TEASPOON SOY SAUCE

    SALT, TO TASTE

KIMCHI

YIELD: 4 CUPS / ACTIVE TIME: 30 MINUTES / TOTAL TIME: 3 TO 7 DAYS

Simple and versatile, kimchi is the perfect introduction to all that fermentation has to offer.

1. Place the cabbage and salt in a large bowl and stir to combine. Work the mixture with your hands, squeezing to remove as much liquid as possible. Let the mixture rest for 2 hours.

2. Add the remaining ingredients, except for the water. Stir the mixture until well combined and squeeze to remove as much liquid as possible.

3. Transfer the mixture to a container and press down so it is tightly packed. The liquid should be covering the mixture. If it is not, add water until the mixture is covered.

4. Cover the jar and let the mixture sit at room temperature for 3 to 7 days, removing the lid daily to release the gas that has built up. When the taste is to your liking, store in an airtight container in the refrigerator.

INGREDIENTS:

1	HEAD NAPA CABBAGE, CUT INTO STRIPS
½	CUP KOSHER SALT
2	TABLESPOONS MINCED GINGER
2	TABLESPOONS MINCED GARLIC
1	TEASPOON SUGAR
5	TABLESPOONS RED PEPPER FLAKES
3	BUNCHES SCALLIONS, TRIMMED AND SLICED
	FILTERED WATER, AS NEEDED

ROASTED BRUSSELS SPROUTS *with* BACON, BLUE CHEESE & PICKLED RED ONION

YIELD: 4 TO 6 SERVINGS / ACTIVE TIME: 15 MINUTES / TOTAL TIME: 40 MINUTES

Brussels sprouts have a bad reputation with a lot of folks, but when seared and seasoned well, their savory, nutty flavor is a revelation, able to go toe-to-toe with rich ingredients like bacon and blue cheese.

1. Place the vinegar, water, sugar, and salt in a saucepan and bring to a boil. Place the onion in a bowl and pour the boiling liquid over the slices. Cover and allow to cool completely.

2. Place the bacon in a large sauté pan over medium heat and cook, stirring occasionally, until crisp, about 8 minutes. Transfer to a paper towel–lined plate and leave the rendered fat in the pan.

3. Place the Brussels sprouts in the pan cut-side down, season with salt and pepper, and cook over medium heat until they are a deep golden brown, about 7 minutes.

4. Transfer the Brussels sprouts to a platter, top with the pickled onions, bacon, and blue cheese, and serve.

INGREDIENTS:

1   CUP CHAMPAGNE VINEGAR

1   CUP WATER

½   CUP SUGAR

2   TEASPOONS KOSHER SALT, PLUS MORE TO TASTE

1   SMALL RED ONION, SLICED

½   LB. BACON, CUT INTO 1-INCH PIECES

1½   LBS. BRUSSELS SPROUTS, TRIMMED AND HALVED

    BLACK PEPPER, TO TASTE

4   OZ. BLUE CHEESE, CRUMBLED

FRIED BRUSSELS SPROUTS
with MAPLE-CIDER GLAZE

YIELD: 2 TO 4 SERVINGS / **ACTIVE TIME:** 10 MINUTES / **TOTAL TIME:** 15 MINUTES

While Vermont may be several hundred miles from the heart of American BBQ turf, the folks at Bluebird Barbeque in Burlington know how to make some fine pulled pork, brisket, and ribs. They put their own mark on this art form, slow smoking the meat and serving it with homemade sauces and pickles. Though all of their meat is exceptional, one of my favorite things on the menu is their seasonal offering of Fried Brussels Sprouts with Maple-Cider Glaze. Chef Dan Miele exercises plenty of restraint with the glaze, ensuring it is just tangy and sweet enough, and he was kind enough to share his recipe with me.

---

1. Place the maple syrup, vinegar, apple cider, and a pinch of salt in a medium saucepan and cook over medium heat, stirring constantly, until reduced it has by one-quarter. Remove from heat and set aside.

2. Add oil to a Dutch oven until it is about 3 inches deep. Warm over medium-high heat until it is 350°F or a scrap of Brussels sprout sizzles upon contact. Place the Brussels sprouts in the oil and fry until they are browned, 1 to 2 minutes. Transfer to a paper towel–lined plate to drain.

3. Place the Brussels sprouts in a bowl, season with salt, and add 1 tablespoon of the glaze for every cup of Brussels sprouts. Toss until evenly coated and serve.

TIP: If you prefer not to deep-fry the Brussels sprouts, toss them with oil and salt and roast at 375°F for 20 minutes, until the Brussels sprouts are tender but still have a crunch to them.

INGREDIENTS:

- ¾ CUP REAL MAPLE SYRUP
- ½ CUP APPLE CIDER VINEGAR
- ½ CUP APPLE CIDER
- SALT, TO TASTE
- VEGETABLE OIL, FOR FRYING
- 1 LB. BRUSSELS SPROUTS, TRIMMED AND HALVED

STOVE-TOP BRUSSELS SPROUTS

YIELD: 4 SERVINGS / ACTIVE TIME: 10 MINUTES / TOTAL TIME: 15 MINUTES

The roasted Brussels sprout was my gateway preparation, but I have since developed a method I like even more. Both achieve that browned, crunchy exterior (I prefer them almost black), but I like the control I have with the stovetop method, and it's very quick.

1. Warm a wide sauté pan over high heat. When it begins to smoke, add all of the Brussels sprouts and a few tablespoons of water. Place the lid on and steam for 2 minutes.

2. Remove the lid and add enough oil to coat the bottom of the pan. Reduce heat to medium and let the Brussels sprouts brown, turning them every so often to brown on all sides.

3. Continue cooking until the desired tenderness is achieved, adding more oil if the pan starts to look dry. Season with salt and pepper and serve.

INGREDIENTS:

1 LB. BRUSSELS SPROUTS, TRIMMED AND HALVED

WATER, AS NEEDED

OLIVE OIL, AS NEEDED

SALT AND PEPPER, TO TASTE

GRILLED CABBAGE

YIELD: 4 SERVINGS / ACTIVE TIME: 15 MINUTES / TOTAL TIME: 45 MINUTES

This deceptively simple preparation of grilled cabbage results in a mellow, tasty side. You could even brush the wedges with oil and place them directly on the grill for a few minutes before placing them in aluminum foil.

1. Preheat your grill to medium heat and cut the head of cabbage into 8 wedges.

2. Remove the core and place the wedges on a large piece of aluminum foil. Season with the garlic powder, salt, and pepper. Create a packet by folding the foil over and crimping the edges.

3. When the grill is about 400°F, place the packet on the grill, cover the grill, and cook until tender, 30 to 40 minutes. Remove from the packet and serve immediately.

INGREDIENTS:

1   LARGE HEAD CABBAGE

1½   TEASPOONS GARLIC POWDER

    SALT AND PEPPER, TO TASTE

BASIC RED CABBAGE SLAW

YIELD: 2 TO 4 SERVINGS / ACTIVE TIME: 10 MINUTES / TOTAL TIME: 2 TO 3 HOURS

This is a topper that should be made a few hours ahead of time to give the cabbage time to soften. Once it is ready, it works on top of tacos and is a nice complement to grilled chicken and steak.

1. Place the cabbage in a large bowl, sprinkle the salt on top, and toss to distribute. Use your hands to work the salt into the cabbage, then let it sit for 2 to 3 hours.

2. Once it has rested, taste to gauge the saltiness: if too salty, rinse under cold water and let drain; if just right, add the lime juice and cilantro, stir to combine, and serve.

INGREDIENTS:

1   SMALL RED CABBAGE, CORED AND SLICED AS THINLY AS POSSIBLE

1   TEASPOON KOSHER SALT, PLUS MORE TO TASTE

    JUICE OF 1 LIME

1   BUNCH FRESH CILANTRO, CHOPPED

SAUTÉED RED CABBAGE *with* APPLES, FENNEL & BALSAMIC

YIELD: 4 SERVINGS / ACTIVE TIME: 25 MINUTES / TOTAL TIME: 30 MINUTES

This is a lovely dish for fall when the weather cools. It is very easy to make vegan by substituting olive oil for the butter.

1. Place the cabbage in a large sauté pan with a tablespoon of the butter and the water. Bring to a boil and cover the pan. Let the cabbage steam until the thick ribs are tender, 5 to 8 minutes, then remove the lid and cook until the water has evaporated.

2. Add the remaining butter, the apple, fennel seeds, and pinches of salt and pepper. Reduce heat to medium-low and cook, stirring occasionally.

3. When the apples and cabbage have caramelized, add the vinegar, cook for another minute, and then serve with brown rice or mashed potatoes.

INGREDIENTS:

- ½ RED CABBAGE, CORED AND SLICED
- 3 TABLESPOONS UNSALTED BUTTER
- ¼ CUP WATER
- 1 APPLE, PEELED, CORED, AND DICED
- 1 TEASPOON FENNEL SEEDS

    SALT AND PEPPER, TO TASTE
- 1-2 TABLESPOONS BALSAMIC VINEGAR

    BROWN RICE OR MASHED POTATOES, FOR SERVING

SAUTÉED RADICCHIO
with BEANS, PARMESAN & BALSAMIC

YIELD: 4 SERVINGS / ACTIVE TIME: 1 HOUR / TOTAL TIME: 5 TO 25 HOURS

There are many good companions to radicchio, and among them are mild, creamy beans. You can use any type of dry bean in this dish, but I would choose a medium-sized one like Jacob's Cattle or Cannellini. The Parmesan cheese and balsamic are considered condiments for this dish, so add as much or as little as you like. If you have a fun, infused balsamic, like fig or pear, this would be a good opportunity to use it.

1. Place the beans in a colander and rinse with cold water. Place them in a pot, cover by 1 inch with water, and leave to soak for at least 4 hours and ideally overnight.

2. Drain the beans, place them in a small saucepan, cover with water, and bring to a boil. Reduce to a simmer and cook for 30 minutes, checking every so often to make sure there is enough liquid in the pan. When the beans are tender but not mushy, remove from heat and let cool.

3. Place the oil in a sauté pan, warm over medium heat, and add the radicchio. Sauté until it starts to wilt and brown, about 3 minutes. Add the shallot and garlic and cook until everything is browned and the garlic is fragrant, about 5 minutes. Deglaze the pan with the wine and stock.

4. Drain the beans and add them to the radicchio mixture. Season with salt and pepper, stir in the thyme, and cook until most of the liquid has evaporated. Remove the pan from heat. Serve warm or at room temperature, topped with Parmesan cheese and a splash of balsamic vinegar.

INGREDIENTS:

- ⅔ CUP DRIED BEANS
- 1 TABLESPOON OLIVE OIL
- 1 SMALL HEAD RADICCHIO, CORED AND SLICED THIN
- 1 SHALLOT, DICED
- 1 GARLIC CLOVE, MINCED
- ¼ CUP WHITE WINE
- ¼ CUP CHICKEN OR VEGETABLE STOCK (SEE PAGES 748 AND 755, RESPECTIVELY, FOR HOMEMADE)
- SALT AND PEPPER, TO TASTE
- ½ TEASPOON CHOPPED FRESH THYME
- PARMESAN CHEESE, GRATED, FOR GARNISH
- BALSAMIC VINEGAR, FOR GARNISH

SAVORY CARROT HALWA

YIELD: 2 SERVINGS / ACTIVE TIME: 15 MINUTES / TOTAL TIME: 20 MINUTES

Carrot Halwa is an Indian dish that is usually prepared as a dessert for special occasions or festivals. Grated carrots are simmered in milk and cardamom until tender and then sugar is added to make a pudding that is sometimes served with raisins. I had a similar dish at a restaurant in Montpelier, Vermont, called Salt that, sadly, no longer exists, and I've wanted to recreate something like it ever since. This version of Halwa omits the sugar, but the carrots ensure it is still plenty sweet.

1. Melt the butter in a medium saucepan, then add the carrots and cardamom and cook over medium heat until the carrots start to soften, about 5 minutes.

2. Add the milk, bring to a simmer, and cook until the milk has reduced and the carrots are very soft. Season with salt and serve.

INGREDIENTS:

1   TABLESPOON UNSALTED BUTTER

½   LB. CARROTS, PEELED AND GRATED

¼   TEASPOON GROUND CARDAMOM

1   CUP WHOLE MILK

    SALT, TO TASTE

CARROT & JICAMA SLAW

Carrots and jicama are both sweet, so they need a zesty dressing. Fresh lime juice will give them some zip and the cilantro adds a citrusy flavor. If you can find toasted pumpkin seed oil, it really gives this slaw some backbone. If not, olive oil also works. Don't go in thinking the ancho chili powder is spicy, as it adds just a hint of smoke.

1. Grate the carrots and jicama into a bowl and stir to combine.

2. Add the remaining ingredients and gently toss to combine. Taste, adjust the seasoning as needed, and serve.

INGREDIENTS:

½ LB. CARROTS, PEELED

½ LB. JICAMA, PEELED

1-2 TABLESPOONS FRESH LIME JUICE

1 TABLESPOON TOASTED PUMPKIN SEED OR OLIVE OIL

¼ TEASPOON ANCHO CHILI POWDER

¼ CUP CHOPPED FRESH CILANTRO

SALT, TO TASTE

STIR-FRIED CARROT NOODLES

YIELD: 4 SERVINGS / ACTIVE TIME: 30 MINUTES / TOTAL TIME: 30 MINUTES

Showing the versatility of carrots, this recipe sends them through the spiralizer to make "noodles" and then tops them with a rich peanut-sesame sauce.

1. Place the sesame seeds in a small skillet and toast over medium heat until golden brown and aromatic, about 2 minutes. Transfer the sesame seeds to a small bowl and set aside.

2. Place the peanut butter, water, vinegar, soy sauce, brown sugar, sesame oil, chili sauce, and ginger in a small saucepan, whisk to combine, and bring to a gentle boil over medium-low heat. Cook, stirring frequently, until the sauce thickens, 4 to 5 minutes. Remove the sauce from heat and set aside.

3. Warm a wok or a large skillet over medium heat for 2 to 3 minutes. Raise heat to medium-high and add the peanut oil. When the oil begins to shimmer, add half of the carrots and a pinch of salt and stir-fry until the carrots have softened, about 2 minutes. Transfer the carrots to a bowl and set aside. Repeat the process with the remaining carrots, adding peanut oil if necessary.

4. Add the sauce to the bowl and toss until the carrots are evenly coated. Garnish with the toasted sesame seeds and scallions and serve.

INGREDIENTS:

- 2 TEASPOONS SESAME SEEDS
- 2 TABLESPOONS SMOOTH PEANUT BUTTER
- 2 TABLESPOONS WATER
- 2 TABLESPOONS SEASONED RICE VINEGAR
- 1 TABLESPOON SOY SAUCE
- 1 TABLESPOON LIGHT BROWN SUGAR
- 2 TEASPOONS TOASTED SESAME OIL
- 1 TEASPOON CHILI SAUCE, PLUS MORE TO TASTE
- 1-INCH PIECE GINGER, PEELED AND GRATED
- 2 TABLESPOONS PEANUT OIL, PLUS MORE AS NEEDED
- 4-6 LARGE CARROTS, PEELED AND SPIRALIZED OR GRATED
- SALT, TO TASTE
- 5-6 SCALLIONS, TRIMMED AND CHOPPED, FOR GARNISH

SPICY BABY CARROTS *with* TOASTED SEED GRANOLA & HONEY-THYME YOGURT

YIELD: 4 TO 6 SERVINGS / ACTIVE TIME: 30 MINUTES / TOTAL TIME: 1 HOUR AND 45 MINUTES

This spice blend is similar to what you would find in a barbecue rub. It works exceptionally well with the sweet carrots and is a nice spring dish to remind you that warmer weather is just around the bend.

1. Preheat the oven to 375°F.

2. Wash and trim the carrots. Drain and pat dry. Place the carrots, oil, the 1½ tablespoons of salt, pepper, cumin, fennel, coriander, paprika, and brown sugar in a bowl and toss to coat evenly. Arrange the carrots in an even layer on a foil-lined baking sheet. Place the carrots in the oven and roast for about 25 minutes, until tender. Remove and let cool slightly.

3. Place the yogurt, honey, remaining salt, and the thyme in the serving dish and stir to combine. Place the carrots on top and sprinkle the granola over the carrots. Garnish with additional thyme and serve.

TOASTED SEED GRANOLA

1. Preheat the oven to 300°F. Place the maple syrup, honey, brown sugar, oil, and salt in a small saucepan and warm over medium heat, stirring until the sugar has dissolved.

2. Place the oats in a mixing bowl, add the honey mixture, and stir until the oats are evenly coated. Transfer to a parchment-lined baking sheet, place it in the oven, and bake for 40 minutes, stirring the mixture every 10 minutes to ensure it bakes evenly.

3. Remove from the oven and let cool slightly. Transfer to a mixing bowl, fold in the cranberries and toasted squash seeds, and serve.

TIP: If using multiple colors of carrots to enhance the presentation, season and roast them separately as the purple variety will bleed and color the others.

INGREDIENTS:

2	LBS. BABY CARROTS
2	TABLESPOONS OLIVE OIL
1½	TABLESPOONS KOSHER SALT, PLUS 1½ TEASPOONS
1	TEASPOON BLACK PEPPER
2	TEASPOONS CUMIN
1	TEASPOON GROUND FENNEL
1	TEASPOON CORIANDER
1	TEASPOON PAPRIKA
2	TEASPOONS BROWN SUGAR
2	CUPS PLAIN GREEK YOGURT
2	TABLESPOONS HONEY
1½	TEASPOONS CHOPPED FRESH THYME LEAVES, PLUS MORE FOR GARNISH
½	CUP TOASTED SEED GRANOLA (SEE RECIPE)

TOASTED SEED GRANOLA

1	TABLESPOON MAPLE SYRUP
2	TABLESPOONS HONEY
2	TABLESPOONS BROWN SUGAR
2	TABLESPOONS OLIVE OIL
1	TEASPOON KOSHER SALT
1½	CUPS OATS
½	CUP DRIED CRANBERRIES
¾	CUP TOASTED SQUASH SEEDS

ROASTED CAULIFLOWER AU GRATIN

YIELD: 2 SERVINGS / ACTIVE TIME: 20 MINUTES / TOTAL TIME: 1 HOUR AND 15 MINUTES

One surefire way to get people excited about cauliflower is poaching it in a flavorful stock and then caramelizing mild, nutty cheeses like Emmental and Parmesan on top.

1. Place all of the ingredients, except for the cauliflower and cheeses, in a large saucepan and bring to a boil. Reduce heat so that the mixture simmers gently, add the head of cauliflower, and poach until tender, about 30 minutes.

2. While the cauliflower is poaching, preheat the oven to 450°F. Transfer the tender cauliflower to a baking sheet, place it in the oven, and bake until the top is a deep, golden brown, about 10 minutes.

3. Remove from the oven and spread the cheeses evenly over the top. Return to the oven and bake until the cheeses have browned. Remove from the oven and let cool slightly before cutting it in half and serving.

INGREDIENTS:

2	CUPS WHITE WINE
2½	CUPS WATER
⅓	CUP KOSHER SALT
2	STICKS UNSALTED BUTTER
6	GARLIC CLOVES, CRUSHED
2	SHALLOTS, HALVED
1	CINNAMON STICK
3	WHOLE CLOVES
1	TEASPOON BLACK PEPPERCORNS
1	SPRIG FRESH SAGE
2	SPRIGS FRESH THYME
1	HEAD CAULIFLOWER, LEAVES AND STALK REMOVED
1	CUP GRATED EMMENTAL CHEESE
¼	CUP GRATED PARMESAN CHEESE

CELERIAC PUREE

YIELD: 4 SERVINGS / ACTIVE TIME: 10 MINUTES / TOTAL TIME: 45 MINUTES

Whenever I work with celeriac, I remind myself to keep it simple and allow the unique flavor to shine.

1. Trim the ends from the celeriac, remove the skin with a vegetable peeler, and use a knife to cut out any recessed or pocked areas. Cut the remainder into thin slices.

2. Place the celeriac, cream, milk, salt, and pepper in a saucepan and bring to a simmer over medium heat, stirring occasionally. Cook until the celery root is fork-tender, about 30 minutes.

3. Transfer the mixture to a blender and puree. Add the butter, season with salt and pepper, and serve.

INGREDIENTS:

1½   LBS. CELERIAC

½   CUP HEAVY CREAM

½   CUP WHOLE MILK

     SALT AND PEPPER, TO TASTE

1   STICK UNSALTED BUTTER

RICED CAULIFLOWER

YIELD: 2 SERVINGS / ACTIVE TIME: 10 MINUTES / TOTAL TIME: 10 MINUTES

This simple dish provides the texture of rice with the nutritional benefits of cauliflower. It can be used in stir-fries or to accompany curries and is excellent on its own with a little butter.

1. Place the cauliflower in a food processor and pulse until it becomes granular.

2. Place the oil in a large skillet and warm over medium heat. When the oil starts to shimmer, add the cauliflower, cover the pan, and cook until tender, 3 to 5 minutes.

3. Season with salt and pepper and serve.

INGREDIENTS:

1   LARGE HEAD CAULIFLOWER, TRIMMED AND CHOPPED

¼   CUP OLIVE OIL

      SALT AND PEPPER, TO TASTE

CAULIFLOWER MASH

YIELD: 4 SERVINGS / ACTIVE TIME: 5 MINUTES / TOTAL TIME: 20 MINUTES

Cauliflower is so versatile; it can take on forms that you would never expect. From pizza crusts and hummus to rice and this version, which puts mashed potatoes to shame, cauliflower deserves a gold medal for its contributions to the dinner table.

1. Bring salted water to a boil in a large saucepan. Add the cauliflower and cook until tender, about 10 minutes. Drain and let cool slightly.

2. Place the cauliflower, butter, cream, salt, and pepper in a food processor and blitz until the mixture is rich and smooth. Serve immediately.

INGREDIENTS:

SALT AND PEPPER, TO TASTE

1   HEAD CAULIFLOWER, TRIMMED AND CUT INTO CROWNS

3   TABLESPOONS UNSALTED BUTTER, PLUS 1 TEASPOON

¼   CUP HEAVY CREAM

HOME-STYLE BAKED BEANS

YIELD: 6 TO 8 SERVINGS / **ACTIVE TIME:** 30 MINUTES / **TOTAL TIME:** 1½ TO 2 HOURS

mages of cowboys and campfires will be dancing in your head thanks to this cast-iron skillet version of baked beans.

1. Preheat the oven to 325°F.

2. Warm a 12-inch cast-iron skillet over medium heat and add half of the bacon pieces. Cook until the bacon is just starting to crisp up, about 6 minutes. Transfer to a paper towel–lined plate.

3. Place the remaining bacon in the skillet, raise heat to medium-high, and cook, turning often, until the pieces are browned and crispy, about 10 minutes. Reduce heat to medium. Add the onion and bell pepper and cook, stirring occasionally, until the vegetables start to soften, about 6 minutes.

4. Add the salt, beans, barbecue sauce, mustard, and brown sugar. Stir, season with salt and pepper, and bring to a simmer.

5. Lay the partially cooked pieces of bacon on top and transfer the skillet to the oven. Bake for 1 hour, until the bacon on top is crispy and browned and the sauce is thick. If the consistency seems too thin, cook for an additional 15 to 30 minutes, checking frequently so as not to overcook the beans.

6. Remove from the oven and allow to cool slightly before serving.

INGREDIENTS:

- 6   STRIPS THICK-CUT BACON
- ½   ONION, DICED
- ½   CUP SEEDED AND DICED BELL PEPPER
- 1   TEASPOON KOSHER SALT, PLUS MORE TO TASTE
- 2   (14 OZ.) CANS PINTO BEANS, RINSED AND DRAINED
- 1   CUP BARBECUE SAUCE
- 1   TEASPOON DIJON MUSTARD
- 2   TABLESPOONS DARK BROWN SUGAR

     BLACK PEPPER, TO TASTE

POTATO & CELERIAC GRATIN
with GRUYÈRE & FIGS

YIELD: 4 SERVINGS / ACTIVE TIME: 25 MINUTES / TOTAL TIME: 1 HOUR

Potato gratin is among my favorite dishes, but sometimes it is fun to put a twist on your favorite classics. Here, I incorporated celeriac and added some figs to bring out the sweetness in both the celeriac and potatoes. When I cook a gratin, I always parboil the vegetables before putting them in the dish with the rest of the ingredients to make sure everything will be cooked through. Plus, the flavor provided by the bay leaf, milk, and crushed garlic is worth the added effort.

1. Preheat the oven to 375°F.

2. Place the potatoes and celeriac in a medium saucepan and cover with water. Add the bay leaf, 1 teaspoon of the salt, the garlic, and milk, bring to a boil, and then reduce heat. Simmer for 1 minute and then drain. Remove the bay leaf and discard.

3. Butter a 10-inch oval gratin dish or casserole dish and add half of the potatoes and celeriac, making sure they are evenly distributed. Sprinkle half of the figs, some salt, half of the Gruyère, and the pinch of nutmeg on top. Repeat with the remaining potatoes and celeriac, seasonings, and Gruyère.

4. Pour the cream over the top and cover the dish with aluminum foil. Place in the oven and bake for 20 minutes. Remove the foil and bake for another 15 minutes, until the top is browned and most of the liquid has cooked off.

5. Remove from the oven and let stand for 15 minutes before serving.

INGREDIENTS:

1½ LBS. RUSSET POTATOES, PEELED AND SLICED THIN

½ LB. CELERIAC, PEELED AND SLICED THIN

1 BAY LEAF

2 TEASPOONS KOSHER SALT

2 GARLIC CLOVES, CRUSHED

2 TABLESPOONS MILK

3 DRIED OR FRESH FIGS, DICED

4 OZ. GRUYÈRE CHEESE, GRATED

PINCH OF NUTMEG

½ CUP HEAVY CREAM

SOUTHERN COLLARD GREENS

YIELD: 4 TO 6 SERVINGS / ACTIVE TIME: 30 MINUTES / TOTAL TIME: 2 HOURS AND 30 MINUTES

For this recipe I went to the source of my favorite collards: A Lowcountry Backyard Restaurant in Hilton Head, South Carolina. The proprietor, Phillip Barr, who has been cooking them for 36 years, learned from his mother and father, who cooked them their entire lives. Mr. Barr was not willing to give me exact amounts for his ingredients, but he did give me some useful information regarding the long cook time: When you think they are done, just keep cooking them.

1. Place the oil in a large saucepan and warm over medium-high heat. When the oil starts to shimmer, add the onion and sauté until translucent, about 3 minutes. Add the ham, reduce heat to medium, and cook until the ham starts to brown, about 5 minutes.

2. Add the remaining ingredients, stir to combine, and cover the pan. Braise the collard greens until they are very tender, about 2 hours. Check on the collards every so often and add water if all of the liquid has evaporated.

INGREDIENTS:

2   TABLESPOONS OLIVE OIL

1   ONION, DICED

½   LB. SMOKED HAM, DICED

4   GARLIC CLOVES, DICED

3   LBS. COLLARD GREENS, STEMS REMOVED, CHOPPED

2   CUPS VEGETABLE STOCK (SEE PAGE 755 FOR HOMEMADE)

¼   CUP APPLE CIDER VINEGAR

1   TABLESPOON BROWN SUGAR

1   TEASPOON RED PEPPER FLAKES

HOT & GARLICKY EGGPLANT NOODLES

YIELD: 4 SERVINGS / ACTIVE TIME: 45 MINUTES / TOTAL TIME: 45 MINUTES

Eggplants make for good veggie noodles because of their fibrous nature. Use an Italian variety and make sure there is enough room in the pan to fry them; otherwise, they will steam instead of brown.

1. Trim the ends of each eggplant and peel them. Using the julienne attachment on a mandoline, carefully cut the eggplant into thin noodles. Alternatively, cut each eggplant into ¼-inch-thick slices, then cut each slice into ¼-inch-wide strips.

2. Place the garlic-chili paste and water in a small bowl and stir until thoroughly combined.

3. Warm a large nonstick skillet over medium heat for 1 minute. Add half of the olive oil, half of the sesame oil, and half of the chili-garlic mixture and raise heat to medium-high. When the oil begins to shimmer, add half of the eggplant noodles and a couple pinches of salt. Cook, stirring frequently, until the strands have softened and started turning golden brown, about 5 minutes. Transfer to a warmed serving platter and tent loosely with foil to keep warm. Wipe out the pan with a paper towel and repeat the process with the remaining eggplant, olive oil, sesame oil, and chili-garlic mixture. Garnish with the cilantro and almonds and serve immediately.

INGREDIENTS:

4 EGGPLANTS

2 TABLESPOONS CHILI-GARLIC PASTE, PLUS MORE TO TASTE

2 TEASPOONS WATER

3 TABLESPOONS OLIVE OIL

1 TABLESPOON TOASTED SESAME OIL

SALT, TO TASTE

2 HANDFULS FRESH CILANTRO LEAVES, MINCED, FOR GARNISH

½ CUP TOASTED ALMONDS (TAMARI ALMONDS PREFERRED), CHOPPED, FOR GARNISH

CHARRED EGGPLANT *with* BONITO FLAKES

YIELD: 4 SERVINGS / ACTIVE TIME: 5 MINUTES / TOTAL TIME: 30 MINUTES

The trick to this incredible dish is to really char the eggplant, ensuring that it is very soft and has a light, smoky flavor. When paired with the bonito flakes and pickled onions, that smoke makes for a complex, flavor-packed dish that works as a side or a late lunch in the summer.

1. Turn the broiler on your oven to high.

2. Place the eggplants in a 12-inch cast-iron skillet and place them under the broiler. Broil, turning occasionally, until the eggplants have collapsed and are charred all over, about 10 minutes. Remove from the oven, transfer the eggplants to a large bowl, and cover with aluminum foil. Let the eggplants steam for another 10 minutes.

3. Place the vinegar and sugar in a saucepan and bring to a simmer over medium heat. Add the onion and a large pinch of salt and cook until the onion is translucent, about 2 minutes. Remove from heat and set aside.

4. When the eggplants are cool enough to handle, peel off the skins, cut off the ends, and discard. Roughly chop the remaining flesh and return it to the large bowl. Add the lemon juice and oil, season with salt, and stir to combine.

5. Grate the tomatoes into the bowl containing the eggplant. Use a slotted spoon to transfer the onion to the bowl. Add the arugula and toss to combine. Garnish with the bonito flakes and serve.

TIP: You can also serve this as a salad. Spread the grated Roma tomatoes over four chilled salad plates. Top with the eggplant and sprinkle the onion and bonito flakes on top. Add the arugula, drizzle with olive oil, and serve.

INGREDIENTS:

2	LARGE EGGPLANTS
1	CUP CHAMPAGNE VINEGAR
½	CUP SUGAR
1	YELLOW ONION, SLICED INTO THIN HALF-MOONS
	SALT, TO TASTE
	JUICE OF 1 LEMON
¼	CUP OLIVE OIL
4	ROMA TOMATOES
2	LARGE HANDFULS WILD ARUGULA
½	CUP BONITO FLAKES, FOR GARNISH

STEAMED JAPANESE EGGPLANT
with BLACK BEAN GARLIC SAUCE *&* BASIL

YIELD: 4 SERVINGS / ACTIVE TIME: 30 MINUTES / TOTAL TIME: 45 MINUTES

This recipe is a great way to showcase the lovely, delicate flavor of steamed Japanese eggplant. The sauce is made from fermented black beans and garlic and is intense and salty. You can find a jarred version in the Asian section of the supermarket. Thai basil is the best accompaniment for this dish, but if you can't find any, Italian basil will work fine.

1. Place 1 inch of water in a saucepan, set a steaming tray above it, and bring the water to a boil.

2. Place the eggplant in the steaming tray and steam until tender, 5 to 8 minutes. Remove from heat and place on a serving plate.

3. Place the garlic and shallot in a small saucepan with enough oil to coat the bottom. Sauté over medium heat until the vegetables start to brown, about 5 minutes.

4. Add the black bean garlic sauce, soy sauce, and vinegar and stir until the sauce starts to thicken. If the sauce thickens so much that it becomes clumpy, add water 1 teaspoon at a time.

5. Taste, adjust the seasoning as needed, remove from heat, and pour over the eggplant. Garnish with the basil and serve.

INGREDIENTS:

- 1½ LBS. JAPANESE EGGPLANT, SLICED LENGTHWISE AND HALVED
- 1 GARLIC CLOVE, SLICED
- 1 TABLESPOON MINCED SHALLOT
- OLIVE OIL, AS NEEDED
- 2 TABLESPOONS BLACK BEAN GARLIC SAUCE
- 2 TEASPOONS SOY SAUCE
- 2 TEASPOONS RICE VINEGAR
- WATER, AS NEEDED
- 8 FRESH BASIL LEAVES, CHIFFONADE, FOR GARNISH

BROWNED FENNEL *with* ORANGE GLAZE

YIELD: 2 TO 4 SERVINGS / ACTIVE TIME: 20 MINUTES / TOTAL TIME: 50 MINUTES

Orange and fennel go together beautifully. This recipe celebrates this duo by first browning the fennel in a pan and then braising it in fresh orange juice. The juice cooks the fennel all the way through and ultimately reduces to a glaze. A little pat of butter creates a sauce with the remaining liquid for a sweet dish that would be a nice side for either grilled chicken or broiled fish and brown rice.

1. Place the oil in a medium saucepan and warm over medium heat. Once the oil is shimmering, place the fennel in the pan, cut-side down, and cook until browned, about 8 minutes. Turn over and cook until the other sides are also brown.

2. Add the orange juice and fennel seeds and scrape the bottom of the pan to remove any browned bits. Cover the pan and let the fennel braise for 5 minutes.

3. Remove the lid and cook until the juice becomes syrupy and clings to the fennel, 5 to 10 minutes. Add the butter, stir until it melts, season with salt, and serve.

INGREDIENTS:

1   TABLESPOON OLIVE OIL

1   LARGE FENNEL BULB, QUARTERED

⅓   CUP FRESH ORANGE JUICE

½   TEASPOON FENNEL SEEDS

½   TABLESPOON UNSALTED BUTTER

SALT, TO TASTE

KALE *with* GARLIC, RAISINS & LEMON

YIELD: 4 SERVINGS / ACTIVE TIME: 10 MINUTES / TOTAL TIME: 25 MINUTES

This is the kale recipe I always recommended to my CSA members. It is quick, healthy, and delicious. I like it with a splash of lemon juice upon serving but not everyone wants that added tartness, so just serve it with lemon wedges on the side.

1. Place the oil in a wide sauté pan and warm over medium heat. Once it is shimmering, add the kale and cook, stirring occasionally, until it starts to wilt, about 5 minutes.

2. Add the garlic and cook until it starts to brown, about 2 minutes.

3. Add the raisins and deglaze the pan with the water, stirring constantly and scraping up any browned bits from the bottom of the pan. Cook until the water evaporates, about 5 minutes. Season with salt and pepper and serve with lemon wedges.

INGREDIENTS:

1 TABLESPOON OLIVE OIL

½ LB. LACINATO OR RED RUSSIAN KALE, STEMS REMOVED, CHOPPED

2 GARLIC CLOVES, MINCED

¼ CUP RAISINS

¼ CUP WATER

SALT AND PEPPER, TO TASTE

LEMON WEDGES, FOR SERVING

KOHLRABI SLAW *with* MISO DRESSING

YIELD: 4 SERVINGS / **ACTIVE TIME:** 10 MINUTES / **TOTAL TIME:** 10 MINUTES

The Asian flavors of this coleslaw are just perfect alongside grilled shrimp or barbecue tempeh. If you have a mandoline, it will make quick work of the vegetables. A hand grater will also work.

1. Place the white miso paste, vinegar, sesame oil, ginger, soy sauce, peanut oil, sesame seeds, and maple syrup in a mixing bowl and stir to combine. Set aside.

2. Place the kohlrabies, carrots, and cilantro in a separate bowl and stir to combine.

3. Drizzle a few spoonfuls of the dressing into the coleslaw and stir until evenly coated. Taste, add more dressing if desired, top with the pistachios, and serve.

INGREDIENTS:

- 1 TABLESPOON WHITE MISO PASTE
- 1 TABLESPOON RICE VINEGAR
- 1 TEASPOON SESAME OIL
- 1 TEASPOON MINCED GINGER
- 1 TEASPOON SOY SAUCE
- 3 TABLESPOONS PEANUT OIL
- 1 TABLESPOON SESAME SEEDS
- 1 TEASPOON REAL MAPLE SYRUP
- 3 KOHLRABIES, PEELED AND JULIENNED OR GRATED
- 2 CARROTS, PEELED AND JULIENNED OR GRATED
- ¼ CUP CHOPPED FRESH CILANTRO
- ¼ CUP SHELLED PISTACHIOS, CRUSHED

GERMAN-STYLE KOHLRABI IN BÉCHAMEL

YIELD: 4 SERVINGS / ACTIVE TIME: 20 MINUTES / TOTAL TIME: 35 MINUTES

Since the Germans are among kohlrabi's biggest fans, it seemed fitting to include one of their favorite preparations. This recipe is very simple but creates a rich and comforting dish. My only twist on the traditional version is to include the kohlrabi greens as well, partly to reduce food waste and partly because they add great flavor.

1. Bring water to a boil in a medium saucepan. Add the kohlrabies and a dash of salt and cook until just tender, about 5 minutes. Remove with a slotted spoon and set aside.

2. Add the reserved greens to the pan and cook until tender, about 8 minutes. Remove with a slotted spoon and add to the kohlrabies.

3. Drain the water and dry the pan. Return it to the stove and add the butter. Melt the butter over low heat, add the flour, and whisk to combine. Cook for 1 minute, then slowly add the milk, whisking constantly to prevent lumps from forming. Continue whisking until the sauce has thickened, about 5 minutes. Season with salt and pepper and the nutmeg.

4. Return the kohlrabies and greens to the pan, cook until heated through, and serve.

INGREDIENTS:

1 LB. KOHLRABIES, PEELED AND SLICED, GREENS RESERVED AND CHIFFONADE

SALT AND PEPPER, TO TASTE

2 TABLESPOONS UNSALTED BUTTER

2 TABLESPOONS ALL-PURPOSE FLOUR

1 CUP WHOLE MILK

PINCH OF NUTMEG

CHARRED SUMMER LEEKS *with* ROMESCO SAUCE

YIELD: 4 SERVINGS / ACTIVE TIME: 15 MINUTES / TOTAL TIME: 25 MINUTES

When summer leeks are cooked on a grill, they develop a sweet and smoky flavor. The first step is to steam them quickly on the stove to make sure they get cooked through on the grill. Pairing that sweetness and smoke with the garlicky Romesco Sauce is a slice of heaven.

1. Preheat your grill to medium heat. Cut the dark green sections off of the leeks and remove the roots, keeping the base that holds the layers together. Cut the leeks lengthwise and rinse between each layer to remove dirt, taking care to keep the layers together.

2. Place 1 inch of water in a saucepan, place a steaming tray in the pan, and bring the water to a boil. When boiling, place the leeks in the steaming tray and steam until tender, about 5 minutes.

3. Drain, drizzle oil over the leeks, and season with salt and pepper. When the grill is about 400°F, place the leeks on the grill and cook until browned all over, about 8 minutes per side. When the leeks are nearly charred, transfer to a platter and serve with the Romesco Sauce.

ROMESCO SAUCE

1. Place all of the ingredients, except for the oil, in a blender or food processor and pulse until smooth.

2. Add the oil in a steady stream and puree until emulsified. Season with salt and pepper and serve.

INGREDIENTS:

- 8   SUMMER LEEKS
- OLIVE OIL, TO TASTE
- SALT AND PEPPER, TO TASTE
- ROMESCO SAUCE (SEE RECIPE), FOR SERVING

ROMESCO SAUCE

- 2   LARGE ROASTED RED BELL PEPPERS
- 1   GARLIC CLOVE, SMASHED
- ½   CUP SLIVERED ALMONDS, TOASTED
- ¼   CUP TOMATO PUREE
- 2   TABLESPOONS CHOPPED FRESH FLAT-LEAF PARSLEY
- 2   TABLESPOONS SHERRY VINEGAR
- 1   TEASPOON SMOKED PAPRIKA
- ½   CUP OLIVE OIL
- SALT AND PEPPER, TO TASTE

FRIZZLED LEEKS

YIELD: 2 TO 4 SERVINGS / ACTIVE TIME: 15 MINUTES / TOTAL TIME: 20 MINUTES

These delectable fried bits are light and airy. While they can be eaten on their own, they are best as a topping for anything from steak to fried rice.

1. Trim the leeks and cut the white part only into 3-inch sections. Slice the sections in half lengthwise and rinse to remove any dirt. Pat dry and then slice into very thin strips.

2. Place the flour in a mixing bowl, add the leek strips, and toss until evenly coated.

3. Add oil to a Dutch oven until it is about 3 inches deep. Heat the oil to 350°F, or until a pinch of flour dropped in sizzles on contact.

4. Working in batches to ensure that the leeks are fully submerged in the oil, shake the leeks to remove any excess flour and add them to the oil. Fry until browned, transfer to a paper towel–lined plate, and repeat with the remaining leeks.

5. Sprinkle the fried leeks with salt and serve.

INGREDIENTS:

1-2 LARGE LEEKS

¼ CUP ALL-PURPOSE FLOUR

VEGETABLE OIL, FOR FRYING

SALT, TO TASTE

POTATO & TOMATO GRATIN

YIELD: 4 TO 6 SERVINGS / ACTIVE TIME: 15 MINUTES / TOTAL TIME: 45 MINUTES

A testament to the brilliance of French cuisine, this layered dish has all the flavor in the world and is as simple as can be to make. Try serving it with grilled chicken and sautéed kohlrabi.

1. Preheat your oven to 350°F.

2. Place the garlic, parsley, and thyme in a small bowl, stir to combine, and set it aside while you prepare the tomatoes.

3. Lightly oil a 12-inch cast-iron skillet or enameled cast-iron gratin dish and then add a layer of the tomato slices. Season with salt and pepper and add a layer of potatoes and a sprinkle of the garlic-and-parsley mixture. Drizzle with olive oil and continue the layering process until all of the tomatoes, potatoes, and garlic-and-parsley mixture have been used.

4. Cover with foil, place in the oven, and bake for 20 minutes. Remove from the oven and remove the foil. If tomatoes haven't released enough liquid to soften the potatoes, add a bit of the stock. Replace the foil and continue baking for 15 minutes.

5. Remove the foil, cook for an additional 5 minutes, and serve warm.

INGREDIENTS:

4   GARLIC CLOVES, MINCED

      LEAVES FROM 1 SMALL
      BUNCH FRESH PARSLEY,
      MINCED

2   TABLESPOONS MINCED
      FRESH THYME LEAVES

      OLIVE OIL, TO TASTE

2   LBS. TOMATOES, SLICED
      ¼-INCH THICK

      SALT AND PEPPER, TO TASTE

4   WAXY POTATOES, SLICED
      ¼-INCH THICK

      CHICKEN STOCK (SEE PAGE
      748 FOR HOMEMADE), AS
      NEEDED

GREEN BEANS & SAUTÉED SHIITAKES

YIELD: 4 SERVINGS / ACTIVE TIME: 20 MINUTES / TOTAL TIME: 30 MINUTES

I am certainly biased, but I think shiitakes are the best-tasting mushroom. Asking where to use them is like asking where to use bacon: everywhere. They are excellent with subtle pairings such as eggs and cream but can also stand up to a zesty garlic sauce. Here, I matched them with sautéed green beans for an easy summer dish.

1. Bring salted water to a boil in a medium saucepan and prepare an ice water bath. Add the green beans and parboil for 2 minutes. Remove with a slotted spoon and transfer to the ice water bath. When they have cooled completely, drain and set aside.

2. Place the olive oil in a large sauté pan and warm over medium-high heat. When the oil starts to shimmer, add the mushrooms and sauté until they begin to brown, about 5 minutes. Add the parboiled green beans and sauté until they are slightly browned, another 5 minutes. Remove from heat, add the soy sauce, and toss to coat.

3. When the green beans and mushrooms have cooled slightly, add the sesame oil, toss to coat, and serve.

INGREDIENTS:

SALT, TO TASTE

1 LB. GREEN BEANS, CLEANED AND TRIMMED

1 TABLESPOON OLIVE OIL

½ LB. SHIITAKE MUSHROOMS, STEMMED AND SLICED

1 TABLESPOON SOY SAUCE

1 TEASPOON SESAME OIL

OKRA *with* TOMATOES & CAJUN SEASONING

YIELD: 4 SERVINGS / ACTIVE TIME: 15 MINUTES / TOTAL TIME: 20 MINUTES

This is a quick, weeknight vegetable stew that would be excellent alongside fish or rice. If you can't find Cajun seasoning, smoked paprika or cumin are good substitutes.

1. Add enough oil to coat the bottom of a medium sauté pan and warm over medium heat. When the oil starts to shimmer, add the onion and sauté until it just starts to brown, about 6 minutes. Add the okra and cook, stirring continuously, until it starts to brown, about 5 minutes.

2. Add the garlic and cook for 1 minute. Add the tomatoes and Cajun seasoning and stir to incorporate. Cook until the tomatoes have completely broken down and the okra is tender, about 8 minutes.

3. Season with salt and serve.

INGREDIENTS:

OLIVE OIL, AS NEEDED

1   ONION, DICED

1   LB. OKRA, WASHED AND CUT INTO 1-INCH PIECES

1   GARLIC CLOVE, CHOPPED

2   TOMATOES, CHOPPED

1   TEASPOON CAJUN SEASONING

SALT, TO TASTE

PATATAS BRAVAS

YIELD: 4 SERVINGS / ACTIVE TIME: 45 MINUTES / TOTAL TIME: 1 HOUR

Native to Spain, this smoky potato dish can be found in tapas bars all across that country.

1. Place the potatoes, onion, and 1 tablespoon of the olive oil in a mixing bowl and toss to coat.

2. Line a large cast-iron wok with foil, making sure that the foil extends over the side. Add the soaked wood chips and place the wok over medium heat.

3. When the wood chips are smoking heavily, place a wire rack above the wood chips and add the potatoes, onion, and garlic. Cover the wok with a lid, fold the foil over the lid to seal the wok as best you can, and smoke for 20 minutes. After 20 minutes, remove from heat and keep the wok covered for another 20 minutes.

4. Meanwhile, to make *salsa brava*, combine the tomatoes, paprika, vinegar, and remaining olive oil in a blender and puree. Set the mixture aside.

5. Remove the garlic and onion from the smoker. Peel and roughly chop. Add the garlic and onion to the mixture in the blender and puree until smooth. Season the *salsa brava* with salt. Serve the potatoes with sour cream and the *salsa brava*.

INGREDIENTS:

4	MEDIUM POTATOES, CUT INTO THICK PIECES AND PARBOILED
1	ONION, WITH SKIN AND ROOT, HALVED
3	TABLESPOONS OLIVE OIL
2	CUPS WOOD CHIPS, SOAKED IN COLD WATER FOR 30 MINUTES
1	HEAD OF GARLIC, TOP ½ INCH REMOVED
1	(14 OZ.) CAN DICED TOMATOES, DRAINED
1	TABLESPOON SWEET PAPRIKA
1	TABLESPOON SHERRY VINEGAR
	SALT, TO TASTE
	SOUR CREAM, FOR SERVING

POTATO & PARSNIP LATKES

YIELD: 4 SERVINGS / ACTIVE TIME: 40 MINUTES / TOTAL TIME: 1 HOUR

The secret to making good latkes is to make sure you've removed as much water as possible from the potatoes before cooking. You don't need any special equipment for this, just take up the shredded potato in your hands and squeeze. Parsnips are actually very dry as vegetables go, so they do not need the squeeze put on them. They brown beautifully, though, and will add not only sweet flavor but a nice, crispy texture to the final product. There are those who like sour cream on their latkes and those who prefer applesauce. Be an accommodating cook and offer both.

1. Preheat the oven to 350°F. Place the grated potatoes in a colander and squeeze one handful at a time until no more liquid can be removed from them. Transfer to a bowl.

2. Add the parsnips, flour, and egg to the potatoes, stir to combine, and season with salt and pepper.

3. Place the oil in a wide sauté pan and warm over medium-high heat. Once the oil is shimmering, add spoonfuls of the latke mixture to the pan and press down to form 3-inch patties, flattening gently with a spatula. Reduce heat to medium-low and cook until browned on both sides, about 8 to 10 minutes per side.

4. When both sides are perfectly browned, test the latkes to see if the interior is fully cooked. If not, place them on a baking sheet and bake in the oven for an additional 10 minutes.

5. Serve hot with the sour cream and applesauce.

INGREDIENTS:

2   RUSSET POTATOES, PEELED AND GRATED

3   PARSNIPS, PEELED, TRIMMED, CORED, AND GRATED

1   TABLESPOON ALL-PURPOSE FLOUR

1   EGG

    SALT AND PEPPER, TO TASTE

1   TABLESPOON OLIVE OIL

    SOUR CREAM, FOR SERVING

    APPLESAUCE, FOR SERVING

ROASTED PARSNIPS & CARROTS
with RAS EL HANOUT & HONEY

YIELD: 4 SERVINGS / ACTIVE TIME: 20 MINUTES / TOTAL TIME: 40 MINUTES

Roasting brings out the best in parsnips and carrots, and adding honey and spice at the end only enhances the deep flavor already there. Ras el hanout is a North African spice blend. Much like Indian curry, there is no official recipe, but it often contains cardamom, cumin, nutmeg, mace, cinnamon, ginger, chilies, allspice, and salt. It's best to adjust your seasonings to taste as you go, to avoid oversalting.

1. Preheat the oven to 400°F. Place the parsnips and carrots in a roasting pan in one layer, add the oil and salt, and toss to coat. Place in the oven and roast for 20 minutes, or until browned.

2. Remove the pan from the oven and pile the vegetables in the center. Drizzle the honey over the top and toss to coat. Sprinkle the ras el hanout over the top and toss to coat.

3. Return the pan to the oven and roast for another 5 to 10 minutes, making sure the vegetables do not burn. Remove from the oven and serve immediately.

INGREDIENTS:

4   LARGE PARSNIPS, PEELED, TRIMMED, AND CORED

4   LARGE CARROTS, PEELED AND SLICED LENGTHWISE

2   TABLESPOONS OLIVE OIL

    SALT AND PEPPER, TO TASTE

2   TABLESPOONS HONEY

1   TABLESPOON RAS EL HANOUT

CONFIT NEW POTATOES

YIELD: 4 TO 6 SERVINGS / ACTIVE TIME: 5 MINUTES / TOTAL TIME: 1 HOUR AND 10 MINUTES

New potatoes are young potatoes that are pulled in early spring. They are sweeter than their mature counterparts, since the sugars haven't had time to develop into starches, and are so soft and tender that they don't need to be peeled.

1. Place the oil in a Dutch oven and bring it to 200°F over medium heat.

2. While the oil is warming, wash the potatoes and pat them dry. Carefully place the potatoes in the oil and cook until fork-tender, about 1 hour.

3. Drain the potatoes, season generously with salt and pepper, and stir to ensure that the potatoes are evenly coated. If desired, garnish with rosemary and serve immediately.

TIP: These potatoes should have plenty of flavor, but if you're looking to take them to another level, replace the canola oil with chicken or duck fat.

INGREDIENTS:

4   CUPS CANOLA OIL

5   LBS. NEW POTATOES

     SALT AND PEPPER, TO TASTE

     FRESH ROSEMARY LEAVES,
     FOR GARNISH (OPTIONAL)

LOW 'N' SLOW POTATOES

YIELD: 4 SERVINGS / ACTIVE TIME: 20 MINUTES / TOTAL TIME: 40 MINUTES

This simple dish is on regular rotation in our house because it is delicious and goes with everything. I wanted a sautéed potato dish that didn't involve the extra step of parboiling but still produced cubes that were tender on the inside and crispy on the outside. The tradeoff for not fussing with parboiling is that they take a while, but they require nothing beyond an occasional stir. The key to doing it well is to give yourself time—around half an hour—and remain patient while everything browns over low heat. Different starch levels will give you different results, but any type of potato will work.

1. Place the oil in a wide sauté pan and warm over medium heat. When the oil is shimmering, add the potatoes so they sit in one layer. Once you hear them start crackling, reduce heat to low and cook, leaving the potatoes undisturbed, until they have a brown crust on the bottom. This can take up to 10 minutes.

2. Once browned, flip and repeat on another side. Continue until the cubes are brown and crispy all over. Season with salt and serve.

INGREDIENTS:

1   TABLESPOON OLIVE OIL

2   LBS. POTATOES, DICED

     SALT, TO TASTE

HERBED POTATO SALAD

YIELD: 4 TO 6 SERVINGS / ACTIVE TIME: 10 MINUTES / TOTAL TIME: 40 MINUTES

The two most common potato salads have either a mayonnaise dressing or, in the German version, a sweet vinegar dressing. The French have a different approach with shallots and herbs and a tangy vinaigrette that lets the natural sweetness of the potatoes come through. The dressing is poured on the potatoes when they are still warm, letting them soak up the flavor.

1. Add the potatoes to a pot of water large enough to hold them all, bring to a boil, reduce heat, and simmer until tender, about 15 minutes.

2. While the potatoes are simmering, whisk together the oil, vinegar, wine, mustard, and teaspoon of salt.

3. When the potatoes are done, drain them and place them in a bowl. Add the vinaigrette and shallot immediately and gently toss, making sure to coat all of the potatoes. Let cool completely.

4. Taste and adjust seasoning as needed. Add the black pepper and fresh herbs, stir to incorporate, and serve.

INGREDIENTS:

- 1½ LBS. LOW-STARCH, NEW, OR RED POTATOES, CUBED
- ½ CUP OLIVE OIL
- 3 TABLESPOONS WHITE WINE VINEGAR
- 2 TABLESPOONS DRY WHITE WINE
- 1 TEASPOON WHOLE-GRAIN DIJON MUSTARD
- 1 TEASPOON KOSHER SALT, PLUS MORE TO TASTE
- 1 SHALLOT, MINCED
- BLACK PEPPER, TO TASTE
- 2 TABLESPOONS CHOPPED FRESH PARSLEY
- 2 TABLESPOONS CHOPPED FRESH CHIVES
- 2 TABLESPOONS CHOPPED FRESH DILL

BLUE CHEESE GRATIN

YIELD: 4 SERVINGS / ACTIVE TIME: 20 MINUTES / TOTAL TIME: 45 MINUTES

Thin slices of potato are baked in cream and blue cheese here, resulting in a heavenly, tangy gratin. No need to splurge on Stilton or other high-end blue cheeses for this one; a decent-quality blue from the supermarket will work best. Also, nutmeg is very strong, so best to be too conservative than too liberal with it—otherwise, the potatoes will taste bitter.

1. Preheat the oven to 375°F. While the oven is heating up, grease an 8 × 5.5-inch gratin dish with butter.

2. Place the potato slices in a saucepan with the garlic, bay leaf, milk, and salt. Bring to a boil over high heat, drain, and discard the bay leaf.

3. Place half of the potatoes in the gratin dish, then sprinkle on half of the blue cheese, a pinch of nutmeg, salt, and pepper. Add the cream and 2 tablespoons of the butter. Place the remaining potatoes on top and repeat with the blue cheese, nutmeg, salt, pepper, and butter.

4. Place the dish in the oven and bake for about 30 minutes, or until the top is brown and crispy. The cream should come halfway up the potatoes at the start and cook down to a rich sauce by the end. If the dish looks too dry, add a little more cream before serving.

INGREDIENTS:

4   TABLESPOONS UNSALTED BUTTER, CUBED, PLUS MORE AS NEEDED

2   LBS. RUSSET POTATOES, PEELED AND SLICED THIN

2   GARLIC CLOVES, SMASHED

1   BAY LEAF

2   TABLESPOONS WHOLE MILK

1   TEASPOON KOSHER SALT, PLUS MORE TO TASTE

4   OZ. BLUE CHEESE

    NUTMEG, TO TASTE

    BLACK PEPPER, TO TASTE

¾   CUP HEAVY CREAM, PLUS MORE AS NEEDED

TWO PEAS IN A POD
& RADISHES *with* MINT

YIELD: 4 SERVINGS / ACTIVE TIME: 15 MINUTES / TOTAL TIME: 20 MINUTES

An easy recipe that is as beautiful as it is quick. Cooking radishes mellows their bite, making them a nice partner to the peas. Plus, red radishes turn a lovely rose pink when cooked, which provides lovely contrast with the bright green peas.

1. Place the oil in a wide sauté pan and warm over medium heat. When the oil starts to shimmer, add the radishes and sauté, stirring occasionally, until they are browned on both of the cut sides, about 10 minutes.

2. Add the sugar snap peas and frozen peas and cook until the peas are heated through and the sugar snap peas are just tender, about 3 minutes. Transfer to a bowl and add the mint. Toss to combine and season with salt, lemon juice, and more olive oil before serving.

INGREDIENTS:

- 1 TABLESPOON OLIVE OIL, PLUS MORE TO TASTE
- 8 RED RADISHES, QUARTERED
- ½ LB. SUGAR SNAP PEAS (OR SNOW PEAS)
- ¼ CUP FROZEN PEAS
- 1 TABLESPOON CHIFFONADE FRESH MINT
- SALT, TO TASTE
- LEMON JUICE, TO TASTE

MOM'S CREAMED SPINACH

YIELD: 4 SERVINGS / ACTIVE TIME: 20 MINUTES / TOTAL TIME: 25 MINUTES

Everyone has family holiday favorites, and one of mine is my mother's creamed spinach. It is rich and tangy, made with cream cheese and lots of onion, and it is perfect alongside roast turkey or beef and Yorkshire pudding. Definitely use frozen spinach for this one, especially if you are feeding a crowd.

1. Place the butter in a wide sauté pan and melt over medium heat. Add the onion and garlic and cook until the onion is just translucent, about 3 minutes.

2. Add the frozen spinach to the pan along with a few teaspoons water, cover the pan, and cook for a minute. Remove the lid, break the spinach up, and cook until it is completely thawed.

3. Add the cream cheese, nutmeg, and marjoram and stir to incorporate. Cook until the sauce has reduced and thickened, about 5 minutes. Season with salt and pepper and serve.

INGREDIENTS:

1   TABLESPOON UNSALTED BUTTER

1   CUP DICED YELLOW ONION

2   GARLIC CLOVES, CHOPPED

1   LB. FROZEN CHOPPED SPINACH

½   LB. CREAM CHEESE, AT ROOM TEMPERATURE

    PINCH OF NUTMEG

1   TEASPOON DRIED MARJORAM

    SALT AND PEPPER, TO TASTE

MISO-MAPLE TURNIPS

YIELD: 2 TO 4 SERVINGS / ACTIVE TIME: 20 MINUTES / TOTAL TIME: 25 MINUTES

Combining miso and maple syrup makes for magic. You can use it as a glaze for most any-thing, from scallops to cauliflower. Miso is that umami-packed fermented soybean paste commonly used in Japanese cuisine, and maple syrup is the nectar of the gods. Get the two working together and you have a savory-sweet topper that seems to bring out the best of what-ever you have chosen to adorn with it. Here, the tang of the caramelized turnip is a perfect foil for this brilliant pair.

1. Place the bok choy in a 12-inch sauté pan and add the water. Raise heat to high, cover the pan, and steam the bok choy for a few minutes. Remove the lid and continue to cook until all of the water has boiled off, about 1 minute more.

2. Remove the pan from heat and season with salt and pepper. Transfer the bok choy to a plate and set aside.

3. Add the oil to the pan and warm over high heat. Add the turnips and reduce heat to medium. Cook the turnips until the cut sides have browned, about 5 minutes per side.

4. While the turnips are cooking, combine the miso, maple syrup, and soy sauce.

5. When the turnips are fully browned and tender, pour the miso-maple mixture over them and toss to coat. Cook for another minute and then remove from heat.

6. Place the turnips on top of the bok choy and serve.

INGREDIENTS:

½ LB. BOK CHOY, QUARTERED

3 TABLESPOONS WATER

SALT AND PEPPER, TO TASTE

1 TABLESPOON OLIVE OIL

¾ LBS. SMALL PURPLE TOP TURNIPS, QUARTERED

1 TABLESPOON WHITE MISO

1 TABLESPOON REAL MAPLE SYRUP

1 TEASPOON SOY SAUCE

TARO ULASS

YIELD: 4 SERVINGS / ACTIVE TIME: 25 MINUTES / TOTAL TIME: 35 MINUTES

This dish is popular in Egypt. Pureed chard and cilantro are combined with cubes of taro and garlic, making for a dish that is lovely beside grilled chicken, lamb, or just rice. A healthy dash of lemon juice in the broth brings out the best in both the chard and the taro. I used red chard here because the contrast in color is so beautiful, but any color will work.

1. Place the stock and lemon juice in a medium saucepan and bring to a simmer over medium heat. Add the taro and simmer until tender, about 8 minutes.

2. Place the chard leaves and cilantro to a pan with about ¼ cup water. Place on the stove and cook over medium-high heat until leaves are fully wilted and most of the liquid has evaporated. Transfer to a food processor and pulse until fully pureed.

3. Place the oil in a sauté pan and warm over medium heat. Add the garlic and chard stems and cook until the garlic starts to brown slightly, about 2 minutes. Add the taro and its cooking liquid as well as the pureed chard. Stir to combine, cook until heated through, and serve.

INGREDIENTS:

½ CUP CHICKEN OR VEGETABLE STOCK (SEE PAGES 748 AND 755, RESPECTIVELY, FOR HOMEMADE)

JUICE FROM ½ LEMON

1 LB. TARO ROOT, PEELED AND CUBED

1 LARGE BUNCH RED CHARD, STEMS CUT INTO 1-INCH PIECES, LEAVES CHOPPED

LEAVES FROM ½ BUNCH FRESH CILANTRO

1 TABLESPOON OLIVE OIL

2 GARLIC CLOVES, CHOPPED

BAKED SWEET POTATOES
with LIME, SALT & BUTTER

YIELD: 4 SERVINGS / ACTIVE TIME: 15 MINUTES / TOTAL TIME: 40 MINUTES

first saw a recipe like this in Alice Waters's *Chez Panisse Vegetables*. She topped a simple baked sweet potato with lime and cilantro. I tried it and loved it so am passing along my version, which includes butter but omits the cilantro (but by all means, go ahead and sprinkle some on if you have it around). Oh, and be sure to eat the skins—not only are they delicious, they're nutritious, too.

1. Preheat the oven to 400°F. Pour the oil on a baking sheet large enough to fit the sweet potatoes without crowding and spread into a thin film.

2. Place the potatoes, cut-side down, on the baking sheet. Place in the oven and bake for about 30 minutes, or until fork-tender.

3. Remove from the oven, turn over the halves, and make a few slash marks through the flesh to break it up. Squeeze one lime wedge over each half, top with some butter and salt, and serve.

INGREDIENTS:

1   TABLESPOON OLIVE OIL

2   LARGE SWEET POTATOES, HALVED

1   LIME, QUARTERED

    UNSALTED BUTTER, TO TASTE

    SALT, TO TASTE

JERK ACORN SQUASH
with BABY KALE SALAD *&* MAPLE VINAIGRETTE

YIELD: 4 SERVINGS / ACTIVE TIME: 25 MINUTES / TOTAL TIME: 2 HOURS

The melding of the sweet-savory taste of the acorn squash and the delicious spice of the jerk marinade is irresistible, especially when accented by the Maple Vinaigrette.

1. Preheat the oven to 400°F.

2. Cut the squash in half lengthwise, remove the seeds, and reserve them. Cut the bottoms of the halves so that they can sit flat, flesh-side up, on a baking sheet. Score the flesh in a crosshatch pattern, cutting approximately ⅛ inch into the flesh. Brush some of the marinade on the squash and then fill each cavity with about 3 tablespoons of marinade. Place the baking sheet in the oven and bake until the squash is tender, about 45 minutes to 1 hour. As the squash is cooking, brush the flesh with some of the marinade in the cavity every 15 minutes.

3. Remove from the oven and let cool. Lower the oven temperature to 350°F.

4. Run the seeds under water to remove any pulp. Pat the seeds dry, place them in a mixing bowl, and add the oil, salt, pepper, and paprika. Toss to combine and then place the seeds on a baking sheet. Place in the oven and bake until they are light brown and crispy, about 7 minutes.

5. Place the toasted seeds, kale, and cranberries in a salad bowl and toss to combine.

6. Add the Maple Vinaigrette to the salad bowl. Toss to coat evenly and top the salad with the crumbled feta. To serve, place a bed of salad on each plate and place one of the roasted halves of squash on top.

INGREDIENTS:

2	ACORN SQUASH
1	CUP JERK MARINADE (SEE PAGE 661)
1	TABLESPOON OLIVE OIL
½	TEASPOON KOSHER SALT
¼	TEASPOON BLACK PEPPER
¼	TEASPOON PAPRIKA
6	CUPS BABY KALE
½	CUP DRIED CRANBERRIES
	MAPLE VINAIGRETTE (SEE RECIPE)
1	CUP CRUMBLED FETA CHEESE

MAPLE VINAIGRETTE

½	CUP APPLE CIDER VINEGAR
½	CUP MAPLE SYRUP
1	TEASPOON ORANGE ZEST
2	TEASPOONS DIJON MUSTARD
1	TABLESPOON KOSHER SALT
1	TEASPOON BLACK PEPPER
2	ICE CUBES
1½	CUPS OLIVE OIL

MAPLE VINAIGRETTE

1. Place all of the ingredients, except for the oil, in a blender. Turn on high and add the oil in a slow stream. Puree until the mixture has emulsified. Season to taste and serve.

BAKED SPAGHETTI SQUASH *with* TOMATO SAUCE, BÉCHAMEL & RICOTTA

YIELD: 4 TO 6 SERVINGS / ACTIVE TIME: 40 MINUTES / TOTAL TIME: 1 HOUR AND 45 MINUTES

This is a great example of how easy it is to substitute spaghetti squash for pasta. Just be sure to remove as much water from the squash as possible to keep the dish from being too watery.

1. Preheat the oven to 425°F. Line a large baking pan, including the sides, with aluminum foil and trim parchment paper to fit the bottom. Cut off the ends of the squash. Using a spoon, scrape out the seeds. Cut each squash widthwise into four medallions and set them in the prepared pan. Place in the oven, lower the temperature to 400°F, and bake until the strands are tender but still firm, 50 to 60 minutes.

2. Remove from the oven and let cool for 10 minutes. Reduce the oven temperature to 375°F. Using a fork, pull the strands into the center of each round. Working in two batches, transfer half of the squash to a kitchen towel and gently twist, in tourniquet-like fashion, to remove as much liquid as possible. Transfer the squash to a large bowl.

3. Add the salt, tomato sauce, and Aromatic Béchamel Sauce to the bowl and gently stir until the squash is coated. Grease a 9 × 5-inch loaf pan with the butter and then place the squash mixture into it. Place in the oven and bake until bubbly and heated through, about 25 minutes.

4. Remove from the oven and dot the top with the ricotta. Turn on the broiler and place a rack on the top level of the oven. Return the pan to the oven and broil until dark golden brown spots develop on the ricotta and squash, 2 to 3 minutes. Top with the basil and serve immediately.

INGREDIENTS:

2   SPAGHETTI SQUASH

1½   TEASPOONS KOSHER SALT

¾   CUP CLASSIC CANNED TOMATO SAUCE (SEE PAGE 793) OR PLAIN TOMATO SAUCE

½   BATCH AROMATIC BÉCHAMEL SAUCE (SEE PAGE 690)

1   TABLESPOON UNSALTED BUTTER

½   CUP WHOLE MILK RICOTTA CHEESE

   HANDFUL FRESH BASIL LEAVES, CHIFFONADE, FOR SERVING

TURNIP & SWEET POTATO POMMES ANNA

YIELD: 4 SERVINGS / ACTIVE TIME: 35 MINUTES / TOTAL TIME: 45 MINUTES

Pommes Anna is a French dish of artfully arranged, thinly sliced potatoes cooked with butter. For a twist on this classic, I switched out the potatoes for sweet potatoes and turnips, which cook at roughly the same rate. If done well, this is worth presenting at a table because the alternating orange and white discs make for a beautiful swirl. The tricky part is knowing when the bottom layer is browned enough to turn, without letting it burn. It is also a bit challenging to flip it without the whole thing going sideways. I generally don't care for Teflon, but this is one instance when it might come in handy.

1. Warm a 10- to 12-inch sauté pan over medium heat. Melt 1 tablespoon of the butter and remove the pan from heat. Place one slice of sweet potato along the edge of the pan, followed by a turnip slice. Continue along the edge, alternating slices of sweet potato and turnip. When the outside edge is complete, make another row in the inner circle and then in the very center.

2. Sprinkle with half of the thyme and a pinch of salt. Make another layer with the remaining slices, thyme, and salt.

3. Dot the top with another tablespoon of butter, place the pan on the stove, and cook over low heat for 5 minutes. Cover the pan with a lid.

4. Remove the lid every 5 minutes to let out steam. Check on the bottom layer after roughly 20 minutes by gently lifting with a spatula. If it isn't browning, remove the lid and continue cooking. If nice and brown, find a plate with flat edges that is the same size as your pan. With one hand on the pan's handle and another on the plate, invert the vegetables onto the plate, then gently slide the vegetables back into the pan, browned-side up.

5. Add the remaining butter if the pan seems dry. Cook until tender all the way through, about 10 minutes.

6. To serve, either invert onto a serving plate or, if it holds in one piece, lift it out with a spatula.

INGREDIENTS:

3 TABLESPOONS UNSALTED BUTTER

1 LB. SWEET POTATOES, PEELED AND SLICED THIN

1 LB. PURPLE TOP TURNIPS, PEELED AND SLICED THIN

1 TEASPOON FRESH OR DRIED THYME

SALT, TO TASTE

ROASTED ACORN SQUASH
with MAPLE SYRUP, BUTTER & CARDAMOM

YIELD: 2 SERVINGS / ACTIVE TIME: 15 MINUTES / TOTAL TIME: 40 MINUTES

Cardamom is a warm spice that pairs beautifully with maple syrup. The earthy sweetness of acorn squash brings out the best of both.

1. Preheat the oven to 400°F. Place the squash on a baking sheet, cut-side down, and roast for 20 minutes. Flip the squash over and place half of the butter on each half. Baste the flesh with the butter, return the baking sheet to the oven, and roast for another 10 minutes.

2. Remove from the oven and divide the maple syrup and ground cardamom between the halves. Season with salt, baste the squash, return the pan to the oven, and roast for another 10 minutes.

3. Remove from the oven, sprinkle the pistachios over each half, and serve.

INGREDIENTS:

- 1 ACORN SQUASH, HALVED AND SEEDED; BOTTOM CUT TO ALLOW TO REST FLAT WITH CUT-SIDE UP
- 1 TABLESPOON UNSALTED BUTTER
- 2 TABLESPOONS REAL MAPLE SYRUP
- ½ TEASPOON GROUND CARDAMOM
- SALT, TO TASTE
- 2 TABLESPOONS SHELLED AND CHOPPED PISTACHIOS

YU CHOY *with* GARLIC & SOY

YIELD: 4 SERVINGS / ACTIVE TIME: 10 MINUTES / TOTAL TIME: 15 MINUTES

Steaming yu choy keeps it tender and light. If the stalks are large, leave them to cook a little longer.

1. Place the yu choy in a sauté pan large enough to fit all of the stalks, cover with the water, cover the pan, and cook over high heat.

2. After about 5 minutes, check the thickest stalk to see if it is tender. If not, cook until it is. Once tender, add the oil and the garlic. Sauté until the garlic is fully cooked but not browned, about 2 minutes.

3. Add the vinegar and soy sauce, toss to combine, and serve.

INGREDIENTS:

1½ LBS. YU CHOY (IF ESPECIALLY LONG, CUT THEM IN HALF)

¼ CUP WATER

1 TABLESPOON OLIVE OIL

2 GARLIC CLOVES, CHOPPED

½ TABLESPOON RICE VINEGAR

1 TABLESPOON SOY SAUCE

YU CHOY *with* BLACK BEAN GARLIC SAUCE & EXTRA GARLIC

YIELD: 4 SERVINGS / ACTIVE TIME: 15 MINUTES / TOTAL TIME: 20 MINUTES

Black bean garlic sauce is made from fermented black beans and soy sauce, and you can find it in Asian markets or in the Asian section of most grocery stores. It is perfect with steamed yu choy because a spoonful makes for an intense, instant sauce. I like to add an extra clove of garlic to give it a fresh element.

1. Place the yu choy in a sauté pan large enough to fit all the greens, add the water, cover the pan, and cook over high heat.

2. After about 5 minutes, remove the lid and cook until most of the water cooks off.

3. Add the oil and garlic and stir-fry until the garlic is fragrant, about 2 minutes.

4. Add the black bean garlic sauce, stir to coat, and cook until heated through. Serve immediately.

INGREDIENTS:

1½ LBS. YU CHOY, CHOPPED INTO 3-INCH PIECES

¼ CUP WATER

½ TABLESPOON OLIVE OIL

1 GARLIC CLOVE, MINCED

1 TABLESPOON BLACK BEAN GARLIC SAUCE

ZUCCHINI *with* TOMATOES, FETA, GARLIC *&* LEMON

YIELD: 4 SERVINGS / ACTIVE TIME: 25 MINUTES / TOTAL TIME: 45 MINUTES

This is my favorite way of preparing zucchini fresh from the garden. They key is to not crowd the squash in the pan; otherwise, they will steam instead of brown. You can substitute yellow summer squash or pattypan squash, just cut them into pieces of a similar size so they cook at the same rate.

1. Place the oil in a large sauté pan and warm over medium-high heat. When it starts to shimmer, add the zucchini, making sure not to overcrowd the pan. Let the squash brown, flip, then brown on the other sides. Season with salt and pepper. If it is necessary to cook in batches, set the browned zucchini aside and repeat, adding oil if the pan starts to look dry.

2. Return the zucchini to the pan and add the garlic. Cook until the garlic starts to soften, about 3 minutes. Add the tomato, cook for 1 more minute to heat everything through, and transfer the mixture to a platter.

3. Sprinkle the feta and parsley on top, season with lemon juice, and serve.

INGREDIENTS:

1   TABLESPOON OLIVE OIL, PLUS MORE AS NEEDED

3   ZUCCHINI, CHOPPED

    SALT AND PEPPER, TO TASTE

2   GARLIC CLOVES, CHOPPED

1   LARGE TOMATO, DICED

2   OZ. FETA CHEESE, CRUMBLED

2   TABLESPOONS CHOPPED FRESH PARSLEY

    FRESH LEMON JUICE, TO TASTE

GINGER & CORN RELISH

YIELD: 4 SERVINGS / ACTIVE TIME: 20 MINUTES / TOTAL TIME: 30 MINUTES

I first ran across this recipe in the *New York Times* in the mid-1990s. It was paired with tuna steaks, but I find it works with any seafood, particularly scallops. I've tweaked it from the original (my tattered copy was lost long ago) and it is easy to prepare when corn and other summer produce is abundant.

1. Find a large bowl. Take an ear of corn and put the tip in the bottom of the bowl. Cut the kernels off with a sharp knife by running the blade down the ear. Repeat with the second ear.

2. Place the oil in a large saucepan and warm over medium-high heat. When the oil starts to shimmer, add the onion and sauté until translucent, about 3 minutes. Add the corn and cook, stirring occasionally, until the vegetables start to brown, about 4 minutes.

3. Add the ginger, garlic, and bell pepper and cook until the pepper starts to soften, about 5 minutes.

4. Pour in the orange juice and vinegar and scrape the bottom of the pan to incorporate the browned bits. Cook until the liquid reduces down into a glaze.

5. Add the cilantro, season with salt and pepper, and stir to combine. Serve warm or at room temperature.

INGREDIENTS:

2   EARS CORN, SHUCKED AND RINSED

1   TABLESPOON VEGETABLE OIL

1   ONION, DICED

2   TABLESPOONS MINCED GINGER

1   GARLIC CLOVE, CHOPPED

1   CUP SEEDED AND DICED RED BELL PEPPER

¼   CUP ORANGE JUICE

1   TABLESPOON BALSAMIC VINEGAR

⅓   CUP CHOPPED FRESH CILANTRO

SALT AND PEPPER, TO TASTE

FRESH CORN & SCALLION CORN BREAD

YIELD: 4 TO 6 SERVINGS / **ACTIVE TIME:** 10 MINUTES / **TOTAL TIME:** 40 MINUTES

Corn bread is always better when you use both cornmeal and fresh corn kernels.

1. Preheat oven to 425°F. Grease a 15 × 10-inch baking pan.

2. In a large bowl, sift together the cornmeal, flour, sugar, baking powder, baking soda, and salt.

3. In a separate bowl, whisk together the eggs and buttermilk until scrambled.

4. Combine the dry mixture and the wet mixture, stir to combine, and then fold in the corn and scallions.

5. Pour the batter into the pan, place in the oven, and bake for about 30 minutes, or until a knife inserted into the center comes out clean. Remove and let cool before serving.

INGREDIENTS:

1½ CUPS YELLOW CORNMEAL

½ CUP ALL-PURPOSE FLOUR

1 TABLESPOON SUGAR

2 TEASPOONS BAKING POWDER

1 TEASPOON BAKING SODA

1 TEASPOON KOSHER SALT

2 LARGE EGGS

1½ CUPS BUTTERMILK

1 CUP CORN KERNELS (PREFERABLY FRESH)

3 SCALLIONS, SLICED THIN

GRILLED CORN *with* CHIPOTLE MAYO

YIELD: 6 SERVINGS / ACTIVE TIME: 25 MINUTES / TOTAL TIME: 1 HOUR AND 15 MINUTES

This dish, more commonly known as Mexican street corn, has it all—sweet corn, spice from the chipotle, and a soft, creamy landing thanks to the goat cheese.

1. Preheat the oven to 400°F.

2. Place the ears of corn on a baking sheet, place it in the oven, and bake for 25 minutes, until the kernels have a slight give to them. Remove from the oven and let cool. When the ears of corn are cool enough to handle, remove the husks and silk.

3. Preheat your gas or charcoal grill to 400°F. Place the chipotles, mayonnaise, sour cream, brown sugar, lime juice, cilantro, salt, and pepper in a food processor and puree until smooth. Set aside.

4. Drizzle the corn with oil, season with salt and pepper, and place on the grill. Cook, turning occasionally, until the ears are charred all over.

5. Spread the chipotle mayonnaise on the corn, sprinkle the goat cheese on top, and garnish with additional cilantro. Serve with lime wedges.

INGREDIENTS:

6   EARS CORN

3   CHIPOTLE PEPPERS IN ADOBO

½   CUP MAYONNAISE

¼   CUP SOUR CREAM

1½   TABLESPOONS BROWN SUGAR

1   TABLESPOON FRESH LIME JUICE

2   TABLESPOONS CHOPPED FRESH CILANTRO, PLUS MORE FOR GARNISH

1   TEASPOON KOSHER SALT, PLUS MORE TO TASTE

½   TEASPOON BLACK PEPPER, PLUS MORE TO TASTE

3   TABLESPOONS OLIVE OIL

½   CUP CRUMBLED GOAT CHEESE

6   LIME WEDGES, FOR SERVING

CORN BEIGNETS

YIELD: 2 SERVINGS / ACTIVE TIME: 25 MINUTES / TOTAL TIME: 35 MINUTES

These make for wonderful party food. Frozen corn works, but if you make these beignets at the height of the season, the added sweetness provided by fresh kernels is unmistakable.

1. In a medium saucepan, add the milk, salt, and butter and bring to a boil.

2. Add the flour and stir constantly until a ball of dough forms.

3. Remove the pan from heat and let the dough cool for 10 minutes.

4. Add the egg to the pan and whisk vigorously.

5. Once the egg has been incorporated, add the corn and cilantro and stir until combined.

6. Place the oil in a Dutch oven and heat to 350°F.

7. Spoon small amounts of the batter into the hot oil and cook until golden brown.

8. Remove with a slotted spoon and set the beignets on a paper towel to drain. Serve immediately.

INGREDIENTS:

¼ CUP MILK

⅛ TEASPOON KOSHER SALT

2 TABLESPOONS UNSALTED BUTTER

¼ CUP ALL-PURPOSE FLOUR

1 EGG

¼ CUP CORN KERNELS

½ TEASPOON CHOPPED FRESH CILANTRO

2 CUPS VEGETABLE OIL

POLENTA CAKE *with* GREENS

YIELD: 4 TO 6 SERVINGS / ACTIVE TIME: 30 MINUTES / TOTAL TIME: 1 HOUR

Polenta is cornmeal cooked into porridge and then baked or fried. It forms a lovely, bright yellow cake that is moist yet firm. It can be topped with all kinds of things, but in this recipe, it is the base for sautéed vegetables. Delicious.

1. Preheat the oven to 400°F.

2. Liberally oil a 12-inch cast-iron skillet and put it in the oven for a few minutes.

3. In a heavy saucepan, whisk together the cornmeal and water. Place over medium heat and bring to a boil, whisking to prevent lumps from forming. When bubbling, reduce heat to low and simmer, uncovered, for a couple of minutes, or until smooth. Season with salt and pepper.

4. Pour the polenta into the skillet. Place the skillet in the oven and bake for about 30 minutes, until the polenta is lightly golden and coming away from the edge of the pan.

5. While the polenta is baking, prepare the greens. Bring a large pot of salted water to a boil, add the greens, and boil until very tender, 15 to 20 minutes. Drain in a colander and squeeze to remove excess moisture. Cut the greens into pieces. Heat the 3 tablespoons of oil in a pan, add the garlic, and cook, stirring, until fragrant, about 2 minutes. Add the red pepper flakes, stir, and then add the greens. Cook until heated through. Season with salt and pepper. Keep warm until polenta is cooked.

6. Cut the polenta into wedges, top with greens, and sprinkle with Romano.

VARIATION: Substitute ½ lb. baby spinach leaves and ½ lb. kale (tough stems removed) for the 1 lb. of mixed greens.

INGREDIENTS:

3 TABLESPOONS OLIVE OIL, PLUS MORE FOR THE SKILLET

1 CUP CORNMEAL

3 CUPS WATER

SALT AND PEPPER, TO TASTE

1 LB. BITTER GREENS (KALE, SWISS CHARD, ESCAROLE, OR DANDELION), STEMMED

3 GARLIC CLOVES, CHOPPED

RED PEPPER FLAKES, TO TASTE

ROMANO CHEESE, GRATED, FOR GARNISH

ENTREES

Vegetables are the stars of this book, and they are the focal points of these dishes. Meat and seafood are featured in several of these preparations, but so too are tofu and seitan, along with mushrooms, legumes, and grains—guaranteeing not only that all dietary needs are met but that anyone you are cooking for will be satisfied.

GARDEN SESAME NOODLES

YIELD: 6 SERVINGS / ACTIVE TIME: 15 MINUTES / TOTAL TIME: 20 MINUTES

Noodles seasoned with sesame sauce can take on just about any vegetable, either raw or cooked. This is a great recipe for cucumbers and everything else out of a garden. For a gluten-free version, you can swap out the Chinese egg noodles for flat, wide rice noodles.

1. Bring a large pot of water to a boil. Add the noodles and stir for the first minute to prevent any sticking. Cook until tender but still chewy, 2 to 3 minutes. Drain and transfer the noodles to a large bowl. Add ½ tablespoon of the oil and toss to coat to prevent the noodles from sticking together.

2. Place the sesame paste or tahini and peanut butter in a small bowl. Add the soy sauce, vinegar, the remaining oil, the brown sugar, chili-garlic sauce (if using), ginger, and garlic and whisk until the mixture is smooth. Taste and adjust the seasoning according to your preference.

3. Add the sauce to the noodles and toss until evenly distributed. Arrange the noodles in a swirled knot in six bowls and top with the pepper slivers, cucumber slices, snow peas, peanuts, sesame seeds, and scallions. Serve with additional chili-garlic sauce at the table.

INGREDIENTS:

- 1 LB. FRESH, FROZEN, OR DRIED CHINESE EGG NOODLES (SEE PAGE 778 FOR HOMEMADE)
- 2½ TABLESPOONS TOASTED SESAME OIL
- 2 TABLESPOONS CHINESE SESAME PASTE OR TAHINI
- 1½ TABLESPOONS SMOOTH PEANUT BUTTER
- ¼ CUP SOY SAUCE
- 2 TABLESPOONS RICE VINEGAR
- 1 TABLESPOON LIGHT BROWN SUGAR
- 2 TEASPOONS CHILI-GARLIC SAUCE (OPTIONAL), PLUS MORE FOR SERVING
-   2-INCH PIECE GINGER, PEELED AND GRATED OR MINCED
- 2 GARLIC CLOVES, MINCED
- 1 YELLOW OR ORANGE BELL PEPPER, STEMMED, SEEDED, AND SLICED THIN
- 1 MEDIUM CUCUMBER, PEELED, SEEDED, AND SLICED THIN
- 1 CUP SNOW PEAS, TRIMMED
- ½ CUP CHOPPED ROASTED PEANUTS
- 2 TABLESPOONS BLACK OR REGULAR SESAME SEEDS, TOASTED
- 5-6 SCALLIONS (WHITE AND LIGHT GREEN PARTS ONLY), TRIMMED AND SLICED INTO ½-INCH PIECES

ROASTED BARLEY & CARROTS
with PASILLA PEPPERS

YIELD: 4 TO 6 SERVINGS / ACTIVE TIME: 10 MINUTES / TOTAL TIME: 2 HOURS

This dish is light, sweet, spicy, and nutty. Considering how affordable all of the ingredients are, that makes for a whole lot of taste for not very much money.

1. Preheat the oven to 375°F. Place the carrots in a 9 × 13-inch baking pan, drizzle with the oil, and season with salt and pepper. Place the pan in the oven and roast for 45 to 50 minutes, or until the carrots are slightly soft to the touch.

2. While the carrots are cooking, open the pasilla peppers and discard the seeds and stems. Place the peppers in a bowl. Place the water in a saucepan and bring to a boil. Pour the boiling water over the peppers and cover the bowl with plastic wrap.

3. When the carrots are done, remove the baking pan from the oven. Chop the reconstituted peppers, add them to the pan, pouring the liquid from the peppers into the pan as well. Add the remaining ingredients and stir to combine. Spread into an even layer so that the liquid is covering the barley. Cover the pan tightly with aluminum foil and put it back in the oven for another 45 minutes, or until the barley becomes tender. Fluff with a fork and serve.

TIP: Adobo is a spice blend consisting of garlic powder, salt, onion powder, oregano, and turmeric. You can find it under the Goya brand, but it is very easy to make your own.

INGREDIENTS:

5   CARROTS, CUT LENGTHWISE INTO 3-INCH PIECES

    OLIVE OIL, TO TASTE

    SALT AND PEPPER, TO TASTE

6   DRIED PASILLA PEPPERS

2¼   CUPS WATER

1   CUP PEARL BARLEY

1   CUP MINCED RED ONION

2   TABLESPOONS ADOBO SEASONING

1   TABLESPOON SUGAR

1   TABLESPOON CHILI POWDER

¼   CUP DRIED OREGANO

ROASTED CAULIFLOWER STEAKS

YIELD: 4 TO 6 SERVINGS / ACTIVE TIME: 10 MINUTES / TOTAL TIME: 30 MINUTES

Roasting cauliflower brings out its best side. It becomes sweet and nutty, converting even the resolute cauliflower resister. Incorporating turmeric, cumin, and coriander adds a warm, spicy kick. Serve with tzatziki and basmati rice for a satisfying fall meal.

1. Preheat the oven to 425°F. In a bowl, combine the oil, salt, pepper, and spices and whisk to mix thoroughly.

2. Cut the cauliflower crosswise into ½-inch slices. Put the slices into a large, oven-safe skillet and brush the tops liberally with the oil mixture. Turn the cauliflower steaks over and brush the other side.

3. Put the skillet in the oven and roast for about 20 minutes, turning the pieces over after 10 minutes. A toothpick inserted in the flesh should go in easily to indicate that the cauliflower is cooked through.

4. Serve the slices hot with the Tzatziki and basmati rice.

INGREDIENTS:

- 1½ TABLESPOONS OLIVE OIL
- 1 TEASPOON KOSHER SALT
- BLACK PEPPER, TO TASTE
- ½ TEASPOON CUMIN
- ½ TEASPOON CORIANDER
- ½ TEASPOON TURMERIC
- ¼ TEASPOON CAYENNE PEPPER
- 1 HEAD CAULIFLOWER, STEM AND GREEN LEAVES REMOVED
- TZATZIKI (SEE PAGE 197), FOR SERVING
- 2 CUPS COOKED BASMATI RICE, FOR SERVING

FONTINA SAUCE *with* ROASTED CAULIFLOWER, MUSHROOMS & BACON

YIELD: 4 SERVINGS / ACTIVE TIME: 40 MINUTES / TOTAL TIME: 2 HOURS

Cauliflower and bacon were meant to be together. Toss in some mushrooms and a creamy fontina sauce and you have the perfect winter supper. The key to coaxing out that coveted deep, earthy flavor is to roast the mushrooms until they are browned and quite crisp on their edges. It gives them a nice texture to boot.

1. Preheat the oven to 450°F. Add the cauliflower to a large bowl along with 2 tablespoons of the oil and rub gently to coat. Place the cauliflower cut-side down on a parchment paper–lined rimmed baking pan. Season with salt and pepper and cover the pan tightly with aluminum foil. Place it in the oven and roast for 15 minutes.

2. As the cauliflower roasts, add the mushrooms to the same bowl you used for the cauliflower, along with another 2 tablespoons of the oil, and mix well. Arrange on another parchment paper–lined rimmed baking sheet, season with salt and pepper, and sprinkle with the thyme.

3. Remove the pan with the cauliflower from the oven and remove the foil (be careful, as the released steam will be hot). Using a narrow spatula, carefully turn the cauliflower over and return to the oven, uncovered. Lower the temperature to 400°F. Place the mushrooms in the oven. Roast for 15 minutes, until the mushrooms release some of their liquid. Remove the pan from the oven, carefully drain the liquid, and return the pan to the oven. Roast for another 25 minutes. Once the vegetables are soft and lightly browned on their edges, remove both pans from the oven.

4. Heat a large skillet over medium-low heat for 2 to 3 minutes. Add 2 tablespoons of the oil and raise heat to medium. Add the bacon and cook, stirring a few times, until it has browned and is crisp, 8 to 10 minutes. Using a slotted spoon, transfer it to a small bowl and set aside.

INGREDIENTS:

- 1   HEAD CAULIFLOWER, STEM AND GREEN LEAVES REMOVED, FLORETS SEPARATED AND HALVED
- 6½   TABLESPOONS OLIVE OIL
- SALT AND PEPPER, TO TASTE
- 1   LB. CREMINI MUSHROOMS, CLEANED AND QUARTERED
- LEAVES FROM 3 SMALL SPRIGS FRESH THYME
- 6   OZ. BACON, CHOPPED INTO ½-INCH PIECES
- 1   LARGE ONION, GRATED
- ½   CUP CHICKEN OR VEGETABLE STOCK (SEE PAGES 748 AND 755, RESPECTIVELY, FOR HOMEMADE)
- 4   OZ. FONTINA CHEESE, GRATED
- ¾   CUP HEAVY CREAM
- ½   TABLESPOON WORCESTERSHIRE SAUCE
- ¾   LB. PREFERRED PASTA
- HANDFUL FRESH PARSLEY LEAVES, CHOPPED, FOR SERVING

Continued . . .

5. Return the same skillet to the stove, add the grated onion and a couple pinches of salt to the rendered bacon fat, and stir. Cook over medium-high heat, stirring frequently, until the onion starts to gently sizzle, about 2 minutes. Adjust heat to low, cover, and cook, stirring occasionally, until the onion becomes very soft, about 15 minutes. Raise heat to medium-high, add the stock, cheese, and cream, and stir until the cheese is melted and the mixture is bubbly. Stir in the Worcestershire sauce. Remove the skillet from heat and cover to keep warm.

6. While the sauce is simmering, bring a large pot of water to a boil. Once it's boiling, add 1 tablespoon salt for every 4 cups water and stir. Add the pasta and stir for the first minute to prevent it from sticking to the bottom. Drain the pasta 2 minutes prior to the directed cooking time, reserving ¼ cup of the pasta water. The pasta will be soft, but firm. Return the empty pot to the stove. Immediately turn heat to high and add the remaining oil and the reserved pasta water. Quickly add the drained pasta and toss until the water is absorbed. Add the sauce and cook, stirring continuously, for 1 to 2 minutes.

7. Divide the pasta among four warmed bowls. Season with pepper, top with the roasted vegetables, crispy bacon bits, and parsley, and serve immediately.

BLACK BEAN BURRITO

YIELD: 6 SERVINGS / ACTIVE TIME: 20 MINUTES / TOTAL TIME: 1 HOUR AND 15 MINUTES

Adding grilled corn, squash, and zucchini gives this protein-packed burrito a nice charred flavor.

1. Begin by cooking the rice according to the instructions on the package. Once it has cooked completely, transfer it to a bowl, stir in the cilantro, and set aside.

2. Preheat your grill to 450°F. Brush the squash, zucchini, and corn with the oil and sprinkle with salt. Place on the grill and cook until they are charred and tender, about 10 minutes. Turn the vegetables while cooking and make sure they do not become too soft. Remove from heat and dice the zucchini and squash. Remove the corn kernels from the cobs and discard the cobs. Place the grilled vegetables in a bowl. Leave the grill on.

3. While the vegetables are grilling, drain and rinse the black beans. If desired, warm them in a saucepan.

4. Layer the rice-and-cilantro mixture, beans, veggies, onion, tomatoes, and cheese on the tortillas. Wrap tightly and place on the grill for about 1 minute per side. Remove from heat and serve with Grilled Peach & Corn Salsa.

INGREDIENTS:

1	CUP BROWN RICE
¼	CUP CHOPPED CILANTRO
1	LARGE YELLOW SQUASH, CUT INTO LONG SLICES
1	LARGE ZUCCHINI, CUT INTO LONG SLICES
2	EARS CORN, SHUCKED
1	TABLESPOON OLIVE OIL
	SALT, TO TASTE
1	(14 OZ.) CAN BLACK BEANS
1	SMALL RED ONION, CHOPPED
2	TOMATOES, DICED
1	CUP GRATED PEPPER JACK CHEESE
6	LARGE FLOUR TORTILLAS (SEE PAGE 797 FOR HOMEMADE)
	GRILLED PEACH & CORN SALSA (SEE PAGE 798), FOR SERVING

BLACK BEAN BURGERS

YIELD: 4 SERVINGS / ACTIVE TIME: 30 MINUTES / TOTAL TIME: 1 HOUR

For those times when you want to take a break from meat but want the great taste and texture of a juicy hamburger, try making these black bean burgers. Be sure you have ripe tomatoes and avocados for toppings.

1. In a food processor or blender, combine half of the beans with the scallions and roasted red peppers. Pulse until you have a thick paste. Transfer to a large bowl.

2. Add the corn, bread crumbs, egg, cilantro, cumin, cayenne, pepper, and lime juice to the bowl. Stir to combine. Add the remaining beans and stir vigorously to get the mixture to hold together. Cover the bowl with plastic wrap and let it sit at room temperature for 30 minutes.

3. Heat a 12-inch skillet over medium-high heat. Form the mixture into four patties.

4. Add the oil to the skillet and, when it starts to shimmer, add the patties. Cover the skillet and cook for about 5 minutes per side, until the patties are browned and warmed through.

5. Serve on hamburger buns with the Creamy Chipotle & Adobo and the slices of tomato, avocado, and red onion.

CREAMY CHIPOTLE & ADOBO

1. Place the ingredients in a small bowl and whisk until the mixture has emulsified.

INGREDIENTS:

1	(14 OZ.) CAN BLACK BEANS, DRAINED AND RINSED
⅓	CUP CHOPPED SCALLIONS
¼	CUP CHOPPED ROASTED RED PEPPERS
¼	CUP COOKED CORN KERNELS
½	CUP PLAIN BREAD CRUMBS
1	EGG, LIGHTLY BEATEN
2	TABLESPOONS CHOPPED FRESH CILANTRO
½	TEASPOON CUMIN
½	TEASPOON CAYENNE PEPPER
½	TEASPOON BLACK PEPPER
1	TEASPOON FRESH LIME JUICE
1	TABLESPOON OLIVE OIL
	HAMBURGER BUNS, FOR SERVING
	CREAMY CHIPOTLE & ADOBO (SEE RECIPE), FOR SERVING)
	TOMATO SLICES, FOR SERVING
1	AVOCADO, SLICED, FOR SERVING
1	RED ONION, SLICED THIN, FOR SERVING

CREAMY CHIPOTLE & ADOBO

½	CUP GREEK YOGURT
2	CHIPOTLES IN ADOBO
1	TEASPOON ADOBO SAUCE
½	TEASPOON KOSHER SALT
½	TEASPOON BLACK PEPPER
1	TEASPOON HONEY
1	TEASPOON DIJON MUSTARD
1	TABLESPOON FRESH LIME JUICE

CREAMY SUCCOTASH

YIELD: 8 TO 10 SERVINGS / ACTIVE TIME: 30 MINUTES / TOTAL TIME: 1 HOUR

Take advantage of the season when fresh corn is plentiful to create this cookout classic. This uses a lot of corn and is a nice alternative to corn on the cob.

1. Bring a medium pot of salted water to a boil over high heat. Add the lima beans and reduce heat to medium. Cook until they are al dente, about 5 minutes. Drain and set aside.

2. Standing each ear up in the middle of a large baking dish, use a sharp knife to cut down the sides and remove all the kernels. With the kernels off, take the blade of a dull knife and press it along each side of the ears to "milk" the cob of its liquid. Discard the milked cobs.

3. Place the bacon in a nonstick skillet and cook over medium heat until it is crispy, about 8 minutes. Transfer to a paper towel–lined plate and let it drain. When cool enough to handle, chop the bacon into bite-sized pieces.

4. Place a 12-inch cast-iron skillet over medium heat. When hot, lower heat and add the butter so it melts slowly. When melted, add the corn kernels and "milk" from the cobs and stir to coat the kernels with the butter. Increase heat to medium-high and add the water and whole milk. Bring to a boil, stirring constantly, and then reduce heat to low. Add the lima beans, salt, and pepper.

5. Add the flour, cherry tomatoes, and bacon pieces to the skillet, stir to incorporate, and cook over low heat until the sauce thickens. If it gets too thick, add some more whole milk. Serve hot.

TIP: You'll want to freeze some of this to enjoy in the dead of winter. It's easy. Allow the succotash to cool, put it in airtight containers, being sure to push all the air out when sealing, and place in the freezer. Put the date it was cooked on the container so you remember.

INGREDIENTS:

SALT AND PEPPER, TO TASTE

4 CUPS FRESH OR FROZEN LIMA BEANS

12 EARS CORN, SHUCKED AND RINSED

½ LB. THICK-CUT BACON

3 TABLESPOONS UNSALTED BUTTER

1 CUP WATER, AT ROOM TEMPERATURE

1 CUP WHOLE MILK, PLUS MORE AS NEEDED

3 TABLESPOONS ALL-PURPOSE FLOUR

1 CUP HALVED CHERRY TOMATOES

BRAISED PORK & CELERIAC
with ORANGE & ROSEMARY

YIELD: 6 SERVINGS / ACTIVE TIME: 2 HOURS / TOTAL TIME: 2½ TO 3 HOURS

I found this recipe on the BBC's website and fell in love. Celeriac is often paired with rich elements such as heavy cream and cheese, but it also takes well to lighter, acidic flavors. Its earthy flavor is well complemented by the rich pork shoulder, and then the whole shebang is perked up by the orange zest and juice, and the piney rosemary.

1. Preheat the oven to 325°F and warm a large sauté pan over medium-high heat. If the pork has a good marbling of fat, there is no need to add oil to the pan. If it is on the lean side, add a tablespoon of oil to the pan and then add the pork. Cook, turning it every so often to get all sides, until browned, about 12 minutes. Transfer the pork to a bowl, season with salt and pepper, and set it aside.

2. Coat the bottom of the pan with oil and then add the leek, celeriac, and carrots. Sauté until the celeriac has browned slightly, 5 to 10 minutes. Add the garlic and cook until it starts to brown, about 2 minutes.

3. Place the meat in a casserole dish and then add all of the remaining ingredients except for the water, butter, and noodles. Deglaze the sauté pan with the water, scrape the bottom to remove any browned bits, and add the pan sauce to the casserole dish. Cover the dish with aluminum foil and place it in the oven. Roast for 2 hours, removing to stir every 45 minutes. Add water as needed to ensure the liquid comes one-third of the way up the meat and vegetables.

4. When the meat and celeriac are fork-tender, remove from the oven and add the butter. Season to taste and serve over the buttered noodles.

INGREDIENTS:

- 1½ **LBS. PORK SHOULDER, CUBED**
- **OLIVE OIL, AS NEEDED**
- **SALT AND PEPPER, TO TASTE**
- 1 **LARGE LEEK, TRIMMED, RINSED WELL, AND SLICED**
- 1 **LARGE CELERIAC, PEELED AND CUT INTO CHUNKS**
- 3 **LARGE CARROTS, PEELED AND CUT INTO CHUNKS**
- 2 **GARLIC CLOVES, MINCED**
- ¾ **CUP DRY WHITE WINE**
- ¾ **CUP CHICKEN STOCK (SEE PAGE 748 FOR HOMEMADE)**
- **ZEST AND JUICE OF 1 LARGE ORANGE**
- 2 **TEASPOONS SOY SAUCE**
- ¼ **CUP WATER, PLUS MORE AS NEEDED**
- 1 **TABLESPOON UNSALTED BUTTER**
- **BUTTERED NOODLES, FOR SERVING**

SPAGHETTI *with* GARLIC & CHILI OIL

YIELD: 4 SERVINGS / ACTIVE TIME: 10 MINUTES / TOTAL TIME: 25 MINUTES

If you really want garlic flavor with just a few supporting players, then this simple pasta dish from central Italy is for you.

1. Bring a large pot of water to a boil.

2. While the water comes to a boil, place the ⅓ cup of oil, the garlic, and the chilies in a skillet and warm over medium-low heat. Let everything warm up together, with the garlic gently sizzling but not coloring at all; if need be, reduce heat to low or turn it off entirely.

3. Once the water is boiling, add salt (1 tablespoon for every 4 cups water) and stir. Add the spaghetti, stirring for the first minute to prevent any sticking. Cook 2 minutes short of the directed cooking time, drain, and reserve ¼ cup of the pasta water. Return the pot to the stove. Immediately turn heat to high and add the remaining oil and the reserved pasta water. Add the drained spaghetti and toss. Pour in the garlic oil and cook, tossing continuously, for 2 minutes.

4. Divide the spaghetti between four warmed bowls. Garnish with the parsley, if desired, and serve piping hot.

INGREDIENTS:

- ⅓ CUP OLIVE OIL, PLUS ½ TABLESPOON
- 3 GARLIC CLOVES, SLICED THIN
- 1-2 DRIED RED CHILI PEPPERS, BROKEN INTO PIECES AND SEEDED TO TASTE
- SALT, TO TASTE
- ¾ LB. SPAGHETTI
- HANDFUL FRESH PARSLEY LEAVES, CHOPPED, FOR GARNISH (OPTIONAL)

OMELET *with* ARUGULA, RICOTTA, SUN-DRIED TOMATOES & OIL-CURED OLIVES

YIELD: 1 SERVING / ACTIVE TIME: 5 MINUTES / TOTAL TIME: 10 MINUTES

Oil-cured olives are sweet and sun-dried tomatoes are tangy, which leaves arugula to be the spicy player in this dish. Fold it in at the last minute of cooking so it is barely wilted and still has some kick to it. I have left the ingredients list flexible depending upon tastes and appetites.

1. Crack the eggs into a bowl and whisk to blend. Season with salt.

2. Melt butter in a small nonstick skillet and heat until it starts to bubble. Add the eggs and swirl to coat the entire bottom of the pan. Let the eggs cook for 1 or 2 minutes, until the bottom starts to set.

3. Using a spatula, gently flip the omelet and immediately put the ricotta, sun-dried tomatoes and olives in the middle. Cook for 1 minute. Place a handful of arugula on top of the other ingredients and fold the omelet in half. Cook for 30 seconds more and remove to a plate.

INGREDIENTS:

3   **EGGS**

     SALT, TO TASTE

1   **TABLESPOON UNSALTED BUTTER**

2   **SUN-DRIED TOMATOES, SLICED**

4   **OIL-CURED OLIVES, PITTED AND ROUGHLY CHOPPED**

2   **TABLESPOONS RICOTTA CHEESE**

     HANDFUL OF ARUGULA

PUERTO RICAN RICE & BEANS

YIELD: 6 SERVINGS / ACTIVE TIME: 25 MINUTES / TOTAL TIME: 24 HOURS

An authentic recipe would utilize kidney beans, but black beans will also work.

1. Place the beans in a Dutch oven and cover with water. Bring to a boil, reduce heat to medium-low, and cover the pot. Cook for 45 minutes to 1 hour, until the beans are tender. Drain and set the beans aside.

2. Place the pot back on the stove and add half of the oil. Add the chicken and cook over medium-high heat until browned, about 5 minutes on each side. Remove the chicken from the Dutch oven, cut it into 12 pieces, and set aside.

3. Add the salt pork and the remaining oil to the pot and cook until some of the salt pork's fat has rendered, about 5 minutes. Add the Sofrito and the tomato sauce. Cook for 5 minutes, stirring constantly.

4. Add the rice to the pot, stir, and cook for 5 minutes. Add the remaining ingredients and return the chicken to the pot. Reduce heat to medium and cook for 10 minutes. Cover the Dutch oven and continue to cook until the liquid has been absorbed and the rice is tender, 20 to 30 minutes. Uncover the pot and add the beans. Stir to combine and serve immediately.

TIP: The rice at the bottom of the Dutch oven might get a little crunchy, which is actually preferable in this dish.

SOFRITO

1. Place all of the ingredients in a blender or food processor and puree until smooth.

INGREDIENTS:

½ LB. KIDNEY BEANS, SOAKED OVERNIGHT AND DRAINED

½ CUP OLIVE OIL

4 BONELESS, SKINLESS CHICKEN THIGHS

2 PIECES SALT PORK, MINCED (ABOUT ½ CUP)

1 CUP SOFRITO (SEE RECIPE)

1 CUP SPANISH-STYLE TOMATO SAUCE, PUREED

2 CUPS WHITE RICE

3 CUPS CHICKEN STOCK (SEE PAGE 748 FOR HOMEMADE)

2 PACKETS SAZÓN WITH ACHIOTE

2 TABLESPOONS DRIED OREGANO

1 CUP SPANISH OLIVES, WITH THE BRINE

ADOBO SEASONING, TO TASTE

SOFRITO

2 POBLANO PEPPERS, STEMMED AND SEEDED

1 WHITE ONION, QUARTERED

1 RED BELL PEPPER, STEMMED AND SEEDED

1 GREEN BELL PEPPER, STEMMED AND SEEDED

3 PLUM TOMATOES

2 GARLIC CLOVES

1 TABLESPOON CUMIN

2 TABLESPOONS ADOBO SEASONING

MOUSSAKA

YIELD: 4 TO 6 SERVINGS / ACTIVE TIME: 45 MINUTES / TOTAL TIME: 1 HOUR AND 30 MINUTES

Moussaka is one of the highest ends for an eggplant. Usually made with layers of seasoned ground lamb and sheets of eggplant, this version makes it a little easier, mixing the two together in the bottom layer. The crust, however, retains the classic richness granted by a béchamel sauce base.

1. Preheat the oven to 350°F.

2. To begin preparations for the filling, place the cold water in a bowl and add the salt. When the salt has dissolved, add the eggplant cubes and stir. Cover the bowl with plastic wrap and let the cubes soak for about 20 minutes. Drain and rinse with cold water. Squeeze the cubes to remove as much water as you can, place them on a pile of paper towels, and blot dry. Set aside.

3. While the eggplant is soaking, warm a large skillet over medium-high heat. Add a tablespoon of the oil and coat the bottom of the pan. Add the ground lamb and cook until browned and cooked through, about 6 minutes. Use a slotted spoon to transfer the cooked meat to a bowl and set aside.

4. Add ¼ cup of the oil and the eggplant to the skillet and cook, stirring frequently, until they start to soften, about 5 minutes. Use the slotted spoon to transfer the cooked eggplant to the bowl containing the lamb.

5. Add the rest of the oil, the onion, and the garlic to the skillet and cook, stirring frequently, until the onion is translucent, about 3 minutes. Add the lamb and eggplant and stir to combine. Add the wine, tomato sauce, parsley, oregano, and cinnamon. Stir to combine, reduce heat to low, and simmer for about 15 minutes, stirring occasionally. Season with salt and pepper and remove from heat.

6. To prepare the crust, place the eggs in a large bowl and beat them lightly. Place a saucepan over medium heat, melt the butter, lower heat slightly, and add the flour. Stir constantly until the mixture is smooth. Slowly add the milk and bring to a boil, stirring constantly. When the mixture reaches a boil, remove from

INGREDIENTS:

FOR THE FILLING

4   CUPS COLD WATER

¼   CUP KOSHER SALT, PLUS MORE TO TASTE

1   LARGE EGGPLANT, TRIMMED AND CUT INTO CUBES

½   CUP OLIVE OIL

1   LB. GROUND LAMB

1   ONION, DICED

3   GARLIC CLOVES, MINCED

½   CUP DRY RED WINE

1   CUP TOMATO SAUCE

2   TABLESPOONS CHOPPED FRESH PARSLEY

1   TEASPOON DRIED OREGANO

½   TEASPOON CINNAMON

    BLACK PEPPER, TO TASTE

FOR THE CRUST

5   EGGS

6   TABLESPOONS UNSALTED BUTTER

⅓   CUP ALL-PURPOSE FLOUR

2½   CUPS MILK

⅔   CUP GRATED PARMESAN CHEESE

⅓   CUP CHOPPED FRESH DILL OR PARSLEY LEAVES

Continued . . .

heat. Add approximately half of the mixture in the saucepan to the beaten eggs, stirring briskly to combine. Add the tempered eggs to the saucepan, stir to combine, and then add the cheese and dill or parsley. Stir to combine and remove from heat.

7. Pour the crust mixture over the lamb mixture in the skillet and use a rubber spatula to smooth the top. Place the skillet in the oven and bake until the crust is set and golden brown, about 35 minutes. Remove from the oven and let rest for 5 minutes before serving.

CRISPY EGGPLANT BALLS
& RICOTTA IN TOMATO SAUCE

YIELD: 4 SERVINGS / ACTIVE TIME: 45 MINUTES / TOTAL TIME: 2 HOURS

The texture of eggplant makes it an excellent meatball ingredient. Bread it, fry it, and serve it with tomato sauce and pasta, and you have a very satisfying meal. If you are partial to sharper cheese, you can swap out the fresh-tasting ricotta for the salty tanginess of its pressed and dried cousin, ricotta salata.

1. Preheat the oven to 400°F and line two baking sheets with parchment paper.

2. To begin preparations for the eggplant balls, peel and quarter the eggplants. Cut away any overly seedy or spongy parts, then cut into 1-inch cubes. Place the cubes in a bowl with the ¼ cup of the olive oil, toss to coat, and then place the eggplant on the baking sheets. Place the sheets in the oven and roast, turning the eggplant occasionally and swapping the positions of the sheets halfway through, until the eggplant is golden brown, about 20 minutes. Remove one sheet from of the oven, add the garlic, return to the oven, and bake until the skins of the garlic have turned a very light brownish color and opened, about 15 minutes. When done, remove from the oven, season with salt and pepper, and mix well. When cool enough to handle, remove the skins from the garlic cloves and roughly chop the mixture.

3. To begin preparations for the sauce, bring a medium saucepan of water to a boil. Place the tomatoes in the boiling water for 1 minute. Use tongs to transfer them to a cutting board and let rest until cool enough to handle. Remove the skins, cut the flesh into quarters, remove the seeds, and roughly chop the flesh. Discard the skins and the seeds.

4. Warm a large, deep skillet over medium heat for 2 to 3 minutes. Add the oil and heat for a minute or two, then add the onion, a pinch of salt, and the red pepper flakes and cook, stirring frequently, until the onion has softened, about 10 minutes. Add the tomatoes, two pinches of salt, and the sugar and bring to a boil. Adjust heat so that the sauce simmers, cover, and cook until it reaches the consistency of tomato sauce, about 30 minutes.

Continued . . .

INGREDIENTS:

FOR THE EGGPLANT BALLS & RICOTTA

- 2 LARGE EGGPLANTS
- ¼ CUP OLIVE OIL, PLUS 1 TEASPOON
- 8 GARLIC CLOVES, UNPEELED
  SALT AND PEPPER, TO TASTE
- 2¼ CUPS PANKO BREAD CRUMBS
- 1 CUP GRATED PARMESAN CHEESE, PLUS MORE FOR SERVING
- 2 HANDFULS FRESH PARSLEY LEAVES, CHOPPED
- 2 LARGE EGGS, LIGHTLY BEATEN
  GRAPESEED OR SAFFLOWER OIL, FOR FRYING
- ¾ LB. PREFERRED PASTA
- ¾ CUP WHOLE-MILK RICOTTA CHEESE
  LEAVES FROM 3 SPRIGS FRESH OREGANO, CHOPPED

FOR THE TOMATO SAUCE

- 4 LBS. RIPE PLUM TOMATOES
- 2 TABLESPOONS OLIVE OIL
- 1 ONION, GRATED OR SLICED INTO THIN HALF-MOONS
  SALT, TO TASTE
- ¼ TEASPOON RED PEPPER FLAKES
- 1 TEASPOON SUGAR

5. As the sauce cooks, make the eggplant balls. Place the eggplant-and-garlic mixture, 1½ cups of the panko bread crumbs, the Parmesan, two-thirds of the parsley, and the eggs in a bowl, season with salt and pepper, and stir to combine. Form the eggplant mixture into golf ball-sized spheres. Place the remaining panko in a small bowl and roll each sphere in the bread crumbs to coat evenly. Place the coated spheres on a plate or parchment–lined baking sheet.

6. Add enough grapeseed or safflower oil to cover the bottom of a large skillet by ½ inch. Turn heat to medium and when the oil begins to shimmer but is not yet smoking, carefully add the balls. Work in batches to prevent overcrowding. Fry, turning the balls gently as needed, until browned all over, 3 to 5 minutes per batch. Use a slotted spoon to transfer the cooked balls to a paper towel–lined plate and tent with aluminum foil to keep them warm.

7. Bring a large pot of water to a boil. Once it's boiling, add salt (1 tablespoon for every 4 cups water) and stir. Add the pasta, stirring for the first minute to prevent any sticking. Cook 2 minutes short of the directed cooking time, drain, and reserve ¼ cup of the pasta water. Return the empty pot to the stove. Immediately turn heat to high and add the remaining teaspoon of olive oil and the reserved pasta water. Add the drained pasta and toss to combine. Add a few ladles of the tomato sauce and cook, tossing continuously, for 2 minutes.

8. Divide the pasta among four warmed bowls and top with a little more sauce. Add a few dollops of ricotta and six of the eggplant balls, sprinkle with the oregano and a dusting of Parmesan, and serve piping hot.

RATATOUILLE

YIELD: 4 TO 6 SERVINGS / ACTIVE TIME: 20 MINUTES / TOTAL TIME: 1 HOUR AND 30 MINUTES

Ratatouille the way I like it: no peppers. I love peppers, but in this dish I feel they add a bitter element that deflates the rich sweetness of the browned eggplant, squash, and onions.

1. Cut the eggplant into ½-inch pieces, cut the squash and zucchini in half lengthwise, and cut the onions into quarters. Wash the eggplant pieces and sprinkle with salt. Let sit for 30 minutes.

2. Preheat the grill to 450°F. In a large bowl, add 2 tablespoons of the oil. Add the eggplant, squash, zucchini, and onion to the bowl and toss to coat. Place the eggplant, squash, and zucchini directly on the grill. Skewer the onions before placing them on the grill. Grill until they are lightly charred: about 10 to 12 minutes for the onions, and 4 to 5 minutes per side for the eggplant, squash, and zucchini. Remove from heat and let cool.

3. Cut the squash and zucchini into slivers. Add the remaining oil to a large saucepan, warm over low heat, and then add the garlic. Cook until golden, about 2 minutes. Stir in the grilled vegetables, stewed tomatoes, parsley, dried basil, and oregano. Season the mixture with salt and pepper, and cook for about 30 minutes. Remove from heat, stir in the basil leaves, and serve over the brown rice.

INGREDIENTS:

1	EGGPLANT
1	YELLOW SQUASH
1	ZUCCHINI
1	ONION
	SALT AND PEPPER, TO TASTE
3	TABLESPOONS OLIVE OIL
2	GARLIC CLOVES, MINCED
1	(14 OZ.) CAN STEWED TOMATOES
¼	CUP CHOPPED FRESH PARSLEY
	PINCH OF DRIED BASIL
	PINCH OF DRIED OREGANO
¼	CUP FRESH BASIL LEAVES
2	CUPS COOKED BROWN RICE, FOR SERVING

SOBA NOODLES
with MARINATED EGGPLANT *&* TOFU

YIELD: 4 SERVINGS / ACTIVE TIME: 45 MINUTES / TOTAL TIME: 2 HOURS AND 15 MINUTES

An easy meal that combines eggplant with its best companions: ginger, soy, and sesame oil. If you are not a fan of tofu, chicken or pork would also be delicious.

1. To prepare the marinade, place all of the ingredients in a small bowl and stir to combine. To prepare the dressing, place all of the ingredients in a separate small bowl and stir to combine. Set the marinade and the dressing aside.

2. To begin preparations for the salad, trim both ends of the eggplants, slice the eggplants in half, and cut them into ½-inch pieces. Place in a mixing bowl, add the marinade, and toss to combine. Let stand for 1 hour at room temperature.

3. Drain the tofu and cut it into ½-inch strips. Arrange the strips in a single layer on a paper towel–lined tray. Cover with paper towels and pat dry. Let them sit for 30 minutes, changing the paper towels after 15 minutes. Cut the strips into ½-inch cubes.

4. Bring a large pot of water to a boil. Add the noodles and stir for the first minute to prevent any sticking. Cook until tender but still chewy, 5 to 7 minutes. Drain, rinse under cold water, drain again, and place in a large bowl. Add the dressing, toss to coat, and set aside.

5. Warm a wok or a large skillet over medium heat for 2 to 3 minutes. Raise heat to medium-high and add 2 tablespoons of the peanut oil. When it begins to shimmer, add the eggplant cubes and a couple pinches of salt and stir-fry until the eggplant softens and turns golden, 5 to 6 minutes. Using a slotted spoon, transfer the eggplant to a paper towel–lined plate. Add the remaining tablespoon of peanut oil and the tofu cubes to the pan and stir-fry until browned all over, 4 to 5 minutes. Using a slotted spoon, transfer them to a separate paper towel–lined plate.

6. Divide the noodles between four bowls. Arrange the eggplant and tofu on top and top with the scallions.

INGREDIENTS:

FOR THE MARINADE

2   TABLESPOONS RICE VINEGAR

3   TABLESPOONS SOY SAUCE

1   TABLESPOON TOASTED SESAME OIL

½   TEASPOON SUGAR

2   GARLIC CLOVES, MINCED

FOR THE DRESSING

1   TABLESPOON RICE VINEGAR

1   TABLESPOON PEANUT OIL

1   TEASPOON SOY SAUCE

1   TABLESPOON TOASTED SESAME OIL

    1-INCH PIECE FRESH GINGER, PEELED AND GRATED

FOR THE SALAD

3   CHINESE OR REGULAR EGGPLANTS (ABOUT 2 LBS.)

¾   LB. FIRM TOFU

½   LB. SOBA NOODLES

3   TABLESPOONS PEANUT OIL, DIVIDED

    SALT, TO TASTE

5-6   SCALLIONS, TRIMMED AND SLICED INTO ¼-INCH PIECES

EGGPLANT PARMESAN

YIELD: 4 SERVINGS / ACTIVE TIME: 20 MINUTES / TOTAL TIME: 1 HOUR AND 30 MINUTES

This recipe bakes the eggplant instead of frying it, which cuts down on the grease significantly.

1. Preheat the oven to 350°F. Trim the top and bottom off the eggplant and slice into ¼-inch slices. Put the slices on paper towels in a single layer, sprinkle salt over them, and let rest for about 15 minutes. Turn the slices over, salt the other side, and let sit for another 15 minutes. Rinse the salt from all the pieces and pat them dry with paper towels.

2. Drizzle the oil over a baking sheet. In a shallow bowl, combine the bread crumbs and Parmesan. Put the beaten egg in another shallow bowl. Dip the slices of eggplant in the egg and then in the bread crumb-and-cheese mixture until both sides are coated. Place the breaded slices on the baking sheet.

3. When all of the eggplant has been breaded, place it in the oven and cook for 10 minutes. Remove, turn the slices over, and bake another 10 minutes. Remove the sheet from the oven and let cool slightly.

4. Place a layer of tomato sauce in a square 8-inch baking dish or a cast-iron skillet and stir in the garlic. Lay some of the eggplant slices on top of the sauce, top them with more sauce, and then place the remaining eggplant on top. Top with the grated mozzarella.

5. Place in the oven and bake for about 30 minutes, until the sauce is bubbling and the cheese is golden. Remove from the oven and let cool for 10 minutes before serving with additional tomato sauce and fresh basil.

INGREDIENTS:

- 1 **LARGE EGGPLANT**

  SALT, TO TASTE
- 2 **TABLESPOONS OLIVE OIL**
- 1 **CUP ITALIAN SEASONED BREAD CRUMBS**
- 2 **TABLESPOONS GRATED PARMESAN CHEESE**
- 1 **EGG, BEATEN**

  TOMATO SAUCE (SEE PAGE 793 FOR HOMEMADE), AS NEEDED
- 2 **GARLIC CLOVES, MINCED**
- ½ **LB. MOZZARELLA CHEESE, GRATED**

  FRESH BASIL, TORN, FOR GARNISH

SEARED SCALLOPS *with* GREEN LENTILS *&* FENNEL CREAM

YIELD: 4 SERVINGS / ACTIVE TIME: 1 HOUR / TOTAL TIME: 1 HOUR AND 30 MINUTES

I first ran across this recipe from Steve Dunn when he posted it on the website *Food52*, and I made it for a dinner party soon after. When I was pondering my favorite fennel recipes to add to this book, I immediately thought of this one.

1. To begin preparations for the scallops and green lentils, rinse the lentils with cold water, discard any debris, and set the lentils aside. Place a medium saucepan over medium heat, add enough oil to coat the bottom of the pan, and then add the shallot, garlic, fennel, and carrot. Reduce heat to medium-low and cook until the vegetables have softened and are just starting to color.

2. Add the lentils, water, and bay leaf, raise heat to high, and bring to a boil. Reduce heat to low and gently simmer until most (if not all) of the water has evaporated and the lentils are al dente, 25 to 30 minutes.

3. While the lentils are simmering, cook the bacon over medium heat until nicely browned and slightly crisp, but still chewy. Transfer to a paper towel–lined plate and set aside.

4. When the lentils have finished cooking, drain away any excess water, remove the bay leaf, and return the lentils to the saucepan. Add the bacon lardons to the lentils, along with the mustard and butter, and season to taste with salt and pepper. Cover and keep warm by the stove.

5. Working in batches, sear the scallops. Place 1 tablespoon butter and some oil per batch in a large, heavy skillet and melt the butter over medium-high heat. Add the scallops and cook until browned, about 2 minutes per side.

6. Divide the lentils between four plates, arrange three scallops atop the lentils, spoon the Fennel Cream around the lentils and scallops, and garnish with the fennel fronds and lemon zest.

INGREDIENTS:

- ¾ CUP FRENCH GREEN LENTILS (LE PUY GREEN LENTILS)
- OLIVE OIL, AS NEEDED
- 1 SHALLOT, MINCED
- 1 GARLIC CLOVE, MINCED
- 1½ FENNEL BULBS, DICED, FRONDS RESERVED FOR GARNISH
- 1 CARROT, DICED
- 3 CUPS WATER
- 1 BAY LEAF
- ¼ LB. SLAB BACON, CUT INTO LARDONS
- 2 TEASPOONS DIJON MUSTARD
- 2 TABLESPOONS UNSALTED BUTTER, PLUS MORE AS NEEDED
- SALT AND PEPPER, TO TASTE
- FENNEL CREAM (SEE RECIPE)
- 12 LARGE SEA SCALLOPS
- ZEST OF 1 LEMON, FOR GARNISH

FENNEL CREAM

1. Place a medium saucepan over medium-low heat, add the garlic, fennel, fennel seeds, shallot, and a little oil, and cook until the onion is translucent, about 3 minutes. Add the wine, raise heat, and reduce until almost all the liquid is gone. Add the stock and reduce in the same manner.

2. Add the cream and cook until reduced by half. Remove the saucepan from heat and let cool slightly.

3. Pour the cream mixture into a blender and puree until very smooth. Strain through a fine-mesh strainer into a small pan, season with salt and white pepper, and cover to keep warm.

FENNEL CREAM

1	GARLIC CLOVE, CHOPPED
½	FENNEL BULB, DICED
⅛	TEASPOON CRUSHED FENNEL SEEDS
1	TABLESPOON CHOPPED SHALLOT
	OLIVE OIL, AS NEEDED
¼	CUP DRY WHITE WINE
½	CUP CHICKEN STOCK (SEE PAGE 748 FOR HOMEMADE)
1	CUP HEAVY CREAM
	SALT AND WHITE PEPPER, TO TASTE

CHEF PROFILE

Steve Dunn has the enviable job of working at *Cook's Illustrated*, the venerated test kitchen where everyday dishes are fine-tuned until they become their best selves. The chefs there deconstruct basics, such as Chicken Piccata, and dissect each step until they have the ultimate Piccata recipe that can be replicated at home.

Dunn is originally from Vermont, but he trained in Boston and France before settling in Massachusetts. He's worked at *Cook's Illustrated* for over four years, a dream job for anyone who loves to get into the nitty-gritty of flavor, texture, and food chemistry.

CHICKEN *with* 40 CLOVES OF GARLIC

YIELD: 6 SERVINGS / ACTIVE TIME: 45 MINUTES / TOTAL TIME: 1 HOUR AND 30 MINUTES

This is a classic French dish. The name does not exaggerate; to make it, one roasts or braises chicken with 40 cloves, but the garlic mellows considerably, which makes for a sweet, oniony sauce. Given that I used to grow about 600 pounds of garlic a year, I had considerable stores of it in my basement, even after I had replanted the best bulbs for the following year and sold much of the rest. One day, I got a hankering for this dish and grabbed a bunch of garlic heads. Absentmindedly, I started breaking them apart, and when I stopped to count how many were in the bowl, it tallied 80 fat cloves. I looked at the pile and decided that if 40 was no big deal, then 80 wouldn't be much different. This turned out to be untrue. I was making a roasted version of the dish, and when all 80 cloves heated up, a cloud of fumes emanated from the oven, causing anyone within 20 feet of the kitchen to well up with tears. I opened all of the windows on the bottom floor of the house, but the area around the kitchen remained a hazardous zone, and it took over a day to fully ventilate. In sum, this recipe comes with these cautionary words: 40 is enough.

1. Preheat the oven to 350°F. Generously season the chicken with salt and pepper and put a Dutch oven over high heat. Add the chicken in one layer, cooking in batches if necessary. Although oil is not necessarily needed when cooking chicken thighs, if the pan looks dry add a drizzle of oil. When brown on one side, flip to the other side and repeat. Transfer to a plate when fully browned but not cooked through.

2. Put the mushrooms in the pot and sauté over medium heat, stirring occasionally, until they are browned all over. After 5 minutes, add the garlic and cook a few minutes more.

3. Add the vermouth and stock to the pot, scrape the brown bits off the bottom, and then return the chicken to the Dutch oven.

4. Cover with a lid, place the pot in the oven, and let the chicken braise for 25 to 30 minutes, or until the thighs are tender and cooked through.

5. Remove from the oven and transfer the chicken and mushrooms to a separate plate. With a fork or large spoon, smash about half of the cooked garlic into the sauce and stir to incorporate. If the sauce is still thin, place over medium-high heat for a few minutes until it has reduced and thickened. Return the chicken and mushrooms to the pot, reduce heat, and cook until warmed through.

6. When ready to serve, add the butter and tarragon to the pot and season to taste.

7. Place one or two thighs and some mushrooms on each plate and spoon the sauce over the top, being sure to include both whole and mashed garlic cloves. Serve with buttered noodles or rice.

INGREDIENTS:

8   BONELESS, SKINLESS
    CHICKEN THIGHS

    SALT AND PEPPER, TO TASTE

    OLIVE OIL, AS NEEDED

8   WHITE OR BABY BELLA
    MUSHROOMS, QUARTERED

40 GARLIC CLOVES

⅓   CUP DRY VERMOUTH

¾   CUP CHICKEN STOCK (SEE
    PAGE 748 FOR HOMEMADE)

1   TABLESPOON UNSALTED
    BUTTER

1   TABLESPOON CHOPPED
    FRESH TARRAGON

    BUTTERED NOODLES OR
    RICE, FOR SERVING

TARHANA *with* GREEN BEANS & TOMATOES

YIELD: 4 SERVINGS / ACTIVE TIME: 30 MINUTES / TOTAL TIME: 1 HOUR AND 15 MINUTES

Green beans are stewed with vine ripe tomatoes and tarhana, a granular Greek pasta, in a dish that is the essence of summer simplicity.

1. Bring a medium saucepan of water to a boil. Cook the tomatoes in the boiling water for 1 minute, use tongs to transfer them to a cutting board, and let cool. When cool enough to handle, remove the skins and discard. Cut the flesh into quarters, remove the seeds and discard, and mince the flesh.

2. Warm a large, deep skillet over medium-low heat for 2 to 3 minutes. Add the oil and raise heat to medium. When it begins to shimmer, add the onion and a couple pinches of salt and cook, stirring occasionally, until the onion begins to gently sizzle. Reduce heat to low, cover, and cook until the onion is very soft, about 15 minutes. Add the garlic and cook, stirring continuously, for 1 minute, until fragrant. Add the tomatoes and a couple pinches of salt and raise heat to medium-high. Once the sauce begins to sizzle, reduce heat to low, cover, and cook, stirring occasionally, until the tomatoes soften and start breaking down, about 10 minutes.

3. Add the green beans, stock, the ¼ teaspoon of salt, and the tarhana. Raise heat to medium-high and bring to a gentle simmer. Reduce heat to medium-low and cook, stirring occasionally, until both the green beans and tarhana are tender, 15 to 20 minutes. Add more stock, if necessary, to ensure that the mixture is covered halfway.

4. Season to taste, remove from heat, and stir in the basil and black pepper. You can serve this hot or at room temperature. Drizzle a thin film of olive oil into each bowl before serving.

INGREDIENTS:

6   VERY RIPE PLUM TOMATOES

3   TABLESPOONS OLIVE OIL, PLUS MORE AS NEEDED

1   ONION, MINCED

¼   TEASPOON KOSHER SALT, PLUS MORE TO TASTE

1   GARLIC CLOVE, MINCED

1½   LBS. FRESH GREEN BEANS, TRIMMED

1½   CUPS CHICKEN OR VEGETABLE STOCK (SEE PAGES 748 AND 755, RESPECTIVELY, FOR HOMEMADE), PLUS MORE AS NEEDED

⅔   CUP DRIED SOUR TARHANA

¼   CUP FRESH BASIL LEAVES, CUT INTO THIN SLIVERS

BLACK PEPPER, TO TASTE

COCONUT-BRAISED KALE *with* HALIBUT

YIELD: 4 TO 6 SERVINGS / ACTIVE TIME: 30 MINUTES / TOTAL TIME: 1 HOUR

The kale is key, as it provides a nice, soft bed for the halibut and ensures that the fish remains moist and full of flavor.

1. Place the oil in a Dutch oven and warm over medium-high heat. Add the bell peppers, habanero pepper, sweet potato, and cabbage. Season with salt and pepper and cook, stirring frequently, until the sweet potato begins to caramelize, 5 to 7 minutes.

2. Add the eggplant, ginger, and garlic and cook for 10 minutes, stirring often. Add the curry paste and stir to coat all of the vegetables. Cook until the contents of the pot are fragrant, about 2 minutes.

3. Add the bok choy, stock, paprika, cilantro, and coconut milk and cook until the liquid has reduced by one-quarter, about 20 minutes.

4. Add the kale to the Dutch oven. Place the halibut fillets on top of the kale, reduce heat to medium, cover, and cook for about 10 minutes, or until the fish is cooked through.

5. Remove the cover and discard the habanero. Ladle the vegetables and the sauce into bowls and top each one with a halibut fillet. Garnish with the scallions and serve immediately.

INGREDIENTS:

¼ CUP OLIVE OIL

1 YELLOW BELL PEPPER, STEMMED, SEEDED, AND DICED

1 RED BELL PEPPER, STEMMED, SEEDED, AND DICED

1 HABANERO PEPPER, PIERCED

1 LARGE WHITE SWEET POTATO

1 CUP DICED RED CABBAGE

SALT AND PEPPER, TO TASTE

3 GRAFFITI EGGPLANT, CUT INTO 2-INCH PIECES

2 TABLESPOONS PEELED AND MASHED GINGER

3-4 GARLIC CLOVES, MINCED

1-2 TABLESPOONS GREEN CURRY PASTE

2-3 BABY BOK CHOY, CHOPPED

4 CUPS FISH STOCK (SEE PAGE 752 FOR HOMEMADE)

1-2 TABLESPOONS SWEET PAPRIKA

2 TABLESPOONS CHOPPED FRESH CILANTRO

3 (14 OZ.) CANS COCONUT MILK

2 BUNCHES TUSCAN KALE, LEAVES REMOVED AND TORN INTO LARGE PIECES

4-6 (4 OZ.) HALIBUT FILLETS

SCALLIONS, CHOPPED, FOR GARNISH

DRY-FRIED BEANS

YIELD: **4 SERVINGS** / ACTIVE TIME: **30 MINUTES** / TOTAL TIME: **45 MINUTES**

Despite its name, the beans in this recipe are not fried but seared over high heat until almost charred. They are then removed and a sauce is made with pork, Chinese pickled veggies, fermented black beans, garlic, and soy sauce. When testing several recipes, I looked for Chinese pickled vegetables in two different markets and could not find any, so I substituted sauerkraut to very good results. If you can find Chinese pickled vegetables, use them, but know that sauerkraut and kimchi will also work. No need to add extra salt—you will get plenty from the soy and black beans.

1. Place the oil in a large sauté pan, warm over high heat, and add the green beans. Let the beans sear on one side, stir, and sear on the other side. Continue until they are well browned all over. Transfer to a bowl and set aside.

2. Add the pork to the pan and brown over medium-high heat, while breaking it up with a wooden spoon, for about 6 minutes. Add the pickled vegetables, sauerkraut, or kimchi, and the garlic. Cook, stirring continuously, until the contents of the pan are fragrant. Add more oil if the pan starts to look dry.

3. Add the Sherry and cook until it is nearly evaporated. Add the soy sauce, fermented black bean garlic sauce, and sugar and stir to incorporate.

4. Return the green beans to the pan, heat through, and serve with white rice.

INGREDIENTS:

1   TABLESPOON OLIVE OIL, PLUS MORE AS NEEDED

1   LB. GREEN BEANS, TRIMMED

4   OZ. GROUND PORK

2   TABLESPOONS CHINESE PICKLED VEGETABLES, SAUERKRAUT, OR KIMCHI (SEE PAGE 470 FOR HOMEMADE), CHOPPED

1   GARLIC CLOVE, CHOPPED

2   TABLESPOONS SHERRY

2   TABLESPOONS SOY SAUCE

1   TABLESPOON FERMENTED BLACK BEAN GARLIC SAUCE

1   TEASPOON SUGAR

    WHITE RICE, FOR SERVING

POTATOES *with* KALE & CHICKPEAS

YIELD: 4 SERVINGS / ACTIVE TIME: 25 MINUTES / TOTAL TIME: 35 MINUTES

Turmeric, garlic, and ginger bring out the best in kale, and the potatoes and chickpeas are good platforms for all that herbaceous flavor. If you're looking for a more filling meal, serve this with basmati rice and perhaps some naan.

1. Bring a small pot of water to a boil. Add the potatoes and a pinch of salt and boil until just tender, about 8 minutes. Drain and set aside.

2. Put the oil in a skillet and warm over medium-high heat. Add the cumin seeds and onion and sauté until the onion is translucent, about 3 minutes. Add the turmeric, garlic, and ginger and cook until the contents of the pan are fragrant, about 2 minutes.

3. Add the kale, water, and the ½ teaspoon of salt and stir to incorporate. Simmer until the kale is cooked through, about 10 minutes. Add the chickpeas, potatoes, and coriander and simmer until everything is cooked through, about 2 minutes. Serve immediately with lemon wedges.

INGREDIENTS:

- ½   LB. FINGERLING POTATOES, SCRUBBED AND SLICED
- ½   TEASPOON KOSHER SALT, PLUS MORE TO TASTE
- 1   TABLESPOON OLIVE OIL
- 1   TEASPOON CUMIN SEEDS
- 1   ONION, DICED
- ¼   TEASPOON GROUND TURMERIC
- 1   GARLIC CLOVE, MINCED
- 1   TABLESPOON PEELED AND CHOPPED GINGER
- 1   LARGE BUNCH KALE, STEMMED AND CHOPPED
- 1   CUP WATER
- 1   (14 OZ.) CAN CHICKPEAS, DRAINED AND RINSED
- 1   TEASPOON CORIANDER

    LEMON WEDGES, FOR SERVING

BEEF & KOHLRABI STIR-FRY
with TAMARIND SAUCE

YIELD: 4 SERVINGS / ACTIVE TIME: 45 MINUTES / TOTAL TIME: 1 HOUR

Sweet-and-sour tamarind paste is made from the pulp that surrounds tamarind seeds. It is commonly used in Indian cooking, but you might not realize it is also a key component of condiments like Worcestershire sauce. In this dish, it builds a bridge between the kohlrabi and beef, with some help from the usual suspects such as ginger and garlic. You can find it as a finished paste with seeds removed or in more pure form with the seeds still in it. I've given instructions for the type with seeds, but if you have the more refined version, just add water.

1. Place the tamarind pulp in a small bowl and add the hot water. Stir, breaking up the paste until it has thinned, and then push the mixture through a strainer to remove the seeds. Discard the seeds. Add the soy sauce and maple syrup to the strained pulp and set the mixture aside.

2. Place the oil in a wide sauté pan and warm over high heat. When the oil is shimmering, add the onion and sauté until translucent before adding the pepper. Cook until the vegetables start to brown, transfer to a bowl, and set aside.

3. Place the kohlrabi in the pan and add more oil if the pan is dry. Sauté until browned and then add the snap peas. Cook until the peas are bright green, about 3 minutes. Transfer to the bowl with the other veggies.

4. Add the beef to the pan and cook until it starts releasing its juices, about 5 minutes. Add the garlic and ginger and continue to cook until the meat is well browned and the pan is starting to get dry. Add the beef to the bowl of vegetables.

5. Deglaze the pan with the room-temperature water, scraping up the browned bits that have accumulated on the bottom. Add the tamarind mixture and cook until the mixture has reduced to a thick sauce. Return the contents of the bowl to the pan and toss to combine.

6. Add the cilantro, stir to incorporate, and serve with rice or noodles.

INGREDIENTS:

1	TABLESPOON TAMARIND PULP
3	TABLESPOONS HOT WATER (125°F)
1	TEASPOON SOY SAUCE
2	TEASPOONS REAL MAPLE SYRUP
1	TEASPOON OLIVE OIL, PLUS MORE AS NEEDED
1	ONION, DICED
½	YELLOW BELL PEPPER, STEMMED, SEEDED, AND SLICED
2	KOHLRABIES, PEELED AND SLICED
4	OZ. SNAP PEAS, TRIMMED
1	LB. BEEF, SLICED THIN
2	GARLIC CLOVES, MINCED
1	TABLESPOON PEELED AND MINCED GINGER
½	CUP ROOM-TEMPERATURE WATER
½	CUP CHOPPED FRESH CILANTRO
	RICE OR NOODLES, FOR SERVING

RISOTTO *with* SAUSAGE, WINTER SQUASH, KALE & ROSEMARY

YIELD: 4 SERVINGS / ACTIVE TIME: 45 MINUTES / TOTAL TIME: 1 HOUR AND 30 MINUTES

This is one of my favorite cold-weather dishes. It is rich and filling but doesn't feel like lead in your stomach. The salty sausage is the perfect complement to the sweet squash, and the earthy kale rounds it all out.

1. Place the stock in a saucepan, bring to a boil, and then turn off heat. Cover and set aside.

2. Place a wide sauté pan over medium heat and add the oil. When it is shimmering, add the sausage. Cook until it is browned all over, transfer to a bowl, and set aside.

3. Place the squash in the pan and brown on two sides, about 2 minutes a side. Transfer to the bowl containing the sausage.

4. If necessary, add a little more oil to the pan and add the shallot, letting it brown for a few minutes before adding the rice. Toast the rice for a few minutes and then deglaze the pan with the wine, scraping up any browned bits that have accumulated on the bottom of the pan. Add the kale and continue to cook.

5. When the wine has reduced by half, add the warmed stock a little at a time. The tactic with risotto is to add enough liquid to just cover the rice and let it simmer and absorb the liquid slowly. Stir the contents of the pan occasionally so the rice does not stick to the bottom. Cook the rice, adding stock gradually, for another 8 to 10 minutes. Then, add the squash, sausage, and rosemary.

6. Continue adding the stock and stirring until the rice is just barely tender. Let the rice absorb all of the remaining liquid and remove from heat.

7. Add the Parmesan and gently stir. Spoon the risotto into bowls and top with additional Parmesan.

INGREDIENTS:

4 CUPS CHICKEN OR VEGETABLE STOCK (SEE PAGES 748 AND 755, RESPECTIVELY, FOR HOMEMADE)

1 TEASPOON OLIVE OIL, PLUS MORE AS NEEDED

6 OZ. PORK OR TURKEY SAUSAGE, CUBED

1 LB. WINTER SQUASH (BUTTERNUT, BUTTERCUP, OR ACORN), PEELED, SEEDED, AND CUBED

2 TABLESPOONS CHOPPED SHALLOT

1 CUP ARBORIO RICE

½ CUP DRY WHITE WINE

3 LARGE KALE LEAVES, STEMMED AND CHIFFONADE

1 TEASPOON CHOPPED FRESH ROSEMARY LEAVES

⅓ CUP GRATED PARMESAN CHEESE, PLUS MORE FOR GARNISH

MUSHROOM VEGGIE BURGER

YIELD: 6 SERVINGS / ACTIVE TIME: 15 MINUTES / TOTAL TIME: 1 HOUR AND 15 MINUTES

Using mushrooms as a substitute for meat in a burger works really well because the texture is so similar, and the flavor remains superb.

1. Place the water in a saucepan, bring it to a simmer, and add the amaranth. Cook for 25 minutes and then transfer the amaranth to a bowl.

2. Add the mushrooms, spinach, carrot, oat flour, and flaxseed to the bowl, season with salt and pepper, and stir to combine. Let the mixture sit at room temperature for 30 minutes.

3. Preheat the grill to 450°F and brush the grates with the oil. Form the mixture into six patties, place them on the grill, and cook until golden brown on each side, about 4 minutes a side. Serve on hamburger buns along with your favorite condiments.

INGREDIENTS:

1½ CUPS WATER

1½ CUPS AMARANTH

3 OZ. BABY PORTOBELLO MUSHROOMS, MINCED

1 CUP SPINACH, MINCED

1 LARGE CARROT, PEELED AND GRATED

½ CUP OAT FLOUR

¼ CUP GROUND FLAXSEED

SALT AND PEPPER, TO TASTE

¼ CUP OLIVE OIL

HAMBURGER BUNS, FOR SERVING

MUSHROOM FAJITAS

YIELD: 4 SERVINGS / ACTIVE TIME: 15 MINUTES / TOTAL TIME: 30 MINUTES

Portobellos are great for grilling due to their size and heft. But since this recipe uses a vegetable basket, you can use any kind of mushroom you like.

1. To prepare the dressing, place all of the ingredients in a small bowl, stir to combine, and set it aside.

2. To begin preparations for the fajitas, remove the stems from the mushrooms and scoop out the gills. Cut the mushrooms into ½-inch slices and place them in a large bowl. Add the pepper, onion, and dressing and toss to coat. Let the mixture stand for about 10 minutes.

3. Preheat the grill to 450°F and lightly oil a grilling basket. Place the vegetables in the basket, place it on the grill, cover the grill, and cook for 10 to 12 minutes, stirring occasionally.

4. When the vegetables are tender, transfer them to a large bowl. Add the lime juice, stir to coat, and serve with tortillas and cheddar cheese.

INGREDIENTS:

FOR THE DRESSING

- 3 TABLESPOONS OLIVE OIL
- 1 TABLESPOON WHITE WINE VINEGAR
- 1 TABLESPOON CHOPPED FRESH PARSLEY
- 2 TEASPOONS FRESH LEMON JUICE
- 1 GARLIC CLOVE, MINCED
- ½ TEASPOON DRIED BASIL
- ¼ TEASPOON RED PEPPER FLAKES

FOR THE FAJITAS

- 4 LARGE PORTOBELLO MUSHROOMS
- 1 LARGE BELL PEPPER, STEMMED, SEEDED, AND SLICED
- ½ LARGE ONION, SLICED
- OLIVE OIL, AS NEEDED
- 2 TABLESPOONS FRESH LIME JUICE
- 4 FLOUR TORTILLAS (SEE PAGE 797 FOR HOMEMADE), FOR SERVING
- ½ CUP GRATED CHEDDAR CHEESE, FOR SERVING

PORCINI & GOAT CHEESE TORTELLONI

YIELD: 6 SERVINGS / ACTIVE TIME: 2 HOURS / TOTAL TIME: 3 HOURS AND 15 MINUTES

This recipe for homemade tortelloni is an excellent example of how dried mushrooms can add an intense umami flavor to dishes.

1. Place the mushrooms in a small bowl and cover with warm water. Soak until they are softened, about 15 minutes. Lightly run your fingers across all the pieces to dislodge any dirt or debris. Gently squeeze the mushrooms over the bowl to remove excess water, and then chop them. Set the mushrooms aside.

2. Trim away the root end and dark green leaves of the leek, keeping only the white and light green parts. With a sharp knife, cut the leek in half lengthwise and remove the two outer layers. Cut the halves vertically into thin slivers. Place them in a large bowl of water and rinse to remove any dirt. Drain well, transfer to a kitchen towel, and set aside.

3. Warm a large skillet over medium-low heat for 2 to 3 minutes. Add the oil and butter. When the butter has melted and stopped foaming, add the leek and a few pinches of salt and stir. Raise heat to medium. When the leek starts to sizzle, reduce heat to low, cover, and cook, stirring occasionally, until the leek is very soft, about 15 minutes. Add the mushrooms and a pinch of salt and stir to incorporate. Raise heat to medium and cook, stirring occasionally, until the mushrooms have softened, about 5 minutes.

4. Transfer the mixture to a bowl and let it cool completely. Add the goat cheese, season with white pepper, and stir to combine.

5. Prepare the dough as directed on page 761, rolling the dough to the thinnest setting (generally notch 5) for pasta sheets that are about 1/16 inch thick. Lightly dust the sheets with the flour and place on parchment–lined baking sheets. Cover loosely with plastic wrap and work quickly to keep the pasta sheets from drying out.

6. Working with one pasta sheet at a time, place it on a lightly floured work surface and, using a round stamp or pastry cutter, cut as many 3-inch rounds or squares as possible, covering them with plastic wrap. Repeat with all the pasta sheets. Gather the scraps together into a ball, put it through the pasta machine to create additional pasta sheets, and cut those into rounds or squares.

INGREDIENTS:

1   CUP DRIED PORCINI MUSHROOMS

1   LARGE LEEK

1   TABLESPOON OLIVE OIL

1   TABLESPOON UNSALTED BUTTER

    SALT, TO TASTE

10 OZ. GOAT CHEESE, AT ROOM TEMPERATURE

    WHITE PEPPER, TO TASTE

1   BATCH THREE-EGG BASIC PASTA DOUGH (PAGE 761)

    SEMOLINA FLOUR, FOR DUSTING

7. Place a generous teaspoon of filling in the center of each round or square. Should the dough have become a little dry, lightly moisten the pasta border with a wet fingertip (it's helpful to have a small bowl of water nearby for this purpose). Fold the dough over to form a half-moon or a triangle. Draw the two corners together; if using a pasta round, this will form a nurse's cap; for a square, it will have a handkerchief shape. Press down around the joined sides to create a tight seal. As you do this, try to push out any air from around the filling. This prevents the tortelloni from coming apart in the water. Press one more time to ensure that the seal is tight.

8. Lightly dust the filled tortelloni with semolina flour and set on parchment–lined baking sheets so that they are not touching. Repeat with the remaining dough and filling. Allow them to air-dry for 2 hours.

9. To cook the tortelloni, bring a large pot of water to a boil. Once it's boiling, add salt (1 tablespoon for every 4 cups water) and stir. Carefully drop the tortelloni, a few at a time, into the boiling water. Stir for the first minute to prevent any sticking. Cook until they are tender but still chewy, about 3 minutes. Drain and serve with the sauce of your choice.

TIP: The filling can be prepared a day ahead of time; just cover, refrigerate, and bring back to room temperature before filling the rounds or squares. Once air-dried, you can place the tortelloni in a bowl, cover with a kitchen towel, and refrigerate for up to 3 days. Or you can freeze them on the baking sheets, transfer to freezer bags, and store in the freezer for up to 2 months. Do not thaw them prior to cooking (they will become mushy), and add an extra minute or two to their cooking time.

TRUFFLED MUSHROOM & PINE NUT SAUCE
with PASTA

YIELD: 6 SERVINGS / ACTIVE TIME: 1 HOUR / TOTAL TIME: 1 HOUR

Truffles are the food of the gods. If you are lucky enough to have access to fresh ones, go ahead and use a few slices in this sauce. If not, truffle oil is very effective for capturing the essence of these exquisite fungi.

1. Trim the bottom of each mushroom stem. Fill a large bowl with cold water and add the vinegar. Add the mushrooms and swirl them around in the water for 30 seconds or so. Drain and rinse them under cold water. Drain again and place on a kitchen towel, stem-side down, so that any remaining water drains. Let them air-dry for 10 minutes and then cut into ⅓-inch slices.

2. Warm a small skillet over medium-low heat for 2 minutes. Add the pine nuts and cook, stirring frequently, until they are golden in spots, 3 to 4 minutes. Remove from heat and add a pinch of salt. Stir to incorporate and set aside.

3. Bring a large pot of water to a boil. Warm a skillet large enough to hold the finished pasta over medium heat for 2 to 3 minutes. Add the butter and 2 tablespoons of the truffle oil to the skillet. When the butter melts and stops foaming, add the garlic and cook, stirring occasionally, until it begins to turn golden, about 2 minutes. Remove the garlic with a slotted spoon and discard it.

4. Add the mushrooms, a couple pinches of salt, and pepper to the pan and stir to combine. Raise heat to medium and cook, stirring occasionally, until the mushrooms release their liquid, about 6 minutes. Continue to cook until the liquid has evaporated and the mushrooms are nice and soft but haven't browned yet, about 8 minutes. Add the nutmeg, stir, and season to taste. Add the cream, stir to incorporate, and heat through. Remove from heat, cover, and keep warm until the pasta is ready.

5. When the pasta water is boiling, add salt (1 tablespoon for every 4 cups water) and stir. Add the pasta, stirring for the first minute to prevent any sticking. Cook 2 minutes short of the directed cooking time, drain, and transfer directly to the skillet with the mushroom sauce. Turn heat to high and cook, stirring continuously, for 2 minutes.

6. Divide the pasta and sauce between four warmed bowls and top with the toasted pine nuts and additional truffle oil.

INGREDIENTS:

- 1   LB. CREMINI MUSHROOMS
- 1   TABLESPOON DISTILLED WHITE VINEGAR
- ¼   CUP PINE NUTS
-     SALT, TO TASTE
- 2   TABLESPOONS UNSALTED BUTTER
- ¼   CUP WHITE TRUFFLE OIL, PLUS MORE FOR DRIZZLING
- 2   GARLIC CLOVES, LIGHTLY CRUSHED
-     WHITE PEPPER, TO TASTE
- 1   TEASPOON GRATED NUTMEG
- ½   CUP HEAVY CREAM
- ¾   LB. PREFERRED PASTA

PORCINI MUSHROOM & BÉCHAMEL LASAGNA

YIELD: 6 SERVINGS / **ACTIVE TIME:** 1 HOUR / **TOTAL TIME:** 3 HOURS AND 15 MINUTES

Mushrooms, cream, and cheese were meant for each other. This recipe combines both dried and fresh mushrooms to create a decadent lasagna.

1. If making with fresh pasta, prepare the dough as directed on page 760, rolling the dough to the thinnest setting (generally notch 5) for pasta sheets that are about ⅟₁₆-inch thick. Cut the pasta sheets into approximately 12-inch pieces. Lay the cut pasta sheets on lightly floured parchment–lined baking sheets and allow them to dry for at least 15 minutes before boiling, as it will prevent the pasta from sticking together in the water.

2. Place the mushrooms in a small bowl with the water and soak until softened, about 15 minutes. Lightly run your fingers over them to dislodge any dirt or debris. Gently squeeze the mushrooms over the bowl to remove excess water and chop them. Strain the soaking liquid through a paper towel–lined strainer, measure out 1½ cups of the soaking liquid, and set aside with the mushrooms.

3. Place the wine in a small saucepan and bring to a boil. Continue to boil until reduced almost by half, about 5 minutes. Remove from heat and set aside.

4. Warm a large, deep skillet over medium heat for 2 to 3 minutes and then add the butter. When the butter melts and stops foaming, add the shallots and a pinch of salt and stir. Once the shallots begin to sizzle, reduce the temperature to low, cover the skillet, and cook, stirring occasionally, until the shallots have softened, about 10 minutes. Stir in the garlic and cook until it becomes fragrant, about 2 minutes.

5. Raise heat to medium-high and add the porcini and cremini mushrooms, the thyme, and a couple pinches of salt. Cook, stirring frequently, until the mushrooms begin to soften and release their liquid, about 6 minutes. Add the reduced wine, the reserved porcini soaking liquid, and a pinch of salt and bring to a gentle boil. Cook, stirring occasionally, until the mushrooms are tender and the liquid has reduced by half, about 12 to 15 minutes. Remove from heat, season to taste, add the Aromatic Béchamel Sauce, and stir until well combined.

INGREDIENTS:

½ BATCH ALL-YOLK PASTA DOUGH (SEE PAGE 760) OR ½ LB. LASAGNA NOODLES

1 CUP DRIED PORCINI MUSHROOMS

2 CUPS WARM WATER (110°F)

1 CUP DRY RED WINE SUCH AS CABERNET SAUVIGNON, PINOT NOIR, OR SANGIOVESE

2 TABLESPOONS UNSALTED BUTTER

3 SHALLOTS, MINCED

SALT, TO TASTE

2 GARLIC CLOVES, MINCED

1 LB. CREMINI MUSHROOMS, TRIMMED AND CUT INTO ⅙-INCH SLICES

LEAVES FROM 2 SPRIGS FRESH THYME, CHOPPED, PLUS MORE FOR GARNISH

BLACK PEPPER, TO TASTE

½ BATCH AROMATIC BÉCHAMEL SAUCE (SEE PAGE 690)

1½ CUPS GRATED PARMESAN CHEESE

6. Preheat the oven to 350°F.

7. Bring a large pot of water to a boil. Once it's boiling, add salt (1 tablespoon for every 4 cups water) and stir. Add the pasta sheets, only one or two at a time, and boil them until slightly softened but still very firm, 1 to 2 minutes for fresh pasta and about three-quarters of the time directed on the package for dried pasta. Once ready, use a slotted spoon (the larger the better) to transfer them to a large bowl of cold water. Allow them to completely cool, then arrange them in a single layer on clean, damp kitchen towels. Continue this process with the remaining lasagna sheets.

8. Assemble the lasagna. Spoon in enough of the mushroom sauce to cover the bottom of a deep (about 3 inches) 9 × 13-inch baking dish. Arrange a single layer of noodles lengthwise, making sure they are slightly overlapping one another. Then spoon enough sauce to cover the first layer of noodles evenly and sprinkle with ½ cup of the Parmesan. Repeat this layering two more times, ending with a layer of the mushroom mixture topped with the remaining cheese. Cover loosely with aluminum foil, place in the oven, and bake for 35 minutes. Remove the foil and continue to bake until the edges of the lasagna sheets are lightly browned, about 12 minutes. For nice, clean slices, allow the lasagna to rest at room temperature for at least 20 minutes before slicing.

SOBA NOODLES *&* MUSHROOMS
with GINGERY LEMON DRESSING

YIELD: 4 SERVINGS / ACTIVE TIME: 40 MINUTES / TOTAL TIME: 1 HOUR

A hearty pasta salad that utilizes three kinds of mushrooms to provide an array of textures and flavors. If you can't find the first two varieties listed, use an equivalent amount of oyster mushrooms.

1. To prepare the dressing, zest the lemon onto a piece of wax paper. Cut the lemon in half and squeeze 2 teaspoons of juice into a small bowl. Put the lemon zest and juice, ginger, soy sauce, vinegar, honey, and Thai seasoning blend in a food processor or blender and puree for 10 seconds. Transfer to a small bowl, add the oils, and whisk to combine. The dressing will keep in the refrigerator for up to 3 days.

2. To begin preparations for the noodles and mushrooms, cut off the bases of the clusters of shimeji and enoki to separate the mushrooms from each other. Remove the stems from the shiitakes and discard. Fill a large bowl with cold water and add the vinegar. Add the mushrooms and swirl them around in the water for 30 seconds or so. Drain and rinse under cold water. Drain again and place on a kitchen towel, stem side down, so that any remaining water drains. Let air-dry for 30 minutes and then mince the shiitakes.

3. Place the sesame seeds in a small skillet over medium heat and toast until golden brown, about 2 minutes, occasionally shaking the pan. Transfer to a plate and set aside.

4. Bring a large pot of water to a boil and add the noodles, stirring for the first minute to prevent any sticking. Cook according to the package instructions until they are tender and chewy. Drain and rinse under cold water to remove excess starch. Drain again, transfer to a medium bowl, and toss with the ½ tablespoon of sesame oil to prevent any sticking. Set the noodles aside.

5. Warm a skillet large enough to hold the finished dish over medium heat for 2 to 3 minutes. Add the remaining sesame oil and the butter and warm for a minute or so, then raise heat to high. Once the butter has melted and starts sizzling, add the mushrooms and of salt and stir. Cook, stirring continuously, for 2 to 3 minutes. Add the noodles, scallions, and ½ cup of the dressing, and toss to combine. Taste and add more salt or dressing as needed. Transfer to a serving bowl, top with the basil leaves and sesame seeds, and serve warm or at room temperature.

INGREDIENTS:

FOR THE DRESSING

1	LEMON
	2-INCH PIECE GINGER, PEELED AND MINCED
¼	CUP SOY SAUCE
¼	CUP RICE VINEGAR
1½	TABLESPOONS HONEY
½	TEASPOON THAI SEASONING BLEND
3	TABLESPOONS OLIVE OIL
2	TEASPOONS TOASTED SESAME OIL

FOR THE NOODLES & MUSHROOMS

4	OZ. SHIMEJI MUSHROOMS
4	OZ. ENOKI MUSHROOMS
2	SHIITAKE MUSHROOMS
1	TABLESPOON DISTILLED WHITE VINEGAR
2	TABLESPOONS SESAME SEEDS, PLUS MORE FOR GARNISH
½	LB. SOBA NOODLES
½	TABLESPOON TOASTED SESAME OIL, PLUS 2 TEASPOONS
1½	TABLESPOONS UNSALTED BUTTER
	SALT, TO TASTE
3	SCALLIONS, TRIMMED AND SLICED THIN
	HANDFUL FRESH BASIL LEAVES, SLICED THIN, FOR SERVING

EGG NOODLES
with BROWNED ONIONS & CABBAGE

YIELD: 4 SERVINGS / ACTIVE TIME: 20 MINUTES / TOTAL TIME: 45 MINUTES

It doesn't get much simpler than this cabbage, onion, and noodle dish, which is called haluski, is found throughout central and eastern Europe. The combination may sound plain, but the deeply browned vegetables have a subtle, smoky sweetness while the sturdy egg noodles provide a satisfying chewiness. It is pure comfort food. Some versions also include caraway seeds or salt pork.

1. Warm a large skillet over medium heat for 1 minute. Add the oil and raise heat to medium-high. When the oil starts shimmering, add the kielbasa and cook, stirring occasionally, until the cubes start to brown and crisp, 3 to 5 minutes. Use a slotted spoon to transfer them to a small bowl.

2. Add 3 tablespoons of the butter to the skillet. When it has melted and stopped foaming, add the onions and a couple pinches of salt and cook, stirring frequently, until softened, 8 to 10 minutes. Add another 3 tablespoons of the butter, the cabbage, a few more pinches of salt, and a few pinches of pepper and stir to combine. When the mixture starts sizzling, cover and reduce heat to medium-low. Cook, stirring occasionally, until very soft and browned, 12 to 15 minutes.

3. As the onions and cabbage cook, bring a large pot of water to a boil. When it's boiling, add salt (1 tablespoon for every 4 cups water) and stir. Add the egg noodles and stir for the first minute to prevent any sticking. Cook them according to the package instructions. Reserve ¼ cup of the pasta water and drain the noodles.

4. Return the pot to the stove. Immediately turn heat to high and add the remaining butter and the reserved pasta water. Add the drained noodles and toss to combine. Once the added water has been absorbed by the noodles, add the kielbasa and onion-and-cabbage mixture and toss to evenly distribute. Cook for 1 to 2 minutes, stirring continuously but gently, so as to not tear the noodles. Season to taste and serve immediately.

INGREDIENTS:

- 2 TABLESPOONS OLIVE OIL
- ½ LB. KIELBASA, CUT INTO SMALL CUBES
- 6½ TABLESPOONS UNSALTED BUTTER
- 2 LARGE ONIONS, DICED
  SALT AND PEPPER, TO TASTE
- 1½ LBS. GREEN CABBAGE, CORED AND CUT INTO BITE-SIZED PIECES
- ¾ LB. WIDE EGG NOODLES

POTATO GNOCCHI
with RADICCHIO CREAM SAUCE

YIELD: 8 SERVINGS / ACTIVE TIME: 1 HOUR AND 30 MINUTES / TOTAL TIME: 2 HOURS AND 15 MINUTES

Nubby, ridged, and slightly creviced, potato gnocchi (*gnocchi di patate*) are arguably the most well known of all Italian dumplings. Extremely versatile because of their neutral flavor, these tender, pillowy mounds can be combined with a variety of sauces for maximum enjoyment.

1. Bring a large pot of water to a boil and add the potatoes. Cook until you can easily insert a knife through the thickest part of a potato, 35 to 40 minutes. Alternatively, you can also bake the potatoes. Prick them several times with a fork and bake them at 425°F for 45 minutes or so. Drain (or remove from the oven) and let cool.

2. When the potatoes are cool enough to handle, peel off their skins if boiled or scoop the flesh out of their skins if baked. Pass them through a potato ricer while still warm. Alternatively, you can place them in a wide, shallow bowl and press them with a potato masher until smooth. Do not use a food processor or blender, as it works the potatoes too thoroughly, which will then affect the texture of the gnocchi. Create a mound of potatoes on your work surface.

3. Make a small well in the center of the mound. Add the eggs, 1½ cups of the flour, and the salt, then start working the mixture with your hands until it is a dough. Knead the dough as you incorporate the remaining 1 cup of flour, pressing down and away from you with the heel of your hand. Fold the dough, turn it 45 degrees, and repeat the process. As soon as it forms into a non-sticky ball of dough, stop adding flour.

4. Lightly flour the work surface and rip off a handful of dough. Use the palms of your hands to roll it into a long, ¾-inch-thick rope. Cut it into ½-inch pieces. Repeat with the remaining dough.

5. After you finish cutting each rope, give the gnocchi ridges. To create the ridges, gently roll each piece over a gnocchi board or on the back of the tines of a fork. This may take a little practice. At times you may find the dough sticking to the board or fork. When this happens, sprinkle the board with (or dip the fork into) flour before you press the gnocchi against it.

INGREDIENTS:

- 3   **LBS. POTATOES (YUKON GOLD ARE BEST, BUT RUSSETS WILL DO)**
- 2   **LARGE EGGS**
- 2½   **CUPS ALL-PURPOSE FLOUR, PLUS MORE FOR DUSTING**
- 1   **TABLESPOON KOSHER SALT, PLUS MORE AS NEEDED**
- ¼   **CUP GRATED PARMESAN CHEESE, PLUS MORE FOR GARNISH**
-   **RADICCHIO CREAM SAUCE (SEE RECIPE)**

RADICCHIO CREAM SAUCE

- 3   **TABLESPOONS UNSALTED BUTTER**
- 1   **LARGE HEAD RADICCHIO, CORED AND GRATED**
-   **SALT AND WHITE PEPPER, TO TASTE**
- 3   **TABLESPOONS WARM WATER (110°F)**
- 1½   **CUPS HEAVY CREAM**

Continued . . .

6. When finished, put the gnocchi on a parchment–lined baking sheet so they don't touch each other and lightly dust with flour. Once you run out of room, cover them with another sheet of parchment and begin stacking them vertically. Repeat with the remaining dough.

7. Place the Parmesan in a large heatproof bowl.

8. Bring a large pot of water to a boil. Once it's boiling, add salt (1 tablespoon for every 4 cups water) and stir. Cook the gnocchi in batches of 20 to 25. They will immediately plummet to the bottom of the pot. Do not touch them. Within a minute or two, they will start to float up to the top. Cook them for another minute or so. Remove them with a strainer, gently shaking them over the pot to remove any excess water, then transfer them to the bowl with the Parmesan. Add a ladleful of Radicchio Cream Sauce and toss gently to coat. Continue in this manner until all the gnocchi are cooked.

9. Divide the gnocchi among warmed bowls, top with more sauce, and garnish with additional Parmesan.

TIP: The gnocchi can be cooked or covered and refrigerated for up to a day. You can also freeze the gnocchi on a baking sheet, transfer to freezer bags, and store in the freezer for up to 3 months.

RADICCHIO CREAM SAUCE

1. Warm a large skillet over medium heat for 2 to 3 minutes and then add the butter. When it melts and stops foaming, add the radicchio, a couple pinches of salt, and white pepper and stir. Cook, stirring occasionally, until the radicchio wilts, about 5 minutes.

2. Add the warm water and cook until the radicchio softens, another 4 to 5 minutes. Using a slotted spoon, transfer the radicchio to a bowl and cover to keep warm. Add the cream to the skillet and bring to a gentle boil. Reduce heat to low and cook until the sauce is thick and reduced, about 15 minutes. Add to the bowl containing the radicchio and stir to combine.

RED BELL PEPPER & SHALLOT PESTO *with* PASTA

YIELD: 4 SERVINGS / ACTIVE TIME: 25 MINUTES / TOTAL TIME: 50 MINUTES

Love bell peppers? If so, this sauce, in all of its delightful summer sweetness, is for you. Feel free to substitute yellow or orange bell peppers for the red if you are so inclined, though the sauce won't be quite as sweet. The secret flavor weapon in this dish is the umami-packed Worcestershire sauce. Made from anchovies, vinegar, onions, molasses, sugar, salt, garlic, tamarind, cloves, chili powder, and water, it brightens the flavor of the cooked peppers and shallots and contrasts nicely with the tanginess of the feta.

1. Preheat the oven to 500°F and then turn on the broiler. Place a wire rack on top of a parchment–lined baking sheet and set the peppers on top. Broil the peppers, turning them occasionally, until their skins are black and charred all over. Be sure to keep a close eye on them while cooking. Once charred on all sides, place the peppers in a mixing bowl and let cool. When cool enough to handle, remove the skins, stems, and seeds and discard.

2. Warm a small skillet over medium-low heat for 2 to 3 minutes. Add the 3 tablespoons of oil and raise heat to medium. Once the oil begins to shimmer, add the shallots and a couple pinches of salt and stir. When they begin to sizzle, reduce heat to medium-low and cook, stirring every few minutes, until the shallots are soft and beginning to turn golden, about 10 minutes.

3. Place the peppers and shallots in a food processor or blender and puree until very smooth. Transfer the puree to the skillet and cover to keep warm. If desired, the sauce can be cooled, covered, and refrigerated for up to 2 days.

4. Bring a large pot of water to a boil. Once it's boiling, add salt (1 tablespoon for every 4 cups water) and stir. Add the pasta and stir for the first minute to prevent any sticking. Cook 2 minutes short of the directed cooking time and drain, reserving ¼ cup of the pasta water. Return the pot to the stove. Immediately turn heat to high and add the remaining oil and the reserved pasta water. Add the drained pasta and toss until the pasta water has been absorbed. Add the sauce and Worcestershire and cook, tossing continuously, for 1 to 2 minutes.

5. Divide the pasta between four warmed bowls and garnish with the feta, parsley, and basil.

INGREDIENTS:

3   VERY FIRM RED BELL PEPPERS

3   TABLESPOONS OLIVE OIL, PLUS 1 TEASPOON

3   SHALLOTS, DICED

    SALT, TO TASTE

¾   LB. PREFERRED PASTA

1   TABLESPOON WORCESTERSHIRE SAUCE

¾   CUP CRUMBLED FETA CHEESE, FOR GARNISH

    HANDFUL FRESH PARSLEY, CHOPPED, FOR GARNISH

    HANDFUL FRESH BASIL, CHOPPED, FOR GARNISH

GRILLED TUNA
with CHARRED RED PEPPERS, CAPERS, PARSLEY *&* LEMON

YIELD: 2 SERVINGS / **ACTIVE TIME:** 30 MINUTES / **TOTAL TIME:** 45 MINUTES

Tuna and peppers are a beautiful match, especially when you add capers, olives, and lemon to keep things zesty. Roasting the peppers and removing the charred skins will result in a more refined preparation. Do not use canned olives; instead, seek out the good-quality ones that are often near the deli section of the supermarket.

---

1. Preheat your grill to 500°F. Place the peppers on the grill and cook, turning occasionally, until the skin is charred. Remove, transfer them to a bowl, and cover with foil. Leave the grill on.

2. When the peppers have had some time to cool, remove the skins, seeds, and stems and discard. Slice the peppers into strips and set aside.

3. Place 1 tablespoon of the oil in a saucepan and warm over medium heat. Add the shallot and sauté until it has softened, about 5 minutes. Add the peppers, capers, and olives and cook, stirring occasionally, until warmed through.

4. Remove from heat and add the remaining oil, the lemon juice, salt, pepper, and parsley. Stir to incorporate and set the mixture aside.

5. Season the tuna steaks with salt and pepper, rub with oil, and place them on the grill. Tuna cooks quickly, so give them roughly 3 minutes a side, less if they are not very thick. Plate and top with the pepper mixture.

INGREDIENTS:

1½ LBS. RED BELL PEPPERS

3 TABLESPOONS OLIVE OIL, PLUS MORE AS NEEDED

1 SHALLOT, DICED

1 TABLESPOON CAPERS

¼ CUP KALAMATA OLIVES, PITTED AND SLICED

FRESH LEMON JUICE, TO TASTE

SALT AND PEPPER, TO TASTE

½ CUP CHOPPED FRESH PARSLEY

2 TUNA STEAKS (ABOUT ½ LB. EACH)

PEPPERS & CHEESE SANDWICH
with TEMPEH BACON

YIELD: 2 SERVINGS / ACTIVE TIME: 20 MINUTES / TOTAL TIME: 30 MINUTES

I am new to the world of tempeh and seitan but have discovered that both are quite good. Tempeh is made from fermented whole soybeans that are pressed into a type of cake. Just like tofu, you can make it into many different shapes to suit your dish. For this one, I used a type of tempeh from the Tofurky brand that is sliced like bacon. This recipe is heavy on the peppers, which is intentional. You can use the red and green recommended or add any pepper that piques your interest at the market: Italian, Mexican, sweet, or hot. I've kept the traditional slice of provolone cheese, but if you want to make it vegan, you can always use a dairy-free cheese.

1. In a wide sauté pan, add the oil and warm over medium heat. Add the onion and peppers, reduce heat to medium-low, and cook until they start to brown, about 10 minutes. Add more oil to the pan if it starts to look dry.

2. Add the garlic and thyme and cook for another 5 minutes. Turn off heat, add the cheese, if using, and season with salt and pepper.

3. Coat the bottom of a small sauté pan with a thin film of oil and warm over medium heat. Add the tempeh and brown each side for a few minutes.

4. Split open the rolls and brush on a little oil. Put the rolls under a broiler or in a toaster oven for a few minutes until toasted and warm. Divide the pepper mixture between the two and add the tempeh.

INGREDIENTS:

1 TABLESPOON OLIVE OIL, PLUS MORE AS NEEDED

1 LARGE ONION, SLICED

1 RED BELL PEPPER, SEEDED AND SLICED

1 GREEN BELL PEPPER, SEEDED AND SLICED

2 GARLIC CLOVES, MINCED

1 TEASPOON CHOPPED FRESH THYME LEAVES

2-4 SLICES PROVOLONE CHEESE (OPTIONAL)

SALT AND PEPPER, TO TASTE

6 SLICES TEMPEH BACON

2 SUB ROLLS

LOVE 'N' HASH

When Eric and I got engaged, we decided to have the wedding on our new farm with about 100 of our friends and family. We had only lived there for two years and were still putting up buildings and reclaiming fields, so we decided to raise a barn on the morning of the event. It was an amusing mix of cultures, with some local friends who knew what they were doing and a lot of city dwellers who were enthusiastic to partake in this rural pastime. Off to the side were Eric's family and old friends from New Jersey, who thought we were nuts, and my family and old friends from Connecticut, who were discussing how they might do it better. We raised the frame with a lot of straps and goodwill, and it has henceforth been called the Wedding Barn.

Another highlight of that weekend was the brisket smoked by two of our friends (one from Tennessee and one from Kansas) who had not met each other previously but bonded over hours tending the smoker and the libations that kept them going. We served it up, along with some ribs, for the rehearsal dinner, and it was so damned good that we still speak of it with reverence. We feasted on it heartily, but there were leftovers, and when the guests left after the wedding, we still had several pounds of brisket in the fridge. Since we were married in September, I had the most beautiful sweet peppers ready for harvest and a storage bin full of onions and potatoes. Thus, the Love 'N' Hash was born.

LOVE 'N' HASH

YIELD: 4 SERVINGS / ACTIVE TIME: 45 MINUTES / TOTAL TIME: 1 HOUR AND 30 MINUTES

Hash may be considered a blue-plate special, but to prepare it well requires skill. The most important part is to cook everything separately and leave plenty of space in the pan so the ingredients brown rather than steam. You can use any cut of meat, whether it be leftover roast or something specially purchased for the dish. A bit of advice: a fatty cut keeps the meat from drying out. If you'd like to make it vegetarian, mushrooms make an excellent substitute.

1. Add the oil to a wide sauté pan and warm over medium-high heat. Add the potatoes and distribute them so they are as close to one layer as possible. Reduce heat to medium and let them brown slowly, turning occasionally and checking to make sure there is enough oil in the pan so they do not burn, about 25 minutes. When they are sufficiently browned all over and tender all the way through, transfer them to a bowl and set side.

2. Add more oil if necessary and add the pepper and onion to the pan. Reduce heat to medium-low and cook, stirring occasionally, until well browned, about 20 minutes. When they have 5 minutes left to cook, add the garlic. Transfer the vegetables to the bowl containing the potatoes.

3. Add the meat and season with salt. Let the meat brown to the point where it is nearly burnt. Stir and brown on the other side, then add the thyme.

4. When the meat is extremely well browned on both sides, add a few splashes of Worcestershire sauce and cook until the meat is glazed and all of the liquid has reduced. Add the potatoes-and-vegetables mixture to the pan with the meat and season generously with salt and pepper. Taste and add more Worcestershire if necessary. Heat everything through and, if desired, serve with horseradish on the side and a fried egg on top of each serving.

INGREDIENTS:

- 1 TABLESPOON OLIVE OIL, PLUS MORE AS NEEDED
- 3 LARGE RUSSET POTATOES, PEELED AND DICED
- 1 LARGE BELL PEPPER, STEMMED, SEEDED, AND DICED
- 1 LARGE ONION, DICED
- 2 GARLIC CLOVES, MINCED
- 1 LB. COOKED OR RAW MEAT, CUT INTO SMALL PIECES
- SALT, TO TASTE
- 1 TEASPOON DRIED THYME
- WORCESTERSHIRE SAUCE, TO TASTE
- HORSERADISH, TO TASTE (OPTIONAL), FOR SERVING
- FRIED EGGS, FOR SERVING (OPTIONAL)

SPINACH FRITTATA

YIELD: 4 SERVINGS / ACTIVE TIME: 20 MINUTES / TOTAL TIME: 30 MINUTES

This delicious combination gives a nod to Greek cuisine with the addition of feta cheese. Serve this for brunch with other classic Greek foods, like olives, pita wedges, and tzatziki sauce.

1. Preheat the broiler to low. In a small bowl, beat the eggs until scrambled.

2. Warm a cast-iron skillet over medium-high heat. Melt the butter in the skillet and add the onion and garlic. Cook, stirring frequently, until the onion is translucent, about 3 minutes.

3. Add the spinach and cook, stirring continuously, until the leaves wilt. Sprinkle the feta over the mixture.

4. Pour the eggs into the skillet over everything and shake the pan to evenly distribute them. Season with salt and pepper, cover the skillet, and cook until set, about 10 minutes. Place the skillet under the broiler and toast the top for about 2 minutes.

5. Remove and let stand for a couple of minutes, season with salt and pepper, and serve.

INGREDIENTS:

6   EGGS

2   TABLESPOONS UNSALTED BUTTER

¼   CUP CHOPPED RED ONION

1   GARLIC CLOVE, MINCED

2   CUPS PACKED SPINACH, COARSE STEMS REMOVED, ROUGHLY CHOPPED

½   CUP CRUMBLED FETA CHEESE

SALT AND PEPPER, TO TASTE

ITALIAN CRÊPES

YIELD: 8 TO 10 SERVINGS (ABOUT 16 CRÊPES) / ACTIVE TIME: 1 HOUR / TOTAL TIME: 6 HOURS AND 20 MINUTES

I'm not sure that the French would think this is a good idea, but as far as flavor combinations go, it works. Using crêpes instead of pizza dough essentially produces a less bready calzone. *Mangia!*

1. To begin preparations for the crêpes, place the eggs in a large mixing bowl and whisk until scrambled. Add the salt and milk and whisk until thoroughly incorporated. Whisk in the flour and, while whisking, add 2 tablespoons of the melted butter. Keep whisking until the batter is smooth and there are no lumps. Cover the bowl with plastic wrap or a clean kitchen towel, put it in a cool, dark place, and let rest for 3 to 4 hours before making the crêpes.

2. While the crêpe batter is settling, begin preparations for the filling. Warm a cast-iron skillet over medium-high heat, add the sausage, and cook until it's only slightly pink inside. Drain the excess fat and add the garlic. Lower heat to medium and cook, stirring frequently, until the sausage is cooked through, about 5 minutes. Add the spinach and tomatoes and stir to combine. Season with salt and pepper, transfer to a bowl, cover, and refrigerate until you are ready to make the crêpes.

3. When the crêpe batter is ready, place a spatula that won't scratch the skillet and a ladle by the stove.

4. Warm the skillet over medium-high heat and coat the bottom with some of the remaining butter. When the skillet is hot but not smoking, stir the crêpe batter and ladle about ¼ cup of the batter into the skillet. When the batter hits the pan, tilt the skillet gently to spread the batter evenly over the bottom. When the bottom is covered, cook for just over 1 minute. The cêepe is ready to be flipped when the edges are set and start to come away from the pan. Flip the crêpe over and cook for about 30 seconds. Tilt the skillet to slide the crêpe out and onto a plate.

5. Repeat with the remaining batter. You should be able to make several crêpes before adding more butter to the pan, but if you think it needs butter, add some. If the pan gets too hot and the butter browns, wipe it out with a paper towel and start over. As the crêpes cool on the plate, put pieces of waxed paper between them to keep them from sticking together.

INGREDIENTS:

FOR THE CRÊPES

3	EGGS
⅛	TEASPOON KOSHER SALT
1	CUP WHOLE MILK, PLUS MORE AS NEEDED
14	TABLESPOONS ALL-PURPOSE FLOUR
4	TABLESPOONS UNSALTED BUTTER, MELTED, PLUS MORE AS NEEDED
2	CUPS GRATED MOZZARELLA CHEESE

FOR THE FILLING

1	LB. ITALIAN SAUSAGE
4	GARLIC CLOVES, MINCED
1	PACKAGE FROZEN SPINACH, THAWED AND SQUEEZED DRY
1	(14 OZ.) CAN DICED TOMATOES, DRAINED
	SALT AND PEPPER, TO TASTE
1	CUP RICOTTA CHEESE

Continued . . .

6. Preheat the oven to 350°F. Remove the filling from the refrigerator and stir in the ricotta cheese. Taste and adjust the seasoning if necessary.

7. Lightly grease a 9 × 13-inch baking dish. Working with one crêpe at a time, put a generous scoop of the filling in the center and fold the crêpe up around the filling. Place the crêpe in the baking dish so that the seam is facing down. When the baking dish is filled with the stuffed crêpes, sprinkle the mozzarella over the top. Cover the dish with foil, place in the oven, and bake for about 20 minutes. Remove the foil and bake for another 5 to 10 minutes, until the cheese is bubbly and starting to brown. Serve immediately.

SPINACH MALFATTI *with* SAGE BROWN BUTTER

YIELD: 4 SERVINGS / ACTIVE TIME: 40 MINUTES / TOTAL TIME: 1 HOUR

*M*alfatti means "badly formed" in Italian. But once matched with a bright tomato sauce or a rich browned-butter sauce, these dumplings prove that looks can be deceiving.

1. Trim the heavy stems from the spinach and swish it around in a large bowl of cold water. Drain, shake the leaves, and set aside. Place a large skillet on the stove and turn heat to medium-high. Add the spinach and cook until the leaves have wilted but are still bright green. Transfer to a colander. When cool enough to handle, squeeze to remove as much water from the spinach as you can, then mince. Transfer to a medium bowl, add the eggs, and mix well. Add the flour, nutmeg, and a few pinches of salt and white pepper. Use a wooden spoon to stir the mixture until it looks like thick muffin batter.

2. Bring a large pot of water to a boil. Once it's boiling, add salt (1 tablespoon for every 4 cups water) and stir. Move the bowl of batter next to the stove and grab two teaspoons. Dip one teaspoon into the dough to draw out a round dollop. Using the second teaspoon, scrape the dough off the first teaspoon into the boiling water. Work quickly to cook about 15 malfatti (no more) at a time. Cook until they float to the surface, 2 to 3 minutes. Using a strainer, remove them from the water, gently shake over the pot to remove excess water, and transfer to a large, warmed bowl. Tent loosely with aluminum foil to keep warm while you cook the remainder. When all of the malfatti have been cooked, toss with the Sage Brown Butter and serve.

INGREDIENTS:

- 2   LBS. FRESH SPINACH
- 4   LARGE EGGS, LIGHTLY BEATEN
- 1¼ CUPS ALL-PURPOSE FLOUR
- 1   TEASPOON GRATED NUTMEG, TO TASTE

  SALT AND WHITE PEPPER, TO TASTE

  SAGE BROWN BUTTER (SEE RECIPE)

SAGE BROWN BUTTER

- 7   TABLESPOONS UNSALTED BUTTER, CUT INTO SMALL PIECES
- 8   FRESH SAGE LEAVES

  SALT AND PEPPER, TO TASTE

SAGE BROWN BUTTER

1. Warm a large skillet over medium-low heat for 2 to 3 minutes. Add the butter to the pan, raise heat to medium, and, once the butter melts and stops foaming, add the sage leaves. Cook, stirring occasionally, until the butter begins to brown on the bottom and the sage leaves become crispy. Be very attentive during this step, as butter can burn quickly. Make sure the sage is sizzling very gently so that it gets nice and crisp when finished, monitoring it carefully to ensure it does not burn in the process. If sizzling too much, lower heat and take the skillet off the stove for 30 seconds or so before returning it to the burner. Take the pan off the heat once the sage leaves are done. Remove the sage leaves from the butter, season with salt and pepper, and serve.

SORCETTI
with MASCARPONE SAUCE

YIELD: 6 SERVINGS / ACTIVE TIME: 1 HOUR / TOTAL TIME: 1 HOUR AND 30 MINUTES

These rustic potato dumplings from the eastern Italian region of the Marches differ from traditional gnocchi in that the potatoes aren't riced, which yields a pleasantly grainy texture. Sorcetti pair well with hearty sauces. Instead of spinach, feel free to substitute Swiss chard, dandelion greens, or mustard greens.

1. Rinse the spinach and drain, leaving some of the water on the leaves. Place a large skillet on the stove and turn heat to medium. Add the spinach by the handful and cook, stirring frequently, until the leaves wilt slightly but are still bright green. Drain in a colander. When cool enough to handle, squeeze to remove as much liquid as possible from the spinach and then mince. Transfer to a paper towel–lined bowl to absorb any remaining moisture.

2. Place the potatoes in a medium saucepan. Cover them with cold water, bring to a gentle boil over medium-high heat, and cook until fork-tender, about 25 minutes. Drain and let cool. When cool enough to handle, remove and discard the skins and chop the potatoes into large pieces. Transfer to a wide, shallow bowl and mash with a potato masher until smooth. Add the spinach, eggs, and salt, season with pepper, and stir to combine. Add the all-purpose flour and use your hands to work the mixture until the dough sticks together as a mass, adding more flour as necessary. The dough will feel very sticky and soft to the touch.

3. Dust a work surface with all-purpose flour and place the dough on it. Knead the dough until it has a smooth, elastic texture.

4. Roll the dough into a 2-inch-thick rope and cut it into 18 rounds of even thickness. Cover all of the pieces with plastic wrap to keep them from drying out.

5. Roll a round of dough into a long, ½-inch-thick rope, dusting with semolina flour to keep it from sticking. Cut the rope into ¾-inch pieces. Lightly dust the pieces with semolina flour and place them on parchment–lined baking sheets so they are not touching. Repeat with the remaining dough.

INGREDIENTS:

- 1¼ LBS. BABY SPINACH
- 1¼ LBS. RUSSET POTATOES
- 2 LARGE EGGS
- 1 TEASPOON KOSHER SALT, PLUS MORE TO TASTE
- BLACK PEPPER, TO TASTE
- ⅔ CUP ALL-PURPOSE FLOUR, PLUS MORE AS NEEDED
- SEMOLINA FLOUR, FOR DUSTING
- MASCARPONE SAUCE (SEE RECIPE)

MASCARPONE SAUCE

- 3 TABLESPOONS PINE NUTS
- ⅛ TEASPOON KOSHER SALT, PLUS MORE TO TASTE
- ½ CUP WALNUT PIECES
- 2 BLACK GARLIC CLOVES
- ½ CUP MASCARPONE CHEESE, AT ROOM TEMPERATURE
- 3½ TABLESPOONS WHOLE MILK
- 3 TABLESPOONS GRATED PARMESAN CHEESE
- WHITE PEPPER, TO TASTE

Continued . . .

6. To cook the sorcetti, bring a large pot of water to a boil. Once it's boiling, add salt (1 tablespoon for every 4 cups water), stir, and lower heat to medium-high to maintain a gentle boil. Add the sorcetti and stir for the first minute to prevent any sticking. Cook until they float to the surface and are tender but still chewy, 2 to 3 minutes. Drain and serve with Mascarpone Sauce.

TIP: The sorcetti can be refrigerated for up to 2 days. You can also freeze them on the baking sheets, transfer to freezer bags, and store in the freezer for 3 to 4 weeks. Do not thaw them prior to cooking (they will become mushy), and add an extra minute or two to their cooking time.

MASCARPONE SAUCE

1. Warm a small skillet over medium-low heat for 2 minutes. Add the pine nuts and cook, stirring frequently, until they begin to brown in spots, 3 to 4 minutes. Remove from heat, add the salt, and stir to incorporate.

2. Place the walnuts and garlic cloves in a food processor and process until the mixture forms coarse crumbs. Transfer the mixture to a small saucepan and add the mascarpone, milk, and Parmesan, season with salt and white pepper, and stir to combine. Heat the mixture over medium-low heat until it becomes very warm, taking care not to let it come to a boil. Remove from heat, stir in the toasted pine nuts, and serve.

BAKED EGG CASSEROLE

YIELD: 6 SERVINGS / ACTIVE TIME: 15 MINUTES / TOTAL TIME: 1 HOUR AND 10 MINUTES

This dish involves little work but is a great alternative to plain scrambled eggs. If you are serving this for brunch, try whipping up an arugula salad with a little truffle oil, shaved Parmesan, and fresh cracked pepper to go on the side.

1. Preheat the oven to 350°F.

2. Place the eggs, water, and half-and-half in a bowl and whisk until scrambled.

3. Place all of the other ingredients, except for the salt and pepper, in the mixing bowl and stir to combine. Pour the mixture into a greased 8 × 8-inch baking dish.

4. Season with salt and pepper and place the casserole in the oven. Bake for 1 hour, or until the eggs are set in the middle.

5. Remove from the oven and let the casserole stand for 5 minutes before serving. Grate additional Parmesan over the top and serve.

TIP: To test whether the eggs are cooked, insert a knife into the center of the casserole. If it comes out dry, the eggs are ready.

INGREDIENTS:

12   LARGE EGGS

¼   CUP WATER

½   CUP HALF-AND-HALF

3   PLUM TOMATOES, CHOPPED

1   CUP CHOPPED SPINACH

½   CUP CHOPPED SCALLIONS

1   CUP GRATED PARMESAN CHEESE, PLUS MORE FOR TOPPING

1   TABLESPOON CHOPPED FRESH THYME LEAVES

    SALT AND PEPPER, TO TASTE

SPINACH & MUSHROOM QUINOA
with FRESH HERBS

YIELD: 6 SERVINGS / ACTIVE TIME: 10 MINUTES / TOTAL TIME: 5 HOURS

Folding in the herbs at the end of your preparation gives this dish tons of fresh flavor.

1. Place all of the ingredients, except for the spinach and fresh herbs, in a slow cooker. Cook on high for 4 hours. After 4 hours, check the quinoa for doneness. It should be slightly fluffy.

2. When the quinoa is slightly fluffy, add the spinach and turn off heat. Cover the slow cooker and let sit for 1 hour.

3. Fluff the quinoa with a fork and fold in the basil, dill, and thyme. Season with salt and pepper and serve.

TIP: For added flavor, sauté your vegetables for 5 to 10 minutes over high heat before adding them to the slow cooker, stirring often to prevent them from burning. To maintain the proper level of moisture, add another ¼ cup of stock to the slow cooker.

INGREDIENTS:

1½ CUPS QUINOA, RINSED

2½ CUPS CHICKEN STOCK (SEE PAGE 748 FOR HOMEMADE)

1 ONION, DICED

½ RED BELL PEPPER, STEMMED, SEEDED, AND DICED

¾ LB. BABY PORTOBELLO MUSHROOMS, RINSED AND ROUGHLY CHOPPED

2 GARLIC CLOVES, MINCED

1 TABLESPOON KOSHER SALT, PLUS MORE TO TASTE

1 TABLESPOON BLACK PEPPER, PLUS MORE TO TASTE

3 CUPS BABY SPINACH

1½ CUPS FRESH BASIL LEAVES, CHOPPED

¼ CUP CHOPPED FRESH DILL LEAVES

2 TABLESPOONS CHOPPED FRESH THYME LEAVES

THAI FRIED RICE *with* SEITAN

YIELD: 4 SERVINGS / ACTIVE TIME: 35 MINUTES / TOTAL TIME: 1 HOUR

Thai fried rice is similar to Chinese fried rice except it includes pineapple and substitues fish sauce for soy sauce. I love making fried rice at the end of the week, because not only does it use up strays in the vegetable bin but it hits all of the right notes of sweet, salty, sour, chewy, and crunchy. The seitan takes on the role of both salty and chewy. I've given directions for kohlrabi and peas, but you can include any vegetable you like: just cut it into very small cubes to give it equal footing with all the other ingredients and cook each one separately until done.

1. Place the rice and water in a saucepan and simmer for 20 minutes. Remove from heat, fluff with a fork, and let cool, uncovered, so that it dries out a little. Set aside.

2. Place 1 tablespoon of the oil in a wide skillet and warm over high heat. When the oil is shimmering, add the seitan and sauté for a few minutes, until it starts to brown.

3. In a small bowl, combine the soy sauce, 1 tablespoon of the vinegar, and the sugar. Pour this mixture over the seitan and cook until the liquid has reduced to a glaze. Transfer the seitan to a bowl and set aside.

4. Place the remaining oil in a larger skillet and warm over high heat. When the oil is shimmering, add the shallot and kohlrabi. Sauté until browned, about 8 minutes, and then transfer to the bowl containing the seitan.

5. Add the ginger to the skillet, and more oil if the pan looks dry. Sauté for a few minutes and then add the rice. It is very likely that the rice will stick to the bottom of the pan. Do your best to scrape it off with a spatula and add oil if needed. Cook the rice until it starts to brown, about 5 to 10 minutes, taking care not to let it become too mushy. Add the fish sauce and the remaining vinegar and stir to incorporate.

6. Add the pineapple, kohlrabi, shallots, frozen peas, and seitan to the pan. Gently fold to incorporate and cook for another minute to heat everything through. Season to taste, garnish with the cilantro, and serve with lime wedges.

INGREDIENTS:

1   CUP JASMINE RICE

2   CUPS WATER

2   TABLESPOONS OLIVE OIL, PLUS MORE AS NEEDED

6   OZ. SEITAN, RINSED AND DICED

2   TABLESPOONS SOY SAUCE

2   TABLESPOONS RICE VINEGAR

1   TABLESPOON SUGAR

1   SHALLOT, DICED

1   KOHLRABI, PEELED AND DICED

1   TABLESPOON PEELED AND MINCED GINGER

1   TABLESPOON FISH SAUCE

½   CUP PINEAPPLE, DICED

½   CUP FROZEN PEAS

¼   CUP CHOPPED FRESH CILANTRO, FOR GARNISH

LIME WEDGES, FOR SERVING

BUDDHA SEITAN

YIELD: 4 TO 6 SERVINGS / ACTIVE TIME: 35 MINUTES / TOTAL TIME: 1 HOUR

There is a restaurant in Burlington, Vermont, called A Single Pebble that has consistently made the best Chinese food I've encountered outside of Beijing. Those in the know get the vegetarian options because while all of their entrees are fabulous, the vegetarian ones really shine. One of our family favorites is Buddha Sesame "Beef," which is made with seitan. Steve Bogart, who was the chef in 2006, agreed to publish the recipe in the *Burlington Free Press*, but it took until writing this cookbook for me to resurrect my copy and attempt it. Having no experience cooking with seitan, I was a little intimidated, but it turned out that it was easy. Also, I am expressing a belated thanks to Chef Bogart for sharing, since it is now a family favorite at home. As I've said, I feel that one should celebrate the food that is in front of you rather than pretend it is something else. In that spirit, I've renamed the recipe Buddha Seitan and have simplified it considerably.

1. To prepare the sauce, place all of the ingredients in a bowl and whisk to combine. Set the sauce aside.

2. Assuming you are using premade seitan, rinse to remove any broth and tear it into large bite-sized pieces. Pat the seitan dry with paper towels. Place the oil in a small bowl and gradually add the cornstarch, stirring constantly. You want to add the cornstarch slowly to prevent lumps from forming.

3. Add oil to a Dutch oven until it is about 3 inches deep. Heat to 350°F or until a pea-sized bit of seitan dropped in the oil sizzles on contact. Dredge the pieces of seitan in the cornstarch mixture until completely coated. Working in batches, gently drop the seitan in the oil and fry for about 3 to 5 minutes, turning the pieces so they cook evenly. Transfer the cooked seitan to a paper towel–lined plate. Do not discard the cornstarch mixture because you will use it to thicken the sauce later on.

4. Place a small amount of oil in a large skillet and warm over medium heat. Add the mushrooms, making sure they are in one layer, and cook until they are browned all over, about 10 minutes. Transfer the mushrooms to a bowl, add the shallot to the pan, and sauté until it is fragrant, about 1 minute. Add the asparagus and cook until slightly browned, about 4 minutes. Transfer the shallot and asparagus to the bowl containing the mushrooms.

5. Pour the sauce into the pan and scrape up any browned bits from the bottom of the pan. Bring to a boil, add a teaspoon of the cornstarch mixture, and stir until the sauce has thickened. If it does not thicken enough, add another teaspoon. If it is too thick, add a little water. When the sauce has reached the desired consistency, return the seitan and vegetables to the pan and toss to coat. Sprinkle with sesame seeds and serve over rice.

INGREDIENTS:

FOR THE SAUCE

½ CUP WATER, PLUS MORE AS NEEDED

⅓ CUP SUGAR

¼ CUP MUSHROOM SOY SAUCE

½ CUP SOY SAUCE

¼ CUP WHITE WINE VINEGAR

2 GARLIC CLOVES, MINCED

1 TABLESPOON PEELED AND MINCED GINGER

FOR THE BUDDHA SEITAN

1 LB. SEITAN

⅓ CUP VEGETABLE OIL, PLUS MORE AS NEEDED

⅓ CUP CORNSTARCH

½ LB. MUSHROOMS, TRIMMED AND QUARTERED

1 SHALLOT, DICED

1 LB. ASPARAGUS, TRIMMED AND CUT INTO 3-INCH PIECES

SESAME SEEDS, FOR GARNISH

RICE, FOR SERVING

LAMB & PEAS CURRY

YIELD: 4 SERVINGS / ACTIVE TIME: 35 MINUTES / TOTAL TIME: 45 MINUTES

One of my favorite recipes featuring shell peas. They are on equal footing with the ground lamb, and both are robed in garlic, ginger, and curry spice. You can serve it with rice or put out some warm naan and scoop it up pita-style.

1. Place the oil in a wide sauté pan and warm over medium-high heat. When the oil is shimmering, add the onion and sauté until just starting to brown, about 10 minutes.

2. Add the garlic and ginger, cook for another 2 minutes, and then add the lamb, using a wooden spoon to break it up as it cooks. Cook the lamb until fully browned, about 10 minutes.

3. Add the curry powder and stir to thoroughly incorporate. Cook for 1 minute, add the tomatoes, and cook until they start to break down, about 5 minutes. Add the frozen peas and stir until they are warmed through. Season with salt, stir in the yogurt, and serve over rice or with naan.

INGREDIENTS:

1   TABLESPOON OLIVE OIL

1   ONION, DICED

2   GARLIC CLOVES, MINCED

1   TABLESPOON PEELED AND GRATED GINGER

1   LB. GROUND LAMB

1   TABLESPOON CURRY POWDER

½   CUP DICED TOMATOES

1   CUP FROZEN PEAS

    SALT, TO TASTE

2   TABLESPOONS PLAIN YOGURT

    RICE, FOR SERVING (OPTIONAL)

    NAAN, FOR SERVING (OPTIONAL)

JERK CHICKEN
with ROOT VEGETABLES

YIELD: 6 SERVINGS / ACTIVE TIME: 15 MINUTES / TOTAL TIME: 24 HOURS

Jerk chicken can be very fiery. Sweet potatoes and beets are the perfect foil to absorb that heat in this ode to Jamaica.

1. Pour the marinade into a large baking dish, add the chicken pieces, cover with plastic wrap, and refrigerate overnight.

2. Preheat the oven to 375°F. Place the vegetables, oil, salt, and pepper in an 15 × 10-inch baking pan and roast for 30 minutes. Remove, add the thyme, return the pan to the oven, and cook for 25 more minutes.

3. Remove the pan from the oven. Shake off any excess marinade and place the chicken on top of the vegetables. Return the pan to the oven and cook for 45 to 50 minutes, until the thickest parts of the chicken reach 165°F. Remove the pan from the oven and serve.

JERK MARINADE

1. Place all of the ingredients in a blender and puree until smooth.

INGREDIENTS:

JERK MARINADE (SEE RECIPE)

5   LBS. BONE-IN CHICKEN PIECES

2   RED BEETS, PEELED AND DICED

3   CARROTS, PEELED AND DICED

1   SWEET POTATO, PEELED AND DICED

2   TURNIPS, PEELED AND DICED

1   YUCA ROOT, PEELED AND DICED

¼   CUP OLIVE OIL

    SALT AND PEPPER, TO TASTE

2   TABLESPOONS CHOPPED FRESH THYME LEAVES

JERK MARINADE

2   TABLESPOONS FRESH THYME LEAVES

3   HABANERO PEPPERS, 2 SEEDED, 1 LEFT WHOLE

½   ONION

½   CUP BROWN SUGAR

½   TABLESPOON CINNAMON

½   TEASPOON NUTMEG

1   TABLESPOON ALLSPICE

2   TABLESPOONS PEELED AND MINCED GINGER

1   CUP OLIVE OIL

2   TABLESPOONS SOY SAUCE

1   SCALLION, CHOPPED

1   TABLESPOON KOSHER SALT

1   TABLESPOON BLACK PEPPER

1   TABLESPOON RICE VINEGAR

SAAG ALOO

YIELD: 2 TO 4 SERVINGS / ACTIVE TIME: 20 MINUTES / TOTAL TIME: 35 MINUTES

One thing Vermont has very few of is Indian restaurants. Whenever we travel as a family, we seek one out, and I almost always order saag aloo, a dish of spinach simmered with potatoes and spices. This is a very good home version that is great alongside grilled chicken, eggplant, or rice. Though fresh spinach will work in this dish, I recommend using frozen to make sure it doesn't reduce down to a tiny portion.

1. Place the oil and potatoes in a wide sauté pan and cook over medium heat until the potatoes just start to brown, about 5 minutes.

2. Add the onion, mustard seeds, and cumin and cook for another 5 minutes, then add the garlic and ginger and cook, stirring constantly, for another 2 minutes.

3. Add the frozen spinach, the red pepper flakes, and water and cover the pan with a lid. Cook, stirring occasionally, until the spinach is heated through, about 10 minutes.

4. Remove the cover and cook until all of the liquid has evaporated. Season with salt, add the yogurt, and stir to incorporate. Add more yogurt if you prefer a creamier dish, stir to incorporate, and serve.

INGREDIENTS:

1	TABLESPOON OLIVE OIL
½	LB. FINGERLING OR RED POTATOES, CHOPPED
1	SMALL ONION, DICED
1	TEASPOON MUSTARD SEEDS
1	TEASPOON CUMIN
1	GARLIC CLOVE, CHOPPED
1	TABLESPOON PEELED AND MINCED GINGER
1	LB. FROZEN CHOPPED SPINACH
1	TEASPOON RED PEPPER FLAKES
½	CUP WATER
	SALT, TO TASTE
2	TABLESPOONS PLAIN YOGURT, OR TO TASTE

KOREAN CHICKEN THIGHS
with SWEET POTATO NOODLES

YIELD: 4 TO 6 SERVINGS / ACTIVE TIME: 45 MINUTES / TOTAL TIME: 3 HOURS

A Korean take on lo mein, the Chinese classic. The umami flavor of the sweet potato noodles, shiitake mushrooms, and cabbage is the perfect complement to the sweetness of the marinated chicken.

1. To prepare the marinade, place all of the ingredients in a blender and puree until smooth. Reserve ¼ cup of the marinade and pour the remaining marinade over the chicken thighs. Marinate in the refrigerator for at least 2 hours.

2. Fill a large saucepan with water and bring to a boil. Add the vermicelli and cook for about 6 minutes. Drain, rinse with cold water, and set aside.

3. Preheat the oven to 375°F. Remove the chicken from the refrigerator and place a 12-inch cast-iron skillet on the stove. Add the olive oil and warm over medium-high heat. When the oil starts to shimmer, remove the chicken thighs from the marinade and place them in the pan, skin-side down.

4. Sear the chicken until a crust forms on the skin, about 5 to 7 minutes. Turn the chicken thighs over, add the reserved marinade, place the pan in the oven, and cook for about 15 to 20 minutes, until the centers of the chicken thighs reach 165°F.

5. Remove the pan from the oven, remove the chicken from the pan, and set it aside. Leave the oven at 375°F. Drain the pan and wipe it clean. Return the pan to the stove, add the cabbage, mushrooms, shallot, onion, garlic, scallion whites, and ginger, and cook for 8 minutes, or until the cabbage is wilted.

6. Add the brown sugar, sesame oil, fish sauce, soy sauce, and vinegar to a small bowl and stir until combined. Add this sauce and the vermicelli to the pan, stir until the noodles are completely coated, and then return the chicken thighs to the pan. Top with the scallion greens and sesame seeds, return to the oven for 5 minutes, and serve.

TIP: Sweet potato noodles can be found at most specialty stores and a few major chains. If you can't find them in a store near you, you can order them online.

INGREDIENTS:

FOR THE MARINADE

1	LEMONGRASS STALK, TENDER PART ONLY (THE BOTTOM HALF)
2	GARLIC CLOVES
1	TABLESPOON PEELED AND MINCED GINGER
1	SCALLION, CHOPPED
¼	CUP BROWN SUGAR
2	TABLESPOONS CHILI PASTE
1	TABLESPOON SESAME OIL
1	TABLESPOON RICE VINEGAR
2	TABLESPOONS FISH SAUCE
1	TABLESPOON BLACK PEPPER

FOR THE CHICKEN & NOODLES

4-6	SKIN-ON, BONE-IN CHICKEN THIGHS
10	OZ. SWEET POTATO VERMICELLI
2	TABLESPOONS OLIVE OIL
2	CUPS CHOPPED NAPA CABBAGE
3½	OZ. SHIITAKE MUSHROOMS, SLICED THIN
1	SHALLOT, SLICED THIN
1	ONION, SLICED THIN
2	GARLIC CLOVES, MINCED
2	SCALLIONS, CHOPPED, GREENS RESERVED
2	TABLESPOONS PEELED AND MINCED GINGER
¼	CUP BROWN SUGAR
2	TABLESPOONS SESAME OIL
2	TABLESPOONS FISH SAUCE
¼	CUP SOY SAUCE
¼	CUP RICE VINEGAR
¼	CUP SESAME SEEDS

FRASCARELLI *with* SWISS CHARD & PARMESAN

YIELD: 4 SERVINGS / ACTIVE TIME: 45 MINUTES / TOTAL TIME: 2 HOURS AND 45 MINUTES

Frascarelli are a specialty of the Umbria region of Italy and are treated like polenta because of their resemblance to porridge. If you don't want to make the frascarelli, you can substitute penne or ziti in their place.

1. Place the flours in a large, deep baking dish and stir until thoroughly combined.

2. Place the eggs, water, lemon zest, and a couple pinches of salt in a medium bowl and whisk to combine. Place the bowl right next to the baking dish.

3. Dip a basting brush into the egg mixture, then let it drip into the flour mixture. Keep repeating this until there are drippings over the entire surface of the flour. Lightly sprinkle more semolina flour over the egg-streaked areas.

4. Using the fingertips and thumb of your dominant hand, gently work the mixture until little nuggets of pasta form. With your hands, gently transfer the pasta nuggets from the flour to a colander, then shake to remove any excess flour. Transfer the frascarelli to a clean kitchen towel. Add more semolina flour to the mixture as needed. Let the frascarelli air-dry for 2 hours.

5. Bring a large pot of water to a boil. Once it's boiling, add salt (1 tablespoon for every 4 cups water) and stir. Add the Swiss chard and, once the water comes back to a boil, blanch for 2 minutes. Using a strainer or tongs, transfer to a colander and rinse under cold water. Reduce heat so that the water is at a gentle boil. Add half of the frascarelli and cook, gently stirring once or twice to prevent any sticking, for 10 minutes. Using a strainer or a large slotted spoon, transfer them to a large, warmed bowl and tent with aluminum foil to keep warm. Repeat with the remaining frascarelli.

6. As the frascarelli cook, flatten out each chard leaf on a cutting board and make incisions with a knife on both sides of each stem. Discard the stems. Pile the leaves on top of each other and slice them into 2-inch-wide ribbons.

7. Place a large skillet over medium-high heat and add the butter. Once it stops foaming and little browned bits develop on the bottom of the skillet, add the frascarelli. Gently toss to coat with the butter. Add the Swiss chard and nutmeg and fold gently to incorporate. Cook until everything is heated through, about 2 minutes. Season with pepper, top with the Parmesan, and serve immediately.

INGREDIENTS:

- 2 **CUPS SEMOLINA FLOUR, PLUS MORE AS NEEDED**
- 2 **CUPS ALL-PURPOSE FLOUR**
- 2 **LARGE EGGS**
- ¼ **CUP WATER**
- **ZEST OF 1 LEMON**
- **SALT AND PEPPER, TO TASTE**
- 1 **LB. SWISS CHARD, STEMS TRIMMED**
- 4 **TABLESPOONS UNSALTED BUTTER**
- 1 **TEASPOON GRATED NUTMEG**
- ⅓ **CUP GRATED PARMESAN CHEESE**

SPRING RAGOUT *with* PEAS, ASPARAGUS & MUSHROOMS IN TARRAGON CREAM

YIELD: **4 SERVINGS** / ACTIVE TIME: **45 MINUTES** / TOTAL TIME: **1 HOUR**

Just because it's spring doesn't mean we are done with chilly, rainy days. This ragout with all my favorite spring veggies is warming but not too heavy. If you are not a fan of tarragon, substitute dill, but add it at the very end. I like to serve this over farro, but rice or barley also works.

1. Fill a large saucepan halfway with water and bring it to a boil. Submerge the artichokes, reduce heat so that the water is at a gentle boil, and cook for about 15 minutes. Remove the artichokes from the water and let cool.

2. Remove the outer leaves. Remove the center choke until you reach the heart. Slice each heart into quarters and set aside.

3. Place the oil in a wide pan and warm over medium-high heat. When the oil is shimmering, add the mushrooms and cook, turning them occasionally, until they are evenly browned, about 10 minutes. Transfer to a bowl and set aside.

4. Add the shallot to the pan and cook until translucent, about 3 minutes. Add the butter and melt. Sprinkle the flour over the contents of the pan and cook, stirring continuously, for 2 minutes. Slowly add the stock, stirring to prevent any lumps from forming. Add the cream and wine and bring to a simmer.

5. When the sauce has thickened slightly, add the asparagus and cook until just tender, about 5 minutes. Add the tarragon, artichoke hearts, frozen peas, mushrooms, and lemon juice to the pan and cook until the peas are warmed through, about 5 minutes. Season with salt and pepper and serve over farro or rice.

INGREDIENTS:

- 2 **ARTICHOKES**
- 1 **TABLESPOON OLIVE OIL**
- ½ **LB. WHITE, SHIITAKE, OR OYSTER MUSHROOMS, SLICED**
- 1 **LARGE SHALLOT, CHOPPED**
- 1 **TABLESPOON UNSALTED BUTTER**
- 1 **TABLESPOON ALL-PURPOSE FLOUR**
- 1 **CUP CHICKEN OR VEGETABLE STOCK (SEE PAGES 748 AND 755, RESPECTIVELY, FOR HOMEMADE)**
- ½ **CUP HEAVY CREAM**
- ½ **CUP DRY WHITE WINE**
- ¾ **LB. ASPARAGUS, TRIMMED AND CUT INTO 2-INCH PIECES**
- 1 **TEASPOON DRIED TARRAGON**
- ½ **CUP FROZEN PEAS**
- 1 **TEASPOON FRESH LEMON JUICE**
  SALT AND PEPPER, TO TASTE
  COOKED FARRO, RICE, OR BARLEY, FOR SERVING

CHARD SPÄTZLE *with* GORGONZOLA CREAM

YIELD: 6 SERVINGS / ACTIVE TIME: 1 HOUR / TOTAL TIME: 1 HOUR AND 45 MINUTES

Spätzle has a consistency somewhere between a pasta and a dumpling. The chard in this recipe gives it a nice herbal note that is perfectly complemented by the Gorgonzola Cream.

1. Remove the stems from the chard and bring a large pot of water to a boil. Once it's boiling, add salt (1 tablespoon for every 4 cups water) and stir. Add the chard greens and cook until wilted, about 3 minutes. Using a strainer, transfer the greens to a colander set in a large bowl (reserve the cooking water to cook the spätzle). Rinse the greens under cold water.

2. Drain well and squeeze the chard to remove as much liquid as possible. Transfer to a clean kitchen towel and pat dry.

3. Place the greens, eggs, 1½ tablespoons salt, and nutmeg in a food processor and pulse until the greens are mostly shredded. Add the flour and water and process until the mixture is smooth, about 3 minutes, occasionally stopping to scrape down the work bowl. Transfer the batter to a medium bowl. At this point, the dough should be more like pancake batter, so if it seems too thick, add milk, 1 teaspoon at a time, until the consistency becomes thinner. Cover with plastic wrap and let rest for 1 hour at room temperature.

4. Bring the pot of water you used to cook the greens back to a boil. Reduce heat so the water gently boils. Grease a spätzle maker with nonstick cooking spray and push handfuls of the dough through it into the boiling water. Stir the pot from time to time with a long, wooden spoon to dislodge any spätzle stuck to the bottom of the pot. Cook until they float to the surface, about 1 minute. Quickly remove them with a strainer and transfer to the prepared baking sheet. Drizzle with olive oil so that they don't stick together and tent loosely with aluminum foil to keep them warm. Repeat until all of the spätzle have been cooked and serve with Gorgonzola Cream.

INGREDIENTS:

- 2 LBS. SWISS CHARD
- 1½ TABLESPOONS KOSHER SALT, PLUS MORE TO TASTE
- 4 EXTRA-LARGE EGGS
- 1 TEASPOON GRATED NUTMEG
- 2 CUPS ALL-PURPOSE FLOUR, PLUS MORE AS NEEDED
- ¼ CUP WATER

  MILK, AT ROOM TEMPERATURE, AS NEEDED

  OLIVE OIL, FOR DRIZZLING

  GORGONZOLA CREAM (SEE RECIPE), FOR SERVING

GORGONZOLA CREAM
- 2 CUPS HEAVY CREAM
- 4 OZ. GORGONZOLA DOLCE CHEESE, CUT INTO PIECES
- ⅔ CUP GRATED PARMESAN CHEESE
- 1 TEASPOON GRATED NUTMEG

  SALT AND WHITE PEPPER, TO TASTE

GORGONZOLA CREAM

1. Place the cream and cheeses in a medium saucepan and cook, stirring occasionally, over medium heat until the cream is gently simmering and the sauce is smooth, about 5 minutes. Continue to simmer the sauce until it is thick enough to coat the back of a wooden spoon, 8 to 9 minutes. Stir in the nutmeg, season with salt and white pepper, and serve with the spätzle.

CURRY NOODLES *with* TOFU

YIELD: 4 SERVINGS / ACTIVE TIME: 30 MINUTES / TOTAL TIME: 1 HOUR

A soul-satisfying dish that beautifully blends chewy noodles with the piquant flavor of red curry paste and the pleasant crunch of bean sprouts.

1. Drain the tofu and cut it into ½-inch-wide strips. Arrange them in a single layer on a paper towel–lined tray. Cover with paper towels and pat dry. Let them sit for 30 minutes, changing the paper towels after 15 minutes.

2. Bring a large pot of water to a boil. While it comes to a boil, pick over the bean sprouts, discarding any discolored or spoiled ones. Put the remaining bean sprouts in a bowl of cold water. Discard the hulls that float to the top, drain the remaining bean sprouts, and rinse them under cold water. Add the sprouts to the boiling water and cook for 2 minutes. Remove them from the water with a strainer and immediately rinse under cold water to stop them from cooking further. Drain well and set aside.

3. Bring the water back to a full boil and add the noodles. Cook until they are tender but still chewy, about 15 minutes. Drain, rinse the noodles under hot water to remove excess starch, and drain well again.

4. While the noodles are cooking, place the oil, curry paste, and coconut cream in a large saucepan or Dutch oven and cook over medium-high heat, stirring occasionally, for 3 to 4 minutes. Add the fish sauce, brown sugar, stock, and coconut milk, stir well, and bring to a simmer. Cook for 4 to 5 minutes. Add the curry powder and tofu, stir to incorporate, and reduce heat to low.

5. Divide the noodles between four warmed bowls. Ladle over the piping hot soup, making sure to space out the tofu. Top with the bean sprouts and half an egg and serve with the cilantro, peanuts, lime wedges, and Thai chili powder.

INGREDIENTS:

- 1   LB. EXTRA-FIRM TOFU
- ½   LB. MUNG BEAN SPROUTS
- ½   LB. DRIED RICE STICK NOODLES
- 1   TABLESPOON OLIVE OIL
- ¼   CUP RED CURRY PASTE
- 3   TABLESPOONS COCONUT CREAM (THE THICK LAYER AT THE TOP OF A CAN OF COCONUT MILK; DON'T SHAKE THE CAN BEFORE OPENING IT)
- 3   TABLESPOONS FISH SAUCE, PLUS MORE TO TASTE
- 2   TABLESPOONS LIGHT BROWN SUGAR
- 3   CUPS CHICKEN STOCK (SEE PAGE 748 FOR HOMEMADE)
- 1½   CUPS UNSWEETENED COCONUT MILK
- 2   TEASPOONS CURRY POWDER
- 2   MEDIUM-BOILED EGGS, PEELED AND HALVED, FOR SERVING
-   FRESH CILANTRO, CHOPPED, FOR SERVING
-   PEANUTS, MINCED, FOR SERVING
-   LIME WEDGES, FOR SERVING
-   RED THAI CHILI POWDER, FOR SERVING

RAMEN NOODLES & TOFU SAN BEI

YIELD: 4 SERVINGS / ACTIVE TIME: 30 MINUTES / TOTAL TIME: 1 HOUR AND 45 MINUTES

*S*an *bei,* which means "3 cups" in Mandarin, is a reference to the quantities of soy sauce, sesame oil, and rice wine used in the sauce. Altering the formula a tad results in this scrumptious ramen dish.

1. Drain the tofu and cut it into ½-inch slices. Arrange them in a single layer on a paper towel–lined tray. Cover with paper towels and pat dry. Let them sit for 30 minutes, changing the paper towels after 15 minutes.

2. Warm the largest skillet you have over medium heat for 2 to 3 minutes. Add the peanut or grapeseed oil and warm until it starts to shimmer. Dredge the tofu slices in a shallow bowl filled with cornstarch and tap to remove any excess. Working in batches, add the tofu in a single layer to the skillet. Raise heat to medium-high and cook until the tofu has browned all over, 3 to 4 minutes per side. Transfer to a paper towel–lined plate to drain.

3. Wipe out the skillet and add the sesame oil to the pan. Reduce heat to medium and add the smashed garlic, ginger pieces, scallions, and two pinches of salt once the oil starts to shimmer. Cook, stirring frequently, until fragrant, about 2 minutes. Add the sugar and stir until it has melted. Add the ¾ cup water, the wine or Sherry, and soy sauce and stir. Raise heat to medium-high and bring to a boil. Reduce heat to low, cover, and simmer, stirring occasionally, for 10 minutes.

4. Place the 1½ teaspoons cornstarch and 1 tablespoon water in a small bowl and stir until the mixture is smooth. Add the mixture to the sauce and stir until thoroughly incorporated. Continue to cook, stirring occasionally, until the sauce slightly thickens, about 5 minutes. Add the tofu slices and cook until warmed through.

5. As the sauce simmers, bring a large pot of water to a boil. Add the ramen noodles and stir for the first minute to prevent any sticking. Cook until tender and chewy, drain, and divide the noodles between four warmed, shallow bowls. Top with the tofu slices, ladle the sauce over the top, garnish with the basil, and serve.

INGREDIENTS:

- 1 LB. EXTRA-FIRM TOFU
- 3 TABLESPOONS PEANUT OR GRAPESEED OIL
- 1½ TEASPOONS CORNSTARCH, PLUS MORE AS NEEDED
- 3 TABLESPOONS TOASTED SESAME OIL
- 8 GARLIC CLOVES, SMASHED
- 2-INCH PIECE GINGER, PEELED AND SLICED INTO 8 PIECES
- 10 SCALLIONS, TRIMMED AND CUT INTO ½-INCH PIECES
- SALT, TO TASTE
- 3 TABLESPOONS SUGAR
- ¾ CUP WATER, PLUS 1 TABLESPOON
- ¾ CUP SHAOXING RICE WINE OR DRY SHERRY
- ⅓ CUP SOY SAUCE
- ⅓ LB. RAMEN NOODLES
- 2 HANDFULS FRESH BASIL LEAVES (THAI BASIL PREFERRED), SLICED THIN, FOR GARNISH

VEGAN TOM YAM GUNG *with* TOFU

YIELD: 4 SERVINGS / ACTIVE TIME: 20 MINUTES / TOTAL TIME: 45 MINUTES

This hot-and-sour soup traditionally contains shrimp. But since it's a very fragrant and healthy soup, I thought putting a vegan twist on it would be a great modification.

1. In a medium saucepan, add 2 tablespoons of the oil and warm over medium heat. When the oil starts to shimmer, add the onion and garlic and cook, stirring frequently, until the onion softens, about 5 minutes. Add the stock, lime juice, lime leaves, chilies, cilantro stalks, lemongrass stalk, and sugar and bring to a boil.

2. Meanwhile, in a large sauté pan, add the remaining oil and warm over medium heat. Add the tofu and cook, stirring frequently, until lightly browned on all sides. Remove from the pan and set aside.

3. Strain the broth through a fine sieve, discard the solids, and place the liquid in a clean pan. Add the soy sauce and shiitake mushrooms and bring to a simmer. Add the tofu and cook for 4 additional minutes.

4. Season with salt and pepper, place in warmed bowls, and garnish with watercress, bean sprouts, and the reserved cilantro.

INGREDIENTS:

¼ CUP OLIVE OIL

1 ONION, MINCED

1 GARLIC CLOVE, MINCED

6 CUPS VEGETABLE STOCK (SEE PAGE 755 FOR HOMEMADE)

¼ CUP FRESH LIME JUICE

3 MAKRUT LIME LEAVES

3 BIRD'S EYE CHILI PEPPERS, STEMMED, SEEDED, AND SLICED

6 CILANTRO STALKS, LEAVES REMOVED, CHOPPED, AND RESERVED FOR GARNISH

1 LEMONGRASS STALK, BRUISED

1 TABLESPOON SUGAR

¾ LB. TOFU, CUT INTO ½-INCH CUBES

¼ CUP SOY SAUCE

8 SHIITAKE MUSHROOMS, SLICED

SALT AND PEPPER, TO TASTE

WATERCRESS, FOR GARNISH

BEAN SPROUTS, FOR GARNISH

SESAME TOFU & GREEN BEAN CASSEROLE

YIELD: 4 SERVINGS / ACTIVE TIME: 5 MINUTES / TOTAL TIME: 2 DAYS

Letting tofu sit in a marinade for two days is one way to really punch up its flavor.

1. To prepare the marinade, place all of the ingredients in a small bowl and stir to combine.

2. To begin preparations for the casserole, place the marinade and the tofu in a resealable 1-gallon plastic bag, removing as much air as possible when sealing. Place in the refrigerator for 2 days, flipping the bag over at the end of the first day.

3. To begin preparations for the casserole, preheat the oven to 375°F. Remove the tofu from the bag. Place the green beans, mushrooms, sesame oil, and soy sauce in the bag and shake.

4. Line a 9 × 13-inch baking pan with parchment paper and place the tofu on it in a single layer. Place the pan in the oven and bake for 35 minutes. Remove the pan, flip the tofu over, and push it to the outer edge of the pan. Add the green bean-and-mushroom mixture, return the pan to the oven, and bake for 15 minutes, or until the green beans are cooked to your preference. Remove the pan from the oven, garnish with the sesame seeds, and serve.

INGREDIENTS:

FOR THE MARINADE

3   TABLESPOONS DARK SOY SAUCE

2   TABLESPOONS RICE VINEGAR

1   TABLESPOON SESAME OIL

1   TABLESPOON HONEY

    PINCH OF CINNAMON

    PINCH OF BLACK PEPPER

FOR THE CASSEROLE

1   (14 OZ.) PACKAGE EXTRA-FIRM TOFU, DRAINED AND CUT INTO 1-INCH CUBES

1   LB. FRESH GREEN BEANS

¼   LB. SHIITAKE MUSHROOMS, SLICED

2   TABLESPOONS SESAME OIL

1   TABLESPOON SOY SAUCE

2   TABLESPOONS SESAME SEEDS, FOR GARNISH

SNOW PEA & CHICKEN STIR-FRY
with GINGER SAUCE

YIELD: **4 SERVINGS** / ACTIVE TIME: **40 MINUTES** / TOTAL TIME: **40 MINUTES**

This is an easy weeknight meal that hits all the right notes: salty, sweet, and tangy. Snow peas hardly require any cooking, so add them at the very last minute. Using cornstarch to coat the chicken not only gives it a nice crust, it also helps to thicken the finished sauce. If you'd like to make this vegetarian, substituting firm tofu for the chicken is delicious.

1. Place a wide sauté pan over high heat and add the olive oil and the onion. Cook the onion is browned, about 7 minutes, transfer it to a bowl, and add the mushrooms to the pan. Cook, stirring occasionally, until browned all over, about 7 minutes. Transfer to a separate bowl.

2. Place the cornstarch in a separate bowl, add the chicken, and toss to coat. Shake to remove any excess cornstarch and add the chicken to the pan. Sauté until browned all over and cooked through, about 8 minutes. Add more olive oil if the pan starts to look dry while the chicken is cooking. Transfer the cooked chicken to the bowl containing the mushrooms.

3. Place the ginger in the pan and cook until fragrant, about 1 minute. Deglaze the pan with the Sherry, scraping up any browned bits from the bottom of the pan, then add the soy sauce and maple syrup. Cook for a few minutes, until the sauce has thickened.

4. Return the onion, mushrooms, and chicken to the pan and add the water chestnuts, snow peas, sesame oil, and sesame seeds. Stir to incorporate, reduce heat to medium, and cook until the snow peas have turned bright green. Serve with white rice.

INGREDIENTS:

2 TABLESPOONS OLIVE OIL, PLUS MORE AS NEEDED

1 SMALL ONION, DICED

½ LB. WHITE MUSHROOMS, SLICED

¼ CUP CORNSTARCH

½ LB. BONELESS, SKINLESS CHICKEN BREASTS, CHOPPED

1 TABLESPOON PEELED AND MINCED GINGER

¼ CUP DRY SHERRY

2 TABLESPOONS SOY SAUCE

1 TEASPOON MAPLE SYRUP

1 CAN SLICED WATER CHESTNUTS, DRAINED AND RINSED

½ LB. SNOW PEAS

1 TEASPOON TOASTED SESAME OIL

2 TEASPOONS SESAME SEEDS

   WHITE RICE, FOR SERVING

ROASTED SUNCHOKES, SHALLOTS, KALE & MUSHROOMS OVER QUINOA

YIELD: 2 SERVINGS / ACTIVE TIME: 15 MINUTES / TOTAL TIME: 1 HOUR

This recipe is convenient in that you can roast the vegetables all at once, but they require different cooking times. I put the sunchokes, mushrooms, and shallot on the same baking sheet but keep them in their own corners. The kale goes on a separate baking sheet. The shallot, kale, and mushrooms are done first and removed; the sunchokes stay in a little longer. With the help of a timer, this approach makes for easy cooking.

1. Preheat the oven to 375°F. Place the sunchokes, mushrooms, and shallot in separate corners of a baking sheet. Pour a little oil over each pile, sprinkle with salt, and lightly toss to make sure everything is coated. Then spread the vegetables out in their respective corners, making sure they are in one layer.

2. Place the kale leaves on a separate baking sheet and lightly drizzle with oil and salt. Place the vegetables in the oven. After 10 minutes, remove the kale and set it aside.

3. After 5 more minutes, remove the other pan; remove the mushrooms and shallot, turn the sunchokes over, and return the pan to the oven. When the sunchokes are brown around the edges, remove the pan from the oven and let the sunchokes cool to room temperature.

4. Prepare the quinoa by putting it in a fine sieve and rinsing under cold water. Place the quinoa in a small pot, add the water, bring to a boil, and then reduce heat so that the quinoa simmers. Simmer until the quinoa has absorbed all of the liquid, about 15 minutes. Remove from the stove and let cool.

5. Place a mound of the quinoa in the bottom of two bowls. Divide the vegetables into two portions and put a portion in each bowl. Dress with the Maple & Mustard Vinaigrette and serve.

MAPLE & MUSTARD VINAIGRETTE

1. Place all of the ingredients in a bowl and whisk to combine.

INGREDIENTS:

- ⅓ LB. SUNCHOKES, SCRUBBED AND TRIMMED
- 4 LARGE WHITE MUSHROOMS, QUARTERED
- 1 SHALLOT, CUT INTO THICK SLICES
- 2 TABLESPOONS OLIVE OIL, PLUS MORE AS NEEDED
- SALT, TO TASTE
- 5 KALE LEAVES, STEMS REMOVED
- ½ CUP QUINOA
- 1 CUP WATER
- MAPLE & MUSTARD VINAIGRETTE (SEE RECIPE)

MAPLE & MUSTARD VINAIGRETTE

- 1 TABLESPOON DIJON MUSTARD
- 1 TABLESPOON MAPLE SYRUP
- 2 TABLESPOONS APPLE CIDER VINEGAR
- ⅓ CUP OLIVE OIL
- SALT AND PEPPER, TO TASTE

SWEET POTATO GNOCCHI *with* CHARD, BROCCOLINI, LEMON MASCARPONE & FRIED SAGE

YIELD: **4 SERVINGS** / ACTIVE TIME: **30 MINUTES** / TOTAL TIME: **2 HOURS AND 30 MINUTES**

This recipe is a little involved, but it turns out very nicely. The ricotta cheese makes for a pillowy gnocchi—just don't work the dough too much. If you cannot find mascarpone cheese, heavy cream is a good substitute.

1. Preheat the oven to 400°F. Place the sweet potato halves cut-side down on a greased baking sheet. Bake for 30 minutes, or until very tender. Remove from the oven, let cool, and scoop the flesh into a bowl.

2. Add the ricotta, flour, egg, and a pinch of salt to the sweet potato flesh. Blend with your hands until a dough forms. If it is very wet, add some more flour. Let the dough sit for an hour.

3. When the dough has rested, take a handful at a time and use your hands to roll it out into a rope that is about 1 inch in diameter. Cut the rope into ¾-inch pieces and lay them on a flour-dusted baking sheet. Repeat until all of the dough is cut into gnocchi shapes.

4. Bring a large pot of water to a boil on the stove. Working in batches, gently lower the gnocchi into the water and cook until they float to the surface. Transfer to a bowl, lightly drizzle with oil to prevent them from sticking, and repeat with the remaining gnocchi.

5. Coat the bottom of a large sauté pan with oil and add the shallot. Sauté until translucent, about 3 minutes. Add the Swiss chard, and more oil if the pan looks dry. When the chard has wilted and the shallot starts to brown, transfer them to a bowl.

6. Add the broccolini to the pan with a few tablespoons of water and cover. Cook until tender, about 4 minutes, and then transfer to the bowl containing the chard and shallot.

7. Add the butter and gnocchi to the pan so they sit comfortably in one layer. Cook until brown on one side and then gently flip them to brown on the other side, about 2 minutes per side. Place them in the bowl with the vegetables and repeat until all of the gnocchi have been cooked.

8. Place the sage leaves in the pan, adding more oil if it looks dry, and fry them until crisp, about 30 seconds per side. Transfer to a paper towel–lined plate to drain.

9. Add the mascarpone to the pan along with the lemon zest and lemon juice. Cook, stirring frequently, until the sauce is combined and warmed through, about 2 minutes. Return all of the ingredients, except the sage, to the pan and gently toss to coat with the sauce and reheat. Season with salt and pepper and garnish with Parmesan and the sage.

INGREDIENTS:

- 1 **SWEET POTATO, HALVED**
- 1 **CUP WHOLE-MILK RICOTTA CHEESE**
- 2 **CUPS ALL-PURPOSE FLOUR, PLUS MORE AS NEEDED**
- 1 **EGG**
- **SALT AND PEPPER, TO TASTE**
- **OLIVE OIL, AS NEEDED**
- 2 **TABLESPOONS CHOPPED SHALLOT**
- 4 **LARGE LEAVES SWISS CHARD, STEMS REMOVED, CHOPPED**
- ½ **LB. BROCCOLINI, CHOPPED**
- 1 **TABLESPOON UNSALTED BUTTER**
- 12 **FRESH SAGE LEAVES**
- ½ **CUP MASCARPONE CHEESE**
- 1 **TEASPOON LEMON ZEST**
- 1½ **TEASPOONS FRESH LEMON JUICE**
- **PARMESAN CHEESE, GRATED, FOR GARNISH**

BUTTERNUT SQUASH CARAMELLE

YIELD: 6 SERVINGS / ACTIVE TIME: 1 HOUR AND 35 MINUTES / TOTAL TIME: 3 HOURS AND 45 MINUTES

Butternut ravioli has become a standard among warming fall dishes. Here, the filling goes into a caramelle and some gorgonzola is added to provide a bit of zing. Top it with the Creamy Leek Sauce, and you have the perfect Sunday-night dinner.

1. Preheat the oven to 400°F. Trim the ends of the squash, place it on its widest end, and slice down vertically. If this is difficult to do, use a rubber mallet to tap gently on the back of the blade. Working slowly, wedge the knife all the way to the base of the squash. When you have the two separated squash halves, use a spoon to scrape out the seeds and fibrous insides. Prick the flesh with a fork. Brush all the cut surfaces lightly with oil and place on a parchment–lined baking sheet, cut-side down.

2. Place the baking sheet in the oven, lower the temperature to 375°F, and roast until fork-tender, 40 to 45 minutes. Remove from the oven and let cool, then scoop the soft flesh into a bowl. Run the flesh through a potato ricer or puree in a blender until smooth. Add the bread crumbs, cheeses, egg yolks, nutmeg, and rosemary to the squash and stir to thoroughly combine. The filling will keep in the refrigerator for up to 1 day; just remember to let it return to room temperature before proceeding with the rest of the preparation.

3. Prepare the dough as directed on page 761. Roll the dough to the thinnest setting (generally notch 5) for pasta sheets that are about ¹⁄₁₆-inch thick. Cut the pasta sheets into approximately 12-inch-long pieces. Lay the cut pasta sheets on lightly floured parchment–lined baking sheets and cover loosely with plastic wrap. Work quickly to keep the pasta sheets from drying out, which makes it harder for the pasta to stick together.

4. Working with one sheet at a time, place it on a lightly floured work surface. Using a ridged pastry cutter, cut each sheet into as many 2½-inch squares as possible. Set the squares on lightly floured parchment–lined baking sheets, making sure they don't touch, and cover them loosely with plastic wrap. Repeat with the remaining pasta sheets. Gather any scraps together into a ball, put it through the pasta machine to create additional pasta sheets, and cut those as well.

INGREDIENTS:

- 1½ LBS. BUTTERNUT SQUASH
- OLIVE OIL, AS NEEDED
- ¼ CUP SOFT BREAD CRUMBS
- ½ CUP GRATED PARMESAN CHEESE, PLUS MORE FOR SERVING
- ¼ CUP CRUMBLED GORGONZOLA CHEESE
- 2 LARGE EGG YOLKS
- 1 TEASPOON GRATED NUTMEG
- 10 FRESH ROSEMARY LEAVES, MINCED
- 1 BATCH THREE-EGG BASIC PASTA DOUGH (SEE PAGE 761)
- SEMOLINA FLOUR, FOR DUSTING
- SALT, TO TASTE
- CREAMY LEEK SAUCE (SEE RECIPE), FOR SERVING

CREAMY LEEK SAUCE

- 4 LEEKS
- 2½ TABLESPOONS UNSALTED BUTTER
- SALT, TO TASTE
- 1 CUP HEAVY CREAM
- ¼ CUP WHOLE MILK
- ½ TEASPOON WHITE PEPPER

Continued . . .

5. To make the caramelle, lay out 12 to 14 pasta squares at a time and place 2 teaspoons of filling in the center of each. Should the dough have dried during this process, lightly moisten it with a fingertip dipped in water. Fold one edge of the square over the filling and align it with the opposite edge so that you have a rectangle. Press down around the joined sides to create a tight seal. As you do this, try to push out any air from around the filling (this will keep the caramelle from coming apart in the water when boiling). Press down one more time to ensure that you have a tight seal. Twist the ends of the rectangle in opposite directions and pinch the end joints to create a tight seal. Set the filled caramelle on flour-dusted parchment–lined baking sheets. Repeat until you have used up all the pasta squares and filling. Allow to air-dry for 2 hours, turning the caramelle over halfway through.

6. To cook the caramelle, bring a large pot of water to a boil. Once it's boiling, add salt (1 tablespoon for every 4 cups water) and stir. Carefully drop the caramelle into the boiling water and stir for the first minute to prevent any sticking. Cook until they are tender but still chewy, 3 to 4 minutes. Using a strainer or large slotted spoon, remove the caramelle, gently shaking them over the pot to remove excess surface moisture. Top with the Creamy Leek Sauce and Parmesan and serve.

CREAMY LEEK SAUCE

1. Prepare the leeks by trimming away the root ends and dark green leaves, keeping only the white and light green parts. With a sharp knife, cut each leek in half lengthwise and remove the two outer layers. Cut the halves vertically into thin slivers. Place them in a large bowl of water and swish them around to remove any dirt. Drain well, then transfer to a clean kitchen towel. Set aside.

2. Warm a large skillet over low heat for 2 to 3 minutes. Add 2 tablespoons of the butter and raise heat to medium. Once the butter has melted and stopped foaming, add the leeks and a couple pinches of salt and stir. When the leeks begin to gently sizzle, reduce heat to low, cover the pan, and cook, stirring occasionally, until the leeks become very soft and turn a slightly darker shade of green, about 20 minutes.

3. Raise heat to medium-high and add the cream, milk, and white pepper, season with salt, and bring to a boil. Reduce heat to low and simmer, uncovered, until it has reduced slightly, about 5 minutes. Serve warm.

SPAGHETTI SQUASH NOODLES
with SWISS CHARD & TOASTED SPICED PECANS

YIELD: 4 SERVINGS / ACTIVE TIME: 30 MINUTES / TOTAL TIME: 1 HOUR AND 15 MINUTES

Vegetarian, gluten-free, or omnivore, this dish satisfies all. The herbal notes of the chard are a nice contrast to the sweet strands of squash.

1. Preheat the oven to 400°F. Line a large baking sheet, including the sides, with aluminum foil and trim a sheet of parchment paper so that it fits in the bottom of the pan. Trim the ends of the squash, scrape out the seeds, and cut them into four medallions. Place them in the sheet, place the sheet in the oven, and bake until the strands are tender but still firm, about 50 minutes. Remove from the oven and let cool for 10 minutes.

2. Using a fork, pull the strands in the center of each round to create long strands of "spaghetti." Working in two batches, transfer half of the strands to a kitchen towel and gently twist it to remove as much liquid from the squash as possible. Transfer the squash to a large bowl and repeat this step with the other half of the squash. Set aside.

3. While the squash is roasting, bring a large pot of water to a boil. Once it's boiling, add salt (1 tablespoon for every 4 cups water) and stir. Add the chard leaves and cook until wilted, about 2 minutes. Using a strainer, transfer to a colander and rinse under cold water until cool. Drain well, squeeze the chard to remove as much liquid as possible, and mince. Set aside.

4. Place the pecans in a small resealable bag and gently crush with a rolling pin. Warm a skillet over low heat for 2 to 3 minutes. Add the 2 teaspoons of oil, the chili powder, and sugar and stir. Once the mixture starts to gently sizzle, add the pecans and stir until coated. Cook until fragrant, about 2 minutes. Add salt to taste and mix well. Transfer to a plate and let cool.

5. Warm a large skillet over low heat for 2 to 3 minutes. Add 1 tablespoon of the oil and warm for a minute, then add the garlic, red pepper flakes, rosemary, and a pinch of salt. Cook until the garlic just starts to turn golden, about 2 minutes. Raise heat to medium-high, add the chard and a pinch of salt, stir to combine, and cook for 3 minutes. Transfer the chard to a warmed bowl and tent to keep warm. Add the remaining oil and let it heat for a minute. Add the spaghetti squash strands and two pinches of salt and toss to coat. Sprinkle the vinegar over the top, season with white pepper, and toss again. Taste and adjust the seasoning as needed. Remove from heat, add the Parmesan, and toss to combine. Divide between four warm bowls and top with the pecans.

INGREDIENTS:

- 2 **SPAGHETTI SQUASH (ABOUT 2 LBS. EACH)**
- **SALT, TO TASTE**
- **LEAVES FROM 1 LB. SWISS CHARD**
- ½ **CUP PECANS**
- 3 **TABLESPOONS OLIVE OIL, PLUS 2 TEASPOONS**
- 1 **TEASPOON CHILI POWDER**
- 1 **TEASPOON SUGAR**
- 2 **GARLIC CLOVES, MINCED**
- ½ **TEASPOON RED PEPPER FLAKES**
- **LEAVES FROM 1 SPRIG FRESH ROSEMARY, MINCED**
- 1 **TEASPOON CHINESE BLACK VINEGAR**
- **WHITE PEPPER, TO TASTE**
- ¾ **CUP GRATED PARMESAN CHEESE**

MAPLE-ROASTED VEGETABLES
with CARAMELIZED ONIONS
& MASHED POTATOES

YIELD: 4 SERVINGS / ACTIVE TIME: 25 MINUTES / TOTAL TIME: 1 HOUR

This hearty recipe is one of my favorite dishes. The beets will color everything red, so if you don't care for that aesthetic, cook them in a separate pan and then combine them with the rest when serving. It may seem like a lot of onions when you first put them in the pan, but they will cook down considerably.

---

1. Preheat the oven to 375°F. Melt 3 tablespoons of the butter in a skillet over medium-high heat and add the onions. Raise heat to high and cook the onions for 2 minutes. Reduce heat to low and cook, stirring occasionally, until the onions have caramelized, 30 to 40 minutes.

2. While the onions are cooking, place the rutabaga, beets, carrots, oil, maple syrup, salt, and pepper in a bowl and toss to combine. Spread evenly in a roasting pan and place the pan in the oven. Bake for 45 minutes, turning the vegetables occasionally until they are browned.

3. As the vegetables roast, put the potatoes in a pot and cover with water. Bring to a boil and cook until tender, about 15 minutes. Drain and immediately transfer to a large mixing bowl. Add 2½ tablespoons of the butter and half of the cream. Use a handheld mixer to slowly combine the ingredients. Once the potatoes are half-mashed, add the remaining butter and cream, season with salt and pepper, and mash until smooth.

4. To serve, place a dollop of the mashed potatoes on a plate and make a well. Spoon some of the roasted vegetables into the well and top with a spoonful of caramelized onions and additional butter.

INGREDIENTS:

1	STICK UNSALTED BUTTER, PLUS MORE FOR SERVING
4	LARGE ONIONS, SLICED
1	RUTABAGA, PEELED AND DICED
1	BUNCH BEETS, PEELED AND DICED
2	LARGE CARROTS, PEELED AND DICED
2	TABLESPOONS OLIVE OIL
3	TABLESPOONS REAL MAPLE SYRUP
	SALT AND PEPPER, TO TASTE
1½	LBS. POTATOES, PEELED AND DICED
¾	CUP HEAVY CREAM

CANNELLONI
with BUTTERNUT SQUASH, RICOTTA & SAGE

YIELD: 8 TO 10 SERVINGS / ACTIVE TIME: 35 MINUTES / TOTAL TIME: 1 HOUR AND 45 MINUTES

Butternut and sage are a classic duo. This cannelloni is rich and decadent, enhanced by the creamy ricotta cheese.

1. Preheat the oven to 400°F. Trim the ends of the squash. Rest it on its widest end and, using a heavy kitchen knife, slice down vertically. If this is difficult, use a rubber mallet to tap gently on the back edge of the blade. Work as slowly as you need to and wedge the knife all the way to the base of the squash. When you have the two halves of squash, scrape out the seeds and fibrous insides and prick the flesh with a fork. Brush all the cut surfaces lightly with 1 tablespoon of the oil and place the squash on a parchment–lined baking sheet, cut-side down.

2. Place the baking sheet in the oven, lower the temperature to 375°F, and roast until the squash is fork-tender, 40 to 45 minutes. Remove the squash from the oven and let cool, then scoop the flesh into a wide, shallow bowl and mash it until smooth.

3. Warm a large skillet over low heat for 2 to 3 minutes. Add 2 tablespoons of the oil and the garlic and raise heat to medium. Once the garlic just starts to brown, remove the skillet from heat and transfer the garlic and oil to the bowl with the mashed squash. Add the cheeses, half of the sage, and the nutmeg, season with salt and pepper, and mix well. Use or cover and refrigerate for up to 3 days. Bring back to room temperature before proceeding.

4. Prepare the dough according to the directions on page 760, rolling the dough to the thinnest setting (generally notch 5 or 6) for pasta sheets that are about 1/16-inch thick. Lay the cut pasta sheets on a lightly floured parchment–lined baking sheet, separating them with more lightly floured sheets of parchment. Make sure to work quickly to keep the pasta sheets from drying out and becoming brittle.

INGREDIENTS:

2   LBS. BUTTERNUT SQUASH

5½   TABLESPOONS OLIVE OIL, PLUS MORE AS NEEDED

5   GARLIC CLOVES, MINCED

1½   CUPS WHOLE-MILK RICOTTA CHEESE

1   CUP GRATED PARMESAN CHEESE

12   FRESH SAGE LEAVES, SLICED THIN

1   TEASPOON GRATED NUTMEG

    SALT AND WHITE PEPPER, TO TASTE

1   BATCH ALL-YOLK PASTA DOUGH (PAGE 760)

    SEMOLINA FLOUR, FOR DUSTING

    PREFERRED SAUCE, FOR SERVING

Continued . . .

5. Working with one sheet at a time, place it on a lightly floured work surface in front of you. Using a pastry cutter, cut each sheet into as many 4½- to 5-inch squares as possible. Place the finished squares on another lightly floured parchment–lined baking sheet and make sure they don't touch. As you run out of room, lightly dust them with flour, cover with another sheet of parchment paper, and arrange more squares on top of that. Repeat with all the pasta sheets. Gather any scraps together into a ball, put it through the pasta machine to create additional pasta sheets, and cut those as well.

6. Bring a large pot of water to a boil. Once it's boiling, add salt (1 tablespoon for every 4 cups water) and stir. Add the squares and carefully stir for the first minute to prevent any sticking. Cook until they are just tender, about 2 minutes. Drain, rinse under cold water, and toss with ½ tablespoon oil to prevent sticking.

7. Generously oil a baking dish large enough to fit all the filled cannelloni in a single layer. To fill the cannelloni, place a cooked pasta square in front of you. Place ¼ cup of the squash mixture in the center of the square and shape it into a rough cylinder. Roll the pasta around the filling into a tube and transfer to the prepared baking dish, seam-side down. Repeat with the remaining sheets and filling. When the baking dish is filled, brush the cannelloni tops with the remaining oil. If desired, the cannelloni can be refrigerated for up to 4 hours before baking. If using a ceramic or glass baking dish, bring back to room temperature before baking to prevent cracking.

8. Preheat the oven to 375°F. Put the baking dish on the center rack and bake until the cannelloni are very hot and begin to turn golden brown, about 20 minutes. Serve directly from the baking dish, topped with a drizzle of the sauce of your choice and the remaining sage.

BAKED SHELLS *with* ZUCCHINI, HAM & AROMATIC BÉCHAMEL SAUCE

YIELD: 6 SERVINGS / ACTIVE TIME: 45 MINUTES / TOTAL TIME: 1 HOUR AND 45 MINUTES

This is a cheesy, rich pasta meal in which the zucchini balances out the salty ham and creamy béchamel.

1. Warm a large skillet over medium heat for 2 to 3 minutes, then add the oil. When the oil begins to shimmer, add the onion and a couple pinches of salt. Cook until translucent, about 3 minutes, stirring occasionally. Add the zucchini and a couple more pinches of salt and cook, stirring occasionally, until it is thoroughly cooked but not falling apart, about 10 minutes. Remove the pan from heat and let cool.

2. Bring a large pot of water to a boil. Once it's boiling, add salt (1 tablespoon for every 4 cups water) and stir. Add the pasta and stir for the first minute to prevent any sticking. Cook for three-quarters of the time directed on the package. The pasta will have softened a bit but still be very firm and clearly not cooked through. Drain, rinse under cold water, and drain well again. Place on clean kitchen towels to dry.

3. Preheat the oven to 375°F.

4. Place the zucchini mixture, bread crumbs, cheese, ham, 1 cup of the Aromatic Béchamel Sauce, and pepper in a large bowl. Stir gently until thoroughly combined. Taste and adjust seasoning as needed. Using a small spoon, carefully fill each shell with the mixture.

5. Spread ¾ cup of the sauce over the bottom of a baking dish large enough to accommodate the pasta in a single layer. Add the filled shells. Pour the remaining béchamel sauce over the top, making sure to cover each shell. Sprinkle the Parmesan over the top and cover the dish with aluminum foil.

6. Place the dish in the oven and lower the temperature to 350°F. Bake for 20 minutes. Remove the foil and continue to bake until the tops of the shells just start to turn golden, about 10 minutes. If desired, run it under the broiler for a couple of minutes so that it just browns on top. Remove from the oven and serve immediately.

INGREDIENTS:

- 2 TABLESPOONS OLIVE OIL
- 1 SMALL ONION, SLICED THIN
- SALT AND PEPPER, TO TASTE
- 3 ZUCCHINI, CUT INTO SMALL CUBES
- ¾ LB. LARGE SHELL PASTA
- ¼ CUP PLAIN BREAD CRUMBS
- ½ LB. UNSMOKED SCAMORZA, SCAMORZARELLA, OR MOZZARELLA CHEESE, GRATED
- ½ LB. THICKLY SLICED HONEY HAM, CUT INTO SMALL CUBES
- 1 BATCH AROMATIC BÉCHAMEL SAUCE (SEE RECIPE)
- 1½ CUPS GRATED PARMESAN CHEESE

Continued . . .

AROMATIC BÉCHAMEL SAUCE

1. Place the milk, bay leaves, onion, and peppercorns in a medium saucepan and warm over low heat. Cook, stirring occasionally, until almost boiling, about 6 minutes. Remove from heat, let the mixture steep for 20 minutes, and then strain. Discard the solids.

2. Melt the butter in a medium saucepan over medium heat, stirring to keep it from browning. Add the flour and briskly whisk until the mixture becomes smooth. Cook, whisking constantly, until the mixture stops foaming and turns golden brown, about 5 minutes.

3. Pour in ½ cup or so of the milk and whisk vigorously until you've thinned the flour mixture. Add the remaining milk and cook, whisking constantly, until the mixture has thickened. Season with salt and pepper and stir to incorporate. Use immediately or let cool, cover, and refrigerate for up to 2 days. Bring back to room temperature before using.

INGREDIENTS:

AROMATIC BÉCHAMEL SAUCE

4	CUPS WHOLE MILK
2	BAY LEAVES
½	WHITE ONION
10	BLACK PEPPERCORNS
1	STICK UNSALTED BUTTER
½	CUP ALL-PURPOSE FLOUR
	SALT AND WHITE PEPPER, TO TASTE

TOFU TACOS

YIELD: 4 SERVINGS / ACTIVE TIME: 15 MINUTES / TOTAL TIME: 20 MINUTES

Crumbled extra-firm tofu assertively seasoned, spooned into tortillas, and topped with your favorite fixings makes for delicious tacos. Browning the tofu close to the point of charring imparts a flavorful, meaty texture. The seasoning amounts should be used as a guide rather than a hard rule, depending on your spice threshold.

1. Place the oil in a large saucepan and warm over medium-high heat. Once the oil is shimmering, add the tofu and all the seasonings, with the exception of the adobo sauce. Stir until the tofu is thoroughly coated and then cook until it starts to brown, about 5 minutes.

2. Scramble the tofu in the pan and brown on the other side.

3. Once the tofu is browned all over, add the adobo sauce and more oil if the pan looks dry. Cook for 5 minutes, then serve with hard taco shells or tortillas and the toppings of your choice.

INGREDIENTS:

1 TABLESPOON OLIVE OIL, PLUS MORE AS NEEDED

1 LB. EXTRA-FIRM TOFU, DRAINED AND CRUMBLED

1 TABLESPOON KOSHER SALT

1 TABLESPOON CUMIN

1 TABLESPOON GARLIC POWDER

1 TABLESPOON CAYENNE POWDER

ADOBO SAUCE, TO TASTE

HARD TACO SHELLS OR TORTILLAS (SEE PAGE 797 FOR HOMEMADE), FOR SERVING

PREFERRED TOPPINGS, FOR SERVING

CHEESY POLENTA
with CORN, PEPPERS & TOMATILLOS

YIELD: 4 SERVINGS / ACTIVE TIME: 25 MINUTES / TOTAL TIME: 35 MINUTES

This great vegetarian meal hits all the right notes. The creamy polenta is the perfect complement to the sweet-and-sour combo of corn and tomatillos. Add jalapeño if you like things spicy.

1. To prepare the corn, peppers, and tomatillos, place the oil in a wide pan and warm over medium-high heat. When the oil starts to shimmer, add the onion and sauté until it starts to brown, about 5 minutes. Add the corn and continue to cook, adding more oil if the pan becomes too dry. When the corn has started to brown, add the pepper, jalapeño (if using), tomatillos, cumin, and salt. Cook until the tomatillos start to collapse, about 5 minutes. Add the garlic and cook until fragrant, about 2 minutes. Remove the pan from heat and set aside.

2. To begin preparations for the polenta, bring the milk, water, and salt to a boil in a medium saucepan.

3. Add the cornmeal slowly, stirring constantly to prevent lumps from forming. Reduce heat so that the mixture simmers and cook, stirring continuously, to keep the polenta from burning. Continue until all of the liquid is absorbed and the cornmeal is tender, about 10 minutes. If the polenta absorbs all of the water before it is cooked, add up to 1 cup of additional water.

4. Add the butter and cheese to the polenta and stir to combine. To serve, ladle the polenta onto a plate and top with a large spoonful of the corn-and-tomatillo mixture. Garnish with the cilantro and additonal cheddar cheese.

INGREDIENTS:

FOR THE CORN, PEPPERS & TOMATILLOS

1   TABLESPOON OLIVE OIL, PLUS MORE AS NEEDED

1   ONION, DICED

1   CUP CORN KERNELS

½   SWEET PEPPER, STEMMED, SEEDED, AND DICED

1   SMALL JALAPEÑO PEPPER, DICED (OPTIONAL)

½   LB. TOMATILLOS, HUSKED, RINSED, AND DICED

1   TEASPOON CUMIN

1   TEASPOON KOSHER SALT

1   GARLIC CLOVE, MINCED

¼   CUP CHOPPED FRESH CILANTRO, FOR GARNISH

FOR THE CHEESY POLENTA

1   CUP WHOLE MILK

2   CUPS WATER, PLUS MORE AS NEEDED

½   TEASPOON KOSHER SALT

1   CUP MEDIUM-GRAIN CORNMEAL

2   TABLESPOONS UNSALTED BUTTER

1   CUP GRATED CHEDDAR CHEESE, PLUS MORE FOR GARNISH

GREEN SHAKSHUKA

YIELD: 4 SERVINGS / ACTIVE TIME: 20 MINUTES / TOTAL TIME: 30 MINUTES

Here, tomatillos add a tangy note to the mild spinach and eggs. The Tabasco™ is optional, but I highly recommend it for finishing this dish off.

1. Place the oil in a large sauté pan and warm over medium-high heat. When the oil starts to shimmer, add the onion and sauté until just starting to brown, about 5 minutes. Add the garlic and cook until fragrant, about 2 minutes. Add the tomatillos and cook until they have collapsed, about 5 minutes.

2. Add the spinach, coriander, and water and cook, breaking up the spinach with a fork, until the spinach is completely defrosted and blended with the tomatillos. Season with salt and pepper.

3. Evenly spread the mixture in the pan and then make 4 evenly spaced indentations in the mixture. Crack 1 egg into each indentation. Reduce heat to medium, cover the pan, and let the eggs cook until the whites are set, 3 to 5 minutes. Serve with Tabasco™, if desired.

INGREDIENTS:

1   TABLESPOON OLIVE OIL

1   ONION, DICED

2   GARLIC CLOVES, MINCED

½   LB. TOMATILLOS, HUSKED, RINSED, AND DICED

1   (12 OZ.) PACKAGE FROZEN SPINACH

1   TEASPOON CORIANDER

¼   CUP WATER

    SALT AND PEPPER, TO TASTE

4   EGGS

    TABASCO™, FOR SERVING (OPTIONAL)

BLT *with* BASIL MAYO

YIELD: 2 SERVINGS / ACTIVE TIME: 10 MINUTES / TOTAL TIME: 10 MINUTES

There are certain foods that I will only have when summer tomatoes are available, and a hearty BLT is one. It is the exquisite flavor of the tomato that makes the sandwich, but since I can't leave well enough alone, I make a basil mayonnaise to go with it.

1. To prepare the sandwiches, spread a layer of the Basil Mayo on a slice of bread. Top with 3 slices of bacon, a leaf or two of lettuce, and as much tomato as desired. Season with salt and pepper.

2. Slather another piece of bread with the Basil Mayo and place on top of the sandwich. Repeat to construct the second sandwich and serve.

BASIL MAYO

1. Place the mayonnaise and basil in a blender and puree until smooth. Serve immediately or refrigerate until chilled.

INGREDIENTS:

BASIL MAYO (SEE RECIPE)

4 SLICES BREAD

6 SLICES BACON, COOKED UNTIL CRISPY

4 LEAVES RED LEAF OR ROMAINE LETTUCE

2 RIPE TOMATOES, CUT INTO THICK SLICES

SALT AND PEPPER, TO TASTE

BASIL MAYO

½ CUP MAYONNAISE

½ CUP FRESH BASIL LEAVES

SPRING RISOTTO *with* WATERCRESS, FENNEL, OYSTER MUSHROOMS *&* CHIVE OIL

YIELD: **4 SERVINGS** / ACTIVE TIME: **45 MINUTES** / TOTAL TIME: **1 HOUR**

Watercress lends its bright green color to this light risotto, but its fire is mostly tamed by cooking. The fennel, shallots, and fontina are background notes that offer sweetness and body. If you like, you can substitute scallops or shrimp for the oyster mushrooms.

1. To prepare the chive oil, place the chives, oil, and salt in a blender and puree in smooth. Set aside.

2. To begin preparations for the risotto, place the watercress and water in a blender and puree until smooth. Set aside.

3. Place the stock in a small saucepan and bring to a simmer over medium heat. Turn off heat and leave the pan on the stove. Place the butter and half of the olive oil in a wide sauté pan and warm over medium heat. Add the shallot and fennel and sauté until they just start to brown, about 5 minutes. Add the rice and toast it slightly, stirring constantly.

4. Deglaze the pan with the wine and scrape up any browned bits from the bottom. When the wine has been fully absorbed by the rice, add the warmed stock a little at a time, stirring constantly to prevent sticking, and cook until the rice absorbs the stock. If the rice is still crunchy by the time you have used up all of the stock, add water in 1-tablespoon increments.

5. When the rice is a few minutes from being done—still a little too firm—add the watercress puree and continue to cook. When the rice is al dente, stir in the cheese, season with salt and pepper, and add the lemon juice. Stir to incorporate and turn off heat.

6. Place the remaining oil in a large sauté pan, warm over medium-high heat, and then add the mushrooms in one layer. Add a pinch of salt and cook until the mushrooms brown, about 5 minutes. Turn the mushrooms over, add another pinch of salt, and cook for another 4 minutes. Divide the risotto between 4 wide bowls and top with a few oyster mushrooms. Drizzle with the chive oil and top with extra fontina.

INGREDIENTS:

FOR THE CHIVE OIL

- ½ CUP CHOPPED FRESH CHIVES
- ½ CUP OLIVE OIL
- ½ TEASPOON KOSHER SALT

FOR THE RISOTTO

- 6 CUPS WATERCRESS
- ¼ CUP WATER, PLUS MORE AS NEEDED
- 2 CUPS CHICKEN OR VEGETABLE STOCK (SEE PAGES 748 AND 755, RESPECTIVELY, FOR HOMEMADE)
- 1 TABLESPOON UNSALTED BUTTER
- 2 TABLESPOONS OLIVE OIL
- 2 TABLESPOONS CHOPPED SHALLOT
- ½ CUP MINCED FENNEL
- 1 CUP ARBORIO RICE
- ¼ CUP DRY WHITE WINE
- ¼ CUP GRATED FONTINA CHEESE, PLUS MORE FOR GARNISH
- SALT AND PEPPER, TO TASTE
- 1 TABLESPOON FRESH LEMON JUICE, OR TO TASTE
- 4 OZ. OYSTER MUSHROOMS, SEPARATED AND TRIMMED

CURRIED EGG SALAD ON PUMPERNICKEL

YIELD: 1 SERVING / ACTIVE TIME: 15 MINUTES / TOTAL TIME: 15 MINUTES

There is nothing revolutionary about this recipe. But it never hurts to be reminded how good a simple thing can be. Omit the curry if you like.

1. Bring water to a boil in a small saucepan. Add the eggs and boil for 10 minutes. Remove from the pan and run under cold water. Peel the eggs and roughly chop them with a fork. Add the mayonnaise and curry powder, stir to combine, and then season with salt.

2. Place the egg salad on a slice of pumpernickel and then top with watercress and the remaining slice of bread.

INGREDIENTS:

2   EGGS

1   TABLESPOON MAYONNAISE

½   TEASPOON CURRY POWDER

    SALT, TO TASTE

2   SLICES PUMPERNICKEL BREAD

1   CUP WATERCRESS

RED KURI SQUASH
with COCONUT CURRY & SPINACH

YIELD: 4 SERVINGS / ACTIVE TIME: 20 MINUTES / TOTAL TIME: 30 MINUTES

The sweetness of winter squash takes on spice beautifully. In this dish, I crafted a classic coconut curry around cubes of Red Kuri squash and added a little spinach for color and an herbal note. If you can't find Red Kuri squash, you can use Blue Hubbard, Buttercup, or Kabocha.

1. Place the oil in a large sauté pan and warm over medium-high heat. When the oil starts to shimmer, add the squash and cook until it just starts to brown, about 5 minutes.

2. Add the onion, garlic, and ginger and cook until the onion starts to brown, about 5 minutes. Stir in the cumin, coriander, fennel seeds, cayenne (if using), turmeric, coconut milk, water, and tamarind paste and stir to combine. Allow the mixture to come back to a simmer, reduce heat to low, and cook until the squash is tender, about 10 minutes.

3. In the last 5 minutes of cooking, add the spinach and stir to incorporate. Season with salt and pepper and serve with a blend of white, brown, and wild rice.

INGREDIENTS:

3   TABLESPOONS OLIVE OIL

1½   LBS. RED KURI SQUASH, PEELED AND CUBED

1   ONION, DICED

2   GARLIC CLOVES, CHOPPED

1   TABLESPOON PEELED AND MINCED GINGER

1   TEASPOON CUMIN

1   TEASPOON CORIANDER

½   TEASPOON FENNEL SEEDS

     PINCH OF CAYENNE PEPPER (OPTIONAL)

½   TEASPOON TURMERIC

½   CUP COCONUT MILK

½   CUP WATER

1   TABLESPOON TAMARIND PASTE

2   CUPS PACKED BABY SPINACH

     SALT AND PEPPER, TO TASTE

     WHITE, BROWN, AND WILD RICE, FOR SERVING

LET'S TALK ABOUT FARMING

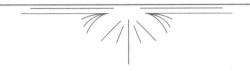

ORGANIC VS. CONVENTIONAL

Going to the produce aisle can be an exercise in existential angst. I stroll through the rows of veggies and see conventionally grown asparagus for $1.99/lb., but the next bin over has organic asparagus for $7/lb. I worry about chemicals on my asparagus but, good heavens, that is more than three times as expensive. Am I too cheap to buy the "better" vegetables for my family? How bad can the conventionally grown asparagus be? It looks the same. But what if I'm poisoning my kids with hidden chemicals that stunt their potential, and it was all because I didn't pay $5/lb. more to ensure their futures as completely healthy adults? What kind of mother am I if I don't get the absolute best for my children at every opportunity? But, sheesh, at $7/lb., does it come with its own butler pouring hollandaise over it?

If you have had such a debate with yourself, you are not alone. I was an organic farmer and even I have this conversation in my head. There are arguments for both bins of asparagus, but it helps to make your purchasing decisions when you are aware of the big picture. When I first started farming, there was no question that I would farm organically. The thought of spraying chemicals on the crops in the field seemed as disagreeable as sprinkling Ajax on my salad. And as I learned about the process of getting my crops certified as organic, I realized that growing vegetables organically is as much about treating my land well as it is about pesticides

and herbicides on the actual vegetables. Half of the questions on the application are about herbicides, fertilizer, and pesticides, but the other half is about how you have treated your farm. To be certified organic, you need to show that you have taken steps to ensure the water quality and soil health of your property. Did you rotate your crops and grow cover crops to reduce pest populations and improve tilth (the condition of soil that has been tilled)? Did you plant buffer zones to prevent runoff? I'm aware that most people choose organic produce because they are concerned about harmful chemicals on their plates, but you should be aware that 50 percent of organic farming is about maintaining a healthy ecosystem around those crops. When you buy organic produce, you are making an environmental choice as much as a choice for personal health.

The downside to organic farming is that it is a costlier way to go about agriculture. Because herbicides are not allowed, more labor is required to keep weeds at bay. Some crops can be cultivated mechanically, but hand weeding or hoeing is a necessity for most crops, and that takes time and labor. There are fewer pesticide options as well. You may be surprised to learn that organic farmers use pesticides at all. But they are a necessary evil. For organic farming they must be organically derived, sparingly used, and must break down into benign substances within a few days. A good

example of an organic pesticide is neem oil, which is derived from the seeds and fruit of the neem tree (*Azadirachta indica*). It is a broad-spectrum repellent that treats for many different kind of pests but does not harm mammals, birds, or bees. Its main ingredient, azadirachtin, breaks down within a few days. But neem oil is very expensive and often not as effective as conventional pesticides.

And then there's fertilizer. Organic farmers can only use organically derived fertilizers: think manure, compost, and commercial fertilizers that come from all-organic sources (i.e., bat guano, rock minerals). Procuring these organic materials is more expensive than the petroleum-based fertilizers of conventional farming.

There is also some debate about which method garners higher yields. Some reports show that organic farming can go toe-to-toe with conventional on yields in a drought year when the water-retaining properties of organically rich soil will sustain crops better. But many more reports show that conventional farming is more efficient and results in higher yields. And that means lower costs for the consumer.

There are other categories in the middle ground, two of which are "sustainably grown" and "low spray." There are some farmers who practice organic methods of growing but do not want to deal with the paperwork and expense of the certification process. They are not allowed to call themselves "organic" with-

out infringing on the organic label, so they often go with "sustainable." In all likelihood, they are identical to organic farms, but without the certification there are no guarantees. I know several farmers who dropped their organic certification because the hassle was not worth it to them. "All my customers are local, and they know I'm organic," said one. Others may find it impossible to grow the types of crops they want organically. For example, strawberries are very challenging to grow since fungi and the tarnished plant bug (TPB) are a relentless menace to them. The strawberry farmer may practice all of the organic methods of soil building and organic fertilizer, but when it comes to mold and TPB

they likely spray with conventional chemicals (though as sparingly as possible).

The low-spray method is pretty much what it sounds like; chemical applications are kept to a minimum. Many tree fruits, like apples and plums, are grown this way. Rather than a regimen of spraying at predetermined intervals, a farmer uses observation to decide whether or not to treat the crops. Some years the pests are not that bad, and a farmer can get away with minimal applications. Other years may be more challenging, and more aggressive treatments are necessary to keep the crop going. In my mind, "low spray" means "I'd rather not, but if you want this fruit at all, I'm going to have to spray it a little." I get it. In a really bad pest year, when all my natural methods had been exhausted and the bugs were still winning the battle, even I would think, *Organic-shmanic, I'm going to kill those $%^&*.* I didn't. But I wanted to.

A conventional farmer uses all means necessary to get the highest yields for their crops: abundant fertilizer, the most effective pesticides, and an herbicide that will knock back all the weeds. They can also use genetically modified (GMO) seeds, which means the plants have been genetically modified to resist a specific herbicide. When the farmer sprays the herbicide, all but the intended crop dies back, leaving no competition for nutrients and light, and a resultant big yield. The advantage of all this modern technology is that it has brought the cost of producing a whole lot of food way down. Organic farmers charge what they need to in order to sustain their business, but unfortunately it results in produce that is beyond the budget of many. Given there are those in our country who can barely afford any food, we have every incentive to make fresh (or frozen) vegetables as affordable as possible. Furthermore, and my organic peers may throw me out of the club for writing this, studies as to whether organically grown vegetables are nutritiously superior are inconclusive. While conventionally grown produce is more likely to have chemicals on it, its bone-strengthening,

skin-healing, immuno-boosting, all-around goodness is largely the same. There is an environmental cost to conventional farming that can also be economically detrimental in the long term, but it is hard to argue against making an inexpensive, nutrient-rich head of broccoli available to a family in a low-income area. We shouldn't have to choose between a healthy environment and affordable vegetables, but the debate on how to solve this issue would fill another book.

Though I chose to grow my crops organically, I would never throw shade at a conventional farmer. Farming is tough. Even with modern equipment, it is a physical job that requires one to deal with the elements every day, whether sleety rain or sweltering heat. A bad storm or a brief drought can ruin everything. New diseases and pests arrive every season. Tariffs and trade wars can upend your plans. Even if you have done everything right, there are myriad ways in which a whole year's worth of work can fail. In short, if you have control issues, you should not become a farmer. Conventional, sustainable, or organic, we all tackle these same challenges. Furthermore, I have never met a farmer of any kind that didn't care about his or her land or the quality of their crops and was not 100 percent passionate about what they do. It's just too much damn work to feel any other way about it.

HYBRID VS. GMO

Since Genetically Modified Organisms (GMOs) arrived, there have been advocates and detractors, and a great deal of conflicting information. As I mention in my explanation of conventional farming, GMO seeds have been genetically altered to express a certain type of behavior. In most cases, they are designed to withstand glyphosate-based herbicides such as Roundup™. The farmer can spray a whole area of crops and the weeds will die back, leaving the crop to thrive without competition. In some cases, a crop is genetically modified to resist or kill a

particular pest. Developers embed a gene that produces a type of bacteria that will kill or repel a specific bug that attacks the plant. The gene is harmful only to the bug and not to humans. Other types of genetically altered plants claim to have a higher yield or nutritional level.

Food is political, and GMOs are perhaps at the top of the list of most controversial topics within the politics of food. As with diets, one could find ample studies to back one's opinion, and given this is a cookbook meant to celebrate vegetables, not to explore agro-politics, I'm going to leave this topic alone. As I've stated, I was an organic farmer and chose not to mess around with genetically modified crops. On the other hand, I believe in science as a force for positive change. Life is complicated.

If there is one thing I can state categorically it is this: don't fear the hybrid. Though the word "hybrid" sounds science-y, the practice is as old as agriculture itself. Vegetables are cross-pollinated in order to produce offspring that will have superior traits: better flavor, disease resistance, a different color. Hybrids got a bad rap for a few decades because the trait most often selected was for storage and appearance, not flavor (see the now-maligned Red Delicious apple). But hybridizers have come back around to selecting for flavor, especially in areas like tomatoes and melons. With the proliferation of farmers markets, shipping is not every farmer's top priority, and seed catalogs are back to trumpeting taste in their descriptions.

Creating a hybrid takes time and patience. One could aim for certain traits with the selection of the parents, but you never know until the fruit emerges; consequently, it can take years to develop a single variety. We all are the beneficiaries of this hard work. Go to any decent market and you will see incredible diversity, making your dinner plate that much more enjoyable.

Heirlooms are open-pollinated varieties that have been around for 50 years or more.

These varieties often have been handed down for generations by gardeners who saved seeds from the best plants. Heirloom tomatoes get all of the attention because of their exquisite taste. Once you've tried a Brandywine tomato, still warm from the vine, you will understand what all of the fuss is about. But other heirlooms, such as dry beans and summer squash, should not be overlooked for their taste and diversity. Flip through the Vermont Bean Seed Company catalog and you will find almost 40 different types of dry beans in pink, red, stripes, black, caramel, and blue.

Heirlooms should certainly be grown and promoted, but there is a reason they do not dominate market shelves. Heirlooms are notorious for being disease-prone and having low yields. Though consumers may love the romance of eating a tomato with history, farmers have taken to grafting heirloom varieties onto rootstock that has more vigor in order to justify the space on their farm. When I first started farming, I was passionate about growing heirlooms whenever available, but after several years of disappointing crops, I started to appreciate hybrids. In the end, I grew a combination of the two, keeping the heirlooms that did well in my soil but selecting the hybrids that could stand up to my less-than-great northern Vermont conditions. My customers seemed very happy with my choices.

GROW IT YOURSELF

PLAN A FARM GARDEN NOW

APPENDIX

CANNING 101

CANNING 101

Proper canning allows you to preserve vegetables no matter the season. This time-honored tradition is simple, but it is important to follow each and every step. Once you get the hang of it, you will be canning everything in sight.

---

1. Bring a pot of water to a boil. Place the mason jars in the water for 15 to 20 minutes to sterilize them. Do not boil the mason jar lids, as this may prevent them from creating a proper seal when the time comes.

2. Bring water to a boil in the large canning pot.

3. Fill the sterilized mason jars with whatever you are canning. Place the lids on the jars and secure the bands tightly. Place the jars in the boiling water for 40 minutes.

4. Use the tongs to remove the jars from the boiling water and let them cool. As they are cooling, you should hear the classic "ping and pop" sound of the lids creating a seal.

5. After 4 to 6 hours, check the lids. There should be no give in them, and they should be suctioned onto the jars. Discard any lids and food that did not seal properly.

TOOLS:

  MASON JARS WITH LIDS
  AND BANDS

1 LARGE CANNING POT

1 PAIR OF CANNING TONGS

DESSERTS

Fear not, if you love both vegetables and desserts, you haven't been forgotten. Here are some sweet vegetable-based desserts that are sure to satisfy a sweet tooth.

LEAF LARD PIECRUST

YIELD: 2 (9-INCH) PIECRUSTS / ACTIVE TIME: 12 MINUTES / TOTAL TIME: 2 HOURS AND 15 MINUTES

Leaf lard is high-grade lard that comes from the fat surrounding a pig's kidneys. While it creates a delicious, flaky, melt-in-your-mouth crust, you can swap out the lard for butter for a vegetarian option.

1. Place the flour, sugar, and salt in a bowl and stir until combined.

2. Add the lard and butter and use a pastry blender to work them into the flour mixture. Work the mixture until it is a coarse meal, making sure to smooth out any large chunks.

3. Add the water and continue to work the mixture until it is a smooth dough. If it feels too dry, add more water in 1-teaspoon increments. Form the dough into a large ball and then cut it in half. Wrap each piece in plastic wrap and place in the refrigerator for 2 hours before using. The dough will keep in the refrigerator for up to 3 days. It also freezes very well and can be stored in a freezer for 3 to 6 months.

INGREDIENTS:

2½ CUPS ALL-PURPOSE FLOUR

1½ TABLESPOONS GRANULATED SUGAR

1 TEASPOON SALT

6 OZ. COLD LEAF LARD, CUBED

2 TABLESPOONS COLD UNSALTED BUTTER, CUBED

5 TABLESPOONS ICE-COLD WATER, PLUS MORE AS NEEDED

GLUTEN-FREE PIECRUST

YIELD: 9-INCH PIECRUST / ACTIVE TIME: 20 MINUTES / TOTAL TIME: 1 TO 24 HOURS

This piecrust works as a replacement for any of the crusts called for in this book and is a great recipe to have in your repertoire, even if you're not gluten-free yourself.

1. In a large bowl, combine the flour blend, sugar, xanthan gum, and salt. Add the butter and work it into the flour mixture with a pastry blender or your fingers to form a coarse meal that includes large chunks of butter.

2. In a small bowl, whisk the egg and lemon juice together briskly until the mixture is very foamy. Add to the dry mixture and stir until the dough holds together. If the dough isn't quite holding, add the cold water in 1-tablespoon increments until it does. Shape into a disk, wrap tightly in plastic wrap, and refrigerate for 30 minutes or overnight.

3. When ready to make the pie, take the dough out of the refrigerator and allow to rest at room temperature for about 10 minutes before rolling out on a lightly floured work surface.

INGREDIENTS:

- 1¼ CUP GLUTEN-FREE MULTI-PURPOSE FLOUR BLEND, PLUS MORE FOR DUSTING
- 1 TABLESPOON GRANULATED SUGAR
- ½ TEASPOON XANTHAN GUM
- ½ TEASPOON SALT
- 6 TABLESPOONS UNSALTED BUTTER, CHILLED AND CUT INTO SMALL PIECES
- 1 LARGE EGG
- 2 TEASPOONS FRESH LEMON JUICE
- 1-2 TABLESPOONS ICE COLD WATER

BLIND BAKING

This technique of baking a piecrust before filling it is also known as "blind baking." When working with a custard filling, as in a lemon meringue or pumpkin pie, baking the crust ahead of time has several advantages. It prevents pockets of steam from forming in the crust once it is filled, which can cause the crust to become puffy and uneven. Blind baking also keeps the bottom of the crust from becoming soggy and allows the edge of the pie to be sturdy, as opposed to saggy. Uncooked rice is the typical weight when blind baking a pie, though dried beans and weights designed specifically for the task can also be utilized.

GRAHAM CRACKER PIECRUST

YIELD: 9-INCH PIECRUST / ACTIVE TIME: 20 MINUTES / TOTAL TIME: 35 MINUTES

The versatility of this crust is what makes it really shine. The sweetness of the graham crackers accents sweet, savory, and citrus fillings, making it a great choice for almost any preparation.

1. Preheat the oven to 375°F. In a large bowl, add the graham cracker crumbs and sugar and stir to combine. Add the maple syrup and 5 tablespoons of the melted butter and stir until thoroughly combined.

2. Liberally grease a 9-inch pie plate with the remaining butter. Pour the dough into the pie plate and lightly press into shape. Line with tin foil and fill with uncooked rice. Bake for 10 to 12 minutes, until the crust is golden.

3. Remove from the oven, discard the rice, and allow the crust to cool before filling.

INGREDIENTS:

- 1½ CUP GRAHAM CRACKER CRUMBS
- 2 TABLESPOONS GRANULATED SUGAR
- 1 TABLESPOON MAPLE SYRUP
- 6 TABLESPOONS UNSALTED BUTTER, MELTED

PILAR'S SWEET CHEESE YUCA CAKE

YIELD: 8 SERVINGS / ACTIVE TIME: 10 MINUTES / TOTAL TIME: 1 HOUR

I confess I have very little experience baking with yuca, so I've called on a friend. Pilar is from Colombia and offered me this beloved family recipe.

1. Preheat the oven to 350°F. Place all of the ingredients in a large bowl and stir until combined.

2. Transfer the mixture to a cake pan that has been greased with nonstick cooking spray. Place in the oven and bake for 45 minutes, or until a knife inserted into the center of the cake comes out clean. Remove and let cool before serving.

INGREDIENTS:

2¾ CUPS FINELY GRATED RAW YUCA

3 CUPS GRATED MOZZARELLA CHEESE

1 CUP GRANULATED SUGAR

1 STICK UNSALTED BUTTER, MELTED

PINCH OF KOSHER SALT

2 LARGE EGGS

1 TEASPOON BAKING POWDER

PURE VANILLA EXTRACT, TO TASTE

SQUASH WHOOPIE PIES *with* GINGER CREAM

YIELD: 12 SERVINGS / ACTIVE TIME: 20 MINUTES / TOTAL TIME: 1 HOUR

The whoopie pie is an incredible dessert that, for whatever reason, remains largely within the boundaries of New England. It's typically made with chocolate, but these sweet treats are even more delicious using autumn squash.

1. Preheat the oven to 350°F. Sift the flour, cinnamon, ground ginger, cloves, nutmeg, baking soda, baking powder, and salt into a mixing bowl.

2. Place the brown sugar, maple syrup, pureed squash, egg, and vegetable oil in a separate mixing bowl and stir until combined. Sift the dry mixture into the squash mixture and stir until it has been incorporated.

3. Use an ice cream scoop to place dollops of the batter on a greased baking sheet. Make sure to leave plenty of space between the scoops. Place the sheet in the oven and bake until the cakes are golden brown, about 10 to 15 minutes. Remove and let cool.

4. While the squash cakes are cooling, place the remaining ingredients in a bowl and beat until combined and fluffy.

5. When the cakes have cooled completely, spread the filling on one of the cakes. Top with another cake and repeat until all of the cakes and filling have been used.

INGREDIENTS:

1⅓	CUPS ALL-PURPOSE FLOUR
1	TEASPOON CINNAMON
1	TEASPOON GROUND GINGER
¼	TEASPOON GROUND CLOVES
½	TEASPOON NUTMEG
½	TEASPOON BAKING SODA
½	TEASPOON BAKING POWDER
1	TEASPOON KOSHER SALT
1	CUP LIGHT BROWN SUGAR
2	TABLESPOONS MAPLE SYRUP
1	CUP PUREED BUTTERNUT OR ACORN SQUASH
1	EGG
1	CUP VEGETABLE OIL
1⅓	CUPS CONFECTIONERS' SUGAR
4	TABLESPOONS UNSALTED BUTTER
8	OZ. CREAM CHEESE, AT ROOM TEMPERATURE
2	TEASPOONS GRATED FRESH GINGER
½	TEASPOON PURE VANILLA EXTRACT

ROASTED PARSNIP ICE CREAM

YIELD: 6 SERVINGS / **ACTIVE TIME:** 20 MINUTES / **TOTAL TIME:** 14 TO 32 HOURS

While you may scoff at the idea of using root vegetables in ice cream, this delicious dessert not only helps reduce waste, it's a great way to use up the last parsnips of the season.

1. Place the cream, milk, roasted parsnip pieces, and salt in a saucepan and cook over medium heat until the mixture starts to bubble. Remove it from heat and allow the mixture to steep for 30 minutes to 1 hour.

2. Strain the mixture through a fine sieve, pressing down on the pieces of parsnip to remove as much liquid as possible. Place the liquid in a saucepan and bring to a simmer. Discard the pieces of parsnip.

3. Place the sugar and egg yolks in a bowl and whisk until combined.

4. Once the liquid is simmering, add a little bit of the milk-and-cream mixture to the egg-and-sugar mixture and whisk constantly. Add the milk-and-cream mixture in small increments until all of it has been incorporated, taking care not to cook the eggs.

5. Return the mixture to the saucepan and cook over low heat, stirring constantly, until it is thick enough to coat the back of a wooden spoon. Remove from heat and let cool. When cool, cover and transfer to the refrigerator for 6 to 24 hours.

6. When you are ready to make the ice cream, add the mixture to your ice cream maker and churn until the desired consistency has been achieved. Place the churned ice cream in the freezer for a minimum of 6 hours before serving.

INGREDIENTS:

1½ CUPS HEAVY CREAM

1½ CUPS WHOLE MILK

3-4 CUPS ROASTED PARSNIP TRIMMINGS (THE STUFF YOU TYPICALLY THROW AWAY)

PINCH OF SALT

⅔ CUP GRANULATED SUGAR

5 EGG YOLKS

CARROT CAKE *with*
MAPLE CREAM CHEESE FROSTING

YIELD: 8 TO 10 SERVINGS / ACTIVE TIME: 30 MINUTES / TOTAL TIME: 1 HOUR AND 30 MINUTES

I will always associate this cake with joy. The first time we reached 100 barrels of maple syrup, I made it to celebrate. There were about 14 of us, working our tails off in the woods and the sugarhouse, and a rich crowd-pleaser like this one was just the ticket. We now produce close to 800 barrels a year. We still high-five when we hit 100 barrels, but it is just a moment that passes, leaving us full of gratitude that the sugaring season is indeed underway.

1. Preheat the oven to 350°F. Grease two 9-inch round cake pans and then line with parchment.

2. Sift together the flour, baking powder, baking soda, salt, and cinnamon into a bowl.

3. In a separate bowl, mix the sugar and oil. Beat the eggs in one at a time, then fold in the carrots, pineapple, and then the nuts (if using).

4. Combine the flour mixture with the carrot mixture and stir until totally blended.

5. Divide the batter into the two pans and put in the oven. Bake for 30 to 45 minutes, or until a knife comes out clean when pierced in the middle. Let cool.

6. While the cake is baking, prepare the frosting by putting the cream cheese in a food processor with a blade or in a stand mixer with the paddle attachment. If you don't have either, use a hand held blender or good old elbow grease to cream the cheese.

7. Add the butter and continue to blend. When there are no visible signs of butter, add the remaining ingredients. Taste the frosting to see if it is to your liking. Add more maple syrup or, if you need to thicken it, add more confectioners' sugar to taste.

8. Remove one of the cooled cakes from the pan and place it on a wide plate or cake stand. Cover with frosting. Repeat with the second cake, placing it on top of the first. Frost the top and sides completely.

INGREDIENTS:

FOR THE CARROT CAKE

2   CUPS ALL-PURPOSE FLOUR

2   TEASPOONS BAKING POWDER

1½   TEASPOONS BAKING SODA

1   TEASPOON KOSHER SALT

2   TEASPOONS GROUND CINNAMON

1¾   CUPS GRANULATED SUGAR

1½   CUPS VEGETABLE OIL

4   EGGS

2   CUPS GRATED CARROT

1   CUP CANNED CRUSHED PINEAPPLE, DRAINED

½   CUP CHOPPED WALNUTS (OPTIONAL)

FOR THE FROSTING

1   LB. CREAM CHEESE, AT ROOM TEMPERATURE

1   STICK UNSALTED BUTTER, AT ROOM TEMPERATURE

½   CUP MAPLE SYRUP, PLUS MORE TO TASTE

1   CUP CONFECTIONERS' SUGAR, PLUS MORE AS NEEDED

1   TEASPOON VANILLA EXTRACT

STRAWBERRY RHUBARB PIE

YIELD: 6 TO 8 SERVINGS / ACTIVE TIME: 20 MINUTES / TOTAL TIME: 1 HOUR AND 20 MINUTES

The summer season just isn't the same without this classic combination of sweet and tart flavors.

1. Preheat the oven to 400°F and grease a 9-inch pie plate.

2. Place the strawberries, rhubarb, sugar, cornstarch, orange zest, and salt in a large mixing bowl and stir to combine. Set the mixture aside.

3. Place the piecrusts on a flour-dusted work surface and roll them out to fit the pie plate. Place one of the crusts into the pie plate, fill it with the strawberry-and-rhubarb mixture, and dot the mixture with the butter.

4. Cut the other crust into 1-inch-wide strips. Lay some of the strips over the pie and trim them so that they fit. To make a lattice crust, lift every other strip and fold them back so you can place another strip across those strips that remain flat. Lay the folded strips back down over the cross-strip. Fold back the strips that you laid the cross-strip on top of, and repeat until the lattice covers the surface of the pie.

5. Brush the lattice crust with the egg, taking care not to get any egg on the filling. Place the pie on a baking sheet, place it in the oven, and bake for 20 minutes. Reduce the temperature to 350°F and bake until the filling is bubbling and the crust is golden brown, about 40 minutes. Remove and let cool before serving.

INGREDIENTS:

2   PINTS STRAWBERRIES, HULLED AND HALVED

4   CUPS CHOPPED RHUBARB

1   CUP GRANULATED SUGAR

¼   CUP CORNSTARCH

    ZEST OF ½ ORANGE

    PINCH OF SALT

2   LEAF LARD PIECRUSTS (SEE PAGE 719), CHILLED

    ALL-PURPOSE FLOUR, FOR DUSTING

2   TABLESPOONS UNSALTED BUTTER

1   EGG, BEATEN

SWEET POTATO PIE

YIELD: 6 TO 8 SERVINGS / ACTIVE TIME: 25 MINUTES / TOTAL TIME: 1 HOUR AND 45 MINUTES

Depending on where you live, the idea of putting sweet potatoes in a pie may be unheard of, but this stunning pie is well worth the leap of faith.

1. Preheat the oven to 400°F. Place the mashed sweet potatoes, evaporated milk, eggs, granulated sugar, salt, cinnamon, ginger, and nutmeg in a bowl and stir until combined.

2. Place a cast-iron skillet over medium heat and melt the butter in it. Add the brown sugar and cook, stirring constantly, until the sugar is dissolved. Remove the pan from heat.

3. Place the piecrust dough on a flour-dusted work surface and roll it out to fit the skillet. Gently place it over the butter-and-brown sugar mixture, line with aluminum foil, and fill the crust with uncooked rice. Place the skillet in the oven and bake for 15 minutes.

4. Remove the skillet from the oven, discard the rice and foil, and briefly let the crust cool. Fill the crust with the sweet potato mixture and use a rubber spatula to evenly distribute. Place the pie in the oven and bake for 15 minutes.

5. Reduce heat to 325°F and bake until the filling is set and a toothpick inserted in the center comes out clean, about 30 minutes. Remove the skillet from the oven and let cool before serving.

INGREDIENTS:

2   CUPS COOKED AND
     MASHED SWEET POTATOES

1½   CUPS EVAPORATED MILK

2   EGGS, LIGHTLY BEATEN

½   CUP GRANULATED SUGAR

½   TEASPOON SALT

1   TEASPOON CINNAMON

¼   TEASPOON GROUND
     GINGER

¼   TEASPOON GROUND
     NUTMEG

1   STICK UNSALTED BUTTER

1   CUP LIGHT BROWN SUGAR

1   BALL OF LEAF LARD
     PIECRUST DOUGH (SEE
     PAGE 719)

     ALL-PURPOSE FLOUR, FOR
     DUSTING

PUMPKIN PIE

YIELD: 6 TO 8 SERVINGS / ACTIVE TIME: 15 MINUTES / TOTAL TIME: 1 HOUR AND 30 MINUTES

A Thanksgiving staple, using pumpkin puree instead of pumpkin pie filling allows you to control the sugar you use but is still more convenient than cutting into your own pumpkin.

1. Preheat the oven to 400°F. In a large bowl, combine the pumpkin puree, evaporated milk, eggs, sugar, salt, cinnamon, ginger, and nutmeg. Stir to combine thoroughly.

2. Working with the crust in the pie plate, fill it with the pumpkin mixture. Smooth the surface with a rubber spatula.

3. Put the pie in the oven and bake for 15 minutes. Reduce heat to 325°F and bake for an additional 30 to 45 minutes, until the filling is firm and a toothpick inserted in the middle comes out clean. Remove the pie from the oven and allow to cool before serving.

INGREDIENTS:

1   (14 OZ.) CAN PUMPKIN PUREE (NOT PUMPKIN PIE FILLING)

1   (12 OZ.) CAN EVAPORATED MILK

2   EGGS, LIGHTLY BEATEN

½   CUP GRANULATED SUGAR

½   TEASPOON SALT

1   TEASPOON CINNAMON

¼   TEASPOON GROUND GINGER

¼   TEASPOON GROUND NUTMEG

1   LEAF LARD PIECRUST (SEE PAGE 719), BLIND BAKED (SEE PAGE 723)

SPICY PUMPKIN PIE

YIELD: 6 TO 8 SERVINGS / **ACTIVE TIME:** 15 MINUTES / **TOTAL TIME:** 1 HOUR AND 30 MINUTES

The earthy flavor of pumpkin is just begging for a hint of spice. The addition of gingersnaps to the base of the crust really makes this dessert sing.

1. Preheat the oven to 375°F.

2. Place the brown sugar, eggs, and pumpkin puree in a mixing bowl and beat until the sugar begins to dissolve. Add spices, rum, salt, and the cream and beat until incorporated.

3. Cover the bottom of the blind-baked crust with gingersnaps.

4. Pour the pumpkin mixture over the gingersnaps and smooth the surface with a rubber spatula. Place in the oven and bake until the filling is set and a toothpick inserted into the center comes out clean, about 45 minutes. Remove and let cool completely before serving.

INGREDIENTS:

⅔ CUP PACKED DARK BROWN SUGAR

4 EGGS

1 (14 OZ.) CAN PUMPKIN PUREE (NOT PUMPKIN PIE FILLING)

1 TEASPOON CINNAMON

1 TEASPOON GROUND GINGER

½ TEASPOON GRATED NUTMEG

¼ TEASPOON GROUND CLOVES

CAYENNE PEPPER, TO TASTE

2 TABLESPOONS SPICED RUM

¼ TEASPOON SALT

1½ CUPS HEAVY CREAM

1 LEAF LARD PIECRUST (SEE PAGE 719), BLIND BAKED (SEE PAGE 723)

12 GINGERSNAPS

PUMPKIN CHEESECAKE

YIELD: 6 TO 8 SERVINGS / **ACTIVE TIME:** 20 MINUTES / **TOTAL TIME:** 24 HOURS

Cheesecake is already almost a meal in and of itself, and adding the heartiness of pumpkin elevates it to the next level. Be sure to serve this with hot apple cider.

1. Place the ground gingersnaps, brown sugar, and melted butter in a mixing bowl and stir to combine. Press the mixture into the bottom of a 9-inch springform pan.

2. Place the pumpkin puree and cream cheese in the mixing bowl of a stand mixer fitted with the paddle attachment. Beat on medium until light and fluffy. Add the allspice, nutmeg, cinnamon, and salt and beat until thoroughly combined.

3. With the mixer running, slowly add the condensed milk. When it has been incorporated, add the whipped cream and fold to incorporate it.

4. Pour the mixture into the crust. Place the cheesecake in the refrigerator overnight. Let sit at room temperature for 30 minutes before serving.

INGREDIENTS:

- 2 CUPS FINELY GROUND GINGERSNAPS
- ½ CUP BROWN SUGAR
- 3 TABLESPOONS UNSALTED BUTTER, MELTED
- 1 CUP CANNED PUMPKIN PUREE (NOT PUMPKIN PIE FILLING)
- 8 OZ. CREAM CHEESE, AT ROOM TEMPERATURE
- ½ TEASPOON ALLSPICE
- ½ TEASPOON GRATED NUTMEG
- 1 TEASPOON CINNAMON
- ½ TEASPOON SALT
- 1 (14 OZ.) CAN SWEETENED CONDENSED MILK
- 1 CUP WHIPPED CREAM (SEE PAGE 744 FOR HOMEMADE)

INDIAN PUDDING

YIELD: 8 SERVINGS / ACTIVE TIME: 10 MINUTES / TOTAL TIME: 9 TO 27 HOURS

This is a New England original, taking inspiration from the hasty pudding found in Britain. It got its start in the early 18th century, when colonists combined molasses and cornmeal (then referred to as "Indian flour") to make this comforting dessert.

1. Preheat the oven to 275°F and grease a square 8-inch baking dish.

2. Place the milk in a large saucepan and cook over medium-high heat until it comes to a boil. Remove the saucepan from heat and set aside.

3. Place all of the remaining ingredients, except for the eggs, butter, and whipped cream, in a mixing bowl and stir to combine. Whisk this mixture into the heated milk.

4. Place the saucepan over medium-low heat and cook, stirring constantly, until the mixture begins to thicken. Remove the saucepan from heat.

5. Crack the eggs into a bowl and beat with a whisk. Add ½ cup of the hot molasses-and-cornmeal mixture and whisk to combine. Continue whisking in ½-cup increments of the mixture until all of it has been incorporated. Add the butter and whisk until it has been incorporated.

6. Pour the mixture into the prepared baking dish. Place the dish in a pan of water, place in the oven, and bake until it is set, about 2 hours.

7. Remove from the oven and let cool. When cool, transfer to the refrigerator for 6 to 24 hours. Serve with the whipped cream.

INGREDIENTS:

3   CUPS WHOLE MILK

1   CUP HEAVY CREAM

½   CUP FLINT CORN (OR CORNMEAL)

½   CUP BLACKSTRAP MOLASSES

½   CUP LIGHT BROWN SUGAR

½   TEASPOON GROUND GINGER

½   TEASPOON NUTMEG

½   TEASPOON ALLSPICE

2   TEASPOONS CINNAMON

2   TEASPOONS SALT

5   EGGS

5   TABLESPOONS UNSALTED BUTTER

WHIPPED CREAM, FOR SERVING (SEE PAGE 744 FOR HOMEMADE)

WHIPPED CREAM

YIELD: 2 CUPS / ACTIVE TIME: 5 MINUTES / TOTAL TIME: 5 MINUTES

Light, fluffy, and satisfying, this topping goes perfectly on pies, cakes, and fresh bowls of fruit.

1. Place the cream and vanilla in a bowl and whisk until soft peaks begin to form. Be sure not to over mix, as this will result in butter.

2. Place in the refrigerator until ready to serve.

INGREDIENTS:

2 CUPS HEAVY CREAM

1 TEASPOON PURE VANILLA EXTRACT

BASIC RECIPES

STOCKS

Depending on dietary needs, ingredients on hand, and personal preference, it is always good to have solid stock recipes close by.

TIPS:
1. Stocks can stay in a freezer for up to six months.

2. This is a large recipe, which can easily be reduced to half or one-quarter the amount. However, as the same amount of time is required, it is always best to make a larger quantity and save some for the future.

VEAL, BEEF, OR LAMB STOCK

YIELD: 6 QUARTS / ACTIVE TIME: 30 MINUTES / TOTAL TIME: 6 TO 7 HOURS

Veal bones make a smoother, lighter stock than pure beef bones. However, beef bones are a more readily available (and cheaper) option. If you are making a lamb stock, try to use half beef or veal bones and half lamb bones, as lamb bones provide a pungent, often overpowering flavor.

1. Preheat oven to 350°F.

2. Lay the bones on a flat baking tray, place in the oven, and cook for 30 to 45 minutes, until they are golden brown. Remove and set aside.

3. Meanwhile, in a large stockpot, add the oil and warm over low heat. Add the vegetables and cook until any additional moisture has evaporated. This allows the flavor of the vegetables to become concentrated.

4. Add the water to the stockpot. Add the bones, aromatics, peppercorns, salt, and tomato paste to the stockpot, raise heat to high, and bring to a boil.

5. Reduce heat so that the stock simmers and cook for a minimum of 2 hours. Skim fat and impurities from the top as the stock cooks. Cook until the desired flavor is achieved, around 4 to 5 hours.

6. When the stock is finished cooking, strain through a fine strainer or cheesecloth. Place the stock in the refrigerator to chill.

7. Once cool, skim the fat layer from the top and discard. Use immediately, refrigerate, or freeze.

INGREDIENTS:

- 10 LBS. VEAL, BEEF, OR LAMB BONES
- ½ CUP VEGETABLE OIL
- 1 LEEK, TRIMMED AND CAREFULLY WASHED, CUT INTO 1-INCH PIECES
- 1 LARGE YELLOW ONION, UNPEELED, ROOT CLEANED, CUT INTO 1-INCH PIECES
- 2 LARGE CARROTS, PEELED AND CUT INTO 1-INCH PIECES
- 1 CELERY STALK WITH LEAVES, CUT INTO 1-INCH PIECES
- 10 QUARTS WATER
- 8 FRESH SPRIGS PARSLEY
- 5 FRESH SPRIGS THYME
- 2 BAY LEAVES
- 1 TEASPOON PEPPERCORNS
- 1 TEASPOON SALT
- 1 CUP TOMATO PASTE

CHICKEN STOCK

YIELD: 6 QUARTS / ACTIVE TIME: 20 MINUTES / TOTAL TIME: 6 TO 7 HOURS

A good homemade chicken stock should be good enough to eat on its own. As with most stocks, the longer they cook, the more flavorful they become, so feel free to increase the cooking time. This recipe will work with most poultry.

1. Preheat the oven to 350°F.

2. Lay the bones on a flat baking tray, place in the oven, and cook for 30 to 45 minutes, until they are golden brown. Remove and set aside.

3. Meanwhile, in a large stockpot, add the oil and warm over low heat. Add the vegetables and cook until any additional moisture has evaporated. This allows the flavor of the vegetables to become concentrated.

4. Add the water to the stockpot. Add the chicken carcasses and/or stewing pieces, the aromatics, the peppercorns, and the salt to the stockpot, raise heat to high, and bring to a boil.

5. Reduce heat so that the stock simmers and cook for a minimum of 2 hours. Skim fat and impurities from the top as the stock cooks. Cook until the desired flavor is achieved, around 4 to 5 hours.

6. When the stock is finished cooking, strain through a fine strainer or cheesecloth. Place stock in the refrigerator to chill.

7. Once cool, skim the fat layer from the top and discard. Use immediately, refrigerate, or freeze.

INGREDIENTS:

10 LBS. CHICKEN CARCASSES AND/OR STEWING CHICKEN PIECES

½ CUP VEGETABLE OIL

1 LEEK, TRIMMED AND CAREFULLY WASHED, CUT INTO 1-INCH PIECES

1 LARGE YELLOW ONION, UNPEELED, ROOT CLEANED, CUT INTO 1-INCH PIECES

2 LARGE CARROTS, CUT INTO 1-INCH PIECES

1 CELERY STALK WITH LEAVES, CUT INTO 1-INCH PIECES

10 QUARTS WATER

8 FRESH SPRIGS PARSLEY

5 FRESH SPRIGS THYME

2 BAY LEAVES

1 TEASPOON PEPPERCORNS

1 TEASPOON SALT

DASHI STOCK

Kombu is an edible dried kelp, while bonito flakes come from dried and fermented fish. Unlike the other stocks provided here, this stock tends to become bitter if cooked at too high a temperature, making it a quick and easy stock to make. While it can be frozen for later, with such a short cooking time it's well worth the effort to make it fresh.

1. In a medium saucepan, add the water and the kombu. Soak for 20 minutes, remove the kombu, and score gently with a knife.

2. Return the kombu to the saucepan and bring to a boil.

3. Remove the kombu as soon as the water boils, so that the stock doesn't become bitter.

4. Add the bonito flakes and return to a boil. Turn off heat and let stand.

5. Strain through a fine sieve and chill in the refrigerator.

INGREDIENTS:

8   CUPS COLD WATER

2   OZ. KOMBU

1   CUP BONITO FLAKES

FISH STOCK

YIELD: 6 QUARTS / ACTIVE TIME: 20 MINUTES / TOTAL TIME: 3 HOURS AND 30 MINUTES

White fish works best for this recipe, as other types of fish tend to add extra oil to the stock and overpower the delicate balance of flavors. However, if you're making a thickened or creamed soup, you can stray from that recommendation, as salmon stock is divine in those types of dishes.

1. In a large stockpot, add the oil and warm over low heat. Add the vegetables and cook until any additional moisture has evaporated. This will allow the flavor of the vegetables to become concentrated.

2. Add the whitefish bodies, the aromatics, the peppercorns, the salt, and the water to the pot.

3. Raise heat to high and bring to a boil. Reduce heat so that the stock simmers and cook for a minimum of 2 hours. Skim fat and impurities from the top as the stock cooks. As for when to stop cooking the stock, let the flavor be the judge, typcally 2 to 3 hours total.

4. When the stock is finished cooking, strain through a fine strainer or cheesecloth. Place the stock in the refrigerator to chill.

5. Once cool, skim the fat layer from the top and discard. Use immediately, refrigerate, or freeze.

INGREDIENTS:

½ CUP VEGETABLE OIL

1 LEEK, TRIMMED AND CAREFULLY WASHED, CUT INTO 1-INCH PIECES

1 LARGE YELLOW ONION, UNPEELED, ROOT CLEANED, CUT INTO 1-INCH PIECES

2 LARGE CARROTS, CUT INTO 1-INCH PIECES

1 CELERY STALK WITH LEAVES, CUT INTO 1-INCH PIECES

10 LBS. WHITEFISH BODIES

8 FRESH SPRIGS PARSLEY

5 FRESH SPRIGS THYME

2 BAY LEAVES

1 TEASPOON PEPPERCORNS

1 TEASPOON SALT

10 QUARTS WATER

VEGETABLE STOCK

YIELD: 6 CUPS / ACTIVE TIME: 20 MINUTES / TOTAL TIME: 3 HOURS

This stock is an excellent way to use up leftover vegetable trimmings you're loath to throw away. However, it's best to avoid starches like potatoes and colorful vegetables like beets, as these will make the stock cloudy or add an unwanted tint. This stock is an ideal replacement for any of the meat stocks in this book.

1. In a large stockpot, add the oil and the vegetables and cook over low heat until any additional moisture has evaporated. This will allow the flavor of the vegetables to become concentrated.

2. Add the aromatics, water, peppercorns, and salt. Raise heat to high and bring to a boil. Reduce heat so that the soup simmers and cook for 2 hours. Skim fat and impurities from the top as the stock cooks.

3. When the stock is finished cooking, strain through a fine strainer or cheesecloth. Place the stock in the refrigerator to chill.

4. Once cool, skim the fat layer from the top and discard. Use immediately, refrigerate, or freeze.

INGREDIENTS:

2   TABLESPOONS VEGETABLE OIL

2   LARGE LEEKS, TRIMMED AND CAREFULLY WASHED

2   LARGE CARROTS, PEELED AND SLICED

2   CELERY STALKS, SLICED

2   LARGE ONIONS, SLICED

3   GARLIC CLOVES, UNPEELED AND SMASHED

2   FRESH SPRIGS PARSLEY

2   FRESH SPRIGS THYME

1   BAY LEAF

8   CUPS WATER

½   TEASPOON BLACK PEPPERCORNS

    SALT, TO TASTE

MUSHROOM STOCK

YIELD: 6 CUPS / ACTIVE TIME: 20 MINUTES / TOTAL TIME: 3 TO 4 HOURS

You can use any mushroom you have on hand in this stock, so feel free to tailor your choice to the dish you have in mind. The trick to a great mushroom stock is to cook down the mushrooms beforehand to reduce their liquid. This cuts down on cooking time and helps concentrate the flavors.

1. In a large stockpot, add the oil and mushrooms and cook over low heat for 30 to 40 minutes. The longer you cook the mushrooms, the better.

2. Add the onion, garlic, bay leaves, peppercorns, and thyme and cook for 5 minutes.

3. Add the wine, cook for 5 minutes, and then add the water.

4. Bring to a boil, reduce heat so that the stock simmers, and cook for 2 to 3 hours, until you are pleased with the taste.

INGREDIENTS:

2 TABLESPOONS VEGETABLE OIL

3 LBS. MUSHROOMS

1 ONION, CHOPPED

1 GARLIC, MINCED

2 BAY LEAVES

1 TABLESPOON BLACK PEPPERCORNS

2 FRESH SPRIGS THYME

1 CUP WHITE WINE

8 CUPS WATER

PASTAS

Store-bought pasta is easy, but making your own is much tastier, and fun besides. If you have the time, be sure to include fresh pastas and noodles in the myriad recipes that call for pasta in this book. There are plenty of variations to choose from, depending on what you're cooking.

WHOLE WHEAT PASTA DOUGH

YIELD: 1¾ LBS. / ACTIVE TIME: 1 HOUR / TOTAL TIME: 2 TO 3 HOURS

Whether you're looking for healthier pasta alternatives or are a fan of chewier pastas like linguine, whole wheat pasta is an excellent conduit for thick, creamy sauces.

1. On a flat work surface, combine the flour and salt and form it into a mountain-like mound. Create a well in the center, then add the egg yolks, oil, and the 2 tablespoons of water. Using a fork or your fingertips, gradually start pulling the flour into the pool of egg, beginning with the flour at the inner rim of the well. Continue to gradually add flour until the dough starts holding together in a single floury mass, adding more water—1 tablespoon at a time—if the mixture is too dry to stick together. Once the dough feels firm and dry and can form a craggy-looking ball, it is time to start kneading.

2. Begin by working the remaining flour on the work surface into the ball of dough. Using the heel of your hand, push the ball of dough away from you in a downward motion. Turn the dough 45 degrees each time you repeat this motion, as doing so incorporates the flour more evenly. The dough should have a smooth, elastic texture. If the dough still feels wet, tacky, or sticky, dust it with flour and continue kneading. If it feels too dry and is not completely sticking together, wet your hands with water and continue kneading. Wet your hands as many times as you need in order to help the dough shape into a ball. Knead for 8 to 10 minutes to create a dough that is smooth and springy and to eliminate any air bubbles and bits of unincorporated flour in the dough. The dough has been sufficiently kneaded when it is very smooth and gently pulls back into place when stretched.

3. Wrap the ball of dough tightly in plastic wrap and let rest for at least 1 hour and up to 2 hours. If using within a few hours, leave it out on the kitchen counter; otherwise, refrigerate it (it will keep for up to 3 days). If refrigerated, the dough may experience some discoloration, but it won't affect the flavor.

4. Cut the dough into four even pieces. Set one piece on a smooth work surface and wrap up the rest in plastic wrap to prevent drying. Shape the dough into a ball, place it on the work surface, and, with the palm of your hand, push down on it so that it looks like a thick pita. Using a rolling pin, roll the dough to ½ inch thick. Try as much as possible to keep the thickness and width of the dough "patty" even, as it will help the dough fit through the pasta maker more easily.

INGREDIENTS:

4   CUPS FINELY GROUND WHOLE WHEAT FLOUR, PLUS MORE AS NEEDED

1½   TEASPOONS SALT

4   LARGE EGG YOLKS

1   TABLESPOON OLIVE OIL

2   TABLESPOONS WATER, PLUS MORE AS NEEDED

ALL-YOLK PASTA DOUGH

YIELD: ¾ LB. / ACTIVE TIME: 1 HOUR / TOTAL TIME: 2 TO 3 HOURS

The use of only egg yolks produces a rich, golden dough that creates tender pasta. It is perfect for thin, fragile, or small, filled pastas.

1. On a flat work surface, form the flours into a mound. Create a well in the center, then add the egg yolks and the 2 tablespoons of water. Using a fork or your fingertips, gradually start pulling the flour into the pool of egg, beginning with the flour at the inner rim of the well. Continue to gradually add flour until the dough starts holding together in a single floury mass, adding more water—1 tablespoon at a time—if the mixture is too dry to stick together. Once the dough feels firm and dry and can form a craggy-looking ball, it is time to start kneading.

2. Begin by working the remaining flour on the work surface into the ball of dough. Using the heel of your hand, push the ball of dough away from you in a downward motion. Turn the dough 45 degrees each time you repeat this motion, as doing so incorporates the flour more evenly. The dough should have a smooth, elastic texture. If the dough still feels wet, tacky, or sticky, dust it with flour and continue kneading. If it feels too dry and is not completely sticking together, wet your hands with water and continue kneading. Wet your hands as many times as you need in order to help the dough shape into a ball. Knead for 8 to 10 minutes to create a dough that is smooth and springy and to eliminate any air bubbles and bits of unincorporated flour in the dough. The dough has been sufficiently kneaded when it is very smooth and gently pulls back into place when stretched.

3. Wrap the ball of dough tightly in plastic wrap and let rest for at least 1 hour and up to 2 hours. If using within a few hours, leave it out on the kitchen counter; otherwise, refrigerate it (it will keep for up to 3 days). If refrigerated, the dough may experience some discoloration, but it won't affect the flavor).

4. Cut the dough into four even pieces. Set one piece on a smooth work surface and wrap up the rest in plastic wrap to prevent drying. Shape the dough into a ball, place it on the work surface, and, with the palm of your hand, push down on it so that it looks like a thick pita. Using a rolling pin, roll the dough to ½ inch thick. Try as much as possible to keep the thickness and width of the dough "patty" even, as it will help the dough fit through the pasta maker more easily.

TIP: This dough is suitable for popular noodles such as linguine and spaghetti.

INGREDIENTS:

- 1½ CUPS ALL-PURPOSE FLOUR
- ⅓ CUP FINELY MILLED "00" FLOUR, PLUS MORE AS NEEDED
- 8 LARGE EGG YOLKS
- 2 TABLESPOONS LUKEWARM WATER (90°F), PLUS MORE AS NEEDED

THREE-EGG BASIC PASTA DOUGH

YIELD: **ABOUT 1 LB.** / **ACTIVE TIME:** 1 HOUR / **TOTAL TIME:** 2 TO 3 HOURS

This simple, delicious pasta recipe is sure to become your go-to.

1. On a flat work surface, form the flour into a mound. Create a well in the center, then add the eggs, egg yolk, and the 2 tablespoons of water. Using a fork or your fingertips, gradually start pulling the flour into the pool of egg, beginning with the flour at the inner rim of the well. Continue to gradually add flour until the dough starts holding together in a single floury mass, adding more water—1 tablespoon at a time—if the mixture is too dry to stick together. Once the dough feels firm and dry and can form a craggy-looking ball, it is time to start kneading.

2. Begin by working the remaining flour on the work surface into the ball of dough. Using the heel of your hand, push the ball of dough away from you in a downward motion. Turn the dough 45 degrees each time you repeat this motion, as doing so incorporates the flour more evenly. The dough should have a smooth, elastic texture. If the dough still feels wet, tacky, or sticky, dust it with flour and continue kneading. If it feels too dry and is not completely sticking together, wet your hands with water and continue kneading. Wet your hands as many times as you need in order to help the dough shape into a ball. Knead for 8 to 10 minutes to create a dough that is smooth and springy, and to eliminate any air bubbles and bits of unincorporated flour in the dough. The dough has been sufficiently kneaded when it is very smooth and gently pulls back into place when stretched.

3. Wrap the ball of dough tightly in plastic wrap and let rest for at least 1 hour and up to 2 hours. If using within a few hours, leave it out on the kitchen counter, otherwise refrigerate it (it will keep for up to 3 days). If refrigerated, the dough may experience some discoloration (but it won't affect the flavor at all).

4. Cut the dough into four even pieces. Set one piece on a smooth work surface and wrap up the rest in plastic wrap to prevent drying. Shape the dough into a ball, place it on the work surface, and, with the palm of your hand, push down on it so that it looks like a thick pita. Using a rolling pin, roll the dough to ½ inch thick. Try as much as possible to keep the thickness and width of the dough "patty" even, as it will help the dough fit through the pasta maker more easily.

TIP: This dough is suitable for popular noodles such as fettuccine, pappardelle, and tagliatelle.

INGREDIENTS:

2¾ CUPS ALL-PURPOSE FLOUR, PLUS MORE FOR DUSTING

3 LARGE EGGS

1 EGG YOLK

2 TABLESPOONS LUKEWARM WATER (90°F), PLUS MORE AS NEEDED

FARFALLE

YIELD: ¾ LB. PASTA / ACTIVE TIME: 45 MINUTES / TOTAL TIME: 1 TO 3 HOURS

*F*arfalle means "butterfly" in Italian, and these lighter-than-air pasta shapes are well worth their elegant name. They work well with tomato- or cream-based sauces, but feel free to experiment with your favorites.

1. Prepare the dough as directed, rolling the dough to the second-thinnest setting (generally notch 4) for pasta sheets that are about ⅛ inch thick. Lay the pasta sheets on lightly floured parchment lined baking sheets and cover loosely with plastic wrap. Work quickly to keep the pasta sheets from drying out, which makes it harder for the pasta to stick together.

2. Working with one pasta sheet at a time, place it on a lightly floured work surface and trim both ends to create a rectangle. Using a pastry cutter, cut the pasta sheet lengthwise into 1- to 1¼-inch-wide ribbons. Carefully separate the ribbons from each other, then, using a ridged pastry cutter, cut the ribbons into 2-inch pieces. To form the butterfly shape, place the index finger of your nondominant hand on the center of the piece of pasta. Then place the thumb and index finger of your dominant hand on the sides of the rectangle—right in the middle—and pinch the dough together to create a butterfly shape. Firmly pinch the center again to help it hold its shape. Leave the ruffled ends of the farfalle untouched. Repeat with all the pasta sheets.

3. Set the farfalle on lightly floured parchment-lined baking sheets so they are not touching. Allow them to air-dry for at least 30 minutes and up to 3 hours, and then cook. Alternatively, you can place them, once air-dried, in a bowl, cover with a kitchen towel, and refrigerate for up to 3 days. Or freeze on the baking sheets, transfer to freezer bags, and store in the freezer for up to 2 months. Do not thaw them prior to cooking (they will become mushy) and add an extra minute or so to their cooking time.

4. To cook the farfalle, bring a large pot of salted water to a boil. Add the farfalle and cook until the pasta is tender but still chewy, 2 to 3 minutes. Drain and serve with the sauce of your choice.

INGREDIENTS:

ALL-YOLK PASTA DOUGH
(SEE PAGE 760)

SEMOLINA FLOUR, FOR
DUSTING

SALT, TO TASTE

FAZZOLETTI

YIELD: ABOUT 1 LB. / ACTIVE TIME: 30 MINUTES / TOTAL TIME: 1 HOUR AND 30 MINUTES

These thin, square or rectangular pasta shapes resemble handkerchiefs, which is where they get their name. Don't worry about making perfect squares; they taste just as good when uneven.

1. Prepare the dough as directed, rolling the dough to the thinnest setting (generally notch 5) for pasta sheets that are about $\frac{1}{16}$ inch thick. Lay the pasta sheets on lightly floured parchment-lined baking sheets and let them air-dry for 15 minutes.

2. Cut each pasta sheet into as many 2½-inch squares or 1½ × 2½-inch rectangles as possible. Set them on lightly floured parchment-covered baking sheets so they are not touching. Gather any scraps together into a ball, put it through the pasta maker to create additional pasta sheets, and cut those as well. Allow them to air-dry for 1 hour, turning them over once halfway through, and then cook. Alternatively, you can place them, once air-dried, in a bowl, cover with a kitchen towel, and refrigerate for up to 3 days.

3. To cook the fazzoletti, cook for about 1 minute in a pot of boiling, salted water, until they are tender but still chewy.

INGREDIENTS:

THREE-EGG BASIC PASTA DOUGH (SEE PAGE 761)

SEMOLINA FLOUR, FOR DUSTING

SALT, TO TASTE

GARGANELLI

YIELD: 1½ LBS. / ACTIVE TIME: 1 HOUR AND 30 MINUTES / TOTAL TIME: 4 HOURS AND 30 MINUTES

This Bolognese pasta requires a delicate touch and a bit of patience, but once you get the hang of rolling the squares around the chopstick, you're sure to want it for every meal.

1. Combine all of the ingredients and prepare the dough as directed on page 760. Then use a pasta maker to roll the dough to the second-thinnest setting (generally notch 4) for pasta sheets that are about ⅛ inch thick. Lay the pasta sheets on flour-dusted, parchment-lined baking sheets and cover them loosely with plastic wrap.

2. Working with one pasta sheet at a time, lightly dust it with flour. Cut it into 1½-inch-wide strips and then cut the strips into 1½-inch squares. Repeat with the remaining pasta sheets. Cover the squares loosely with plastic wrap. Gather any scraps together into a ball, put it through the pasta maker to create additional pasta sheets, and cut those as well.

3. To make each garganello, place one square of pasta dough on a lightly floured work surface with one of the corners pointing toward you. Using a chopstick, gently roll the square of pasta around the chopstick, starting from the corner closest to you, until a tube forms. Once completely rolled, press down slightly as you seal the ends together, then carefully slide the pasta tube off the chopstick and lightly dust with flour. Set them on flour-dusted, parchment-lined baking sheets and allow them to air-dry for 1 hour, turning them over halfway through.

4. To cook the garganelli, cook for 2 to 3 minutes in a pot of boiling, salted water, until they are tender but still chewy.

INGREDIENTS:

2¼ CUPS SEMOLINA FLOUR, PLUS MORE FOR DUSTING

1½ TEASPOONS SALT, PLUS MORE FOR THE PASTA WATER

3 LARGE EGGS

2 TABLESPOONS OLIVE OIL

2 TABLESPOONS WATER

NODI

YIELD: ABOUT 1 LB. / ACTIVE TIME: 1 HOUR AND 30 MINUTES / TOTAL TIME: 3 TO 4 HOURS

This gondola-inspired pasta is formed by creating a knot in the center of a thin noodle.

1. Put the flour, salt, and fennel seeds in a large bowl and add the water. Begin mixing with a fork until the mixture starts to roughly stick together and look coarse. Gather it together with your hands and transfer it to a lightly floured work surface.

2. Using the heel of your hand, push the ball of dough away from you in a downward motion. Turn the dough 45 degrees each time you repeat this motion, as doing so incorporates the flour more evenly. If the dough feels too dry, wet your hands as many times as you need in order to help shape the dough into a ball. Knead for 10 minutes.

3. Cover the dough tightly with plastic wrap to keep it from drying out and let rest for at least 1 hour, but 2 hours is even better. If using within a few hours, leave out on the kitchen counter. Otherwise, put it in the refrigerator, where it will keep for up to 3 days.

4. Between the palms of your hands or on a lightly floured work surface, roll the dough into a 2-inch-thick log and cut it across into 18 rounds of even thickness (the easiest way to do this is to cut the roll in half and continue cutting each piece in half until you have 18 pieces). Cover all the pieces but the one you are working with to keep them from drying out.

5. With the palms of your hands, roll the piece of dough left out into a long rope ⅛ inch thick. Now make the knots. Starting on one end of the rope, tie a simple knot, gently pull on both ends to slightly tighten the knot, then cut the knot off the rope, leaving a tail on each side of about ⅜-inch long. Keep making and cutting off knots in this manner until you use up all of the rope. Repeat with the remaining pieces of dough. Set the finished knots on lightly floured, parchment-lined baking sheets so they are not touching. Allow them to air-dry for 2 hours, turning them over once halfway through, and then cook. Alternatively, you can place them, once air-dried, in a bowl, cover with a kitchen towel, and refrigerate for up to 3 days.

6. To cook the nodi, place in a large pot of boiling, salted water for 2 to 3 minutes, until they are tender but still firm.

INGREDIENTS:

1¾ CUPS SEMOLINA FLOUR, PLUS MORE FOR DUSTING

1   TEASPOON SALT, PLUS MORE FOR THE PASTA WATER

½   TEASPOON FENNEL SEEDS, FINELY GROUND

⅔   CUP WARM WATER

ORECCHIETTE

YIELD: ABOUT 1 LB. / ACTIVE TIME: 1 HOUR AND 30 MINUTES / TOTAL TIME: 4 HOURS

*O*recchiette means "little ears" and refers to this pasta's flattened shape. Orecchiette provide an interesting texture contrast when cooked, as the center is soft while the outer edge is just the slightest bit chewy.

1. Combine the flour and salt in a large bowl. Add the water a little at a time while mixing with a fork. Continue mixing the dough until it starts holding together in a single floury mass. If it is still too dry to stick together, add more water, 1 teaspoon at a time, until it does. Work the dough with your hands until it feels firm and dry and can be formed into a craggy-looking ball.

2. Transfer the dough to a lightly floured work surface and knead it for 10 minutes. Because it is made with semolina flour, the dough can be quite stiff and hard. You can also mix and knead this in a stand mixer; don't try it with a handheld mixer—the dough is too stiff and could burn the motor out. Using the heel of your hand, push the ball of dough away from you in a downward motion. Turn the dough 45 degrees each time you repeat this motion, as doing so incorporates the flour more evenly. Wet your hands as needed if the dough is too sticky. After 10 minutes of kneading, the dough will only be slightly softer (most of the softening is going to occur when the dough rests, which is when the gluten network within the dough will relax). Shape into a ball, cover tightly with plastic wrap, and let rest in the refrigerator for at least 2 hours and up to 2 days.

3. Cut the dough into four equal sections. Take one dough section and shape it into an oval with your hands. Cover the remaining sections with plastic wrap to prevent it from drying out. Place on a lightly floured work surface and, with the palms of your hands, roll it against the surface until it becomes a long ½-inch-thick rope. Using a sharp paring knife, cut the rope into ¼-inch discs, lightly dusting with semolina flour so they don't stick together.

4. To form the orecchiette, place a disc on the work surface. Stick your thumb in flour, place it on top of the disc, and, applying a little pressure, drag your thumb, and the accompanying dough, across to create an ear-like shape. Flour your thumb before making each orecchiette for best results. Lightly dust the orecchiette with flour and set them on lightly floured, parchment-covered baking sheets so they are not touching. Allow them to air-dry for 1 hour, turning them over once halfway through, and then cook. Alternatively, you can place them, once air-dried, in a bowl, cover with a kitchen towel, and refrigerate for up to 3 days.

5. To cook the orecchiette, place in a large pot of boiling, salted water until they are tender but still chewy, 3 to 4 minutes.

INGREDIENTS:

2 CUPS SEMOLINA FLOUR, PLUS MORE FOR DUSTING

1 TEASPOON SALT, PLUS MORE FOR THE PASTA WATER

¾ CUP WATER, PLUS MORE AS NEEDED

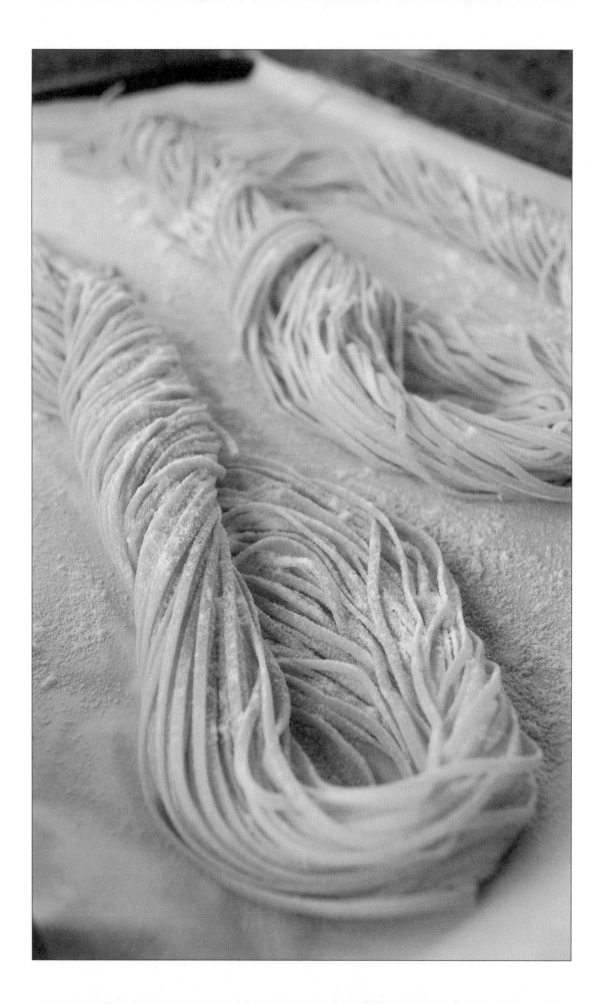

RIBBON PASTA

YIELD: ABOUT 1 LB. / ACTIVE TIME: 20 MINUTES / TOTAL TIME: 1 HOUR

Ribbon pasta includes things like pappardelle, tagliatelle, and the classic fettuccine, and it is one of the easiest pasta types to make on your own. With a little practice, you can have these churned out in as little as a half hour—so long as you don't mind using a little elbow grease.

1. Prepare the dough as directed, rolling the dough to the second thinnest setting (generally notch 4) or thinnest setting (generally notch 5 or 6) to form pasta sheets that are, respectively, ⅛ or 1/16 inch thick. Lay the pasta sheets on lightly floured, parchment-lined baking sheets. Let the sheets air-dry for 15 minutes, turning them over halfway through (doing this will make them easier to cut).

2. Lightly flour the surface of a pasta sheet and gently roll it up, starting from a short end, to create a pasta roll. Use a very sharp knife to gently slice the roll across to your preferred width. Cut into 1- to 1½-inch-wide strips for pappardelle; ¾-inch-wide strips for tagliatelle; and ½- to ¼-inch-wide strips for fettuccine.

3. Lightly dust the cut roll with flour, then begin to gently unfold the strips, one by one, as you shake off any excess flour. Arrange them straight and spread out or lay them down by shaping them in a coil (referred to as a bird's nest). Repeat with all the pasta sheets. Let air-dry for 30 minutes and then cook. Alternatively, cover them with a kitchen towel and refrigerate for up to 3 days.

4. To cook the pasta ribbons, bring a large pot of water to a boil. Once it is boiling, add salt (1 tablespoon for every 4 cups water) and stir. Add the pasta and stir for the first minute to prevent any sticking and to untangle the strands of pasta. Tagliolini will not require additional cooking, so drain them as soon as they hit the water and you stir to disentangle them. Cook the remaining pasta ribbons until tender but still chewy, anywhere from 1 to 3 minutes. Drain and add them to the sauce of your choice.

INGREDIENTS:

1 RECIPE THREE-EGG BASIC PASTA DOUGH (SEE PAGE 761)

SEMOLINA FLOUR, FOR DUSTING

SALT, PLUS MORE FOR THE PASTA WATER

TAJARIN

YIELD: ½ LB. / ACTIVE TIME: 20 MINUTES / TOTAL TIME: 1 HOUR

These delicate, flat noodles are best broken up in a soup or served alongside roasted proteins and vegetables.

1. Prepare the dough as directed, rolling the dough to the thinnest setting (generally notch 5) for pasta sheets that are about ⅟16 inch thick. Cut into 8-inch-long sheets. Lay the pasta sheets on lightly floured parchment-lined baking sheets. Air-dry for 15 minutes.

2. Working with one pasta sheet at a time, lightly dust it with semolina flour, then gently roll it up, starting from a short end. Using a very sharp knife, gently slice the roll across into ⅟12-inch-wide strips. Lightly dust the cut roll with flour, then gently begin unfolding the strips, one by one, as you shake off any excess flour. Arrange them either straight and spread out or curled in a coil. Repeat with all the pasta sheets. Allow them to air-dry for 30 minutes and then cook. Alternatively, you can place them, once air-dried, on a baking sheet, cover with a kitchen towel, and refrigerate for up to 3 days.

3. To cook the tajarin, bring a large pot of salted water to a boil. Cook until the pasta is tender but still chewy, typically no more than 2 minutes. Drain and serve with the sauce of your choice.

INGREDIENTS:

ALL-YOLK PASTA DOUGH
(SEE PAGE 760)

SEMOLINA FLOUR, FOR
DUSTING

SALT, TO TASTE

TROFIE

YIELD: ABOUT 1 LB. / ACTIVE TIME: 40 MINUTES / TOTAL TIME: 4 TO 5 HOURS

Trofie are thin, spiraled noodles that work best with strong sauces, including pesto and ragùs.

1. Put the flour and salt in a large bowl, mix well with a fork, and add the water. Mix with the fork until all the water has been absorbed, then start working the dough with your hands. In a few minutes the crumbly mixture will begin to come together as a grainy dough.

2. Transfer the dough, along with any bits stuck to the bowl, to a lightly floured work surface. Begin to knead the dough. Using the heel of your hand, push the ball of dough away from you in a downward motion. Turn the dough 45 degrees each time you repeat this motion, as doing so incorporates the flour more evenly. Knead the dough for about 10 minutes. Cover the dough with plastic wrap to keep it from drying out and let rest at room temperature for 1 hour, but 2 hours is even better.

3. Between the palms of your hands or on a lightly floured work surface, roll the dough into a 2-inch-thick log and cut it across into eight pieces (the easiest way to do this is to cut the roll in half and continue cutting each piece in half until you have eight pieces). Cover all the dough pieces but the one you are working with to keep them from drying out. Shape each piece of dough into a ball, and then roll it until it is a long, ½-inch-thick rope. Cut into ½-inch pieces and dust them with flour.

4. Working with one piece at a time, press down on the dough with your fingertips and roll the dough down the palm of your other hand. This action will cause the piece of dough to turn into a narrow spiral with tapered ends. Repeat with the remaining pieces of dough. Dust the spirals with flour, set them on flour-dusted, parchment-lined baking sheets, and allow them to air-dry for 2 hours, turning them over halfway through.

5. To cook the trofie, cook for 3 to 4 minutes in a pot of boiling, salted water, until they are tender but still chewy.

INGREDIENTS:

2¾ CUPS ALL-PURPOSE FLOUR

1 TEASPOON SALT, PLUS MORE TO TASTE

1 CUP WATER

SEMOLINA FLOUR, FOR DUSTING

CHINESE EGG NOODLES

YIELD: ABOUT 1 LB. / ACTIVE TIME: 45 MINUTES / TOTAL TIME: 2 HOURS

This noodle is a staple of recipes like lo mein and chow mein, as well as many Asian soups. It is incredibly easy to make and, of course, delicious.

1. Mix the flour and salt together in a large bowl. Add the eggs and mix until a floury dough forms. Add the 3 tablespoons of water and continue to mix until you almost cannot see any remaining traces of flour. If you find, even after adding the water, that your dough is still very floury, add more water, 1 tablespoon at a time, and continue mixing it with your hands until the dough starts coming together more easily. Start kneading the dough in the bowl with your dominant hand. Continue kneading in the bowl until a smooth ball forms; this may take about 10 minutes. Wrap the dough tightly in plastic wrap and let rest at room temperature for 40 to 50 minutes to allow the gluten in the dough to relax.

2. Unwrap the dough and place it on a lightly floured work surface. Using a rolling pin, begin "beating" the dough, turning it over after every 10 whacks or so. Continue doing this for 6 minutes. Then, shape the dough into a ball, cover with plastic wrap, and let rest at room temperature for another 30 minutes.

3. Return the dough to the work surface (no need to flour again). Cut it in half and wrap one half in plastic wrap to prevent drying. Roll the other half into a large, thin sheet about twice the length and breadth of the length of your rolling pin (you should be able to almost see your hand through it). Lightly flour both sides of the sheet of dough and then fold the sheet of dough twice over itself to create a three-layered fold (like a letter).

4. Using a very sharp knife, slice across the roll into evenly spaced strands. You can make them as thin or thick as you'd like. As you cut the dough, be sure to hold the knife perpendicular to the surface and lightly push the newly cut strip away from the roll with the knife to completely separate it. Continue until you have cut the entire roll, then lightly dust the slivered noodles with flour to prevent any sticking. Transfer the noodles to a parchment-lined baking sheet, shaking off any excess flour if necessary. You can leave them nested or unspool them according to your preference, as they will unravel and straighten once boiled. Repeat with the remaining dough. Cook in a pot of boiling, salted water for 3 to 4 minutes, or cover and refrigerate for up to 1 day.

INGREDIENTS:

- 2 CUPS ALL-PURPOSE FLOUR, PLUS MORE FOR DUSTING
- 1 TEASPOON SALT, PLUS MORE FOR THE PASTA WATER
- 2 LARGE EGGS, LIGHTLY BEATEN
- 3 TABLESPOONS WATER, PLUS MORE AS NEEDED

UDON NOODLES

YIELD: 1 LB. / ACTIVE TIME: 1 HOUR / TOTAL TIME: 2 TO 3 HOURS

Japanese udon noodles are best when homemade, as the packaged versions lack some of the chewiness and bulk of the fresh variety.

1. Stir the water and salt together in a small bowl until the salt dissolves. Put the flour in a large bowl and make a well in the center. Add the salted water in a stream while stirring the flour. Once all the water has been added, begin working the dough with your hands to incorporate all the flour. If the dough is too dry, add water in 1-teaspoon increments until the dough sticks together.

2. Transfer the dough to a work surface that you have dusted very lightly with the potato starch or cornstarch. Knead the dough with the palm of your dominant hand, turning it 45 degrees with each pressing, until the dough becomes uniformly smooth and slowly springs back when pressed by a finger, about 10 minutes. Cover the dough tightly with plastic wrap and let rest for 1 to 2 hours to relax the gluten.

3. Cut the dough into two pieces. Set one on a lightly dusted work surface and wrap the other in plastic wrap to prevent drying. Pat the piece of dough into a rectangular shape and, using a lightly dusted rolling pin, roll the dough into a ⅛-inch-thick rectangle. Lightly dust the dough and then fold it twice over itself to create a three-layered fold, as you would a letter.

4. Using a very sharp knife, slice the roll into ⅛-inch-wide strands. As you cut the dough, be sure to hold the knife perpendicular to the surface and lightly push the newly cut strip away from the roll with the knife to completely separate it. Continue until you have cut the entire roll, then lightly dust the slivered pasta to prevent any sticking. Transfer the noodles to a parchment-lined baking sheet, shaking off any excess starch if necessary. Repeat with the remaining dough. Udon noodles quickly turn brittle and break when handled, so cook as soon as you finish making them.

5. To cook the udon, cook for about 1 minute in a pot of boiling, salted water, until they are tender but still chewy.

INGREDIENTS:

- ¼ CUP WARM WATER, PLUS MORE AS NEEDED
- 1 TEASPOON FINE SEA SALT
- 2¼ CUPS CAKE FLOUR OR FINELY MILLED "00" FLOUR

  POTATO STARCH OR CORNSTARCH, FOR DUSTING

DUMPLING WRAPPERS

All of these doughs are used in recipes in this book, but you can fill them with anything you like.

BASIC DUMPLING WRAPPERS

YIELD: 32 WRAPPERS / ACTIVE TIME: 35 MINUTES / TOTAL TIME: 2 HOURS AND 35 MINUTES

Dumplings are some of the most versatile foods on the planet. Steam them, boil them, deep-fry or panfry them—the results will have your guests coming back for seconds (and thirds).

1. Place the flour in the mixing bowl of a stand mixer fitted with the paddle attachment. With the mixer running on low, add the water in a steady stream. Beat until the dough just holds together, adding water in 1-teaspoon increments if needed.

2. Place the dough on a flour-dusted work surface and knead until smooth and elastic, about 5 minutes. Wrap tightly in plastic wrap and let rest at room temperature for 2 hours.

3. Cut a resealable freezer bag at the seams so that you have two squares of plastic. Place the dough on a flour-dusted work surface and cut it in half. Cover one half with plastic wrap and roll the other into a 1-inch-thick log. Cut the log into 16 pieces. Dust each piece with flour, cover with plastic wrap, and press down gently until the rounds are ¼ inch thick.

4. You will want the filling prepared before starting on this step, as the dough sticks together better when it has not been exposed to the air for too long. Place the disks between the two squares of plastic and press down with a rolling pin until they are ⅛ inch thick. Transfer to a flour-dusted work surface and fill the wrappers as desired or freeze, in layers separated by parchment paper, for up to 1 month.

INGREDIENTS:

2   CUPS ALL-PURPOSE FLOUR, PLUS MORE FOR DUSTING

¾   CUP JUST-BOILED WATER, PLUS MORE AS NEEDED

CRYSTAL DUMPLING WRAPPERS

YIELD: 18 WRAPPERS / ACTIVE TIME: 35 MINUTES / TOTAL TIME: 35 MINUTES

These beautiful dumplings have a limited shelf life, so it's best to have your filling prepared ahead of time.

1. Cut a resealable freezer bag at the seams so that you have two squares of plastic and set aside. Place the wheat starch and cornstarch in a heatproof bowl. Add the boiling water and oil. Using a rubber spatula, stir the ingredients until a loose dough forms. Turn the dough out onto a work surface dusted with wheat starch and knead until it is smooth and slowly bounces back into place when pressed with a finger. This should take about 10 minutes.

2. Roll the dough into a 1½-inch-thick log. Cut it into 18 equal pieces, dust them with wheat starch, and cover with plastic wrap. Press down lightly on the pieces to create a disk that is roughly ¼ inch thick. Place the disks between the two squares of plastic and press down with a rolling pin until they are ⅛ inch thick. Dredge any disks that feel sticky with wheat starch, place on a parchment-lined baking sheet, and fill as desired.

INGREDIENTS:

1   CUP WHEAT STARCH, PLUS
     MORE FOR DUSTING

½   CUP CORNSTARCH

1¼   CUPS BOILING WATER

1   TABLESPOON GRAPESEED
     OR SAFFLOWER OIL

EMPANADAS

YIELD: 4 SERVINGS / ACTIVE TIME: 45 MINUTES / TOTAL TIME: 1 HOUR AND 30 MINUTES

While this preparation includes pork, you can substitute any meat or vegetable combination that comes to mind.

1. To prepare the dough, dissolve the salt in the warm water. Place the flour in a mixing bowl, add the lard or butter, and work the mixture with a pastry blender until the mixture is crumbly. Add the salted water and knead the mixture until a stiff dough forms. Cut the dough into eight pieces, cover them with plastic wrap, and place in the refrigerator for 20 minutes.

2. To prepare the filling, place the oil in a skillet and warm over medium heat. Add the onion and cook until soft, about 5 minutes. Add the garlic, cook for 2 minutes, and then add the ground pork. Cook, breaking the pork up with a spoon, until lightly browned, about 5 minutes. Drain off any excess fat and add the tomatoes, salt, pepper, cinnamon stick, cloves, raisins, and vinegar. Simmer until the filling is thick, about 30 minutes. Remove from heat and let cool before folding in the toasted almonds.

3. Add oil to a Dutch oven until it is 2 inches deep and bring it to 350°F. Preheat the oven to 200°F and place a baking sheet in the oven. Place the dough on a flour-dusted work surface and roll each piece into a 5-inch circle. Place 3 tablespoons of the filling in the center of a circle, brush the edge of each circle with water, and fold into a half-moon. Press down on the edge with a fork to seal the empanada tight, trying to remove as much air as possible. Repeat with the remaining pieces of dough and filling.

4. Working in two batches, place the empanadas in the hot oil and fry until golden brown, about 5 minutes. Drain on paper towels and then place them in the warm oven while you cook the next batch.

INGREDIENTS:

FOR THE DOUGH

¼ TEASPOON KOSHER SALT

6 TABLESPOONS WARM WATER (110°F)

1½ CUPS ALL-PURPOSE FLOUR, PLUS MORE FOR DUSTING

3 TABLESPOONS LARD OR UNSALTED BUTTER, CUT INTO SMALL PIECES

FOR THE FILLING

2 TEASPOONS VEGETABLE OIL, PLUS MORE FOR FRYING

1 YELLOW ONION, MINCED

1 GARLIC CLOVE, MINCED

¾ LB. GROUND PORK

1 (14 OZ.) CAN CRUSHED TOMATOES

½ TEASPOON KOSHER SALT

¼ TEASPOON BLACK PEPPER

1 CINNAMON STICK

2 WHOLE CLOVES

2 TABLESPOONS RAISINS

2 TEASPOONS APPLE CIDER VINEGAR

2 TABLESPOONS SLIVERED ALMONDS, TOASTED

SAMOSA WRAPPERS

YIELD: 16 WRAPPERS / ACTIVE TIME: 20 MINUTES / TOTAL TIME: 20 MINUTES

Maida flour is similar to cake flour, as it is finely milled and has all of the wheat bran removed. The result is a soft, light flour.

1. Place the flour and salt in a mixing bowl and use your hands to combine. Add the oil and work the mixture with your hands until it is a coarse meal.

2. Add the water and knead the mixture until a smooth, firm dough forms. If the dough is too dry, incorporate more water, 1 tablespoon at a time.

3. Divide the dough into eight pieces and roll each one out into a 6-inch circle on a flour-dusted work surface. Cut the circles in half and brush the flat edge of each with water. Fold one corner of the flat edge toward the other to make a cone and pinch to seal. Fill each cone one-third of the way with your chosen filling, brush the opening with water, and pinch to seal. Place the sealed samosas on a parchment-lined baking sheet.

4. Add vegetable oil to a Dutch oven until it is 2 inches deep and heat it to 325°F over medium heat. When all of the wrappers have been filled, add them to the hot oil in batches and fry, stirring and turning them over occasionally, until they are golden brown, about 5 minutes. Transfer the cooked samosas to a paper towel–lined plate and serve.

INGREDIENTS:

- 2 **CUPS MAIDA FLOUR, PLUS MORE FOR DUSTING**
- ¼ **TEASPOON KOSHER SALT**
- 2 **TABLESPOONS VEGETABLE OIL, PLUS MORE FOR FRYING**
- ½ **CUP WATER, PLUS MORE AS NEEDED**

WONTON WRAPPERS

YIELD: 48 WRAPPERS / ACTIVE TIME: 1 HOUR / TOTAL TIME: 3 HOURS

Wonton wrappers can be used to make wontons or other preparations that require a thin, delicate wrapper. They can also be fried for a crisp, satisfying appetizer or garnish.

INGREDIENTS:

¼ CUP WATER, PLUS MORE AS NEEDED

1 LARGE EGG

¾ TEASPOON KOSHER SALT

1½ CUPS ALL-PURPOSE FLOUR, PLUS MORE AS NEEDED

CORNSTARCH, FOR DUSTING

1. Place the water, egg, and salt in a measuring cup and whisk to combine. Place the flour in the bowl of a stand mixer fitted with the paddle attachment. With the mixer running on low speed, add the egg mixture in a steady stream and beat until the dough holds together. Add water or flour in ½-teaspoon increments if the dough is too dry or too wet, respectively. Fit the mixer with the dough hook and knead at medium speed until the dough is soft, smooth, and springs back quickly when pressed with a finger, about 10 minutes. Cover the dough tightly with plastic wrap and let rest for 2 hours.

2. Cut the dough into three even pieces. Working with one piece at a time (cover the others tightly in plastic), shape the dough into a ball. Place the dough on a flour-dusted work surface and roll it out until it is ½ inch thick. Feed the dough through a pasta maker, adjusting the setting to reduce the thickness with each pass, until the dough is thin enough that you can see your hand through it. Place the sheets on a parchment-lined baking sheet.

3. Dust a work surface with cornstarch and cut the sheets into as many 4-inch squares or 3-inch rounds as possible. Pile the cut wrappers on top of each other and fill as desired, or cover in plastic wrap and refrigerate for up to 3 days.

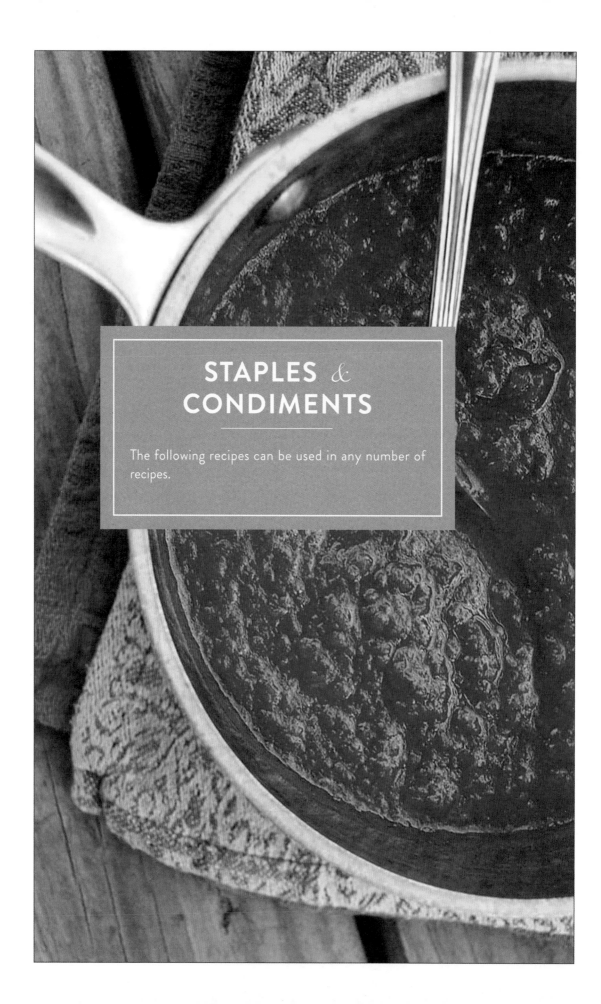

STAPLES & CONDIMENTS

The following recipes can be used in any number of recipes.

CLASSIC CANNED TOMATO SAUCE

YIELD: 10 SERVINGS / ACTIVE TIME: 25 MINUTES / TOTAL TIME: 1 HOUR

Everyone should have a basic tomato sauce in their repertoire that can be made with pantry basics, as it is the foundation of so many great dishes. The simplicity of this recipe belies a robust, complex flavor.

1. Warm a Dutch oven over low heat for 2 to 3 minutes. Add the oil and raise heat to medium. When it begins to shimmer, add the onion and a couple pinches of salt and stir to combine. Once the onion begins to sizzle, reduce heat to low and stir. Cover and cook, stirring occasionally, until the onion becomes very soft, about 20 minutes.

2. While the onion cooks, use a food processor or blender to puree the tomatoes, working with one can at a time.

3. Pour the tomato puree into the pot and add a few more pinches of salt and the sugar. Raise heat to medium-high and bring to a boil. Reduce heat to medium-low and simmer until the sauce has thickened, about 30 minutes, stirring every 10 minutes or so.

4. If using, place the basil leaves on the surface of the sauce and cover the pot for 5 minutes. Remove the basil before using. Use immediately or let cool, transfer to an airtight container, and refrigerate for up to 3 days or freeze for up to 2 months.

INGREDIENTS:

3   TABLESPOONS OLIVE OIL

1   WHITE OR VIDALIA ONION, GRATED

     SALT, TO TASTE

2   (28 OZ.) CANS WHOLE PEELED PLUM TOMATOES (PREFERABLY SAN MARZANO)

1   TEASPOON SUGAR

     HANDFUL FRESH BASIL LEAVES (OPTIONAL)

FERMENTED HOT SAUCE

YIELD: 2 CUPS / ACTIVE TIME: 10 MINUTES / TOTAL TIME: 30 DAYS TO 6 MONTHS

If you're addicted to hot sauce, fermented hot sauce will take that addiction to the next level.

1. Remove the tops of the peppers and split them down the middle.

2. Place the split peppers and the garlic, onion, and salt in a mason jar and cover with the water. Cover the jar and shake well.

3. Place the jar away from direct sunlight and let stand for at least 30 days and up to 6 months. Occasionally unscrew the lid to release some of the gases that build up. Based on my own experience, a longer fermenting time is very much worth it.

4. Once you are ready to make the sauce, reserve most of the brine, transfer the mixture to a blender, and puree to desired thickness. If you want your sauce to be on the thin side, keep adding brine until you have the consistency you want. Season with salt, transfer to a container, cover, and store in the refrigerator for up to 3 months.

INGREDIENTS:

2   LBS. CAYENNE PEPPERS

1   LB. JALAPEÑO PEPPERS

5   GARLIC CLOVES

1   RED ONION, QUARTERED

3   TABLESPOONS SALT, PLUS MORE TO TASTE

    FILTERED WATER, AS NEEDED

TORTILLAS

YIELD: ABOUT 12 LARGE TORTILLAS / ACTIVE TIME: 25 MINUTES / TOTAL TIME: 35 MINUTES

Tortillas are great for more than just tacos. They can be used to make homemade wraps or as a side to larger dishes to help mop up all the extra flavors left behind.

1. Put the flour in a large bowl. Mix in the salt and baking powder.

2. Add the shortening or butter, and, using your fingers, blend it into the flour mix until you have a crumbly dough. Add 1 cup of the water and work it in, then gradually add the remaining ½ cup, working it in with your hands, so that you create a dough that's not too sticky.

3. Lightly flour a work surface and turn out the dough. Knead it for about 10 minutes, until it is soft and elastic. Divide it into 12 equal pieces.

4. Using a lightly floured rolling pin, roll each piece out to almost the size of the bottom of the skillet.

5. Heat the skillet over high heat. Add a tortilla. Cook for just 15 seconds a side. Keep the cooked tortillas warm by putting them on a plate covered with a damp kitchen towel. Serve warm.

INGREDIENTS:

3   CUPS FLOUR, PLUS MORE FOR DUSTING

1   TEASPOON SALT

2   TEASPOONS BAKING POWDER

3   TABLESPOONS VEGETABLE SHORTENING OR 4 TABLESPOONS UNSALTED BUTTER, CHILLED

1½   CUPS WATER, AT ROOM TEMPERATURE

GRILLED PEACH & CORN SALSA

YIELD: 6 SERVINGS / ACTIVE TIME: 15 MINUTES / TOTAL TIME: 20 MINUTES

The juicy peaches complement the natural sweetness of the grilled corn in a salsa that is hard to resist. This can be served alongside chips, over rice, or as a topping for any meat or vegetable dish that needs some extra flavor.

1. Preheat grill to medium heat. Brush olive oil onto the ears of corn and grill for about 5 minutes, turning throughout. Remove from heat once grill marks appear.

2. Remove kernels from the cobs into a large bowl. Add the chopped peaches, tomatoes, onion, jalapeño, and cilantro. Mix together and gently stir in the avocado.

3. Add lime juice, salt, and pepper. Stir gently and serve.

INGREDIENTS:

- 1 TABLESPOON OLIVE OIL
- 2 EARS SWEET CORN
- 3 MEDIUM PEACHES, PEELED, PIT REMOVED AND CHOPPED
- 1 CUP CHERRY OR GRAPE TOMATOES, HALVED
- ⅓ CUP RED ONION, DICED
- 1 JALAPEÑO, MINCED
- ¼ CUP CHOPPED FRESH CILANTRO
- 1 LARGE AVOCADO, PIT REMOVED AND DICED
- 2 TABLESPOONS LIME JUICE
  SALT AND PEPPER, TO TASTE

HOMEMADE TOMATO SALSA

YIELD: ABOUT 6 SERVINGS / ACTIVE TIME: 35 MINUTES: TOTAL TIME: 2 HOURS AND 35 MINUTES

While you can easily buy your own salsa at the store, nothing beats the fresh zing of home-made salsa. This recipe calls for cherry tomatoes. They are slightly tarter in flavor than other tomatoes, depending on the type you purchase, but you can use whatever tomatoes you have on hand.

1. Place a cast-iron skillet on a grill at medium-low heat. Combine the oil, tomatoes, onion, garlic, and jalapeño in a bowl. Next, transfer the mixture to the heated cast-iron skillet and grill for about 20 minutes, stirring every now and then until the tomatoes are charred.

2. Once charred, transfer the contents of the skillet to a food processor along with the remaining ingredients. Pulse until smooth and then cover for at least 2 hours before serving.

INGREDIENTS:

2   TABLESPOONS OLIVE OIL

2   CUPS CHERRY TOMATOES

1   YELLOW ONION, CHOPPED

6   GARLIC CLOVES, CRUSHED

2   JALAPEÑO PEPPERS, DICED

½   CUP FRESH CILANTRO LEAVES

    JUICE FROM 1 LIME

1   TEASPOON GROUND CUMIN

    BLACK PEPPER, TO TASTE

    SALT, TO TASTE

TOMATILLO SALSA

YIELD: ABOUT 6 SERVINGS / ACTIVE TIME: 15 MINUTES / TOTAL TIME: 15 MINUTES

The tomatillos provide a bright, acidic, fruity flavor to this salsa that is unmatched.

1. Place the tomatillos in a saucepan and cover with water. Place over medium-high heat on the stovetop, bring to a boil, and cook for 10 minutes.

2. After 10 minutes, remove the tomatillos from the saucepan and place in a food processor along with the remaining ingredients. Pulse until smooth.

INGREDIENTS:

10   TOMATILLOS, HUSKED AND RINSED

1   SMALL ONION, CHOPPED

2   GARLIC CLOVES, MINCED

¼   CUP CHOPPED FRESH CILANTRO

1   JALAPEÑO PEPPER, CHOPPED

     BLACK PEPPER, TO TASTE

     SEA SALT, TO TASTE

CHIMICHURRI REDUX

YIELD: 1 CUP / ACTIVE TIME: 5 MINUTES / TOTAL TIME: 5 MINUTES

I could have called this "salsa verde," or any of the names given to parsley-based sauces, but "chimichurri" sounds the best. The one variable is the herb other than parsley. I listed rosemary, but you can use cilantro, basil, thyme, dill, or any combination. Thyme, rosemary, and oregano have strong flavors, so use them sparingly, but basil, cilantro, and dill can be tossed in liberally. Use this on anything: grilled steak, steamed corn, roasted potatoes, rice—the list is endless.

1. Place all of the ingredients, except for the oil, in a food processor and puree until it nearly smooth, scraping down the work bowl as needed.

2. With the food processor running, slowly add the oil and puree until emulsified.

3. If not using immediately, refrigerate and allow it to come to room temperature before serving.

INGREDIENTS:

1   CUP FLAT-LEAF PARSLEY
     LEAVES

1   GARLIC CLOVE

     JUICE OF ¼ LEMON

     LEAVES FROM 1 SPRIG
     FRESH ROSEMARY OR
     PREFERRED HERB

1   TEASPOON KOSHER SALT

1   STRIP LEMON ZEST

1   TABLESPOON CAPERS

½   TEASPOON RED PEPPER
     FLAKES

     BLACK PEPPER, TO TASTE

¼   CUP OLIVE OIL

TECHNIQUES

*T*he following techniques are used in multiple recipes; for specific techniques only used in a single recipe, the instructions are found with the respective recipes.

REMOVING THE OUTER LEAVES AND EXPOSING THE MEAT OF AN ARTICHOKE

The tough leaves of the artichoke protect its edible heart. It looks like a lot of work to remove them, but with this method it's not so bad. First, cut the stem and pull off the outer leaves. When you get to the tender yellow leaves, grab the top of the leaves in the center and pull them off, revealing the heart. Dig out the heart with a spoon, and use a small paring knife to remove the bottom leaves and anything clinging to the stem.

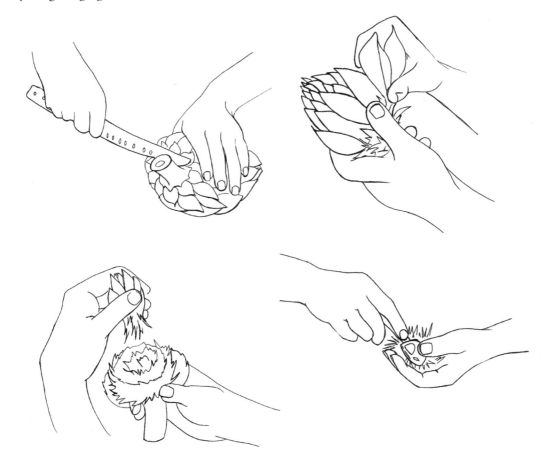

TOMATO CONCASSE

Boil enough water for a tomato to be submerged and add a pinch of salt. While it is heating, prepare an ice bath and score the top of the tomato with a paring knife, taking care not to cut into the meat of the tomato. Place the tomato in the boiling water for 30 seconds, or until the skin begins to blister. Carefully remove it from the boiling water and place it in the ice bath. Once the tomato is cool, remove it from the ice bath and use a paring knife to peel the skin off, starting at the scored top. Cut the tomato into quarters, remove the seeds, and cut according to recipe instructions.

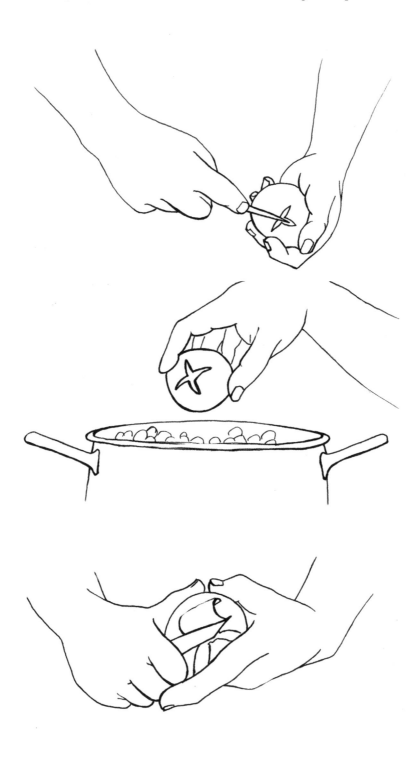

SACHET D'ÉPICES

Cut a 4-inch square of cheesecloth and a 12-inch piece of butcher twine. Place 3 parsley stems, ¼ teaspoon thyme leaves, ½ bay leaf, ¼ teaspoon cracked peppercorns, and ½ garlic clove, minced, in the middle of the cheesecloth and lift each corner to create a purse. Tie one side of the twine around the corners and make a knot. Tie the other side of the twine to the handle of your pot and then toss the sachet d'épices in.

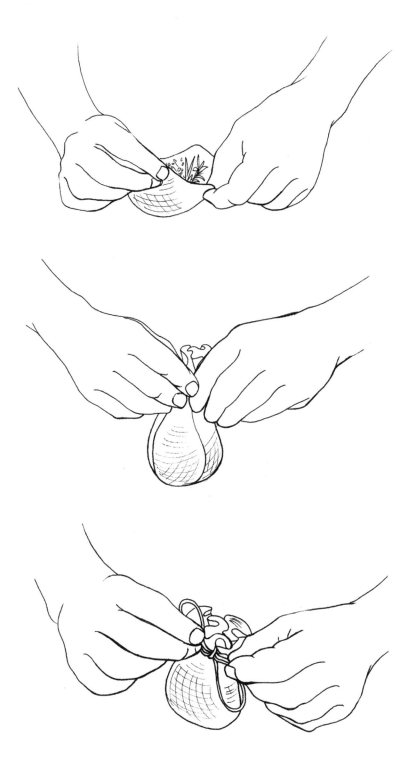

FILLING AND SHAPING WONTONS

When working with wonton dough, you want to leave it covered until you're going to use it. When you are ready, lay a few wrappers out on your work surface and place your filling in the center. Dip your finger into some water and wet the edge of the wonton wrapper—not too much water, or the dough will become sticky and unworkable. Take two opposite corners and lift until they meet. Secure with a little pinch, and then lift the two remaining corners, one at a time.

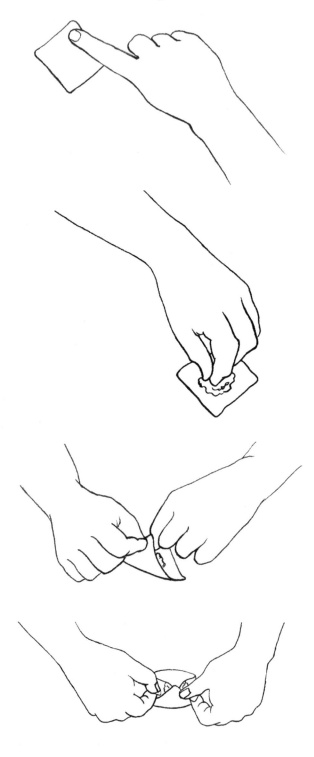

METRIC CONVERSION CHART

WEIGHTS

1 oz. = 28 grams
2 oz. = 57 grams
4 oz. (¼ lb.) = 113 grams
8 oz. (½ lb.) = 227 grams
16 oz. (1 lb.) = 454 grams

VOLUME MEASURES

⅛ teaspoon = 0.6 ml
¼ teaspoon = 1.23 ml
½ teaspoon = 2.5 ml
1 teaspoon = 5 ml
1 tablespoon (3 teaspoons) = ½ fluid oz. = 15 ml
2 tablespoons = 1 fluid oz. = 29.5 ml
¼ cup (4 tablespoons) = 2 fluid oz. = 59 ml
⅓ cup (5 ⅓ tablespoons) = 2.7 fluid oz. = 80 ml
½ cup (8 tablespoons) = 4 fluid oz. = 120 ml
⅔ cup (10 ⅔ tablespoons) = 5.4 fluid oz. = 160 ml
¾ cup (12 tablespoons) = 6 fluid oz. = 180 ml
1 cup (16 tablespoons) = 8 fluid oz. = 240 ml

TEMPERATURE EQUIVALENTS

°F	°C	Gas Mark
225	110	¼
250	130	½
275	140	1
300	150	2
325	170	3
350	180	4
375	190	5
400	200	6
425	220	7
450	230	8
475	240	9
500	250	10

LENGTH MEASURES

1/16 inch = 1.6 mm
⅛ inch = 3 mm
¼ inch = 1.35 mm
½ inch = 1.25 cm
¾ inch = 2 cm
1 inch = 2.5 cm

PHOTO CREDITS

Pages 10, 12–15, 84 (top): Carol Sullivan, photographer, courtesy of Laura Sorkin; page 18: "Bauscher's Seed & Plant Guide" (1899), courtesy of Library of Congress; page 28: "Vegetables in and Around a Basket" (1904), courtesy of Library of Congress; page 31: Manuscripts and Archives Division, The New York Public Library. "Artichoke" (1739), courtesy of New York Public Library Digital Collections; page 32 (bottom): The Miriam and Ira D. Wallach Division of Art, Prints and Photographs: Photography Collection, The New York Public Library. "Artichoke. Monterey County, California" (1939), courtesy of New York Public Library Digital Collections; page 34: Rare Book Division, The New York Public Library. "*Eruca, latifolia, alba, sativa Discoridis = Ruchetta di Orto = Roquette* [Arugula/ Rocket]" (ca. 1772), courtesy of New York Public Library Digital Collections; page 36: United States Office Of War Information; Rosener, Ann, photographer. "Women in war. Summer canning workers. A skilled and vastly important job in this Rochelle, Illinois, asparagus canning factory is performed by this woman grading expert. The grade of vegetables, their water content, and the relative excellence of the product determines the price which the canner will pay the farmer for his crop" (1942), courtesy of Library of Congress; page 45: "Just arrived! Alfred Wright's perfumery. For sale by Sharpless & Sons, Philadelphia" (ca. 1880), courtesy of Library of Congress; page 48: Rothstein, Arthur, photographer. "Weslaco, Texas. Preparing broccoli for packing. Packing shed. Hidalgo County Texas United States" (1942), courtesy of Library of Congress; page

51: Rothstein, Arthur, photographer. "Weslaco, Texas. Packing broccoli in the packing shed. Hidalgo County Texas United States" (1942), courtesy of Library of Congress; page 56: Rare Book Division, The New York Public Library. "*Brassica capitata alba, et viridis = Cauolo Bolognese = Chou* [Cabbage]" (ca. 1772), courtesy of New York Public Library Digital Collections; page 59: The Miriam and Ira D. Wallach Division of Art, Prints and Photographs: Picture Collection, The New York Public Library. "Little Black Rabbit" (1917), courtesy New York Public Library Digital Collections; page 60: The Miriam and Ira D. Wallach Division of Art, Prints and Photographs: Photography Collection, The New York Public Library. "Tying carrots, near Edinburg, Texas" (1939), courtesy of New York Public Library Digital Collections; page 63: American Colony; photo Dept., photographer. "Peasant Women Carrying Cauliflower on Her Head" (ca. 1934), courtesy of Library of Congress; page 66: "Fresh celery from the Kalamazoo Celery Co., for sale here" (1887), courtesy of Library of Congress; page 71: Vachon, John, photographer. "Nebraska Farmer Shucking Corn. Nebraska. United States" (1938), courtesy of Library of Congress; page 72: Lee, Russell, photographer. "Corn near Muskogee, Oklahoma. Muskogee Oklahoma United States" (1939), courtesy of Library of Congress; page 73: Harrison, Lloyd, artist. "Wholesome – Nutritious Foods From Corn" (1918), courtesy of Library of Congress; page 74: Rare Book Division, The New York Public Library. "*Cucumis sativus, vulgaris, maturo fructu subluteo = Cetriuolo = Cocombre* ordinaire [Cucumber]"(ca. 1772), courtesy of New York Public Library Digital Collections; pages 77, 84 (bottom), 101, 121: Laura Sorkin, photographer; page 81 (bottom right): Rare Book Division, The New York Public Library. "*Ferula faemina Plinii = Fenocchione Salvatico = La Ferule* [Giant fennel]"(ca. 1772), courtesy of New York Public Library Digital Collections; page 82: The Miriam and Ira D. Wallach Division of Art, Prints and Photographs: Photography Collection, The New York Public Library. "*Prodavets chesnoku* [Garlic Seller]"(ca. 1890), courtesy of New York Public Library Digital Collections; page 85: Highsmith, Carol M, photographer. "Garlic strings at the French Quarter Market, New Orleans, Louisiana. Louisiana New Orleans United States" (between 1980 and 2006), courtesy of Library of Congress; page 94 (top right): Rare Book Division, The New York Public Library. "*Porrum commune capitatum = Porro = Porreau* [Leek]" (ca. 1772), courtesy of New York Public Library Digital Collections; page 96 (left): "Mushroom Story" (ca. 1920), courtesy of Library of Congress; page 96 (right): The Miriam and Ira D. Wallach Division of Art, Prints and Photographs: Print Collection, The New York Public Library. "Mushrooms" (ca. 1701), courtesy of New York Public Library Digital Collections; page 104: Bain News Service, publisher. 'Anti-onion' gas mask. Camp Kearny, California" (ca. 1917), courtesy of Library of Congress; page 107: The Miriam and Ira D. Wallach Division of Art, Prints and Photographs: Photography Collection, The New York Public Library. "Harvesting onions, truck farming, near Buffalo, N.Y., U.S.A." (1906), courtesy of New York Public Library Digital Collections; page 109: Science, Industry and Business Library: General Collection, The New York Public Library. "Garden parsley" (1739), courtesy of New York Public Library Digital Collections; page 112: Rare Book Division, The New York Public Library. "*Capsicum fructu, subrotundo, ventricoso dulci in summitate tetragono = Peperoni di Spagna grandi,*

e dolci = Poivre d'Inde ou de Guinée [Pepper]" (ca. 1772), courtesy of New York Public Library Digital Collections; page 117: The Miriam and Ira D. Wallach Division of Art, Prints and Photographs: Print Collection, The New York Public Library. "*La récolte des pommes de terre [d'après Breton]*" (ca. late 1800s), courtesy of New York Public Library Digital Collections; page 122: Rothstein, Arthur, photographer. "Packing plant. Icing radishes. Nueces County, Robstown, Texas"(1942), courtesy of Library of Congress; page 125: Batchelder, John Davis, collector. "Girl cutting a Japanese radish. Japan" (ca. 1890), courtesy of Library of Congress; page 132: The Miriam and Ira D. Wallach Division of Art, Prints and Photographs: Print Collection, The New York Public Library. "Gathering seaweed (*nori*)" (ca. early 1800s), courtesy of New York Public Library Digital Collections; pages 131, 133: Morgan Ione Yeager, photographer; page 140: Lee, Russell, photographer. "Wife of FSA Farm Security Administration client shelling peas on porch of old shack home, New Madrid County, Missouri"(1938), courtesy of Library of Congress; page 143: Lee, Russell, photographer. "Monument erected to Popeye, Crystal City, Texas. This is in the spinach growing center" (1939), courtesy of Library of Congress; page 148: Keystone View Company, publisher. "Slicing sweet potatoes, China" (1905), courtesy of Library of Congress. 1905; page 154: The Miriam and Ira D. Wallach Division of Art, Prints and Photographs: Print Collection, The New York Public Library. "Women preparing fried tofu (*dengaku*) at Gion" (1795), courtesy of New York Public Library Digital Collections; page 158: Rare Book Division, The New York Public Library. "*Lycopersicon Galeni = Pomidoro + Pomme d'ammour* [Tomato]" (ca. 1772), courtesy of New York Public Library Digital Collections; page 160: Loag, Samuel, publisher. "Ripe Red Tomatoes for Sale Here" (ca. 1869), courtesy of Library of Congress; page 161: Lee, Russell, photographer. "Truck farmer with an armload of turnips at early morning market,

San Angelo, Texas" (1939), courtesy of Library of Congress; page 163: Rare Book Division, The New York Public Library. "*Rapa Sativa, rotonda, radice candida = Rapa vusuale = Rave* [Turnip]"(ca. 1772), courtesy of New York Public Library Digital Collections; page 166: Keystone View Company, publisher. "Vegetable and grain display, state fair, Pueblo, Colorado" (1919), courtesy of Library of Congress; page 169 (left): Rare Book Division, The New York Public Library. "*Pepo fructu parvo, Pyriformi. Cucurbita aspera Pyriformis, parva = Zucca = Citrouille* [Pumpkin]" (ca. 1772), courtesy of New York Public Library Digital Collections; page 173: Schomburg Center for Research in Black Culture, Jean Blackwell Hutson Research and Reference Division, The New York Public Library. "Cultivating a patch of cassava on the agricultural experiment plot" (1904), courtesy of New York Public Library Digital Collections.

The following images and recipes are courtesy of Cider Mill Press: page 94 (top left), 179, 183, 187, 189, 190, 193–194, 198, 205–206, 212–213, 216, 219, 222, 225, 234, 238, 241, 248, 250, 252–253, 254, 257–258, 260, 261–262, 266, 270, 281–285, 288–309, 314–319, 324, 326–327, 330–332, 337–343, 348–359, 362–367, 370–383, 390–399, 406–409, 412–415, 424–425, 429, 436–437, 443, 452, 456–457, 460, 470, 472–473, 481, 488, 490–492, 496–500, 508, 523, 532, 534–535, 550–551, 564, 568, 571, 575–577, 580, 585–586, 589, 592, 595, 597, 600, 603, 604, 612–613, 619, 620, 624, 627, 628, 630, 633, 634, 644, 647, 649–653, 660–661, 664–665, 666, 668, 671–672, 674–677, 680–683, 685, 687–689, 693, 694, 716, 719–720, 723, 726–727, 728, 732, 735–736, 739–740, 742–743, 744, 747–749, 751–756, 759–762, 765–766, 769–770, 773–774, 777–778, 781, 783–784, 787–788, 791, 793–795, 797–798, 801–802.
All other images used under official license from Shutterstock.com.

RESOURCES

These books were of immense help when putting together *Vegetables*.

Derek Bissonnette
Soup
(Cider Mill Press, 2018)

Serena Cosmo
The Ultimate Pasta and Noodle Book
(Cider Mill Press, 2017)

Mamie Fennimore
Dressings
(Cider Mill Press, 2017)

Shane Hetherington
One Pot, Big Pot
(Cider Mill Press, 2018)

Rachel Narins
Cast Iron
(Cider Mill Press, 2019)

Elizabeth Orsini
From Garden to Grill
(Cider Mill Press, 2017)

Keith Sarasin & Chris Viaud
The Farmers Dinner
(Cider Mill Press, 2019)

ACKNOWLEDGMENTS

There are many subjects that one learns by studying a book. Farming and cooking are learned by watching and doing, quite literally getting your hands dirty to understand how it all works. Everything I know about these subjects comes from apprenticing under others first and I am grateful to all who shared their knowledge.

Thanks to Tim and Suzanne of Luna Bleu Farm for taking on a city kid for a summer and giving me a foundation in organic farming that I have used ever since. I am also grateful for all of the Vermont farmers and those in the Northeast Organic Farming Association (NOFA) who give of their time to teach newbies the tricks of the trade. Special thanks to Ann Hazelrigg at UVM Extension who is the CSI of the plant world. There is no spot, wilt, or bite mark that Ann cannot diagnose and her help was critical on many occasions.

Special shout out to Carol Sullivan who has not only photographed my farm and cooking, but has accompanied me on assignment from sheep farms to breweries for the past twelve years. Your gorgeous pictures make my work better and your friendship makes my life better.

In cooking, I first have to thank my mom who not only made the best homemade meals but took my brother, sister, and me around the world to explore other cuisines. The most important thing she taught me about food, though, was that sitting down together for a family meal is sacred, no matter what is on the table.

I also have to thank the bloggers who contributed recipes to this book: Steve Dunn, Joanne Rappos, and Priscilla McDonald. They expand our worlds by sharing their lives and culinary knowledge through their blogs and we are all beneficiaries. Friends such as Pilar Velasquez and Chef Dan Miele also generously handed over cherished recipes, in the case of Pilar, helping me with ingredients with which I had very little experience. Big hugs to Joe Poricelli and Jones Deady who not only shared recipes but are my culinary brothers who I would wield a spatula with anytime.

Thanks to Buzz Poole and Cider Mill Press for giving me this opportunity. Writing this book has been an opportunity to reflect on the past 20 years on the farm, which has been a true pleasure. Buzz, you have given me just the right amount of guidance, keeping me on task but letting me keep my voice. It has been a delight to work with you.

Much appreciation to Lucy for tolerating a half year of vegetable recipe testing. You were a good sport through this process, enduring episodes like the Week of Peas and the Chard Fiasco. I promise the next book will be titled, *Dunkin' vs Krispy Kreme: An Analysis*. And thanks to Heather and Buck for providing a daily dose of sanity so I can have a calm enough mind to face a blank page.

Lastly, thank you to my love, Eric, who supports me no matter how harebrained the idea. I'll go on an adventure with you anytime. What's next?

ABOUT THE AUTHOR

Laura Sorkin was born in New York City and grew up in Connecticut. She has a BA from McGill University, a Culinary degree from the French Culinary Institute, and a Masters of Environmental Management from Duke University. She ran an organic vegetable farm for over 15 years and has been co-owner of Runamok Maple since 2009. Laura has written for *Edible Green Mountains*, *Kids VT*, *Seven Days*, *Modern Farmer*, *Local Banquet*, *Northern Woodlands*, and *Better Homes and Gardens*. She lives in northwestern Vermont with her husband and two children.

INDEX

ABOUT CIDER MILL PRESS BOOK PUBLISHERS

Good ideas ripen with time. From seed to harvest, Cider Mill Press brings fine reading, information, and entertainment together between the covers of its creatively crafted books. Our Cider Mill bears fruit twice a year, publishing a new crop of titles each spring and fall.

"Where Good Books Are Ready for Press"

Visit us online at

cidermillpress.com

or write to us at

PO Box 454
12 Spring St.
Kennebunkport, Maine 04046